DISCARDED

Swinburne as Critic

The Routledge Critics Series

GENERAL EDITOR: B. C. SOUTHAM, M.A., B.LITT. (OXON.)
Formerly Department of English, Westfield College, University of London

Swinburne
as Critic

Edited by

Clyde K. Hyder

Professor Emeritus of English
University of Kansas

Routledge & Kegan Paul
London and Boston

Upsala College
Library
East Orange, N. J. 07019

821.8
S978sw

*First published 1972
by Routledge & Kegan Paul Ltd
Broadway House, 68–74 Carter Lane,
London EC4V 5EL and
9 Park Street,
Boston, Mass. 02108, U.S.A.
Printed in Great Britain by
W & J Mackay Limited, Chatham*

137044

*© Clyde K. Hyder 1972
No part of this book may be reproduced in
any form without permission from the
publisher, except for the quotation of brief
passages in criticism*

ISBN 0 7100 7343 7

to the memory of
Allena Hicks Hyder (1912–68)
Carl Turner Hyder (1896–1971)

General editor's preface

The purpose of the Routledge Critics Series is to provide carefully chosen selections from the work of the most important British and American literary critics, the extracts headed by a considerable Introduction to the critic and his work, to the age in which he was writing, and to the influence and tradition to which his criticism has given rise.

Selections of a somewhat similar kind have always existed for the great critics, such as Johnson, Wordsworth, Arnold, Henry James, and the argument for their appearance in this series is that of re-appraisal and re-selection: each age has its own particular needs and desiderata and looks in its especial own way at the writing of the past—at criticism as much as literature. And in the last twenty years or so there has also been a much more systematic and intelligent re-reading of other critics, particularly the lesser-known essayists and reviewers of the Victorian period, some of whose writing is now seen to be criticism of the highest order, not merely of historical interest, but valuable to us now in our present reading of nineteenth-century literature, and so informing us in our living experience of literature as well as throwing light upon the state of literature and criticism at particular moments in the past.

B.C.S.

Contents

Preface

Re-reading his prose has strengthened my conviction that Swinburne belongs among the great critics, not merely among the great poets. The selections in this book illustrate various aspects of his criticism. Mindful of how those who choose selections tend to differ in their choices, I can claim for mine only that they include what I consider to be his best and most representative work and that they are chosen with some regard for his favourite opinions and authors, particularly those of whose rank he was an effective advocate. Though 'John Webster', for instance, may not be his most felicitous essay on Elizabethan dramatists, Swinburne was not alone in thinking that Webster is more important than Ford, Dekker, or Massinger.

Swinburne's prose abounds in allusions and quoted phrases. These I have tried to identify, trusting that, even if not always in the interest of clarity, such identification will at least satisfy intellectual curiosity. Because Swinburne read so widely and remembered so much of what he read, I cannot claim to have carried out this purpose in every instance. Since Swinburne's own notes, particularly in the earlier selections, are sometimes long, all notes come at the end of each selection, Swinburne's initials being placed after notes for which he is responsible.

Though I have relied primarily on a fresh examination of Swinburne's prose, including his letters, some titles listed in the Bibliography may have influenced my choice of material and my point of view. The notes to my Introduction acknowledge specific obligations. It is pleasant to name persons who also have been helpful. Professor Cecil Y. Lang of the University of Virginia, whose *Swinburne Letters* I quote by his permission and that of the Yale University Press, saw my tentative list of contents and suggested an addition. He and his wife, Violette Lang, who have an unusual command of the French language, have suggested desirable changes in the translations of the passages Swinburne composed and assigned to 'a French critic' in 'Matthew Arnold's New Poems'; thanks to them, these passages are more accurate and idiomatic than they originally were. The Translations in the notes, chiefly in the review of *Les Fleurs du Mal*, aim at exactness rather than elegance. Professor Mattie Crumrine of the University of Kansas looked over them and suggested improvements. Since neither she nor Professor and Mrs Lang had an opportunity to read final versions of what they had respectively seen, only the editor is accountable for possible oversights. That staunch champion of Swinburne and student and collector of Swinburniana, John S. Mayfield, Curator of Manuscripts and Rare Books in the Syracuse University Library, has sent me Xerox copies of certain texts; in one instance, acknowledged on a later page, he identified a difficult allusion. Professors R. H. Super of the University of Michigan, Frederic E. Faverty of Northwestern University and Arthur A. Adrian of Case-Western Reserve University have courteously answered inquires. The Watson Library and the Spencer Library at the University of Kansas have once more proved indispensable.

C.K.H.

Introduction

I

A critic of any century is likely to be remembered for his judgment, which should be based on knowledge, and taste. Critical aims, whether professed openly or merely implicit, may differ in emphasis. It has been pointed out that nineteenth-century critics tended to conceive of literature as expressive of an author's ideas and emotions, as a mirror of nature (both human and wild) or reality, as a work of art conforming to accepted standards, and as an organic whole.[1] Among the Romantic critics, those of the generation preceding his, Algernon Charles Swinburne (1837–1909) particularly admired Samuel Taylor Coleridge and Charles Lamb, both of whom he surpassed in range, in catholicity of taste, and in sharpness of perception. The influence of Coleridge was more seminal than his, for Coleridge has contributed more to recent critical theories, but Swinburne's judgment has affected the standing of more authors. Furthermore, his opinions on subjects dealt with by both men, such as the characters of Shakespeare, are sounder. In stimulating interest in Elizabethan drama he carried on a labour of love begun by Lamb, but he did this more amply and systematically, Lamb's work being mainly that of an anthologist. Swinburne's contemporary, Matthew Arnold, deeply aware of the relationship between literature and society, was a social as well as a literary critic, but Arnold had little to say either of the older English drama or of contemporary authors, at any rate publicly; and though Arnold may be in some respects more important, Swinburne's understanding and appraisal of French literature were more trustworthy.

Like Arnold and Coleridge, he was both poet and critic, and his outlook on the poetic art and his insights and style were often those of a poet. In 1879 he wrote to Theodore Watts (*The Letters of Algernon Charles Swinburne*, ed. Cecil Y. Lang, hereafter cited as 'Lang', iv, 83): 'I have just given an hour this morning before breakfast . . . to the composition of a little poem in prose on the subject of Shakespeare's Cleopatra'—a passage that was written for his *Study of*

Shakespeare. Highly imaginative and emotional prose is not unusual in Swinburne's books. His poetry, too, contains several bits of literary appreciation, the best-known being perhaps his sonnets on Elizabethan dramatists. As a critic of poetry, Swinburne exalted the lyric and the dramatic and, himself a virtuoso of metres, often noticed metrical qualities. A poet's sensibility may enhance his sensitiveness to the poetry of others, and, being a creative artist, he does not need to find in criticism an outlet for a frustrated creative instinct—a besetting temptation, T. S. Eliot thought, of poor critics.

A statement in the preface of his *Miscellanies* comes nearer than any other short passage to setting forth Swinburne's credo: 'Reserving always as unquestionable and indisputable the primal and instinctive truths of aesthetics as of ethics, of art as of character, of poetry as of conduct, we are bound under penalty of preposterous failure, of self-convicted and self-conscious injustice, to take into full and fair account the circumstances of time and accident which affected for better or for worse the subjects of our moral or critical sentence.' Though Swinburne emphasized aesthetic criteria in judging literature, it is an error to suppose that he disregarded moral standards or historic considerations. While he learned from the Romantic critics to write from his personal experience and to express his enthusiasms, he also drew on his knowledge of the ancient classics. He is impressionistic in responding to literature in such a way as to communicate his own feeling; he is also judicial in comparing authors and estimating their rank. Besides using some of their methods—to a far greater extent he introduced metaphorical analogies and indulged in what he called 'the noble pleasure of praising'—Swinburne accepted certain ideas found in the Romantic critics of England and France, such as the organic nature of art and the inseparability of form and content, and helped to transmit them to modern times. Particularly in his writings about the drama he insisted on the integrity of texts and used artistic standards of judgment rather than the merely mechanical methods of some of his contemporaries.

The younger contemporary on whom Swinburne made the strongest impression, Walter Pater, more restricted in his critical range, avoided extremes of praise or blame and the recurring vices of style that have tended to obscure Swinburne's merits, but of Swinburne's critical insights and their importance for the twentieth century, and indeed of his critical stature, there can be no reasonable doubt.

II

In 'Charles Dickens' (No. 18) Swinburne described 'the merely personal element of the critic, the natural atmosphere in which his mind or his insight works, and uses its faculties of appreciation' as 'really the first and last thing to be taken into account'. In time Swinburne's 'personal element' is felt and cannot be captured through hasty analysis, but it is rooted in his family background and experience. His grandfather, Sir John Swinburne, was a staunch republican who had spent several years in France, and the poet's early republican views and French sympathies may be attributed partly to the grandfather he admired. Both influences are reflected in his writings. In 'Charles Dickens', again, Swinburne recalled his grandfather's liking for a novel by Dickens and deprecated, too, the identification of Dickens's Harold Skimpole with Leigh Hunt. Swinburne's admiration of Hunt as a writer and a critic of sorts was partly due to his grandfather's friendship with that author, who in his autobiography had written of Sir John as 'a refutation of all that can be said against' human nature. Swinburne's father, Admiral Charles Henry Swinburne, unlike his son in many ways, seems to have done most to waken in that son, while still tiny, the passionate love of the sea of which both his poetry and his critical analogies often remind us. His maternal uncle, the fourth Earl of Ashburnham, made available to the boy the resources of a large and remarkable library. Before he entered Eton, he had acquired a command of French and under his mother's tutelage had read several masterpieces in Italian. Attendance at church familiarized him with the Book of Common Prayer. Like that of his friend John Ruskin, his writing is studded with reminiscences from the Bible.

The places that he knew and came to love left their mark on his prose as well as his verse. The country around Capheaton, his grandfather's estate in Northumberland, was not less dear than his own home in the Isle of Wight. He loved the popular ballads because of hearing them sung in what he regarded as their natural territory and could even become indignant over the claims made for minstrels of the Scottish as opposed to the English border. Like the Brontës, he knew the fascination of the moors and once wrote in regard to Charlotte: 'To me as to other northcountrymen she is, as I believe you know, a much greater light than the now more popular Warwickshire woman [George Eliot]' (Lang, iii, 260–1).

Swinburne formed his most intense literary attachments while he was young. His reading of Shakespeare, the source of 'the chief intellectual business' and 'the chief spiritual delight of my whole life' (*A Study of Shakespeare*), began when he was six. Here is what he says of those who belittle the text of Thomas Bowdler: 'More nauseous and more foolish cant was never chattered than that which would deride the memory or depreciate the merits of Bowdler. No man ever did better service to Shakespeare than the man who made it possible to put him into the hands of intelligent and imaginative children; it may well be, if we consider how dearly the creator of Mamillius must have loved them, that no man has ever done him such good service' ('Social Verse'). The reference to Mamillius, the little boy in *A Winter's Tale*, reminds us of something as fundamental to Swinburne's nature as his love of the sea or of books—his love of children. No reader should be surprised to find Mrs Browning's portrait of a baby regarded as the high point of *Aurora Leigh* or Hugo's *L'Art d'être grand-père* called 'the most absolutely and adorably beautiful book ever written'—a note 'from the heaven of heavens in which little babies are adored by great poets, the frailest by the most potent of divine and human kind'.

This great poet was still a boy when he discovered the power of Shakespeare's fellow dramatists, even before fuller realization of it came from Charles Lamb's *Specimens of English Dramatic Poets Contemporary with Shakespeare*. Charles Lamb he was often to praise (see No. 22), thinking of him as 'the most supremely competent judge and exquisite critic of lyrical and dramatic art that we have ever had' (*William Blake*).

At Eton Swinburne was reading the old dramatists while pursuing his classical studies. There he acquired familiarity with Catullus, Horace, and Vergil, as well as with two authors whom he could name along with Shakespeare: 'Æschylus is the greatest poet who ever was also a prophet, Shakespeare is the greatest dramatist who ever was also a poet; but Sappho is simply nothing less—as she is certainly nothing more—than the greatest poet who ever was at all.—There, at all events, you have the simple and sincere profession of my life-long faith' (Lang, iv, 124). This brilliant student of the classics did not lay aside his Greek after leaving Oxford but set out to memorize Æschylus, and succeeded, as we infer from Henry Adams's account of him in 1862. Having previously read only parts of it in school exercises, in 1874 he read all of the *Iliad*, 'with great comfort and benefit to my spirits' (Lang, ii, 335). His extraordinary memory made possible his linguistic accomplishments—the memory that enabled him to write to Browning that 'at nineteen I knew *Sordello* by heart from end to end' (Lang, iii, 20). His memory explains certain aspects of Swinburne's style—the readiness of his illustrations and his frequent use of quoted phrases.

Strong emotion sometimes lurks behind Swinburne's literary opinions, particularly when those opinions concerned his idols. With the three most important of them he became personally acquainted. In 1864 he visited Walter Savage Landor in Florence. He commemorated the occasion in a verse-tribute from which comes a quotation now on Landor's tomb. Like Shelley, considered by Swinburne to be the greatest of English lyric poets, Landor was a lover of freedom and a hater of tyranny. Both Hugo and Mazzini, the Italian idealist whom Swinburne met in London in 1867, supplied inspiration, especially in *Songs before Sunrise* (1871). *Chastelard* (1865) had been dedicated to Hugo, and the two men occasionally corresponded before their meeting in Paris in 1885. Swinburne's account of that meeting explains why he once referred to 'my dear Father's and Master's work': '. . . almost his first words to me when we met were "*mon fils*"'(Lang, v, 109).

Even before he had met any of his three acknowledged masters Swinburne had met other poets—the first and more important of these, Wordsworth, when he was twelve. Since the sale catalogue of Swinburne's library lists a copy of Samuel Rogers's *Poems* as inscribed to Swinburne by the author on 28 February 1852, one may safely assume that he was nearly fifteen when he met Rogers. He was much impressed by the old man, who laid his hand solemnly upon the boy's head. The early Christians were believed to transmit spiritual power by the laying on of hands; Swinburne's feelings about the poet's mission, especially that of the poet-prophet, were not far from being religious. Because in his youth he seemed rebellious and iconoclastic, one may easily overlook the poet's reverence for his art.

In the fall of 1857, when D. G. Rossetti, William Morris, and Edward Burne Jones (later, Burne-Jones) were working on the frescoes of the Oxford Union debating room, Swinburne met all three. Swinburne profited from studying the poetry of both Morris and Rossetti, but Rossetti's personal influence was stronger; it was he who interested Swinburne most in the direction of '*l'art pour l'art*' (discussed below). The poet-painter and his brother William Michael, Swinburne's friend thenceforth, were familiar with contemporary French writing; the latter indeed gave him a copy of Baudelaire's

Fleurs du Mal and was himself to touch upon the question of art and morality (he was not indifferent to the claims of morality, as the chief apologist of 'art for art's sake', Théophile Gautier, was) in his important defence of Swinburne's *Poems and Ballads*.[2]

Though, in contrast to that of *Atalanta in Calydon* (1865), the reception of *Chastelard* in the same year was unfavourable, *Poems and Ballads* (1866), Swinburne's fourth book and first book of poems, created a sensation without parallel in England since Byron's day. Admired for its technical excellence as poetry, it was widely condemned for sensuality and paganism. The publication of this volume affected Swinburne's fortunes both as poet and as critic. He has been judged adversely because of his harsh comments on certain writers. To be sure, he could be as intemperate in defending his favourites as in replying to attacks, nor can one always separate these two purposes. Owing to what the book says of three authors, especially Charles Lamb, he wrote a bitter poem on Carlyle's *Reminiscences*. When in his discussion of Lamb (No. 22) he tags Carlyle as 'Cloacinus', he remembered that, in the hardly agreeable phraseology ascribed to him by Emerson, Carlyle had consigned Swinburne to 'a cesspool'.[3]

By 1867 Swinburne had met John Morley, known to him as the author of the anonymous attack on *Poems and Ballads* in the *Saturday Review*. In that year Morley became editor of the *Fortnightly Review*, and Swinburne's critical essays began to appear in it. According to Edmund Gosse, these essays, which seemed more novel because of their impressionistic and even impassioned character, attracted much attention, particularly among the young 'aestheticians'.[4] A less important outlet, beginning a few years later, was the ninth edition of the *Encyclopædia Britannica*. The editor who arranged for Swinburne's contributions to it was Thomas Spencer Baynes, who had apparently written a hostile article on Swinburne for the *Edinburgh Review*.[5]

Swinburne's most important critical volumes include *William Blake* (1868), *Essays and Studies* (1875), *A Note on Charlotte Brontë* (1877), *A Study of Shakespeare* (1880), *Miscellanies* (1886), *A Study of Ben Jonson* (1889), *Studies in Prose and Poetry* (1894), and *The Age of Shakespeare* (1908).

III

In his early years Swinburne rebelled against the literary standards then current. His letter in the *Spectator* of 7 June 1862 defending George Meredith's sequence *Modern Love* declares that 'if some poetry, not without merit of its kind, has at times dealt in dogmatic morality, it is all the worse and all the weaker for that' (Lang, i, 52). This forecasts the point of view in *Notes on Poems and Reviews* (1866), in which he defends himself for having overlooked the contemporary intolerance of literature not intended for children and girls. For Swinburne, Baudelaire's morality in *Les Fleurs du Mal* (No. 1) is artistically right because it is implicit, not obtrusive. *William Blake* contains a more extended statement about art: 'Her business is not to do good on other grounds, but to be good on her own.' Victor Hugo's work 'is in its essence artistic, in its accident alone philanthropic or moral'.[6] Though he was influenced by D. G. Rossetti and Gautier, Swinburne could have acquired fundamental convictions from Shelley: 'Didactic poetry is my abhorrence; nothing can be equally well expressed in prose that is not tedious and supererogatory in verse'[7]—a statement nearly echoed by Swinburne in a letter to E. C. Stedman: 'I believe you know my theory that nothing which can possibly be *as well* said in prose ought ever to be said in verse' (Lang, iii, 67). Late in life he defended the 'aesthete' as by definition 'an intelligent, appreciative, quick-witted person; in a word, as the lexicon has it, "one who perceives"' ('Whistler's Lecture on Art') and denounced Tennyson's scornful verse on 'art for art's sake' ('Changes of Aspect', accessible in *New Writings by Swinburne*, ed. Cecil Y. Lang). Before he published *Songs before Sunrise* (1871), which aims at the inculcation of faith and principles, according to his own statement, he had foreseen the limitations of 'art for art's sake'. Whether or not his admiration of Hugo had anything to do with his modification of his earlier statements, he chose to announce his repudiation of the 'negative' aspects of '*l'art pour l'art*' in a discussion of Hugo (No. 8).

Swinburne often makes judgments on other than aesthetic grounds. He does not say that the poet is necessarily a prophet, as at times Wordsworth and Tennyson imply a poet should be, nor does he portray the poet as 'God's spy' in Browning's phrase, but he acknowledges the existence of 'the poet-prophet'. For him Blake is an example, but Æschylus, Hugo, and Dante are better examples. In short, Swinburne, who regarded the *Oresteia* as 'the greatest work of the greatest among poets', could be an 'aesthete' in his sense of the term but not in the more usual pejorative sense.

The outcry over *Poems and Ballads* rather obscured Swinburne's utterances on artistic reserve. 'If anything can justify the serious and deliberate display of merely physical emotion in literature or in art, it must be one of two things: intense depth of feeling expressed with inspired perfection of simplicity, as by Sappho; or transcendent supremacy of actual and irresistible beauty in such revelation of naked nature as was possible to Titian' ('Whitmania'). Coprology, he thought, 'should be left to Frenchmen' (*A Study of Ben Jonson*). 'By the very law of her life, by the very condition of her being, she [art] is bound to reject whatever is brutal, whatever is prurient' ('John Ford'). Swinburne's distaste for Zola was not inconsistent with his belief in the writer's freedom of selection; he simply thought Zola's selection of material sordid.

To Swinburne art, in the general sense, was 'the highest, deepest, most precious and serious pleasure to be got out of life' (Lang, ii, 47). One cannot doubt the intensity of his feelings about literature. He exalts the character of the poet because of his own emotions, not merely because of tradition. In 'Thalassius' ('sea-born') he portrays himself, in Shelleyan fashion, as the child of the Oceanid Cymothoë and Apollo, god of the sun and of poetry. The child acquires a foster-father—allegorically, Landor, 'a warrior grey with glories'—who taught him 'high things', love of liberty and hatred of what oppresses, hope for the triumph of good, fear of what is unworthy. Nevertheless, he experiences unworthy passion before he realizes the nature of his unique poetic mission, to which he is consecrated by his father Apollo:

> Child of my sunlight and the sea, from birth
> A fosterling and fugitive on earth;
> Sleepless of soul as wind or wave or fire,
> A manchild with an ungrown God's desire;
> Because thou hast loved nought mortal more than me,
> Thy father, and thy mother-hearted sea; . . .
> Because thou hast heard with world-unwearied ears
> The music that puts light into the spheres;
> Have therefore in thy heart and in thy mouth
> The sound of song that mingles north and south,
> The song of all the winds that sing of me,
> And in thy soul the sense of all the sea.

In a companion-piece, 'On the Cliffs', Apollo and the sea again have dominant roles. The nightingale becomes the incarnation of Sappho:

Being bird and God in one,
With throat of gold and spirit of the sun;
The sun whom all our souls and songs call sire. . . .

Apollo's gift to Sappho is the gift of eternal inspiration, for this nightingale, like Keats's, lives on, but, unlike that poet's, is 'woman and god and bird'. The note is again one of consecration, and Sappho is hailed as 'sister':

We were not marked for sorrow, thou nor I,
For joy nor sorrow, sister, were we made,
To take delight and grief to live and die,
Assuaged by pleasures or by pains affrayed
That melt men's hearts and alter; we retain
A memory mastering pleasure and all pain,
A spirit within the sense of ear and eye,
A soul behind the soul, that seeks and sings. . . .

Both poems stress the poet's inspiration—an inspiration that was really the test Swinburne used to distinguish the gods and the giants among the great poets (cf. No. 23).

The emotional tone of the two poems is religious, though Apollo, symbolical source of poetic inspiration and the pervading light, is the only deity mentioned. What is the highest gift from a god to a poet? It is the gift of harmony: 'Now it is a poor thing to have nothing but melody and be unable to rise above it into harmony, but one or the other, the lesser if not the greater, you *must* have' (Lang, iii, 9). This 'harmony' is the product of the happiest alliance between thought and the words chosen for the thought, and the thought must reflect 'nature' (reality). Such a generalization would not have surprised many previous authors, some of whom conceived of 'reality' in Platonic terms or even of the Deity as the 'reality' sought. In his *Defence of Poetry* Shelley explains that poetry 'strips the veil of familiarity from the world, and lays bare the naked and sleeping beauty, which is the spirit of its forms'. Indeed the very distinction Swinburne makes, as has been plausibly suggested,[8] was made by Shelley: 'But there is a principle within the human being, and perhaps within all sentient beings, which acts otherwise than in the lyre, and produces not melody alone, but harmony, by an internal adjustment of the sounds or motions thus excited to the impressions which excite them.' Coleridge had found in Wordsworth's poems 'a perfect appropriateness of words to the meaning' (*Biographia Literaria*), but

Swinburne considered that Shelley had penetrated closer to the heart of nature: Shelley had power 'to rise beyond these regions of contemplation and sensation into that other where the emotion of Keats and the emotion of Wordsworth become one, and are superseded by a greater; to breathe, in Shakespeare's audaciously subtle and successful phrase, the very "spirit of sense" itself, to transcend at once the sensuous and the meditative elements of poetry, and to fuse their highest, their keenest, their most inward and intimate effects, in such verse as utters what none before could utter, and renders into likeness of form and sound such truths of inspired perception, such raptures of divine surprise, as no poet of nature can think to render again. At the sound of the "Ode to the West Wind", the stars of Wordsworth's heaven grow fainter in our eyes, and the nightingale of Keats's garden falls silent in our ears' ('Wordsworth and Byron').

When he made a distinction between 'inner music' and 'outer music', Swinburne had in mind a distinction similar to that between 'melody' and 'harmony'.[9] 'Outer music' may spring from technical devices like rhythm, rhyme, or assonance, whereas 'inner music' stems from a kind of concord between a poem and nature itself. Victor Hugo's 'magnificent quality of communion with the great things of nature and translation of the joyous and terrible sense they give us of her living infinity' (*Under the Microscope*) is illustrative. This view of the relation between 'music' and insight into nature is, again, not uniquely Swinburne's. Carlyle, for instance, had written: 'A *musical* thought is one spoken by a mind that has penetrated into the inmost heart of the thing; detected the inmost mystery of it, namely the *melody* that lies hidden in it; the inward harmony of coherence which is its soul' ('The Hero as Poet').

Like the Romantic poets, Swinburne assigns a central role to the imagination. If 'the two primary and essential qualities of poetry are imagination and harmony' ('Wordsworth and Byron'), the first is indispensable as a means of achieving 'harmony': '. . . the crowning gift of imagination, the power to make us realise that thus and not otherwise it was, that thus and not otherwise it must have been, was given—except by exceptional fits and starts—to none of the poets of their time but only to Shakespeare and Webster' (No. 25). Similarly, the high gift of 'those great twin sisters in genius who were born to the stern and strong-hearted old Rector of Haworth' is 'to make us feel in every nerve, at every step forward which our imagination is compelled to take under the guidance of another's, that thus and not otherwise, but in all things altogether even as we are told and shown, it was and it must have been with the human figures set before us in their action and their suffering' (No. 15). Only the imagination can create sublimity, the high quality of Marlowe's poetry (No. 24), and achieve 'harmony', the conviction of reality whether in poetry or fiction.

Coleridge had identified the imagination as 'that synthetic and magical power' essential to poetic creation—itself 'a repetition in the finite mind of the eternal act of creation in the infinite I AM'. Only the imagination can fuse disparate elements so as to create something organic. Though at least one passage in Aristotle's *Poetics* assumed the organic nature of art, Coleridge emphasized this view more than his predecessors. Like his older contemporaries, Carlyle and Ruskin, Swinburne accepted it. He hoped that it could be said of his own tragedy *Erechtheus* that the whole is greater than any part of it ('Dedicatory Epistle'). The organic view presupposes a unity of form and content: 'It should be superfluous and impertinent to explain that the expression is not to be considered apart from the substance' (*George Chapman*).

Though Swinburne owed much to the Romantic writers and their emphases, he also accepts classical standards. To be sure, he is aware that 'the test of the highest poetry is that it eludes all tests' ('Wordsworth and Byron'), and so he does not resort to such tests mechanically. In 'Matthew Arnold's New Poems' (No. 3) he deprecates the use of 'tags' like 'romantic'[10] or 'classic', 'form or harmony' being 'the high one law of all art'. Remembering Aristotle's famous definition in the *Poetics*, he observes: 'It will never be [admitted], by any unperverted judgment, that this eternal canon of tragic art, the law which defines terror and pity as its only proper objects, . . . may ever be disregarded or ignored' (*A Study of Ben Jonson*). A reason for his choice of material for *The Tale of Balen* was that 'there is no episode in the cycle of Arthurian romance more genuinely Homeric in its sublime simplicity and its pathetic sublimity of submission to the masterdom of fate' ('Dedicatory Epistle'). This element of fate, so prominent in ancient epic and drama, was neglected by Tennyson in his treatment of Arthurian legend, with the result that the moral tone of the story was lowered, as Swinburne explains in *Under the Microscope*; and by way of comparison he refers to the *Oresteia*.

Swinburne had in mind another distinction made by Aristotle, that between poetry and history, when he declared that Achilles is 'more actual' than Wellington (No. 8). Some have thought that in its treatment of tragedy Aristotle's *Poetics* subordinates character to plot, though this view disregards the nature of Greek drama and the attention Aristotle devotes to the heroes of tragedy. With the principle at any rate Swinburne would not have agreed. With him character is primary: the action must be consistent with the character. In 'Charles Reade' he states that Reade sacrifices consistency of characterization to his dramatic instincts. The 'single defect of moral harmony' in the story of *Griffith Gaunt* is the inadequate motivation of Gaunt's 'betrayal of her trust and innocence' in his offer to marry (though himself already married) the woman who has saved his life. Swinburne considers the betrothal of Oliver and Celia in *As You Like It* unsatisfactory because of Oliver's earlier baseness and Celia's higher status as Rosalind's friend.

The example of the Greeks did supply standards of judgment, and, like Arnold, Swinburne greatly admired their achievement. His 'Dedicatory Epistle' indicates that he had tried to make his *Erechtheus* conform more closely to the Greek model than his *Atalanta in Calydon*. Browning's translation of the *Agamemnon*, he explained to his friend John Nichol, was 'the last straw that broke this camel's back. I wrote a line of thanks, and went straight to bed. . . . Some devil possesses him whenever he touches on anything Hellenic' (Lang, iv, 31). Swinburne thought that the Greek form of the ode, 'with its regular arrangement of turn, return, and after-song, is not to be imitated because it is Greek, but to be adopted because it is best'; 'without an accurately corresponsive or antiphonal scheme of music even the master of masters, who is Coleridge, could not produce, even through the superb and enchanting melodies of such a poem as his "Dejection", a fit and complete companion, a full and perfect rival, to such a poem as his ode on France' ('Dedicatory Epistle').

Charles Lamb and William Hazlitt wrote frankly of their experience in reading, seeking to communicate their own 'gusto' (Hazlitt's word). Lamb tells how the reading of *The Revenger's Tragedy* could make his ears 'tingle', and Hazlitt remarks, 'I could be in love with Mrs. Inchbald, romantic with Mrs. Radcliffe, and sarcastic with Madame D'Arblay.' Swinburne similarly shares his feelings and experiences, trusting that his enthusiasms will be contagious.

A critical method of the Romantic critics, and one which Swinburne used more than any other critic has used it, was the employment of imagery, often metaphorical, to suggest an analogy, a kind of co-ordination of the world of experience and the world of books. As in his poetry, nature in general and particularly the sea supplied many images. In Byron's *Don Juan* there is 'a tidal variety of experience and emotion' which 'gives to the poem something of the breadth and freshness of the sea' (No. 2). In Hugo's *Les Châtiments*, 'Between the prologue "Night" and the epilogue "Light" the ninety-eight poems . . . roll and break and lighten and thunder like waves of a visible sea' (*A Study of Victor Hugo*). The most extended analogy, used (as Swinburne explains) also by Hugo, comes at the beginning of *A Study of Shakespeare* (No. 21, 'Shakespeare and the Sea'). One could easily multiply examples. Again as in his poems, the imagery is often elemental: 'There never was such a thunderstorm of a play' ('Cyril Tourneur'). Though storms had a special fascination for Swinburne, the elements need not be violent: Blake's *Book of Thel* has 'the clearness and sweetness of spring-water'. 'The Blessed Damozel' has 'the odour and colour of cloudless air, the splendour of an hour without spot' ('The Poems of Dante Gabriel Rossetti'). Morris's *Life and Death of Jason* is 'fresh as wind, bright as light, full of the spring and the sun'. Of a poet very different from Rossetti or Morris, Chaucer, Swinburne comments: 'But the wide warm harvest-field of Chaucer's husbandry was all glorious with gold of ripening sunshine while all the world beside lay in darkness and in bonds' (No. 11).

The poet's imagery is not limited to wild nature. Charles Lamb's charm 'pervades his work as with an odour of sweet old-world flowers or spices long laid by among fine linens and rare brocades in some such old oaken or cedarn cabinet as his grandmother might have opened to rejoice the wondering senses of her boyish visitor at "Blakesmoor"' (No. 22). Of Chapman's continuation of Marlowe's *Hero and Leander*: 'Faultless indeed this lovely fragment is not; it also bears traces of the Elizabethan barbarism, as though the great queen's ruff and farthingale had been clapped about the neck and waist of the Medicean Venus.' Of course Chapman was attempting the impossible, for 'The poet was not alive, among all the mighty men then living, who could worthily have completed the divine fragment of Marlowe. As well might we look now to find a sculptor who could worthily restore for us the arms of the Venus of Melos—"Our Lady of Beauty", as Heine said when lying at her feet stricken to death, "who has no hands, and cannot help us".'[11]

The last quotations remind us how often Swinburne's comparisons are based on art, especially pictorial art, with which he had unusual familiarity. It was natural for him to say of the poet Collins that 'Corot on canvas might have signed his "Ode to Evening"' (No. 12). He wrote criticism of art, too (cf. Nos. 5, 6), both in prose and verse. One conscious of the interrelationships of the arts and sensitive to analogies of various kinds of experience could easily, like some of the Romantic poets, develop an interest in synaesthesia. The poems of William Blake suggest 'a fragrance of sound, a melody of colour'. In reading 'Kubla Khan' 'we seem rapt into that paradise revealed to Swedenborg, where music and colour and perfume were one' (No. 7).

Critics of all times have made comparisons between authors; it may be one way of measuring achievement by a standard, that of what others have achieved. Swinburne's literary comparisons are abundant and illuminating, though sometimes recondite. He believed that 'it is always more interesting, as it is always more profitable, to find instances of likeness than to find instances of contrast to the work of a poet or the speculation of a thinker' (from his essay on Hugo's *Dieu*), but his contrasts can be fruitful: 'Mr Reade, by far the greatest master of narrative whom our country has produced since the death of Scott, was as much his superior in dramatic dexterity as he was inferior to Dumas in the art of concealing rather than obtruding his natural command and his practical comprehension of this peculiar talent.' Swinburne notes, too, a way in which Trollope vies with Reade: 'More delightfully actual and lifelike groups of figures than the Grantlys, the Luftons, and the Proudies, it would be impossible to find on any canvas of Mr Reade's: and these leading figures or groups of Barsetshire society are sketched with such lightness of hand, such an attractive ease and simplicity of manner, that the obtrusive and persistent vehemence of presentation which distinguishes the style and method of Charles Reade appears by comparison inartistic and ineffectual.' Sometimes the critic's special knowledge may lead him into comparison too involved for some readers: 'Nabbes is to Shirley what Shirley is to Massinger . . .' ('Thomas Nabbes').

In using his reading to form judgments, Swinburne did not neglect his experience of human nature. Like Arnold, and Schiller before Arnold, he renounces any 'art' that brings depression, preferring to associate art with joy: 'Nothing which leaves us depressed is a true work of art. We must have light though it be lightning, and air though it be storm' (No. 3). He says of Ben Jonson's comedy, 'Scorn and indignation are but too often the motives or the mainsprings of his comic art; and when dramatic poetry can exist on the sterile and fiery diet of scorn and indignation, we may hope to find life sustained in happiness and health on a diet of aperients and emetics' (*A Study of Ben Jonson*).

Swinburne always does honour to literature, his main aim being to exalt, not to denigrate. If at times he may seem worshipful or dogmatic, he was not without a sense of humour even in regard to his own convictions. He ends a letter to Theodore Watts thus: '. . . those two admirable poets [Arnold and Rossetti], to my lifelong perplexity and disgust, can see nothing almost in each other's work to admire or enjoy. "It is really singular" as Mme. de Sévigné's candid and charming old friend said to her "that I should be the one only person I know in the world whose judgment is invariably right" —is it not?' (Lang, iii, 226)

IV

Probably more important than a critic's theories or his methods are the range of his knowledge and the quality of his taste. Though Coleridge knew more of German literature and philosophy, Swinburne's acquaintance with German authors apparently including little besides Goethe and Heine in translation, Swinburne's familiarity with belles-lettres was probably more extensive than that of any other English poet-critic. He seldom mentions Spanish literary works, not often even *Don Quixote*, or those of the Orient, except for the Bible and the *Rubáiyát*. But his reading of English and French literature was unrivalled among English authors of his day, and his knowledge of the ancient classics and the greater Italians was remarkable. His taste knew no chronological boundaries or taint of provincialism, whether of time or place. He could appreciate the work of W. S. Gilbert, and the lines of an old song,

> He came all so still
> To his mother's bower
> As dew in April
> That falleth on the flower,

were to him 'unspeakable in their loveliness' ('Social Verse').

Who among English critics has done so much to awaken interest in so many different authors? He was a champion of Blake, of Charlotte and Emily Brontë—particularly in the rank assigned to the latter he was far ahead of his time—and of George Chapman. He emphasized the merits of Collins as a lyrist (No. 12). His essay on Byron (No. 2) was a landmark in the appreciation of that poet. Swinburne was also an early champion of FitzGerald's *Rubáiyát* and a discriminating apologist in behalf of Browning (No. 10). His essay on Dickens (No. 18) came at a time when it was needed; he anticipated recent critics in naming Dickens with Shakespeare. Following in the footsteps of Charles Lamb, he not only extolled the merits of the greater dramatists like Marlowe and Webster but also urged the claims of their less renowned contemporaries like Tourneur. His appraisal of Shakespeare's great characters and scenes is discerning. As for French authors, he was an early and probably the first English defender of Baudelaire (No. 1). He overrated Gautier and seemed unaware of certain limitations of Hugo but saw in them beauties not apparent to his countrymen. He was a warm admirer of Balzac and Flaubert. He shared in the revival of interest in François Villon (cf. No. 11). He did not share Arnold's warmth of enthusiasm for Sainte-Beuve, nor did he make use of the critical theories of Taine, though at least once he praised the latter critic: 'A better and keener estimate of Ford, of Dryden, and of Swift can hardly be found than M. Taine's' ('John Ford'). Like George Saintsbury, he disliked the naturalists, though admitting Zola's possession of 'potent and indisputable genius'.

Swinburne's relatively few adverse judgments, by the way, have often been cited in his disfavour. His early recognition of Whitman in *William Blake* has been partly overshadowed by his 'Whitmania', written because of his disgust with those who had overpraised Whitman or praised him for the wrong reasons. Once more in the company of Saintsbury, he disliked Ibsen, but laudation of Ibsen and repeated disparagement of Shakespeare and the Elizabethans by Shaw help to account for overemphasis in his opinions on Ibsen. This is clearly indicated in his 'Short Notes': 'The celebrity of Ibsen is the very reason why a loyal Shakespearean and Hugoist should and must feel bound—or shall we say free?—to protest, by no means against the recognition of his unquestioned capacity, but against the cult of his iconoclastic idolators who blaspheme and revile the name that is above every name.'[12] Among the ancients, Euripides was a favourite object of aversion ('that fluent and facile dealer in flaccid verse and sentimental sophistry')—aversion shared with his friend Benjamin

Jowett, the eminent Greek scholar, from whom Swinburne won the admission, however, 'of the charm and grace and sweetness of some of the shorter and simpler lyrics' in Euripides ('Recollections of Professor Jowett').

Disparagers of Swinburne's criticism also point to intemperance in 'the noble pleasure of praising' (a phrase from his *Notes on Poems and Reviews*) and in denunciation. Though this complaint is not always unwarranted, readers sometimes overlook how he qualifies his praise, whether in his use of superlatives or elsewhere. As an illustration of intemperance, Churton Collins once quoted Swinburne's reference to a passage in Marlowe as 'perhaps the noblest in the literature of the world, ever written by one of the greatest masters of poetry', omitting 'in loving praise of the glorious delights and sublime submission to the everlasting limits of his art' (No. 24)—an omission which Swinburne compared to omitting the Psalmist's 'The fool hath said in his heart' and quoting the Psalmist as saying, 'There is no God' (Lang, v, 171). Swinburne's praise even of his favourites is rarely unmodified. Though 'no sane or candid student will question the value of Coleridge's finest critical work', he regarded Coleridge as 'one of the most untrustworthy of verbal critics' (preface to *Miscellanies*), and in another passage illustrated the 'fusion of malevolence with incompetence' in one of Coleridge's statements about Beaumont and Fletcher. Swinburne can even differ with Charles Lamb or Victor Hugo, though respectfully and deferentially. T. S. Eliot's remark that 'with all his superlatives, his judgment, if carefully scrutinized, appears temperate and just' is pertinent here. Swinburne's use of superlatives is related to the intensity of his convictions, as well as to his desire to be emphatic. He was known to feel that 'all but the meanest and most perverse of dunces and malignants' would agree with his opinion of a work by Hugo.

A final objection to Swinburne as a critic relates to other aspects of his style. His 'Byron' is clear and forcible; one may add that much of his earlier prose is imaginative, even poetic—the prose of a poet. One must not measure it with a twentieth-century yardstick; to judge it fairly, one must remember that the nineteenth century fostered such styles as those of De Quincey and Ruskin. Swinburne's later and usually more prosaic style, instead of becoming simpler and more natural, tends to be more involved; it is over-elaborate and even redundant, pairs being used where single words would suffice. The balance aimed at has sometimes been regarded as faintly Johnsonian. The elaboration is often not unrelated to Swinburne's desire to refine a definition or make an exact qualification. Perhaps the critic may even want to be conversational and allow us to see his mental processes in detail. Otherwise why write that *A Midsummer Night's Dream* is 'probably or rather surely one of the most beautiful works of man'? After all admissions about Swinburne's style, particularly its effect on a twentieth-century reader, one may still insist that Swinburne's vigour and wit may arrest attention. A passage in *A Study of Shakespeare* seems characteristic: 'Upon the Sonnets such a preposterous pyramid of presumptuous commentary has long since been reared by the Cimmerian speculation and Bœotian "brain-sweat" of sciolists and scholiasts, that no modest man will hope and no wise man will desire to add to the structure or subtract from it one single brick of proof or disproof, theorem or theory.' This discourse with a pattern of alliterative balance is obviously not the kind of prose that Molière's M. Jourdain spoke. Its tone does justice to its content, and in later sentences Swinburne voices the hope, not unfulfilled, that Dr Grosart will edit 'the one contemporary book which has ever been supposed to throw any direct or indirect light on the mystic matter'.[13] Another poet and critic, John Addington Symonds, at one time Swinburne's friend and an ardent admirer of his poetry,[14] warned Arthur Symons that Swinburne's prose style was 'catching': 'Nobody can read it without finding himself writing to its tune.'[15]

T. S. Eliot says of Swinburne: 'His great merit as a critic is really one which, like many signal virtues, can be stated so simply as to appear flat. It is that he is sufficiently interested in his subject-matter and knew quite enough about it; and this is a rare combination in English criticism. . . . And it is because this elementary virtue is so rare that Swinburne must take a very respectable place as a critic.'[16] To some extent he combined the methods of the man of letters with those of the scholar. He respected the historical point of view, though as a rule he seeks to stimulate and interpret rather than to explain. He concerned himself little with the history of thought or, except in his encyclopaedia articles and to some extent in his study of the Brontës and his 'Tennyson and Musset', with biographical considerations.

Swinburne would justifiably have claimed his scholarly specialty to be the Elizabethan drama. He thought of the drama as literature, primarily to be read rather than performed. What one may gain from watching a play is more obvious to most people than what one may gain from a careful reading, giving free rein to one's imagination in visualizing the scenes and to one's emotions in feeling the poetry. In reading, the texts are not mangled, nor is the poetry smothered, by actors. Edmund Gosse relates that Swinburne was so much disgusted by a performance of *Othello* in which the actor Fechter looked in a mirror when he said, 'It is the cause, it is the cause, my soul', that he decided not to see Shakespeare on the stage again.[17] In Charles Lamb's 'On the Tragedies of Shakespeare' he would have found the best defence for reading Shakespeare rather than seeing Shakespeare performed. Not unaware of the dramatic quality of great scenes, he chooses to emphasize most the characters and the poetry.

As a student of Shakespeare, Swinburne quarrelled with F. J. Furnivall, founder of the New Shakspere Society (even the spelling of the name seemed new), over what the poet considered to be too mechanical a method of solving questions like the authorship of *Henry VIII*. Though Swinburne did not take into account the possible bearing of metrical considerations upon questions of chronology, Furnivall seemed to forget that Swinburne's *Study of Shakespeare* did not aim at chronological distinctions but instead sought to divide Shakespeare's work into periods according to the nature of the plays. The opposition between the 'scientific' and the 'artistic' approach in deciding Shakespearean questions did not die with the invention of the computer or other mechanical devices, for in the end critical intelligence must make choices. F. G. Fleay and others, some whose names are now forgotten, were making wild assumptions about the authorship of plays in the accepted canon, using fallacious tests. Swinburne deserves credit for ridiculing the 'disintegrators' who tried to assign portions of this or that play to an author other than Shakespeare. His 'Report of the Proceedings on the First Anniversary Session of the Newest Shakespeare Society', in the Appendix of his *Study*, justly satirized what he elsewhere calls 'fruitless learning and bootless ingenuity', including absurd readings of the plays as allegorical interpretations of historical events. Only a reader versed in the 'scholarly' writings of the time can fairly suspect Swinburne of exaggerating their absurdity. One should not overlook his satire of the Baconians in 'Tennyson or Darwin?', a humorous work ridiculing the Baconians by using 'evidence' similar to theirs in order to 'prove' that Darwin wrote *In Memoriam*.

Swinburne repeatedly deplored indifference to the accuracy of texts of Elizabethan dramatists in an age that did insist on accurate texts of the ancient classics; he also used his personal influence to make better texts accessible. He encouraged the labours of older scholars like Alexander Dyce and younger ones like A. H. Bullen, who dedicated his edition of Middleton to Swinburne and who made accessible the texts of several unpublished plays.[18]

The leading Shakespearean critic of the early twentieth century, A. C. Bradley, in his *Shakespearean Tragedy* more than once acknowledged obligations to Swinburne. One finds Bradley and Swinburne largely in agreement on subjects like the character of Hamlet, Othello, or Falstaff and in the view that Shakespeare was a conscious artist who served the ends of art and not merely the requirements of the theatre.

Walter Pater was the chief younger contemporary indebted to the criticism of Swinburne, who once wrote to John Morley: 'I admire and enjoy Pater's work so heartily that I am somewhat shy of saying how much, ever since on my telling him once at Oxford how highly Rossetti (D. G.) as well as myself estimated his first papers in the *Fortnightly*, he replied to the effect that he considered them as owing their inspiration entirely to the example of my own work in the same line: and though of course no one else would dream of attributing the merit to a study of my style of writing on such matters, I suppose, as Rossetti said, that something of the same influence was perceptible in them to him, there is just such a grain of truth in the pound of compliment as to impede the free expression of all my opinion as to their excellence. But in effect they seem to me throughout as full of original character and power as of grace and truth' (Lang, ii, 240–1). Among the younger critics, Arthur Symons has been the most appreciative: 'He was the only critic of our time who never, by design or by accident, praised the wrong things.'[19] T. S. Eliot, though he places Swinburne among the 'imperfect critics', calls him an almost unerring judge of Elizabethan drama and can think of only two pronouncements with which to differ. The most accomplished of the twentieth-century academic critics, Oliver Elton, regards him as 'the acutest judge of drama and of lyrical poetry, and perhaps also of fiction, in his age'.[20] Swinburne's best praise is that his appreciation of literary and especially poetic beauty has been a source of pleasure to many readers.

NOTES

1 This classification is similar to that made by M. H. Abrams in *The Mirror and the Lamp: Romantic Theory and the Critical Tradition* (New York, 1953).

2 W. M. Rossetti's text is reprinted in my *Swinburne: The Critical Heritage* (London, 1970). The relation of 'artistic excellence' to 'moral truth' is discussed on pages 73ff.

3 See *ibid.*, 118. Swinburne's Latin epigrams on Cloacinus (Lang, ii, 277) make clear the connection between them and the Emerson interview.

4 Edmund Gosse, *The Life of Algernon Charles Swinburne* (London, 1927), 156.

5 *Swinburne: The Critical Heritage*, 133.

6 In *The Times Literary Supplement* for 25 December 1959 (p. 755), Robert H. Tener demonstrated that two of the selections on Hugo in the Bonchurch Edition have been incorrectly attributed to Swinburne. See my headnote for No. 9.

7 From the 'author's preface' to *Prometheus Unbound*; quoted in William K. Wimsatt, Jr., and Cleanth Brooks, *Literary Criticism: A Short History* (New York and London, 1957), 423.

8 Robert L. Peters, *The Crowns of Apollo* (Detroit, 1965), 151.

9 Thomas E. Connolly, who developed this contrast in an earlier article, has a chapter on it in *Swinburne's Theory of Poetry* (State University of New York, 1964).

10 This introduction uses 'Romantic' (with a capital) chiefly as an indication of chronology.

11 Heine's epilogue to his *Romanzero* tells how in 1848 he had gone out 'for the last time' (he did not die till 1856) and had collapsed in the Louvre near 'Our Beloved Lady of Milo'.

12 *New Writings by Swinburne*, ed. Cecil Y. Lang (Syracuse, New York, 1964), 77.

13 In Appendix XI (on *Willobie His Avisa*) of the New Variorum edition of Shakespeare's *Sonnets*, ed. H. E. Rollins (Philadelphia and London, 1944), Marie Louise Edel notes (ii, 302 n.) that Charles Hughes's edition of *Willobie His Avisa* (1904) is dedicated to Swinburne. Grosart's had appeared in 1880.

14 Symonds's comments in a copy of *Tristram of Lyonesse* are quoted in *A Catalogue of the First Editions of the Works of Algernon Charles Swinburne in the Library of Edward K. Butler*: 'We yearly grow more and more to love and admire this poet for his overflowing generosity and intellectual humility; for his unsparing recognition of excellence and greatness wherever he may find it among dead men and living men of letters.'

15 *The Letters of John Addington Symonds*, ed. Herbert M. Schueller and Robert L. Peters (Detroit, 1967–69), iii, 129.

16 T. S. Eliot, *The Sacred Wood: Essays on Poetry and Criticism* (New York and London, 1930), 24.

17 Gosse's *Life*, 75.

Upsala College
Library
East Orange, N. J. 07019

18 Cf. Lang, iv, 279, Swinburne's letter to Bullen: 'I am sincerely gratified to know that my studies on Ford and Chapman did for you something of what Lamb did for me when a boy at Eton.'

19 In the *Fortnightly Review*, May 1917, 795.

20 *A Survey of English Literature* 1780–1880 (New York, 1920), iv, 81.

Note on the text

Except for the review of Baudelaire's *Fleurs du Mal* and 'Charles Dickens', which appeared only in periodicals, the texts are based upon Swinburne's published books and take account of possible changes in his lifetime, though I may add that nearly all later 'editions', as T. J. Wise's *Bibliography* calls them, are, in the bibliographical sense, new issues rather than new editions; apart from revealing Swinburne's correction of misprints, examining them does not usually reveal important differences. I have compared the essays with texts appearing earlier in periodicals or encyclopaedias, and in headnotes or notes at the end of selections have mentioned some interesting changes.

The treatment of quotation marks and italics, especially in the handling of titles, has been made consistent. Swinburne was of course not unique in writing 'awhile' in phrases like 'for a while', but it does not seem desirable to reproduce this misspelling, historically anomalous and still unacceptable in good usage. I have silently corrected a few misprints. Otherwise the texts are faithfully reproduced.

Poetry and Art

1 Charles Baudelaire: *Les Fleurs du Mal* 1862

'Charles Baudelaire: *Les Fleurs du Mal*', which appeared in the *Spectator* for 6 September 1862, was not published again in Swinburne's lifetime. After reading it, the French poet expressed his appreciation but suggested that Swinburne had overstated the moral grounds for his defence (Lang, i, 87–8). In his only public address, given at the Royal Literary Fund dinner in May 1866, Swinburne referred to the author of *Les Fleurs du Mal* as 'one of the most exquisite, most delicate, most perfect poets of the century'. The report of Baudelaire's death led him to insert a note in *William Blake* and to compose his finest tribute, the elegy '*Ave atque Vale*'. Swinburne's comment in 1901, 'I never had really much in common with Baudelaire, though I retain all my early admiration for his genius at its best' (Lang, vi, 153), was not, as some have construed it, a repudiation but a simple statement of fact. The poet may have recalled allegations, like Robert Buchanan's, that he had taken over Baudelaire's 'animalism'. Similarities stressed by the early critics were largely due to shared interests, tastes, and kind of sensibility.

It is now some time since France has turned out any new poet of very high note or importance; the graceful, slight, somewhat thin-spun classical work of M. Théodore de Banville hardly carries weight enough to tell across the Channel; indeed, the best of this writer's books, in spite of exquisite humorous character and a most flexible and brilliant style, is too thoroughly Parisian to bear transplanting at all. French poetry of the present date, taken at its highest, is not less effectually hampered by tradition and the taste of the greater number of readers than our own is. A French poet is expected to believe in philanthropy, and break off on occasion in the middle of his proper work to lend a shove forward to some theory of progress. The critical students there, as well as here, judging by the books they praise and the advice they proffer, seem to have pretty well forgotten that a poet's business is presumably to write good verses, and by no means to redeem the age and remould society. No other form of art is so pestered with this impotent appetite for meddling in quite extraneous matters; but the mass of readers seem actually to think that a poem is the better for containing a moral lesson or assisting in a tangible and material good work. The courage and sense of a man who at such a time ventures to profess and act on the conviction that the art of poetry has absolutely nothing to do with didactic matter at all, are proof enough of the wise and serious manner in which he is likely to handle the materials of his art. From a critic who has put forward the just and sane view of this matter with a consistent eloquence, one may well expect to get as perfect and careful poetry as he can give.

To some English readers the name of M. Baudelaire may be known rather through his admirable translations, and the criticisms on American and English writers appended to these, and framing them in fit and sufficient commentary, than by his volume of poems, which, perhaps, has hardly yet had time to make its way among us. That it will in the long run fail of its meed of admiration, whether here or in France, we do not believe. Impeded at starting by a foolish and shameless prosecution, the first edition was, it appears, withdrawn before anything like a fair hearing had been obtained for it. The book now comes before us with a few of the original poems cancelled, but with important additions. Such as it now is, to sum up the merit and meaning of it is not easy to do in a few sentences. Like all good books, and all work of any original savour and strength, it will be long a debated point of argument, vehemently impugned and eagerly upheld.

We believe that M. Baudelaire's first publications were his essays on the contemporary art of France, written now many years since. In these early writings there is already such admirable judgment, vigour of thought and style, and appreciative devotion to the subject, that the worth of his own future work in art might have been foretold even then. He has more delicate power of verse than almost any man living, after Victor Hugo, Browning, and (in his lyrics) Tennyson. The sound of his metres suggests colour and perfume. His perfect workmanship makes every subject admirable and respectable. Throughout the chief part of this book, he has chosen to dwell mainly upon sad and strange things—the weariness of pain and the bitterness of pleasure—the perverse happiness and wayward sorrows of exceptional people. It has the languid lurid beauty of close and threatening weather—a heavy heated temperature, with dangerous hothouse scents in it; thick shadow of cloud about it, and fire of molten light. It is quite clear of all whining and windy lamentation; there is nothing of the blubbering and shrieking style long since exploded. The writer delights in problems, and has a natural leaning to obscure and sorrowful things. Failure and sorrow, next to physical beauty and perfection of sound or scent, seem to have an infinite attraction for him. In some points he resembles Keats, or still more his chosen favourite among modern poets, Edgar Poe; at times, too, his manner of thought has a relish of Marlowe, and even the sincerer side of Byron. From Théophile Gautier, to whom the book is dedicated, he has caught the habit of a faultless and studious simplicity; but, indeed, it seems merely natural to him always to use the right word and the right rhyme. How supremely musical and flexible a perfect artist in writing can make the French language, any chance page of the book is enough to prove; every description, the slightest and shortest even, has a special mark on it of the writer's keen and peculiar power. The style is sensuous and weighty; the sights seen are steeped most often in sad light and sullen colour. As instances of M. Baudelaire's strength and beauty of manner, one might take especially the poems headed 'Le Masque', 'Parfum Exotique', 'La Chevelure', 'Les Sept Vieillards', 'Les Petites Vieilles', 'Brumes et Pluies';[1] of his perfect mastery in description, and sharp individual drawing of character and form, the following stray verses plucked out at random may stand for a specimen:—[2]

Sur ta chevelure profonde
Aux âcres parfums,
Mer odorante et vagabonde
Aux flots bleus et bruns,

Comme un navire qui s'éveille
Au vent du matin,
Mon âme réveuse appareille
Pour un ciel lointain.

Tes yeux où rien ne se révèle
De doux ni d'amer
Sont deux bijoux froids où se mêle
L'or avec le fer.

Et ton corps se penche et s'allonge
Comme un fin vaisseau
Qui roule bord sur bord et plonge
Ses vergues dans l'eau.

The whole poem is worth study for its vigorous beauty and the careful facility of its expression. Perhaps, though, the sonnet headed 'Causerie' is a still completer specimen of the author's power. The way in which the sound and sense are suddenly broken off and shifted, four lines from the end, is wonderful for effect and success. M. Baudelaire's mastery of the sonnet form is worth remarking as a test of his natural bias towards such forms of verse as are most nearly capable of perfection. In a book of this sort, such a leaning of the writer's mind is almost necessary. The matters treated of will bear no rough or hasty handling. Only supreme excellence of words will suffice to grapple with and fitly render the effects of such material. Not the luxuries of pleasure in their simple first form, but the sharp and cruel enjoyments of pain, the acrid relish of suffering felt or inflicted, the sides on which nature looks unnatural, go to make up the stuff and substance of this poetry. Very good material they make, too; but evidently such things are unfit for rapid or careless treatment. The main charm of the book is, upon the whole, that nothing is wrongly given, nothing capable of being re-written or improved on its own ground. Concede the starting point, and you cannot have a better runner.

Thus, even of the loathsomest bodily putrescence and decay he can make some noble use; pluck out its meaning and secret, even its beauty, in a certain way, from actual carrion; as here, of the flies bred in a carcase.[3]

Tout cela descendait, montait comme une vague;
  Ou s'élançaint en pétillant.
On eût dit que le corps, enflé d'un souffle vague,
  Vivait en se multipliant.

Et ce monde rendait une étrange musique,
  Comme l'eau courante et le vent,
Ou le grain qu'un vanneur d'un mouvement rhythmique
  Agite et tourne dans son van.

Another of this poet's noblest sonnets is that 'À une Passante', comparable with a similar one of Keats, 'Time's sea hath been five years at its slow ebb', but superior for directness of point and forcible reality. Here for once the beauty of a poem is rather passionate than sensuous. Compare the delicate emblematic manner in which Keats winds up his sonnet to this sharp perfect finale:—[4]

> Fugitive beauté
> Dont le regard m'a fait soudainement renaître,
> Ne te verrai-je plus que dans l'éternité?
> Ailleurs, bien loin d'ici, trop tard! jamais peut-être!
> Car j'ignore où tu fuis, tu ne sais où je vais,
> O toi que j'eusse aimée, ô toi qui le savais!

There is noticeable also in M. Baudelaire's work a quality of *drawing* which recalls the exquisite power in the same way of great French artists now living. His studies are admirable for truth and grace; his figure-painting has the ease and strength, the trained skill, and beautiful gentle justice of manner, which come out in such pictures as the 'Source' of Ingres, or that other splendid study by Flandrin, of a curled-up naked figure under full soft hot light, now exhibiting here. These verses of Baudelaire's are as perfect and good as either.[5]

> —Tes sourcils méchants
> Te donnent un air étrange,
> Qui n'est pas celui d'un ange,
> Sorcière aux yeux alléchants,
>
> . . . . . .
>
> Sur ta chair le parfum rôde
> Comme autour d'un encensoir;
> Tu charmes comme le soir,
> Nymphe ténébreuse et chaude.
>
> . . . . . .
>
> Le désert et la forêt
> Embaument tes tresses rudes;
> Ta tête a les attitudes
> De l'énigme et du secret.
>
> *Tes hanches sont amoureuses*
> *De ton dos et de tes seins*,
> Et tu ravis les coussins
> Par tes poses langoureuses.

Nothing can beat that as a piece of beautiful drawing.

It may be worth while to say something of the moral and meaning of many among these poems. Certain critics, who will insist on going into this matter, each man as deep as his small leaden plummet will reach, have discovered what they call a paganism on the spiritual side of the author's tone of thought. Stripped of its coating of jargon, this may mean that the poet spoken of endeavours to look at most things with the eye of an old-world poet; that he aims at regaining the clear and simple view of writers content to believe in the beauty of material subjects. To us, if this were the meaning of these people, we must say it seems a foolish one; for there is not one of these poems that could have been written in a time when it was not the fashion to dig for moral motives and conscious reasons. Poe, for example, has written poems without any moral meaning at all; there is not one poem of the *Fleurs du Mal* which has not a distinct and vivid background of morality to it. Only this moral side of the book is not thrust forward in the foolish and repulsive manner of a half-taught artist; the background, as we called it, is not out of drawing. If any reader could extract from any poem a positive spiritual medicine—if he could swallow a sonnet like a moral prescription—then clearly the poet supplying these intellectual drugs would be a bad artist; indeed, no real artist, but a huckster and vendor of miscellaneous wares. But those who will look for them may find moralities in plenty behind every poem of M. Baudelaire's; such poems especially as 'Une Martyre'. Like a mediæval preacher, when he has drawn the heathen love, he puts sin on its right hand and death on its left. It is not his or any artist's business to warn against evil; but certainly he does not exhort to it, knowing well enough that the one fault is as great as the other.

But into all this we do not advise any one to enter who can possibly keep out of it. When a book has been so violently debated over, so hauled this way and that by contentious critics, the one intent on finding that it means something mischievous, and the other intent on finding that it means something useful, those who are in search neither of a poisonous compound nor of a cathartic drug had better leave the disputants alone, or take only such notice of them as he absolutely must take. Allegory is the dullest game and the most profitless taskwork imaginable; but if so minded a reader might extract most elaborate meanings from this poem of 'Une Martyre'; he might discover a likeness between the Muse of the writer and that strange figure of a beautiful body with the head severed, laid apart

Sur la table de nuit comme une renoncule.[6]

The heavy 'mass of dark mane and heap of precious jewels' might mean the glorious style and decorative language clothing this poetry of strange disease and sin; the hideous violence wrought by a shameless and senseless love might stand as an emblem of that analysis of things monstrous and sorrowful, which stamps the whole book with its special character. Then again, the divorce between all aspiration and its results might be here once more given in type; the old question re-handled:—

What hand and brain went ever paired?
What heart alike conceived and dared?[7]

and the sorrowful final divorce of will from deed accomplished at last by force; and the whole thing summed up in that noble last stanza:—[8]

Ton époux court le monde; et ta forme immortelle
  Veille près de lui quand il dort;
Autant que toi sans doute il te sera fidèle,
  Et constant jusque à la mort.

All this and more might be worked out if the reader cared to try; but we hope he would not. The poem is quite beautiful and valuable enough as merely the 'design of an unknown master'. In the same way one might use up half the poems in the book; for instance, those three beautiful studies of cats (fitly placed in a book that has altogether a feline style of beauty—subtle, luxurious, with sheathed claws); or such carefully tender sketches as 'Le Beau Navire';[9] or that Latin hymn 'Franciscæ meæ [Laudes]':—[10]

Novis te cantabo chordis,
O novelletum quod ludis
In solitudine cordis.

Esto sertis implicata,
O fœmina delicata
Per quam solvuntur peccata!

Some few indeed, as that *ex-voto* poem 'À une Madone', appeal at once to the reader as to an interpreter; they are distinctly of a mystical moral turn, and in that rich symbolic manner almost unsurpassable for beauty.[11]

Avec mes Vers polis, treillis d'un pur métal
Savamment constellé de rimes de cristal,
Je ferai pour ta tête une énorme Couronne;

Et dans ma Jalousie, ô mortelle Madone,
Je saurai te tailler un manteau, de façon
Barbare, roide et lourd et doublé de soupçon,
Qui comme une guérite enfermera tes charmes;
Non de Perles brodé, mais de toutes mes Larmes!
Ta Robe, ce sera mon Désir, frémissant,
Onduleux, mon Désir qui monte et qui descend,
Aux pointes se suspend, aux vallons se repose,
Et revêt d'un baiser tout ton corps blanc et rose.

Before passing on to the last poem we wish to indicate for especial remark, we may note a few others in which this singular strength of finished writing is most evident. Such are, for instance, 'Le Cygne', 'Le Poison', 'Tristesse de la Lune', 'Remord Posthume', 'Le Flacon', 'Ciel Brouillé', 'Une Mendiante Rousse' (a simpler study than usual, of great beauty in all ways, noticeable for its revival of the old fashion of unmixed masculine rhymes), 'Le Balcon', 'Allegorie', 'L'Amour et le Crâne',[12] and the two splendid sonnets marked xxvii. and xlii. We cite these headings in no sort of order, merely as they catch one's eye in revising the list of contents and recall the poems classed there. Each of them we regard as worth a separate study, but the 'Litanies de Satan', as in a way the key-note to this whole complicated tune of poems, we had set aside for the last, much as (to judge by its place in the book) the author himself seems to have done.

Here it seems as if all failure and sorrow on earth, and all the cast-out things of the world—ruined bodies and souls diseased—made their appeal, in default of help, to Him in whom all sorrow and all failure were incarnate. As a poem, it is one of the noblest lyrics ever written; the sound of it between wailing and triumph, as it were the blast blown by the trumpets of a brave army in irretrievable defeat.[13]

O toi qui de la Mort, ta vieille et forte amante,
Engendras l'Espérance—une folle charmante!
  O Satan, prends pitié de ma longue misère!

Toi qui fais au proscrit ce regard calme et haut
Qui damne tout un peuple autour d'un échafaud,
  O Satan, prends pitié de ma longue misère!

. . . .

Toi qui, magiquement, assouplis les vieux os
De l'ivrogne attardé foulé par les chevaux,
  O Satan, prends pitié de ma longue misère!

Toi qui, pour consoler l'homme frêle qui souffre,
Nous appris à mêler le salpêtre et le soufre,
O Satan, prends pitié de ma longue misère!

These lines are not given as more finished than the rest; every verse has the vibration in it of naturally sound and pure metal. It is a study of metrical cadence throughout, of wonderful force and variety. Perhaps it may be best, without further attempts to praise or to explain the book, here to leave off, with its stately and passionate music fresh in our ears. We know that in time it must make its way; and to know when or how concerns us as little as it probably concerns the author, who can very well afford to wait without much impatience.

NOTES

1 'The Mask', 'Exotic Perfume', 'The Hair', 'The Seven Old Men', 'The Little Old Women', 'Mists and Rains'.
2 From '*Le Serpent qui danse*': 'Upon your heavy hair with pungent perfumes, a fragrant tossing sea with blue and brown billows, like a ship that rouses in the morning breeze my soul in its reverie sets off for a distant sky. Your eyes, in which nothing of sweet or bitter is revealed, are two cold gems where gold is mingled with iron. And your body bends and stretches out like a splendid ship that rolls from side to side and plunges its sail-yards in the water.'
3 From '*Une Charogne*': 'All of that descended, [then] rose like a wave, or darted forth sparkling; one would have said that the corpse, swollen by a faint breath, was living and even multiplying itself. And this retinue [a swarm of flies] made a strange music like running water and wind, or the grain which a winnower shakes and tosses in his [winnowing] basket with rhythmic motion.'
4 From 'To a Woman Passing by': 'Fleeting beauty whose glance has suddenly given me new life, shall I see you no more but in eternity? Somewhere else, far, far from here, too late! never, perhaps! for I do not know whither you are fleeing, you do not know where I am going, O you whom I would have loved, O you who knew it.'
5 From '*Chanson d'après-midi*' ('Afternoon Song'): 'Your wicked eyebrows give you a strange air—not that of an angel, you sorceress with alluring eyes. Perfume roams on your flesh as around a censer: nymph dark and warm, you charm like the evening. Your rugged tresses savour of desert and forest. Your head has an air of the secret and mysterious. Your hips are enamoured of your back and your breasts, and with your languorous poses you ravish the cushions.'
6 From 'A Martyr': 'On the night-table, like a ranunculus.'

7 Browning's 'The Last Ride Together', ll. 56–7.

8 From 'A Martyr': 'Your husband roams the world, and your immortal form watches near him when he sleeps; as much as you, no doubt, he will be faithful to you and constant till death.'

9 'The Beautiful Ship.'

10 'Praises of My Frances': 'I shall sing to you with new strings, O garden of my delight, which you play in loneliness of heart. You should be entwined with garlands, O delicate woman through whom sins are absolved.'

11 From 'To a Madonna: a Votive Poem in the Spanish Manner': 'With my polished verse, lattice-work of pure metal, skilfully studded with rimes of crystal, I shall make an enormous crown for your head; and out of my jealousy, O mortal Madonna, I shall be able to cut a mantle for you, of uncouth fashion, stiff, heavy, and lined with suspicion, which shall enclose your charms like a sentry-box; not embroidered with pearls, but with all my tears! Your robe shall be my desire, quivering, sinuous—my desire which rises and falls, clings to itself on peaks and reposes in hollows and clothes with kisses your pink and white body.'

12 'The Swan', 'The Poison', 'Sadness of the Moon', 'Remorse after Death', 'The Flask', 'Murky Sky', 'A Red-headed Beggar', 'The Balcony', 'Allegory', 'Love and the Skull'.

13 From 'Satan's Litanies': 'O you who from Death, your old and strong love, beget Hope—a mad charmer! O Satan, have pity on my long misery! You who give to the outlaw that calm and lofty glance which condemns all the rabble around a scaffold! . . . You who, magically, make supple the old bones of the loitering drunkard trampled on by horses [so that his bones are not broken]. . . . You who, to console the frail, suffering man, taught us to mix saltpeter and sulphur [material used in gunpowder, by whose means a sufferer may end his troubles]....'

2 Byron
1866, 1875

'Byron', which was originally a 'preface' to a selection of Byron's poems (1866) and was reprinted in *Essays and Studies* (1875), became, according to the historian of Byron's fame, Samuel C. Chew, a turning point in the story of that poet's reputation. Alfred Austin's *Poetry of the Period*, which exalted Byron and depreciated contemporary poets, was one reason why Swinburne's *Under the Microscope* (1872) emphasized Tennyson's superiority to Byron as a lyrist. In his essay on Byron, Matthew Arnold quoted, making it a key passage, Swinburne's reference to Byron's 'splendid and imperishable excellence which covers all his offences and outweighs all his defects: the excellence of sincerity and strength'. But Arnold's ranking Byron and Wordsworth above Shelley and Coleridge led Swinburne, in his 'Wordsworth and Byron' (*Miscellanies*, 1886), to over-emphasize Byron's faults as a man and as a lyric poet, though he had written in 1879 that he had 'nothing to add or recant, and little if anything to modify, on reconsideration of my early essay' (Lang, iv, 105).

In revising the 'preface' for *Essays and Studies*, Swinburne added the first three of his footnotes and omitted his concluding paragraph.

[Prefatory note.—This, like the following essay, was prefixed to a small volume of selections from the poems of the author whose genius is the subject of discussion. To the work of Coleridge this process of selection, if adequately carried out, must have been, as Leigh Hunt long since suggested, a real and great service; for his work is distinctly divisible into good and bad, durable and perishable; and it would be a clear gain to have the priceless parts of that work detached from the worthless; but to Byron, who rarely wrote anything either worthless or faultless, it could not be otherwise than injurious. He can only be judged or appreciated in the mass; the greatest of his works was his whole work taken altogether; and to know or to honour him aright he must be considered with all his imperfections and with all his glories on his head.[1]]

The most delicate and thoughtful of English critics has charged the present generation of Englishmen with forgetfulness of Byron.[2] It is not a light charge: and it is not ungrounded. Men born when this century was getting into its forties were baptized into another church than his with the rites of another creed. Upon their ears, first after the cadences of elder poets, fell the faultless and fervent melodies of Tennyson. To them, chief among the past heroes of the younger century, three men appeared as predominant in poetry; Coleridge, Keats, and Shelley. Behind these were effaced, on either hand, the two great opposing figures of Byron and Wordsworth. No man under twenty can just now be expected to appreciate these. The time was when all boys and girls who paddled in rhyme and dabbled in sentiment were wont to adore the presence or the memory of Byron with foolish faces of praise. It is of little moment to him or to us that they have long since ceased to cackle and begun to hiss. They have become used to better verse and carefuller workmen; and must be forgiven if after such training they cannot at once appreciate the splendid and imperishable excellence which covers all his offences and outweighs all his defects: the excellence of sincerity and strength. Without these no poet can live; but few have ever had so much of them as Byron. His sincerity indeed is difficult to discover and define; but it does in effect lie at the root of all his good works: deformed by pretension and defaced by assumption, masked by folly and veiled by affectation; but perceptible after all, and priceless.

It is no part of my present office to rewrite the history of a life in which every date and event that could be given would now seem trite and stale to all possible readers. If, after so many promises and hints, something at once new and true shall at length be unearthed or extricated, which may affect for the better or the worse our judgment of the man, it will be possible and necessary to rewrite it. Meantime this among other chances 'lies on the lap of the gods';[3] and especially on the lap of a goddess who still treads our earth. Until she speaks, we cannot guess what she may have to say; and can only pass by with reverent or with sceptical reticence.[4]

Thus much however we may safely assert: that no man's work was ever more influenced by his character; and that no man's character was ever more influenced by his circumstances. Rather from things without than from things within him did the spirit of Byron assume colour and shape. His noblest verse leapt on a sudden into life after the heaviest evils had fallen upon him which even he ever underwent. From the beginning indeed he had much to fight against; and three impediments hung about him at starting, the least of which would have weighed down a less strong man: youth, and genius, and an ancient name.[5] In spite of all three he made his way; and suffered for it. At the first chance given or taken, every obscure and obscene thing that lurks for pay or prey among the fouler shallows and thickets of literature flew against him; every hound and every hireling lavished upon him the loathsome tribute of their abuse; all nameless creatures that nibble and prowl, upon whom the serpent's curse has fallen, to go upon his belly and eat dust all the days of his life,[6] assailed him with their foulest venom and their keenest fangs. And the promise given of old to their kind was now at least fulfilled: they did bruise his heel. But the heads of such creatures are so small that it is hard to bruise them in return; it would first be necessary to discern them.

That Byron was able to disregard and to outlive the bark and the bite of such curs as these is small praise enough: the man who cannot do as much is destructible, and therefore contemptible. He did far more than this; he withstood the weight of circumstances to the end; not always without complaint, but always without misgiving. His glorious courage, his excellent contempt for things contemptible, and hatred of hateful men, are enough of themselves to embalm and endear his memory in the eyes of all who are worthy to pass judgment upon him. And these qualities gave much of their own value to verse not otherwise or not always praiseworthy. Even at its best, the serious poetry of Byron is often so rough and loose, so weak in the screws and joints which hold together the framework of verse, that it is not easy to praise it enough without seeming to condone or to extenuate such faults as should not be overlooked or forgiven. No poet is so badly represented by a book of selections. It must show something of his weakness; it cannot show all of his strength. Often, after a noble overture, the last note struck is either dissonant or ineffectual. His magnificent masterpiece, which must endure for ever among the precious relics of the world, will not bear dissection or extraction. The merit of *Don Juan* does not lie in any part, but in the whole. There is in that great poem an especial and exquisite balance and sustenance of alternate tones which cannot be expressed or explained by the utmost ingenuity of selection. Haidée is supplanted by Dudù, the shipwreck by the siege, the Russian court by the English household; and this perpetual change, this tidal variety of experience and emotion, gives to the poem something of the breadth and freshness of the sea. Much of the poet's earlier work is or seems unconsciously dishonest; this, if not always or wholly unaffected, is as honest as the sunlight, as frank as the sea-wind. Here, and here alone, the student of his work may recognise and enjoy the ebb and flow of actual life. Here the pulse of vital blood may be felt in tangible flesh. Here for the first time the style of Byron is beyond all praise or blame: a style at once swift and supple, light and strong, various and radiant. Between *Childe Harold* and *Don Juan* the same difference exists which a swimmer feels between lake-water and sea-water: the one is fluent, yielding, invariable; the other has in it a life and pulse, a sting and a swell, which touch and excite the nerves like fire or like music. Across the stanzas of *Don Juan* we swim forward as over 'the broad backs of the sea';[7] they break and glitter, hiss and laugh, murmur and move, like waves that sound or that subside. There is in them a delicious resistance, an elastic motion, which salt water has and fresh water has not. There is about them a wide wholesome air, full of vivid light and constant wind, which is only felt at sea. Life undulates and death palpitates in the splendid verse which resumes the evidence of a brave and clear-sighted man concerning life and death. Here, as at sea, there is enough and too much of fluctuation and intermission; the ripple flags and falls in loose and lazy lines: the foam flies wide of any mark, and the breakers collapse here and there in sudden ruin and violent failure. But the violence and weakness of the sea are preferable to the smooth sound and equable security of a lake: its buoyant and progressive impulse sustains and propels those who would sink through weariness in the flat and placid shallows. There are others whom it sickens, and others whom it chills; these will do well to steer inshore.

It is natural in writing of Byron to slide into remembrances of what is likest to his verse. His work and Shelley's, beyond that of all our other poets, recall or suggest the wide and high things of nature; the large likeness of the elements; the immeasurable liberty and the stormy strength of waters and winds. They are strongest when they touch upon these; and it is worth remark how few are the poets of whom this can be said. Here, as elsewhere, Shakespeare is supreme when it pleased him; but it pleased him rarely. No poetry of shipwreck and the sea has ever equalled the great scene of *Pericles*; no such note of music was ever struck out of the clash and contention of tempestuous elements. In Milton the sublimity is chiefly of sound; the majesty of melodies unsurpassed from all time wellnigh excludes and supplants all other motives of material beauty.[8] In the minds of mediæval poets there was no width or depth to receive and contain such emotion. In Spenser, despite his fertile and fluent ingenuity, his subtle and sleepy graces, the effeminacy of colour no less than the monotony of metre makes it hopeless to look for any trace of that passionate sense of power and delight in great outer things of which we speak here. Among later men, Coleridge and Keats used nature mainly as a stimulant or a sedative; Wordsworth as a vegetable fit to shred into his pot and pare down like the outer leaves of a lettuce for didactic and culinary purposes.[9] All these doubtless in their own fashion loved her, for her beauties, for her uses, for her effects; hardly one for herself.

Turn now to Byron or to Shelley. These two at least were not content to play with her skirts and paddle in her shallows. Their passion is perfect, a fierce and blind desire which exalts and impels their verse into the high places of emotion and expression. They feed upon nature with a holy hunger, follow her with a divine lust as of gods chasing the daughters of men.[10] Wind and fire, the cadences of thunder and the clamours of the sea, gave to them no less of sensual pleasure than of spiritual sustenance. These things they desired as others desire music or wine or the beauty of women. This outward and indifferent nature of things, cruel in the eyes of all but her lovers, and even in theirs not loving, became as pliant to their grasp and embrace as any Clymene or Leucothea to Apollo's.[11] To them the large motions and the remote beauties of space were tangible and familiar as flowers. Of this poetry, where description melts into passion and contemplation takes fire from delight, the highest sample is Shelley's 'Ode to the West Wind'. An imperfect mastery of his materials keeps the best things of Byron some few degrees below an equal rank. One native and incurable defect grew up and strengthened side by side with his noblest qualities: a feeble and faulty sense of metre. No poet of equal or inferior rank ever had so bad an ear. His smoother cadences are often vulgar and facile; his fresher notes are often incomplete and inharmonious. His verse stumbles and jingles, stammers and halts, where there is most need for a swift and even pace of musical sound. The rough sonorous changes of the songs in *The Deformed Transformed* rise far higher in harmony and strike far deeper into the memory than the lax easy lines in which he at first indulged; but they slip too readily into notes as rude and weak as the rhymeless tuneless verse in which they are so loosely set, as in a cheap and casual frame. The magnificent lyric measures of *Heaven and Earth* are defaced by the coarse obtrusion of short lines with jagged edges: no small offence in a writer of verse. Otherwise these choral scenes are almost as blameless as they are brilliant. The poet who above others took delight in the sense of sounding storms and shaken waters could not but exult over the vision of deluge with all his strength and breadth of wing. Tempest and rebellion and the magnificence of anguish were as the natural food and fire to kindle and sustain his indomitable and sleepless spirit. The godless martyrdom of rebels; the passion that cannot redeem; the Thebaid whose first hermit was Cain,[12] the Calvary whose first martyr was Satan; these, time after time, allured and inspired him. Here for once this inner and fiery passion of thought found outer clothing and expression in the ruin of a world. Both without and within, the subject was made for him, and lay ready shapen for the strong impressure of his hand. His love of wide and tempestuous waters fills his work throughout as with the broad breath of a sea-wind. Even the weakest of his poems, a thing still-born and shapeless, is redeemed and revived by one glorious verse:—[13]

When the Poles crashed, and water was the world.

This passion and power in dealing with the higher things of nature, with her large issues and remote sources, has been bestowed upon Victor Hugo alone among our contemporaries. He also can pass beyond the idyllic details of landscape, and put out from shore into the wide waste places of the sea. And this of course is the loftiest form of such poetry as deals with outward nature and depends upon the forms of things. In Byron the power given by this passion is the more conspicuous through his want of dramatic capacity. Except in the lighter and briefer scenes of *Don Juan*, he was never able to bring two speakers face to face and supply them with the right words. In structure as in metre his elaborate tragedies are wholly condemnable; filled as they are in spirit with the overflow of his fiery energy. *Cain* and *Manfred* are properly monologues decorated and set off by some slight appendage of ornament or explanation. In the later and loftier poem there is no difference perceptible, except in strength and knowledge, between Lucifer and Cain. Thus incompetent to handle the mysteries and varieties of character, Byron turns always with a fresh delight and a fresh confidence thither where he feels himself safe and strong. No part of his nature was more profound and sincere than the vigorous love of such inanimate things as were in tune with his own spirit and senses. His professions of contempt were too loud to express it; scorn is brief or silent; anger alone finds vent in violent iteration and clamorous appeal. He had too much of fury and not enough of contempt; he foams at things and creatures not worth a glance or a blow. But when once clear of men and confronted with elements, he casts the shell of pretence and drops the veil of habit; then, as in the last and highest passage of a poem which has suffered more from praise than any other from dispraise, his scorn of men caught in the nets of nature and necessity has no alloy of untruth; his spirit is mingled with the sea's, and overlooks with a superb delight the ruins and the prayers of men.

This loftiest passage in *Childe Harold* has been so often mouthed and mauled by vulgar admiration that it now can scarcely be relished. Like a royal robe worn out, or a royal wine grown sour, it seems the worse for having been so good. But in fact, allowing for one or two slips and blots, we must after all replace it among the choice and high possessions of poetry. After the first there is hardly a weak line; many have a wonderful vigour and melody; and the deep and glad disdain of the sea for men and the works of men passes into the verse in music and fills it with a weighty and sonorous harmony grave and sweet as the measured voice of heavy remote waves. No other passage in the fourth canto will bear to be torn out from the text; and this one suffers by extraction. The other three cantos are more loosely built and less compact of fabric; but in the first two there is little to remember or to praise. Much of the poem is written throughout in falsetto; there is a savour in many places as of something false and histrionic. This singular and deep defect, which defaces so much of Byron's work, seems also to have deformed his personal character, to have given a twist to his enmities and left a taint upon his friendships. He was really somewhat sombre and sad at heart, and it pleased him to seem sadder than he was. He was impressible and susceptible of pleasure, able to command and enjoy it; and of this also it pleased him to make the most in public. But in fact he was neither a Harold nor a Juan; he was better than these in his own way, and assumed their parts and others with a hypocrisy but half insincere. The fault was probably in great part unconscious, and transparent as a child's acting. To the keen eye and cool judgment of Stendhal it was at once perceptible. Byron's letter to him in defence of Scott[14] was doubtless not insincere; yet it is evident that the writer felt himself to be playing a graceful part to advantage. This fretful and petulant appetite for applause, the proper apanage[15] of small poets and lowly aspirants, had in Byron's case to wrestle with the just pride of place and dignity of genius; no man ever had more of these; yet they did not always support him; he fell even into follies and vulgarities unworthy of a meaner name than his. In effect, when his errors were gravest, he erred through humility and not through pride. Pride would have sustained him far above the remarks and reviews of his day, the praise or dispraise of his hour. As it was, he was vulnerable even by creeping things; and at times their small stings left a poison behind which turned his blood. The contagion of their touch infected him; and he strove under its influence to hiss and wound as they. Here and there in his letters and reflections, in the loose records of his talk and light fragments of his work, the traces of infection are flagrant.

But these defects were only as scars on the skin, superficial and removable; they are past and done with; while all of him that was true and good remains, as it will to all time. Justice cannot be done to it here or now. It is enough if after careful selection as little injustice be done as possible. His few sonnets, unlike Shelley's, are all good; the best is that on Bonnivard, one of his noblest and completest poems. The versified narratives which in their day were so admirable and famous have yielded hardly a stray sheaf to the gleaner. They have enough of vigour and elasticity to keep life in them yet; but once chipped or broken their fabric would crumble and collapse. The finest among them is certainly either *The Giaour* or *The Siege of Corinth*; the weakest is probably either *Parisina* or *The Bride of Abydos*.[16] But in none of these is there even a glimpse of Byron's higher and rarer faculty. All that can be said for them is that they gave tokens of a talent singularly fertile, rapid and vivid; a certain power of action and motion which redeems them from the complete stagnation of dead verses; a command over words and rhymes never of the best and never of the worst. In *The Giaour*, indeed, there is something of a fiery sincerity which in its successors appears diluted and debased.[17]

The change began in Byron when he first found out his comic power, and rose at once beyond sight or shot of any rival. His early satires are wholly devoid of humour, wit, or grace; the verse of *Beppo*, bright and soft and fluent, is full at once of all. The sweet light music of its few and low notes was perfect as a prelude to the higher harmonies of laughter and tears, of scorn and passion, which as yet lay silent in the future. It is mere folly to seek in English or Italian verse a precedent or a parallel. The scheme of metre is Byron's alone; no weaker hand than his could ever bend that bow, or ever will. Even the Italian poets, working in a language more flexible and ductile than ours, could never turn their native metre to such uses, could never handle their national weapon with such grace and strength. The *terza rima* remains their own, after all our efforts to adapt it; it bears here only forced flowers and crude fruits;[18] but the *ottava rima* Byron has fairly conquered and wrested from them. Before the appearance of *Beppo* no one could foresee what a master's hand might make of the instrument; and no one could predict its further use and its dormant powers before the advent of *Don Juan*. In *The Vision of Judgment* it appears finally perfected; the metre fits the sense as with close and pliant armour, the perfect panoply of Achilles. A poem so short and hasty, based on a matter so worthy of brief contempt and long oblivion as the funeral and the fate of George III, bears about it at first sight no great sign or likelihood of life. But this poem which we have by us stands alone, not in Byron's work only, but in the work of the world. Satire in earlier times had changed her rags for robes; Juvenal had clothed with fire, and Dryden with majesty, that wandering and bastard Muse. Byron gave her wings to fly with, above the reach even of these. Others have had as much of passion and as much of humour; Dryden had perhaps as much of both combined. But here and not elsewhere a third quality is apparent: the sense of a high and clear imagination. The grave and great burlesque of King George and St. Peter is relieved and sustained by the figures of Michael and Satan. These two, confronted and corresponding as noon and night, lift and light up the background of satire, blood-red or black according to the point of view. Above all, the balance of thought and passion is admirable; human indignation and divine irony are alike understood and expressed: the pure and fiery anger of men at sight of wrongdoing, the tacit inscrutable derision of heaven. Upon this light and lofty poem a commentary might be written longer than the text and less worth reading; but here it shall not be. Those who read it with the due delight, not too gravely and not too lightly, will understand more than can now be set down; those who read it otherwise will not understand anything. Even these can hardly fail to admire the vigour and variety of scorn, the beauty and the bitterness of verse, which raise it beyond comparison with any other satire. There is enough and too much of violence and injustice in the lines on Southey; but it must be remembered that he was the first to strike, and with an unfair weapon. A poet by profession, he had assaulted with feeble fury another poet, not on the fair and open charge of bad verses, but under the impertinent and irrelevant plea that his work was an affliction or an offence to religion and morality—the most susceptible, as the most intangible, among the creatures of metaphor. A man less irritable and less powerful than Byron might be forgiven for any reprisals; and the excellence of his verses justifies their injustice. But that Southey, who could win and retain for life the love and the praise of Landor, was capable of conscious baseness or falsity, Byron himself in sober moments should hardly have believed. Between official adoration and not less official horror—between George deified and Byron denounced—the Laureate's position was grotesque enough. It was almost a good office to pelt him with the names of hireling and apostate; these charges he could reject and refute. The facts were surely sufficient: that, as to religion, his 'present Deity'[19] was the paltriest maniac among kings and Cæsars; as to morality, his feelings or his faith obliged him to decry as pernicious the greatest work of his opponent.

Side by side with the growth of his comic and satiric power, the graver genius of Byron increased and flourished. As the tree grew higher it grew shapelier; the branches it put forth on all sides were fairer of leaf and fuller of fruit than its earlier offshoots had promised. But from these hardly a stray bud or twig can be plucked off by way of sample. No detached morsel of *Don Juan*, no dismembered fragment of *Cain*, will serve to show or to suggest the excellence of either. These poems are coherent and complete as trees or flowers; they cannot be split up and parcelled out like a mosaic of artificial jewellery, which might be taken to pieces by the same artisan who put it together. It must then be remembered that any mere selection from the verse of Byron, however much of care and of goodwill be spent upon the task, must perforce either exclude or impair his very greatest work. Cancel or select a leaf from these poems, and you will injure the whole framework equally in either case. It is not without reluctance that I have given any extracts from *Don Juan*; it is not without a full sense of the damage done to these extracts by the very act of extraction. But I could only have left them untouched with a reluctance even greater; and this plea, if it can, must excuse me. As fragments they are exquisite and noble, like the broken hand or severed foot of a Greek statue; but here as much is lost as there. Taken with their context, they regain as much of beauty and of force as the sculptured foot or hand when, reunited to the perfect body, they resume their place and office among its vital and various limbs. This gift of life and variety is the supreme quality of Byron's chief poem; a quality which cannot be expressed by any system of extracts. Little can here be given beyond a sample or two of tragic and serious work. The buoyant beauty of surrounding verse, the 'innumerable laughter'[20] and the profound murmur of its many measures, the fervent flow of stanzas now like the ripples and now like the gulfs of the sea, can no more be shown by process of selection than any shallow salt pool left in the sand for sunbeams to drain dry can show the depth and length of the receding tide.

It would be waste of words and time here to enlarge at all upon the excellence of the pure comedy of *Don Juan*. From the first canto to the sixteenth; from the defence of Julia, which is worthy of Congreve or Molière, to the study of Adeline, which is worthy of Laclos or Balzac; the elastic energy of humour never falters or flags. English criticism, with a mournful murmur of unanimous virtue, did at the time, and may yet if it please, appeal against the satire which strikes home and approve the satire that flies abroad. It was said, and perhaps is still said, that the poem falls off and runs low towards the end. Those who can discover where a change for the worse begins might at least indicate the landmark, imperceptible to duller eyes, which divides the good from the bad. Others meantime will retain their belief that this cry was only raised because in these latter cantos a certain due amount of satire fell upon the false and corrupt parts of English character, its mealy-mouthed vices and its unsound virtues. Had the scene been shifted to Italy or France, we might have heard little of the poet's failing power and perverse injustice.

It is just worth a word of notice that Byron, like Fielding before him, has caught up a well-known name and prefixed it to his work, without any attempt or desire to retain the likeness or follow the tradition attached to it. With him Don Juan is simply a man somewhat handsomer and luckier than others of his age. This hero is not even a reduced copy of the great and terrible figure with which he has nothing in common but a name. The Titan of embodied evil, the likeness of sin made flesh, which grew up in the grave and bitter imagination of a Spanish poet,[21] steeped in the dyes and heated by the flames of hell, appears even in the hands of Molière diminished, and fallen as it were from Satan to Belial; but still splendid with intellect and courage that tower above the meaner minds and weaker wills of women and of men; still inflexible to human appeal and indomitable by divine anger. To crush him, heaven is compelled to use thunder and hell-fire; and by these, though stricken, he is not subdued. The sombre background of a funereal religion is not yet effaced;

but it tasked the whole strength of Molière, gigantic as that strength was, to grapple with the shadow of this giant, to transfigure upon a new stage the tragic and enormous incarnation of supreme sin. As it is, even when playing with his debtors or his peasants, the hero of Molière retains always some feature of his first likeness, some shadow of his early shape. But further than France the terrible legend has never moved. Rigid criticism would therefore say that the title of Byron's masterpiece was properly a misnomer: which is no great matter after all, since the new Juan can never be confounded with the old.

Of Byron's smaller poems there is less to say, and less space to say it. Their splendid merits and their visible defects call neither for praise nor blame. Their place and his, in the literature of England, are fixed points: no critical astronomy of the future can lower or can raise them: they have their own station for all time among the greater and the lesser stars. As a poet, Byron was surpassed, beyond all question and all comparison, by three men at least of his own time; and matched, if not now and then overmatched, by one or two others. The verse of Wordsworth, at its highest, went higher than his; the verse of Landor flowed clearer. But his own ground, where none but he could set foot, was lofty enough, fertile and various. Nothing in Byron is so worthy of wonder and admiration as the scope and range of his power. New fields and ways of work, had he lived, might have given room for exercise and matter for triumph to 'that most fiery spirit'.[22] As it is, his work was done at Missolonghi; all of his work for which the fates could spare him time. A little space was allowed him to show at least a heroic purpose, and attest a high design; then, with all things unfinished before him and behind, he fell asleep after many troubles and triumphs. Few can ever have gone wearier to the grave; none with less fear. He had done enough to earn his rest. Forgetful now and set free for ever from all faults and foes, he passed through the doorway of no ignoble death out of reach of time, out of sight of love, out of hearing of hatred, beyond the blame of England and the praise of Greece. In the full strength of spirit and of body his destiny overtook him, and made an end of all his labours. He had seen and borne and achieved more than most men on record. 'He was a great man, good at many things, and now he has attained this also, to be at rest.'[23]

NOTES

1 Cf. *Hamlet*, I, v, 78–9: '. . . sent to my account/With all my imperfections on my head.'

2 Matthew Arnold, in 'Heinrich Heine', *Essays in Criticism*.

3 *Iliad*, xvii, 514.

4 It will be evident that these lines were written before the appearance of the book in which Madame de Boissy thought fit to let the world know that she had nothing to tell worth its hearing with regard to the man whose love had made her famous, but was not the less willing to put forth that nothing in two leaden volumes of verbiage. The worst consequence of this miscarriage was not the collapse of such faint hopes or surmises as we might yet have cherished of some benefit to be received in the way of biography, some new and kindly light to be thrown on the life and character of Byron; it was the opportunity given to a filthy female moralist and novelist who was not slow to avail herself of such an occasion 'to expound her beastly mind to all'. Evidently the laurels of Mrs. Behn had long kept her successor from sleeping; it was not enough to have copied the authoress of *Oroonoko* in the selection of a sable and a servile hero; her American imitator was bent on following her down fouler ways than this. But I feel that an apology is due to the virtuous memory of the chaste Aphra; she was indeed the first 'nigger novelist', and she was likewise a vendor and purveyor of obscene fiction; but here the parallel ends; for I am not aware that she ever applied her unquestionable abilities in that unlovely line of business to the defamation at second hand of the illustrious and defenceless dead. (ACS)

'To expound . . . all' is adapted from *Cymbeline*, I, vi, 152–3: 'To expound his beastly mind to us.'

Madame de Boissy was known to Byron as the Countess Guiccioli, whose *My Recollections of Lord Byron* was translated and in 1868–9 appeared in England. 'Filthy female moralist' alludes to Harriet Beecher Stowe's sensational article 'The True Story of Lady Byron's Life' (1869). Mrs Stowe is compared to Aphra Behn (1640–89), a writer of coarse plays and of novels, of which the best-known is *Oroonoko*.

5 That his youth and his rank were flung in his face with vulgar insolence on the publication of his first little book it can hardly be necessary to remind any reader of Byron; but possibly even these offences might have been condoned in a scribbler whose work had given no offensive promise of greatness yet to be. In the verses on Lochnagar at least an ominous threat or presage of something new and splendid must have been but too perceptible to the discerning eye of criticism. (ACS)

6 Cf. Gen. 3: 14–15.

7 *Iliad*, ii, 159.

8 The 'preface' to *Selections* omits both 'wellnigh' and 'material'.

9 I remember some critical cackling over this phrase when it first appeared as over a senseless insult offered to the name and genius of a great poet. Insult is no habit of mine; and the term here used implies no more than he that runs may read in the text of Wordsworth; in whom, after the somewhat early subsidence of that 'simple, sensuous, and passionate' delight in nature of which in two of his most famous poems he has for ever embalmed his recollection, the place of this rapturous instinct of submission and absorption, which other poets have seen who never have ceased to feel in sight of natural glory and beauty, was taken by a meditative and moralizing spirit too apt to express itself in the tone of a preacher to whom all the divine life of things outside man is but as raw material for philosophic or theological cookery. How far this method of contemplating and interpreting the splendours and terrors of nature differs from that of his greatest contemporaries it is surely neither irrelevant nor impertinent to point out once more. Wide apart as lay their lines of work, it is true alike of Shelley and of Keats that for them it was not fated, nor could it ever have been possible, to outlive

The hour
Of splendour in the grass, of glory in the flower;

nor could Byron, while retaining as did Wordsworth the freshness and the force of his genius, have outlived his more fiery delight in the triumphant life of sea and cloud and storm. (ACS)

'Critical cackling' refers to a review in the *Spectator* for 31 March 1866. The two poems showing 'simple, sensuous, and passionate' delight in nature (the quoted phrase is from Milton's famous statement in *Of Education*) are presumably 'Tintern Abbey' and 'Ode on Intimations of Immortality', the latter containing the lines quoted.

10 Cf. Gen. 6: 2, 4: '. . . the sons of God . . . the daughters of men.'

11 Ovid states that Clymene was mother of Phaëthon by the sun-god (*Metamorphoses*, i, 751) and tells of Apollo's love for Leucothea, or Leucothoë (*ibid.*, iv, 196ff.).

12 The early hermits, such as Saint Anthony of Egypt, lived in the country around Thebes.

13 'The Island', iv, 150.

14 A letter from Geneva, 29 May 1823, *Letters and Journals*, vi, 219–21.

15 'Appanage' in the 'preface'.

16 'Or *The Siege of Corinth*' and 'or *The Bride of Abydos*' were not in the 'preface'.

17 Remembering the success of these stories, we may believe that Byron's contempt for the critical fashions of a time which extolled his worst work was not wholly affected or assumed; and understand how the instincts of opposition and reaction drove him back into that open idolatry of Pope and his school which he expressed loudly and foolishly enough. Probably at heart he did really prefer Pope to all men. His

critical faculty, if I may steal one phrase from a treasury that may well spare me the loan, was 'zero, or even a frightful *minus* quantity'; his judgment never worth the expense of a thought or a word. Besides, he had striven to emulate or at least to copy the exquisite manner of Pope in his satires, and must have seen how great and impassable a gulf lay between the master and his pupil. This would naturally lead him to over-estimate what he could not attain: the delicate merit, the keen perfection, the equable balance of force and finish, of sense and style, which raised his favourite so high among writers, if they left him somewhat low among poets; and having himself so bad an ear for metre, he may even have imagined that Pope's verse was musical. (ACS)

Lang (*The Swinburne Letters*, iv, 89) assigns the quotation ('zero . . . quantity') to Carlyle's 'Latter Stage of the French-German War, 1870–71'.

18 I do not of course forget that our own time has produced two noble poems in this foreign and alien metre; but neither *Casa Guidi Windows* nor 'The Defence of Guenevere' will suffice to establish its general excellence or fitness. The poets have done so well because they could do no less; but there may be at once good material and good workmanship without good implements. Neither of them has done more to give footing in England to the metre of their poems than did Byron himself by his 'Prophecy of Dante'. They have done better than this; but this they have not done. (ACS)

19 From Dryden's 'Alexander's Feast', l. 35.

20 From Æschylus, *Prometheus Bound*, ll. 89–90.

21 'Tirso de Molina' (pseudonym of Gabriel Tellez, *c.* 1571–1648). After Molière's time, Mozart's opera *Don Giovanni* (1787) and its interpretation by Mozart's German admirer, E. T. A. Hoffmann (1776–1822), gave new life to the legend, which, strictly speaking, had in Swinburne's day moved 'further than France'.

22 The noble verses of Shelley are fitter to be spoken over Byron than over any first or last Napoleon. To no other man could they be so well applied: for the world indeed took more of warmth from the fire of his spirit while alive than from any other then kindled:—

What! alive and so bold, O Earth?
    Art thou not over-bold?
    What! leapest thou forth as of old
In the light of thy morning mirth,
    The last of the flock of the starry fold?

. . . . . .

    Thou wert warming thy fingers old
    O'er the embers covered and cold
Of that most fiery spirit, when it fled:
What, Mother, do you laugh now he is dead? (ACS)

23 Not identified. Swinburne ended his 'preface' to the *Selections* with a paragraph which in the later essay would have seemed both irrelevant and anticlimactic:

> Of the workman and his work there is here no space to say more; and of the present book of selections not much need be said. It bears on the face of it the marks of imperfection and inadequacy; for these the very circumstances and conditions of its existence must be in some part answerable. Adequate and complete such a book cannot be: it must have fallen yet further short of its proper aim, but for the courtesy of those with whom it rested to determine whether the attempt should be made at all. Thanks are therefore due to the publisher and proprietor of Byron's poems, if there should be anything here worth thanks, from the reader; from the editor and publisher of this book, they are due in any case. Much that should be found here will be missed, and by none more than by me; but nothing at least will be found unworthy to share or unfit to secure the fame of Byron.

3 Matthew Arnold's New Poems

1867, 1875

In 'Matthew Arnold's New Poems' Swinburne recalls his early interest in Arnold, some of whose lectures as Professor of Poetry he had heard at Oxford. Indeed the young Swinburne had disagreed with one of them, as shown by 'Modern Hellenism' in the *Undergraduate Papers*, a publication of the Old Mortality Club, of which he was a member. Though Swinburne did not acknowledge authorship of this paper, its attribution to him, proposed by Georges Lafourcade, who reprinted it in *La Jeunesse de Swinburne* (ii, 221–3), is convincing. George Birkbeck Hill, Swinburne's friend, ascribed it to Swinburne, in a letter written in 1857, as did the editor, John Nichol; and it contains characteristic phraseology like 'the scorn of sciolists and the ridicule of fools' and 'the yet more shameful than mournful ruin of the Syracusan expedition'. In it Swinburne defended the Elizabethan age and Sir Walter Raleigh, contrasted unfavourably by Arnold with the ancient Greeks and the historian Thucydides.

Arnold appreciated Swinburne's valuation of his poetry, and the two men were friendly. Unfortunately an early reference in Arnold's letters, published posthumously, led Swinburne to make harsh comments in 'Charles Dickens' (see No. 18, note 30) and in 'Changes of Aspect' (in *New Writings by Swinburne*, ed. Lang). Though the title of 'Matthew Arnold's New Poems' may not be sufficiently inclusive, since about a third of it concerns Arnold's essays, it remains one of the best discussions of its subject. Arnold's greatest poems are justly praised. The estimate of his treatment of French authors is discerning, and most writers on metrics agree with what Swinburne says of the hexameter.

In revising his article in the *Fortnightly Review* (October 1867) for *Essays and Studies* (1875) Swinburne added the first long passage assigned to the fictitious 'French critic' and the word 'again' in citing the 'critic' on page 85. He also added six notes, those on David Gray, the *Rubáiyát*, Christina Rossetti's 'great new-year hymn', and Arnold's 'New Sirens' and '*In Utrumque Paratus*', as well as the note on a remark by 'a French critic'. The comments in French imply a criticism of Browning's point of view—possibly one of several reasons for assigning them to the imaginary critic.

There are two things which most men begin by hating until they have won their way, and which when combined are more than doubly hateful to all in whose eyes they are not doubly admirable: perfection of work, and personality in the workman. As to perfection, it must be seen to be loved, and few have eyes to see it. To none but these few can it be acceptable at first; and only because these few are the final legislators of opinion, the tacit and patient lawgivers of time, does it ever win acceptance. A strong personal tone of character stamped and ingrained into a man's work, if more offensive at first to the mass, is likelier to find favour before long in the sight of some small body or sect of students. If not repulsive, it must be attractive and impressive; and there are always mental cripples in plenty to catch at a strong man's staff and cut it down into a crutch for themselves. But the more love a man has for perfection, the more faith in form, the more instinct for art, the fewer will these early believers be, and the better worth having; the process of winning their suffrages will be slower, and surer the hold of them when won.

For some years the immediate fame of Mr. Matthew Arnold has been almost exclusively the fame of a prose writer. Those students could hardly find hearing—they have nowhere of late found expression that I know of—who, with all esteem and enjoyment of his essays, of their clearness, candour, beauty of sentiment and style, retained the opinion that if justly judged he must be judged by his verse and not by his prose; certainly not by this alone; that future students would cleave to that with more of care and of love; that the most memorable quality about him was the quality of a poet. Not that they liked the prose less, but that they liked the verse more. His best essays ought to live longer than most, his best poems cannot but live as long as any, of their time. So it seemed to some who were accordingly more eager to receive and more careful to study a new book of his poems than most books they could have looked for; and since criticism of the rapid and limited kind possible to contemporaries can be no more than the sincere exposition of the writer's belief and of his reasons for it, I, as one of these, desire, with all deference but with all decision, to say what I think of this book, and why. For the honour of criticism, if it is to win or to retain honour at all, it must be well for the critic to explain clearly his personal point of view, instead of fighting behind the broad and crestless shield of a nameless friend or foe. The obscurest name and blazon are at least recognisable; but a mere voice is mere wind, though it affect to speak with the tongues and the authority of men and of angels.[1]

First on this new stage is the figure of an old friend and teacher. Mr. Arnold says that the poem of *Empedocles on Etna* was withdrawn before fifty copies of the first edition were sold. I must suppose then that one of these was the copy I had when a schoolboy—how snatched betimes from the wreck and washed across my way I know not; but I remember well enough how then as now the songs of Callicles clove to my ear and memory. Early as this was, it was not my first knowledge of the poet; the 'Reveller', the 'Merman', the 'New Sirens', I had mainly by heart in a time of childhood just ignorant of teens. I do not say I understood the latter poem in a literal or logical fashion, but I had enjoyment enough of its music and colour and bright sadness as of a rainy sunset or sundawn. A child with any ear or eye for the attraction of verse or art can dispense with analysis and rest content to apprehend it without comprehension; it were to be wished that adults equally incapable would rest equally content. Here I must ask, as between brackets, if this beautiful poem is never to be reissued after the example of its younger?[2] No poet could afford to drop or destroy it; I might at need call into court older and better judges to back my judgment in this; meantime 'I hope here be proofs'[3] that, however inadequate may be my estimate of the poet on whom I am now to discourse, it is not inadequate through want of intimacy with his work. At the risk of egotism, I record it in sign of gratitude; I cannot count the hours of pure and high pleasure, I cannot reckon the help and guidance in thought and work, which I owe to him as to all other real and noble artists whose influence it was my fortune to feel when most susceptible of influence, and least conscious of it, and most in want. In one of his books, where he presses rather hard upon our school as upon one wholly void of spiritual or imaginative culture, he speaks of his poems as known to no large circle—implies this at least, if I remember:[4] he will not care to be assured that to some boys at Eton Sohrab and Rustum, Tristram and Iseult, have been close and common friends, their stream of Oxus and bays of Brittany familiar almost as the well-loved Thames weirs and reaches. However, of this poem of *Empedocles* the world it seems was untimely robbed, though I remember on searching to have found a notice of it here and there. Certain fragments were then given back by way of dole, chiefly in the second series of the author's revised poems. But one, the largest if not the brightest jewel, was withheld; the one long and lofty chant of Empedocles. The reasons assigned by Mr. Arnold in a former preface for cancelling the complete poem had some weight: the subject-matter is oppressive, the scheme naked and monotonous; the blank verse is not sonorous, not vital and various enough; in spite of some noble interludes, it fails on the whole to do the work and carry the weight wanted; its simplicity is stony and grey, with dry flats and rough whinstones. To the lyrics which serve as water-springs and pastures I shall have to pay tribute of thanks in their turn; but first I would say something of that strain of choral philosophy which falls here 'as the shadow of a great rock in a weary land'.[5] It is a model of grave, clear, solemn verse; the style plain and bare, but sufficient and strong; the thought deep, lucid, direct. We may say of it what the author has himself said of the wise and sublime verses of Epictetus, that 'the fortitude of that is for the strong, for the few; even for them, the spiritual atmosphere with which it surrounds them is bleak and grey';[6] but the air is higher and purer, the ground firmer, the view clearer; we have a surer foothold on these cold hills of thought than in the moist fragrance of warmer air which steeps the meadows and marshes of sentiment and tradition.

Thin, thin the pleasant human noises grow,
      And faint the city gleams;
Rare the lone pastoral huts; marvel not thou!
The solemn peaks but to the stars are known,
But to the stars, and the cold lunar beams;
Alone the sun arises, and alone
      Spring the great streams.

These noble verses of another poem clipped from Mr. Arnold's first book, and left hanging in fragments about one's memory—I here make my protest against its excision[7]—may serve as types of the later, the more immediate and elaborate discourse of thought here embodied and attired in words of stately and simple harmony. It is no small or common comfort, after all the delicate and ingenious shuffling of other English poets about the edge of deep things, to come upon one who speaks with so large and clear and calm an utterance; who begins at the taproot and wellspring of the matter, leaving others to wade ankle-deep in still waters and weave river-flags or lake-lilies in lieu of stemming the stream. Nothing in verse or out of verse is more wearisome than the delivery of reluctant doubt, of half-hearted hope and half-incredulous faith. A man who suffers from the strong desire either to believe or disbelieve something he cannot may be worthy of sympathy, is certainly worthy of pity, until he begins to speak; and if he tries to speak in verse, he misuses the implement of an artist. We have had evidences of religion, aspirations and suspirations of all kinds, melodious regrets and tortuous returns in favour or disfavour of this creed or that—all by way of poetic work; and all within the compass and shot-range of a single faith; all, at the widest, bounded north, south, east, and west by material rivers or hills, by an age or two since, by a tradition or two; all leaving the spirit cramped and thirsty. We have had Christian sceptics, handcuffed fighters, tongue-tied orators, plume-plucked eagles; believers whose belief was a sentiment, and free-thinkers who saw nothing before Christ or beyond Judæa. To get at the bare rock is a relief after acres of such quaking ground.

A French critic[8] has expressed this in words which I may quote here, torn out from their context:— 'Le côté fort du caractère d'un peuple fait souvent le côté faible de sa poésie. Ces poëtes anglais pèchent du côté de la raison religieuse. Ce n'est pas que les anglais soient effectivement ou trop religieux ou trop raisonnables. C'est qu'ils ont la manie de vouloir réconcilier les choses irréconciliables. On voit cela partout, dans la politique, dans les beaux arts, dans la vie pratique, dans la vie idéale. Leur république est juchée sur des échasses féodales, attifée des guenilles étincelantes d'une royauté usée jusqu'à la corde; tout le bric-à-brac monarchique lui plaît; ses parfums rances, ses lambris dédorés, sa défroque rapiécée; elle n'ose se montrer sans mettre son masque de reine, sans rajuster ses jupons de pairesse. Pourquoi se donne-t-elle cette peine? quel profit espère-t-elle en retirer? c'est ce qu'un anglais même ne saurait dire,[9] tout en répondant que Dieu le sait, il est permis de douter que Dieu le sache. Venons aux arts; que veut-on d'un peintre? de la peinture? fi donc! Il nous faut un peu de morale, un peu d'intention, le beau vrai, le vrai beau, l'idée actuelle, l'actualité idéale, mille autres choses très-recommandables dans ce genre-là. C'est ce malin esprit, très-peu spirituel, qui est venu souffler aux poëtes la belle idée de se poser en apôtres réconciliateurs entre le croyant et le libre penseur. L'un d'eux fait foudroyer M. Renan par Saint Jean expirant en pleine odeur de philosophie, écrase sous son talon le pauvre évêque Colenso,[10] et démontre que si le Christ n'est pas "le Dieu incommensurable", il doit être tout bonnement un homme "perdu" (c'est son mot); vu que d'après la tradition de sa parole écrite plusieurs millions de gens plus ou moins honnêtes sont morts dans cette foi, et que voilà apparemment le seul Dieu, et que voilà la seule religion, qui ait jamais produit un effet pareil. Sous des vers plus soigneusement limés, plus coquettement ajustés, nous ne trouverons qu'une plus profonde stérilité de raisonnement. Voici une belle âme de poëte qui pleure, qui cherche, qui envisage la mort, le néant, l'infini;[11] qui veut peser les faits, trier les croyances, vanner la foi; et voici son dernier mot: Croyons, afin de moins souffrir; tâchons au moins de nous faire accroire à nous-mêmes que nous croyons à quelque chose de consolant. Il est douloureux de ne pas croire qu'on doit revivre un jour, revoir ses amis morts, accomplir de nouveaux destins. Posons donc que cela est, que cela doit être, qu'il faut absolument y croire, ou du moins faire semblant à ses propres yeux d'y croire, se persuader, se réitérer à haute voix que cela est. La vie sans avenir est impossible. Plus de raisonnements d'incrédule. Le cœur se lève comme un homme irrité et répond: J'ai senti! Vous manquez de foi, dites-vous, vous manquez de preuves, mais il suffit que vous ayez eu des sensations. À ce compte-là, il vaut bien la peine de faire rouler le wagon poétique sur les rails de la philosophie, de s'embourber les roues dans les ornières de la théologie. Aimez, souffrez, sentez, c'est très-bien; vous êtes là dans votre droit. Cela ne prouve rien, mais cela est fort joli, mis en de beaux vers. On perd un objet aimé, on désire le revoir, on épreuve des émotions douloureuses à songer qu'on ne le reverra point. Après? La mort, la douleur, l'oubli, la misère, voilà sans doute des choses pénibles, et que l'on voudrait éviter; il est clair que nous ferions tous notre possible pour y échapper. Cela prouve-t-il que ces choses-là n'existent pas? On est tenté de répondre une bonne fois à ces bonnes gens: Messieurs, vous raisonnez en poëtes, vous poétisez en raisonneurs. De grâce, soyez l'un ou l'autre: ou bien, si vous avez les deux dons réunis, raisonnez en raisonneurs, poétisez en poëtes. Faites-nous grâce en attendant de cette poésie démontée, de cette philosophie déraillée.

'Encore un mot. La poésie n'a que faire de tout cela. Il n'y a pas de religion possible dont elle ne sache prendre son parti. Toute croyance qui émeut, qui fait vibrer, résonner, tressaillir une seule corde intérieure—toute véritable religion, sombre ou radieuse, tragique ou riante, est une chose essentiellement poétique. Partout où puisse aller la passion, l'émotion, le sentiment qui fait les martyrs, les prophètes, les vierges mystérieuses, les apôtres effrayants du bien ou du mal, partout où puissent pénétrer les terreurs mystiques, les joies énormes, les élans obscurs de la foi, il y a pour les poëtes un milieu respirable. Vénus ou Moloch, Jésus ou Brahma, n'importe. Un poëte enfermé chez lui peut être le meilleur chrétien du monde, ou bien le plus affreux païen; ce sont là des affaires de foyer où la critique n'a rien à voir; mais la poésie propre ne sera jamais ni ceci ni cela. Elle est tout, elle n'est rien. . . . Toute émotion lui sert, celle de l'anachorète ni plus ni moins que celle du blasphémateur. Pour la morale, elle est mauvaise et bonne, chaste et libertine; pour la religion, elle est incrédule et fidèle, soumise et rebelle. Mais l'impuissance religieuse ou morale, mais la pensée qui boite, l'esprit qui louche, l'âme qui a peur et de se soumettre et de se révolter, la foi manquée qui pleure des larmes sceptiques, les effluves fades, tristes, nauséabonds, de la caducité spirituelle, les plantes étiolées, les sources desséchées, les pousses sans sève d'une époque douteuse et crépusculaire—que voulez vous qu'elle fasse de tout cela? Pour elle, la négation même n'est pas stérile; chez elle, Lucrèce a sa place comme Moïse, Omar[12] comme Job; mais elle ne saurait où glisser les petites questions d'évidence, les petites tracasseries théologiques. Même en cette époque cependant nous ne manquons pas de poëtes qui sachent manier des choses hautes et sombres. Nous ne renverrons pas des écrivains anglais au sixième livre des *Contemplations*, aux sommets pour eux inabordables de la poésie actuelle, où la lumière se mêle au vertige; sans citer le grand maître, nous pourrions leur indiquer un des leurs qui a mieux fait qu'eux.' [The strong side of a people's character often produces the feeble side of its poetry. The English poets go astray with rational religion. Not that the English are actually either too religious or too rationalistic but rather that they always want to reconcile things irreconcilable. You see it everywhere—in politics, in the fine arts, in daily life, in ideas. Their republic is perched on feudal stilts, decked in the glittering rags of a royalty thoroughly threadbare. All the royal bric-à-brac pleases it: rancid perfumes, ungilded woodwork, patched cast-offs. It dares not appear without its regal mask, without arranging its noble petticoats. Why bother? What does it hope to gain? An Englishman himself could not say; even in answering that God knows, one may doubt whether God does know. Let us turn to the arts: What do you want from a painter? Paintings? Not at all! We want a little morality, a bit of purpose, the beautiful true, the true beautiful, the actual idea, the ideal actuality, a thousand other respectable things of that sort.

It is that evil spirit—not very spiritual—which has come to suggest to poets the fine idea of playing the part of apostle-reconcilers between the believer and the freethinker. One of them blasts M. Renan with St. John's dying in the full odour of philosophy, crushes under his heel the poor Bishop Colenso, and shows that if Christ is not 'the incommensurable God', he has to be quite simply a man 'lost' (that is his word); seeing that according to the tradition of his written word many millions of more or less upright people have died with that faith and that *there* is the only God, *there* the only religion, that has ever produced a like result. Underneath verses more carefully polished, more coquettishly adjusted, we find only a more profound sterility of argument. Here is a beautiful poet's soul who weeps, who searches, who envisions death, nothingness, the infinite; who wishes to weigh facts, sort out beliefs, sift faith; and here is his last word: Let us believe, in order to suffer less; let us endeavour at least to make ourselves believe that we believe in something consoling. It is sad not to believe that we are to live once more sometime, see again our dead friends, fulfil new destinies. Let us affirm, then, that this is true, that it has to be; that it is absolutely necessary to believe in it, or at least to pretend to ourselves to believe in it, to persuade ourselves, to repeat loudly that it is true. Life without a future is impossible. No more reasonings of the unbeliever. The heart starts up like a man incensed and answers: I have felt! You lack faith, you say, you lack proofs, but it is enough that you have had feelings. This being true, it is well worth the trouble to set the poetic car rolling on the rails of philosophy, to mire the wheels in the muddy ruts of theology. Love, suffer, feel—very well: it is your right. That proves nothing, but is very pretty when put into beautiful verse. You lose a beloved object, you long to see it again, you feel sorrowful in dreaming that you will never see it again. Afterwards? Death, grief, oblivion, distress—these are undoubtedly painful things that one would wish to avoid. Clearly, we would all do our best to escape them. Does that prove that these things do not exist? One is tempted to respond once for all to these good people: Messieurs, you reason as poets, you poetize as reasoners. For mercy's sake, be one or the other: or rather, if you have both gifts together, reason as reasoners, poetize as poets. Meantime spare us this disjointed poetry, this derailed philosophy.

One word more: poetry has no use for all that. You cannot imagine a religion that poetry could not accept. Every creed that rouses, that makes vibrate, reverberate, strike just one inner chord—every veritable religion, sombre or radiant, tragic or gay, is a thing essentially poetic. Wherever passion may go, emotion, the sentiment that makes martyrs, prophets, and mysterious virgins, fearsome apostles of good or of evil, wherever mystic terrors, vast joys, obscure transports of faith can penetrate, *there* is for poets a breathable atmosphere. Venus or Moloch, Jesus or Brahma—it doesn't matter. A poet imprisoned in his own house can be the best Christian in the world, or else the most frightful pagan; these are domestic matters with which the critic has no concern; but poetry as such would never be this or that. It is all, it is nothing. . . . All emotion is serviceable to it, that of the anchorite neither more nor less than that of the blasphemer. For morals, it is bad and good, chaste and libertine; for religion, unbelieving and faithful, submissive and rebellious. But religious or moral impotence, the thought that lisps, the spirit that squints, the soul that fears both to submit and to revolt, the halfway faith that weeps sceptical tears, the tasteless emanations, sorrowful and loathsome, of spiritual decay, the sickly plants, the dried-up springs, the sprouts without sap of an uncertain and twilight epoch—what do you expect to make of all that? For it, even negation is not sterile; with it, Lucretius has his place as well as Moses, Omar as well as Job. But it would not know where to tuck away little questions of evidence, little theological bickerings. Even in this epoch, however, we do not lack poets who know how to handle high and serious subjects. We shall not refer English writers to the sixth book of *Contemplations*, to the unapproachable summits of present-day poetry where light blends with dizziness. Without citing the grand master, we can indicate to them one of their own who has done better than they.] Here follows the reference to Mr. Arnold's poem and to the exact passages supposed to bear upon the matter at issue. 'Ce monologue lyrique est d'une ampleur, d'une droiture poétique dont on ne saurait ailleurs retrouver une trace. C'est un rude évangile qu'on vient là nous prêcher; on sent dans cette cratère des flammes éteintes; c'est lugubre pour les âmes faibles, pour les esprits à l'œil chassieux; c'est une poésie froide et ferme et forte. Voici enfin quelqu'un qui a le regard haut, le pied sûr, la parole nette, la vue large; on sait ce qu'il nous veut. Sa philosophie âpre, escarpée, impassible, est après tout meilleure consolatrice que la théologie douteuse, pleureuse, tracassière de ses rivaux.'[13] [This lyric monologue is of an amplitude, of a poetic rightness of which no trace could be found elsewhere. It is a tough gospel that is preached here. We feel flames extinguished in that crater; it is lugubrious for the feeble souls, for the blear-eyed spirits. It is a poetry cold and firm and strong. Here is finally someone who has the lofty look, the sure foot, the clear word, the large view. We know what he wants for us. His austere philosophy, rugged, undisturbed, is after all a better consoler than the doubtful, sorrowful theology, so annoying, of his rivals.] In spite of his flippancy and violence of manner, I am disposed in part to agree with this critic.

Elsewhere, in minor poems, Mr. Arnold also has now and then given signs of an inclination for that sad task of sweeping up dead leaves fallen from the dying tree of belief; but has not wasted much time or strength on such sterile and stupid work. Here, at all events, he has wasted none; here is no melodious whine of retrospective and regretful scepticism; here are no cobwebs of plea and counterplea, no jungles of argument and brakes of analysis. 'Ask what most helps when known';[14] let be the oracular and the miraculous, and vex not the soul about their truth or falsehood; the soul, which oracles and miracles can neither make nor mar, can neither slay nor save.

> Once read thy own breast right,
> And thou hast done with fears.
> Man gets no other light,
> Search he a thousand years.
> Sink in thyself; there ask what ails thee, at that shrine.

This is the gospel of *αὐτάρκεια*, the creed of self-sufficience,[15] which sees for man no clearer or deeper duty than that of intellectual self-reliance, self-dependence, self-respect; an evangel not to be cancelled or supplanted by any revelation of mystic or prophet or saint. Out of this counsel grows the exposition of obscure and afflictive things. Man's welfare—his highest sphere and state of spiritual well-doing and well-being—this indeed is his true aim; but not this is the aim of nature: the world has other work than this to do; and we, not it, must submit; submit, not by ceasing to attempt and achieve the best we can, but by ceasing to expect subservience to our own ends from all forces and influences of existing things; it is no reason or excuse for living basely instead of nobly, that we must live as the sons and not as the lords of nature. 'To tunes we did not call our being must keep chime'; but this bare truth we will not accept. Philosophy, as forcibly and clearly as religion, indicates the impediments of sin and self-will; 'we do not what we ought, what we ought not we do'; but there religion stops, as far as regards this world, and passes upward into a new world and life; philosophy has further to go without leaving her hold upon earth. Even were man pure, just, wise, instead of unwise, unjust, and impure, this would not affect the 'other existences that clash with ours'.

Like us, the lightning fires
Love to have scope and play;
The stream, like us, desires
An unimpeded way;
Like us, the Libyan wind delights to roam at large.

Streams will not curb their pride
The just man not to entomb,
Nor lightnings go aside
To leave his virtues room;
Nor is that wind less rough which blows a good man's barge.

Nature, with equal mind
Sees all her sons at play;
Sees man control the wind,
The wind sweep man away:
Allows the proudly-riding and the founder'd bark.

Again, there are 'the ill-deeds of other men' to fill up the account against us of painful and perilous things. And we, instead of doing and bearing all we can under our conditions of life, must needs 'cheat our pains' like children after a fall who 'rate the senseless ground':

So, loth to suffer mute,
We, peopling the void air,
Make gods to whom to impute
The ills we ought to bear;
With God and Fate to rail at, suffering easily.

Yet grant—as sense long miss'd
Things that are now perceiv'd,
And much may still exist
Which is not yet believ'd—
Grant that the world were full of Gods we cannot see;

All things the world which fill
Of but one stuff are spun,
That we who rail are still,
With what we rail at, one;
One with the o'er-labour'd Power that through the breadth and length

Of earth, and air, and sea,
  In men, and plants, and stones,
Hath toil perpetually,
  And struggles, pants, and moans;
Fain would do all things well, but sometimes fails in strength.

And, patiently exact,
  This universal God
Alike to any act
  Proceeds at any nod,
And quietly declaims the cursings of himself.

This is not what man hates,
  Yet he can curse but this.
Harsh Gods and hostile Fates
  Are dreams; this only *is*;
Is everywhere; sustains the wise, the foolish elf.

Again, we must have comfortable Gods to bless, as well as these discomfortable to curse; 'kind Gods who perfect what man vainly tries'; we console ourselves for long labour and research and failure by trust in their sole and final and sufficient knowledge. Then comes the majestic stroke of reply to rebuke and confute the feeble follies of inventive hope, the futile forgeries of unprofitable comfort; scornful and solemn as the forces themselves of nature.

Fools! that in man's brief term
  He cannot all things view,
Affords no ground to affirm
  That there are Gods who do;
Nor does being weary prove that he has where to rest.

In like manner, when pleasure-seekers fail of pleasure in this world, they turn their hearts Godward, and thence in the end expect that joy which the world could not give; making sure to find happiness where the foiled student makes sure to find knowledge. Again the response from natural things unseen, or from the lips of their own wisest, confronts their fancies as before.

Fools! that so often here
  Happiness mocked our prayer,
I think, might make us fear
  A like event elsewhere;
Make us, not fly to dreams, but moderate desire.

Nor finally, when all is said, need the wise despair or repine because debarred from dreams of a distant and dubious happiness in a world outside of ours.

Is it so small a thing
  To have enjoyed the sun,
To have lived light in the spring,
  To have loved, to have thought, to have done?

The poorest villager feels that it is not so small a thing that he should not be loth to lose the little that life can yield him. Let the wiser man, like him, trust without fear the joys that are; life has room for effort and enjoyment, though at sight of the evil and sorrow it includes one may have abjured false faith and foolish hope and fruitless fear.

The majesty and composure of thought and verse, the perfect clearness and competence of words, distinguish this from other poetry of the intellect now more approved and applauded. The matter or argument is not less deep and close than clear and even in expression; although this lucidity and equality of style may diminish its material value in eyes used to the fog and ears trained to the clatter of the chaotic school. But a poem throughout so flowerless and pallid would miss much of the common charm of poetry, however imbued with the serene and severe splendour of snows and stars. And the special crown and praise of this one is its fine and gentle alternation of tone and colour. All around the central peak, bathed in airs high as heaven and cloven with craters deep as hell, the tender slopes of hill and pasture close up and climb in gradual grace of undulation, full of sunbeams and murmurs, winds and birds. The lyric interludes of the *Empedocles* are doubtless known by heart to many ignorant of their original setting, in which they are now again enchased. We have no poet comparable for power and perfection of landscape. This quality was never made more of by critics, sought after by poets with so much care; and our literature lies in full flowerage of landscape, like Egypt after the reflux of the Nile. We have galleries full of beautiful and ingenious studies, and an imperial academy of descriptive poets. The supreme charm of Mr. Arnold's work is a sense of right resulting in a spontaneous temperance which bears no mark of curb or snaffle, but obeys the hand with imperceptible submission and gracious reserve. Other and older poets are to the full as vivid, as incisive and impressive; others have a more pungent colour, a more trenchant outline; others as deep knowledge and as fervid enjoyment of natural things. But no one has in like measure that tender and final quality of touch which tempers the excessive light and suffuses the refluent shade; which as it were washes with soft air the sides of the earth, steeps with dew of quiet and dyes with colours of repose the ambient ardour of noon, the fiery affluence of evening. His verse bathes us with fresh radiance and light rain, when weary of the violence of summer and winter in which others dazzle and detain us; his spring wears here and there a golden waif of autumn, his autumn a rosy stray of spring. His tones and effects are pure, lucid, aërial; he knows by some fine impulse of temperance all rules of distance, of reference, of proportion; nothing is thrust or pressed upon our eyes, driven or beaten into our ears. For the instinctive selection of simple and effectual detail he is unmatched among English poets of the time, unless by Mr. Morris, whose landscape has much of the same quality, as clear, as noble, and as memorable—memorable for this especially, that you are not vexed or fretted by mere brilliance of point and sharpness of stroke, and such intemperate excellence as gives astonishment the precedence of admiration: such beauties as strike you and startle and go out. Of these it is superfluous to cite instances from the ablest of our countrymen's works; they are taught and teach that the most remote, the most elaborate, the most intricate and ingenious fashions of allusion and detail make up the best poetical style; they fill their verse with sharp-edged prettinesses, with shining surprises and striking accidents that are anything but casual; upon every limb and feature you see marks of the chisel and the plane: there is a conscious complacency of polish which seems to rebuke emulation and challenge improvement. It is otherwise with the two we have named; they are not pruned and pared into excellence, they have not so much of pungency and point; but they have breadth and ease and purity, they have largeness and sureness of eyesight; they know what to give and to withhold, what to express and to suppress. Above all, they have *air*; you can breathe and move in their landscape, nor are you tripped up and caught at in passing by intrusive and singular and exceptional beauties which break up and distract the simple charm of general and single beauty, the large and musical unity of things. Their best verse is not brought straight or worked right; it falls straight because it cannot fall awry; it comes right because it cannot go wrong. And this wide and delicate sense of right makes the impression of their work so durable. The effect is never rubbed off or worn out; the hot suffering eastern life of 'The Sick King in Bokhara'; the basking pastures and blowing pines about 'The Church of Brou'; the morning field and midday moorland so fondly and fully and briefly painted in 'Resignation'; above all, to me at least, the simple and perfect sea-side in the 'Merman'—'the sandy down where the sea-stocks bloom', the white-walled town with narrow paved streets, the little grey church with rain-worn stones and small leaded panes, and blown about with all the breath of wind and sound of waves—these come in and remain with us; these give to each poem the form and colour and attire it wants, and make it a distinct and complete achievement. The description does not adorn or decorate the thought; it is part of it; they have so grown into each other that they seem not welded together, but indivisible and twin-born.

Of the five songs of Callicles—whom we have left somewhat too long midway on Etna—that of Marsyas seems to me the highest and sweetest in tone, unless the first place be rather claimed for that of Cadmus and Harmonia. Others may prefer the first for its exquisite grace of scenery, or the last for its fresh breath and light, shed on softer places than the fiery cone of Etna—for its sweetness and calm, subduing, after all, the force of flames and darkness with the serenity of stars and song; but how fine in each one alike is the touch which relieves the scenery with personal life, Chiron's or Typho's or the sleeping shepherds' and passing Muses'. We have no word but the coarse and insufficient word *taste* to express that noble sense of harmony and high poetic propriety shown in the arrangement and composition of these lyrics; the first, full of the bright moist breath of well-watered glen and well-wooded ford, serving as prelude with its clear soft notes to the high monotone of Empedocles; the second, when that has ceased upon the still keen air, rising with fuller sweetness from below. Nothing can be more deep and exquisite in poetical tact than this succession of harmonies, diverse without a discord. For the absolute loveliness of sound and colour in this and the next song there are no adequate words that would not seem violent; and violence is too far from this poetry to invade even the outlying province of commentary. It must be accepted as the 'warm bay among the green Illyrian hills' accepts the sunlight, as the frame of maiden flowers and enclosure of gentle grass accept the quiet presence of the sacred snakes. No ear can forget the cadence, no eye the colour; I am half shaken in my old preference of the next ode until I recall it from end to end:

That triumph of the sweet persuasive lyre,
   That famous, final victory,
When jealous Pan with Marsyas did conspire;
When, from far Parnassus' side,

Young Apollo, all the pride
Of the Phrygian flutes to tame,
To the Phrygian highlands came.

Verse stately as the step and radiant as the head of Apollo; not 'like to the night' this time, but coming as the morning to the hills. How clear it makes the distance between Parnassus and Phrygia, the beautiful scorn and severe youth of the God, leaving for these long reed-beds and rippled lakes and pine-clad ridges of hill the bays and olives of his Greece; how clear the presence of the listening Muses, the advent of the hurrying Mænads, the weeping Olympus, and the implacable repose of Apollo. No poet has ever come so near the perfect Greek; he has strung with a fresh chord the old Sophoclean lyre; he has brought back the Muses from Phrygia even to Colonus;

ἔνθ'
ἁ λίγεια μινύρεται
θαμίζουσα μάλιστ' ἀηδὼν
χλωραῖς ὑπὸ βάσσαις·[16]

he has watered afresh the fruitful foliage of that unfooted grove of the God, sunless and stormless in all seasons of wind or sun; and for him the sleepless wellsprings of Cephisus are yet unminished and unfrozen,

οὐδὲ Μουσᾶν
χοροί νιν ἀπεστύγησαν, οὐδ' ἁ
χρυσάνιος 'Αφροδίτα.[17]

Even after his master, the disciple of Sophocles holds his high place; he has matched against the Attic of the Gods this Hyperborean dialect of ours, and has not earned the doom of Marsyas.[18] Here is indeed the triumph of the lyre; and he has had to refashion it for himself among a nation and in an age of flute-players and horn-blowers.

For the rest, the scheme of this poem is somewhat meagre and inefficient. Dramatic or not, the figure of Empedocles as here conceived is noble, full of a high and serene interest; but the figure as here represented is a ghost, without form and void; and darkness is upon the face of the deep in which his life lies stagnant; and we look in vain for the spirit to move upon the face of the waters.[19] Dimly and with something of discomfort and depression we perceive the shadow of the poet's design; we discern in rough and thin outline the likeness of the wise world-wearied man, worn down and worsted in the struggle of spirit against unwisdom and change and adverse force of men and things. But how he stands thus apart among the saints and sophists, whence and whither he comes and goes, what ruin lies behind or what revolution before, we hardly see at all. Not only do we contemplate a disembodied spirit, but a spirit of which we cannot determine how it was once embodied, what forms of thought or sense it once put on, what labour and what life it once went through. There is a poetry of the bodiless intellect, which without touching with finger-tip or wing-tip the edge of actual things may be wise and sweet and fruitful and sublime; but at least we must see the light and feel the air which guides forward and buoys upward the naked fleshless feet of the spirit. Grant that we want no details of bodily life and terrene circumstance, no touch of local or temporal colour; we want at least an indication of the spiritual circumstance, the spiritual influence, without which this poetry would have no matter to work upon. 'Il fallait nous faire sentir l'entourage, l'habillement, le milieu respirable de cette âme nuageuse, de cet esprit fatigué.'[20] After the full effusion of spirit in his one great utterance, Empedocles has little to bring forth but fragments and relics of the soul, shadows of thin suggestion and floating complaint. The manliness and depth, the clearness and sufficiency of thought have passed from him; he is vague and weak, dissatisfied much as the commonest thinker is dissatisfied with whom all things have not gone well, to whom all things are visibly imperfect and sensibly obscure. Now the prophet of nature who spoke to us and to Pausanias in the solemn modulation of his lyric speech was more than that. There needs no ghost come from the grave[21]—there needs no philosopher scale the summit of Etna—to tell us this that we find here: that a man had better die than live who can neither live with other men as they do nor wholly suffice to himself; that power and cunning and folly are fellows, that they are lords of life in ages of men with minds vulgar and feeble, and overcome the great and simple servants of justice and the right; that the lord of our spirit and our song, the god of all singers and all seers, is an intolerable and severe god, dividing and secluding his elect from full enjoyment of what others enjoy, in the stress and severity of solitude—sacrificing the weaker and sequestering the strong; that men on whom all these things beat and bear more heavily than they need can find no fullness of comfort or communion in the eternal elements made of like matter with us, but better made, nor in any beauty nor in any life of the laborious and sleepless soul of things; that even when all other components of our transient nature are duly and happily resolved into those durable elements, the insoluble and inevitable riddle of mind and thought must vex us to the last as at the first.

> We know all this, we know!
> Cam'st thou from heaven, O child
> Of light! but this to declare?
> Alas! to help us forget
> Such barren knowledge awhile,
> God gave the poet his song.[22]

Not that such barren knowledge is ignoble or inadequate matter for poetry; only it must assume something of the dramatic form and circumstance which here are scantily supplied. Less scanty is the supply of noble verses such as these:

> But we received the shock of mighty thoughts
> On simple minds with a pure natural joy;[23]

verses in the highest tone of Wordsworth's, as clear and grave as his best, as close and full and majestic. The good and evil influence of that great poet, perverse theorist, and incomplete man, upon Mr. Arnold's work is so palpable and so strong as to be almost obtrusive in its effects. He is the last worth reckoning whom *The Excursion* is ever likely to misguide. The incalculable power of Wordsworth on certain minds for a certain time could not but be and could not but pass over. Part of this singular power was doubtless owing to the might of will, the solid individual weight of mind, which moulded his work into the form he chose for it; part to the strong assumption and high self-reliance which grew in him so close to self-confidence and presumption; part to the sublimity and supremacy of his genius in its own climate and proper atmosphere—one which forbids access to all others and escape to him, since only there can he breathe and range, and he alone can breathe and range there; part to the frequent vapour that wraps his head and the frequent dust that soils his feet, filling the simpler sort with admiration of one so lofty at once and so familiar; and part, I fear, to the quality which no other great poet ever shared or can share with him, to his inveterate and invincible Philistinism, his full community of spirit and faith, in certain things of import, with the vulgarest English mind—or that which with the Philistine does duty for a mind. To those who like Shelley and Landor could see and mark this indomitable dullness and thickness of sense which made him mix with magnificent and flawless verse the 'enormous folly' of 'those stupid staves',[24] his pupils could always point out again the peculiar and unsurpassable grandeur and splendour of his higher mood; and it was vain to reply that these could be seen and enjoyed without condonation or excuse of his violent and wearisome perversities. This is what makes his poetry such unwholesome and immoral reading for Philistines; they can turn round upon their rebukers, and say, 'Here is one of us who by your own admission is also one of the great poets'; and no man can give them the lie; and the miserable men are confirmed in their faith and practice by the shameful triumph.

It will be a curious problem for the critics of another age to work at, and if they can to work out, this influence of men more or less imbued with the savour and spirit of Philistia upon the moral Samson who has played for our behoof the part of Agonistes or protagonist in the new Gaza where we live.[25] From the son of his father and the pupil of his teacher none would have looked for such efficient assault and battery of the Philistine outworks; none but those who can appreciate the certain and natural force, in a strong and well-tempered spirit, of loyal and unconscious reaction. I say reaction, and not revolt; he has assuredly nothing of the bad, perhaps not enough of the good stuff, which goes to make a rebel. He is loyal, not to a fault, but to the full; yet no man's habit of mind or work can be less like that which men trained in other schools expect from a scholar of Rydal or of Rugby.[26] A profane alien in my hearing once defined him as 'David the son of Goliath'; and when rebuked for the flat irreverence, avowed himself unable to understand how such a graft could have ever been set by the head gardener of the main hot-bed of Philistine saplings now flourishing in England. It is certain that the opinion put forth with such flippant folly of phrase is common to many of the profane, and not explicable by mere puerile prejudice or sentiment; and that students of Rugby or of Rydal, vocal and inarticulate, poetic and prosaic, are not seldom recognisable through certain qualities which, if any be, are undeniably Philistine. Whatever these schools have of good, their tendency is to cultivate all the merits recognised and suppress all the merits unrecognised in Ascalon or in Gath.[27] I will not call up witnesses past or present from the realms of prose or verse, of practice or theory: it would be a task rather invidious than difficult.

Son of Goliath or son of Jesse, this David or Samson or Jephthah[28] of our days, the man who has taught our hands to war and our fingers to fight[29] against the Philistines, must as a poet have sat long and reverently at the feet of their Gamaliel.[30] And as when there is high and pure genius on either side a man cannot but get good from the man he admires, and as it was so in this case if ever in any, he must have got good from that source over and above the certain and common good which the sense of reverence does to us all. The joy of worship, the delight of admiration, is in itself so excellent and noble a thing that even error cannot make it unvenerable or unprofitable; no one need repent of reverence, though he find flaws or cavities in his idol; it has done him good to worship, though there were no godhead behind the shrine. To shut his eyes upon disproof and affirm the presence of a god found absent, this indeed is evil; but this is not an act of reverence or of worship; this is the brute fatuity of cowardice, the violent impotence of fear; wanting alike what is good and fruitful in belief and what is heroic and helpful in disbelief; witness (for the most part) the religious and political, moral and æsthetic scriptures of our own time, the huge canonical roll of the Philistine. Nothing can be more unlike such ignoble and sluggard idolatry than the reverence now expressed and now implied by Mr. Arnold for the doctrine and example of Wordsworth. His memorial verses at once praise and judge the great poet then newly dead better than any words of other men; they have the still clear note, the fresh breath as of the first fields and birds of spring awakened in a serene dawn, which is in Wordsworth's own verse. With wider eyes and keener, he has inherited the soothing force of speech and simple stroke of hand with which Wordsworth assuaged and healed the weariness and the wounds of his time; to his hands the same appeasing spells and sacred herbs that fell from the other's when they relaxed in death have been committed by the gods of healing song. The elder physician of souls had indeed something too much of Æsculapius in him, something too little of Apollo his father; nevertheless the lineal and legitimate blood was apparent.

This elegy[31] and the poem headed 'Resignation' are in my eyes the final flower of Mr. Arnold's poems after Wordsworth—as I take leave to qualify a certain division of his work. The second of these is an unspotted and unbroken model of high calm thought couched in pure and faultless words; the words more equal and the vision more clear than his old teacher's, more just in view and more sure in grasp of nature and life. Imbued with the old faith at once in the necessity of things and in the endurance of man, it excels in beauty and in charm the kindred song of Empedocles; from first to last there rests upon it a serene spell, a sad supremacy of still music that softens and raises into wisdom the passionless and gentle pain of patience; the charm of earth and sorrowful magic of things everlasting; the spell that is upon the patient hills and immutable rocks, at work and asleep in 'the life of plants and stones and rain';[32] the life to which we too may subdue our souls and be wise. At times he writes simply as the elder poet might have written, without sensible imitation, but with absolute identity of style and sentiment; at times his larger tone of thought, his clearer accent of speech, attest the difference of the men. So perfect and sweet in speech, so sound and lucid in thought as the pupil is at his best, the master seldom was; and at his best the pupil is no more seen, and in his stead is a new master. He has nothing of Wordsworth's spirit of compromise with the nature of things, nothing of his moral fallacies and religious reservations; he can see the face of facts and read them with the large and frank insight of ancient poets; none of these ever had a more profound and serene sense of fate. But he has not grasped, and no man I suppose will ever grasp, the special and imperial sceptre of his elder. The incommunicable, the immitigable might of Wordsworth when the god has indeed fallen upon him cannot but be felt by all, and can but be felt by any; none can partake or catch it up. There are many men greater than he; there are men much greater; but what he has of greatest is his only. His concentration, his majesty, his pathos have no parallel; some have gone higher, many lower, none have touched precisely the same point as he; some poets have had more of all these qualities, and better; none have had exactly his gift. His pathos for instance cannot be matched against any other man's; it is trenchant, and not tender; it is an iron pathos. Take for example the most passionate of his poems, 'The Affliction of Margaret'; it is hard and fiery, dry and persistent as the agony of a lonely and a common soul which endures through life, a suffering which runs always in one groove without relief or shift. Because he is dull and dry and hard, when set by the side of a great lyrist or dramatist; because of these faults and defects, he is so intense and irresistible when his iron hand has hold of some chord which it knows how to play upon. How utterly unlike his is the pathos of Homer or Æschylus, Chaucer or Dante, Shakespeare or Hugo; all these greater poets feel the moisture and flame of the fever and the tears they paint; their pathos when sharpest is full of sensitive life, of subtle tenderness, of playing pulses and melting colours; his has but the downright and trenchant weight of swinging steel; he strikes like the German headsman, one stroke of a loaded sword. This could not be done even by the poets who could do more and better than this. His metre too is sublime, his choice or chance of language casual or chosen has miraculous effects in it, when he feels his foot firm on ground fit for him; otherwise his verse is often hard as wood and dry as dust and weak as water. In this as in other ways his influence has been now good and now bad. The grave cadence of such a poem as the 'Resignation', in this point also one of Mr. Arnold's most noble and effective, bears with it a memory and a resonance of the master's music, such as we find again in the lovely single couplets and lines which now and then lift up the mind or lull it in the midst of less excellent verse; such for instance as these, which close a scale of lower melodies, in a poem not wholly or equally pleasurable: but these are faultless verses and full of the comfort of music, which tell us how, wafted at times from the far-off verge of the soul,

> As from an infinitely distant land,
> Come airs, and floating echoes, and convey
> A melancholy into all our day.[33]

These have a subtle likeness to Wordsworth's purer notes, a likeness undefined and unborrowed; the use of words usually kept back for prose (such as 'convey') is a trick of Wordsworth's which either makes or mars a passage; here the touch, it may be by accident, strikes the exact chord wanted, elicits the exact tone.

But indeed, as with all poets of his rank, so with Mr. Arnold, the technical beauty of his work is one with the spiritual; art, a poet's art above all others, cannot succeed in this and fail in that. Success or achievement of an exalted kind on the spiritual side ensures and enforces a like executive achievement or success; if the handiwork be flawed, there must also have been some distortion or defect of spirit, a shortcoming or a misdirection of spiritual supply. There is no such thing as a dumb poet or a handless painter. The essence of an artist is that he should be articulate. It is the mere impudence of weakness to arrogate the name of poet or painter with no other claim than a susceptible and impressible sense of outward or inward beauty, producing an impotent desire to paint or sing. The poets that are made by nature are not many; and whatever 'vision' an aspirant may possess, he has not the 'faculty divine'[34] if he cannot use his vision to any poetic purpose. There is no cant more pernicious to such as these, more wearisome to all other men, than that which asserts the reverse. It is a drug which weakens the feeble and intoxicates the drunken; which makes those swagger who have not learnt to walk, and teach who have not been taught to learn. Such talk as this of Wordsworth's is the poison of poor souls like David Gray's.[35] Men listen, and depart with the belief that they have this faculty or this vision which alone, they are told, makes the poet; and once imbued with that belief, soon pass or slide from the inarticulate to the articulate stage of debility and disease. Aspiration foiled and impotent is a piteous thing enough, but friends and teachers of this sort make it ridiculous as well. A man can no more win a place among poets by dreaming of it or lusting after it than he can win by dream or desire a woman's beauty or a king's command; and those encourage him to fill his belly with the east wind[36] who feign to accept the will for the deed, and treat inarticulate or inadequate pretenders as actual associates in art. The Muses can bear children and Apollo can give crowns to those only who are able to win the crown and beget the child; but in the school of theoretic sentiment it is apparently believed that this can be done by wishing.

Small things suffice to give immediate proof or disproof of the requisite power. In music or in painting all men admit this for a truth; it is not less certain in poetry. There is nothing in either of the poets I speak of more distinctive and significant than the excellence of their best sonnets. These are almost equally noble in style; though the few highest of Wordsworth's remain out of reach of emulation, not out of sight of worship. Less adorable and sublime, not less admirable and durable, Mr. Arnold's hold their own in the same world of poetry with these. All in this new volume are full of beauty, sound and sweet fruits of thought and speech that have ripened and brought forth together; the poetry of religious thought when most pure and most large has borne no fairer than that one on the drawing in the Catacombs of the Good Shepherd bearing the young, not of a sheep, but of a goat;[37] or that other on the survival of grace and spirit when the body of belief lies dead;[38] but all, I repeat, have a singular charm and clearness. I have used this word already more than once or twice; it comes nearest of all I can find to the thing I desire to express; that natural light of mind, that power of reception and reflection of things or thoughts, which I most admire in so much of Mr. Arnold's work. I mean by it much more than mere facility or transparency; more than brilliance, more than ease or excellence of style. It is a quality begotten by instinct upon culture; one which all artists of equal rank possess in equal measure.

There are in the English language three elegiac poems so great that they eclipse and efface all the elegiac poetry we know; all of Italian, all of Greek. It is only because the latest born is yet new to us that it can seem strange or rash to say so. The 'Thyrsis' of Mr. Arnold makes a third with 'Lycidas' and 'Adonais'. It is not so easy as those may think who think by rote and praise by prescription to strike the balance between them. The first however remains first, and must remain; its five opening lines are to me the most musical in all known realms of verse; there is nothing like them; and it is more various, more simple, more large and sublime than the others; lovelier and fuller it cannot be.

The leader is fairest,
But all are divine.[39]

The least pathetic of the three is 'Adonais', which indeed is hardly pathetic at all; it is passionate, subtle, splendid; but 'Thyrsis', like 'Lycidas', has a quiet and tender undertone which gives it something of sacred. Shelley brings fire from heaven, but these bring also 'the meed of some melodious tear'.[40] There is a grace ineffable, a sweet sound and sweet savour of things past, in the old beautiful use of the language of shepherds, of flocks and pipes; the spirit is none the less sad and sincere because the body of the poem has put on this dear familiar raiment of romance; because the crude and naked sorrow is veiled and chastened with soft shadows and sounds of a 'land that is very far off';[41] because the verse remembers and retains a perfume and an echo of Grecian flutes and flowers,

Renews the golden world, and holds through all
The holy laws of homely pastoral,
Where flowers and founts, and nymphs and semi-gods,
And all the Graces find their old abodes.[42]

Here, as in 'The Scholar Gipsy', the beauty, the delicacy and affluence of colour, the fragrance and the freedom as of wide wings of winds in summer over meadow and moor, the freshness and expansion of the light and the lucid air, the spring and the stream as of flowing and welling water, enlarge and exalt the pleasure and power of the whole poem. Such English-coloured verse no poet has written since Shakespeare, who chooses his field-flowers and hedgerow blossoms with the same sure and loving hand, binds them in as simple and sweet an order. All others, from Milton downward to Shelley and onward from him, have gathered them singly or have mixed them with foreign buds and alien bloom. No poem in any language can be more perfect as a model of style, unsurpassable certainly, it may be unattainable. Any couplet, any line proves it. No countryman of ours since Keats died has made or has found words fall into such faultless folds and forms of harmonious line. He is the most efficient, the surest-footed poet of our time, the most to be relied on; what he does he is the safest to do well; more than any other he unites personality and perfection; others are personal and imperfect, perfect and impersonal; with them you must sometimes choose between inharmonious freedom and harmonious bondage. Above all, he knows what as a poet he should do, and simply does that; the manner of his good work is never more or less than right; his verse comes clean and full out of the mould, cast at a single jet; placed beside much other verse of the time, it shows like a sculptor's work by an enameller's. With all their wealth and warmth of flowers and lights, these two twin poems are solid and pure as granite or as gold. Their sweet sufficiency of music, so full and calm, buoys and bears up throughout the imperial vessel of thought. Their sadness is not chill or sterile, but as the sorrow of summer pausing with laden hands on the middle height of the year, the watershed that divides the feeding fountains of autumn and of spring; a grave and fruitful sadness, the triumphant melancholy of full-blown flowers and souls full-grown. The stanzas from the sixth to the fourteenth of 'Thyrsis', and again from the sixteenth to the twentieth, are if possible the most lovely in either poem; the deepest in tone and amplest in colour; the choiceness and sweetness of single lines and phrases most exquisite and frequent.

O easy access to the hearer's grace,
  When Dorian shepherds sang to Proserpine!
    For she herself had trod Sicilian fields,
  She knew the Dorian water's gush divine,
    She knew each lily white which Enna yields,
      Each rose with blushing face;
  She loved the Dorian pipe, the Dorian strain.
    But, ah! of our poor Thames she never heard!
    Her foot the Cumnor cowslips never stirred;
  And we should tease her with our plaint in vain.

She has learnt to know them now, the river and the river-meadows, and access is as easy for an English as a Dorian prayer to the most gentle of all worshipped gods. It is a triumphal and memorial poem, a landmark in the high places of verse to which future travellers studious of the fruits and features of the land may turn and look up and see what English hands could rear.

This is probably the highest point of Mr. Arnold's poetry, though for myself I cannot wholly resign the old preference of things before familiar; of one poem in especial, good alike for children and men,

'The Forsaken Merman'; which has in it the pathos of natural things, the tune of the passion we fancy in the note of crying birds or winds weeping, shrill and sweet and estranged from us; the swift and winged wail of something lost midway between man's life and the life of things soulless, the wail overheard and caught up by the fitful northern fancy, filling with glad and sad spirits the untravelled ways of nature; the clear cry of a creature astray in the world, wild and gentle and mournful, heard in the sighing of weary waters before dawn under a low wind, in the rustle and whistle and whisper of leaves or grasses, in the long light breaths of twilight air heaving all the heather on the hills, in the coming and going of the sorrowful strong seas that bring delight and death, in the tender touch and recoil of the ripple from the sand; all the fanciful pitiful beauty of dreams and legends born in grey windy lands on shores and hill-sides whose life is quiet and wild. No man's hand has pressed from the bells and buds of the moors and downs by cape or channel of the north a sweeter honey than this. The song is a piece of the sea-wind, a stray breath of the air and bloom of the bays and hills: its mixture of mortal sorrow with the strange wild sense of a life that is not after mortal law—the childlike moan after lost love mingling with the pure outer note of a song not human—the look in it as of bright bewildered eyes with tears not theirs and alien wonder in the watch of them—the tender, marvellous, simple beauty of the poem, its charm as of a sound or a flower of the sea—set it and save it apart from all others in a niche of the memory. This has all the inexplicable inevitable sweetness of a child's or a bird's in its note; 'Thyrsis' has all the accomplished and adult beauty of a male poem. In the volume which it crowns there is certainly no new jewel of equal water. 'Palladium' is a fresh sample of the noble purity and clearness which we find always and always praise in his reflective poetry; its cool aërial colour like that of a quiet sky between full sunset and full moonrise, made ready for the muster of the stars, swept clean of cloud and flame, and laved with limpid unruffled air from western green to eastern grey; a sky the cenotaph of unburied sunlight, the mould of moonlight unborn. 'A Southern Night' is steeped in later air, as gentle and more shining; the stanzas on the Grande Chartreuse are stamped with the impression of a solemn charm, and so the new verses on Obermann,[43] the new verses on Marguerite, strange to read for those who remember reading the first at the time when all the loves we read of assume a form and ascend a throne in our thoughts, the old and the new side by side, so that now this poem comes under our eyes like a new love-song of Petrarca to Laura or Coleridge to Geneviève.[44] It is fine and high in tone, but not such as the famous verses, cited and admired even by critics sparing of their priceless praise, beginning

Yes, in this sea of life enisled—.[45]

These in their profound and passionate calm strike deeper and sound fuller than any other of the plaintive dejected songs of Switzerland. 'Dover Beach' marks another high point in the volume; it has a grand choral cadence as of steady surges, regular in resonance, not fitful or gusty but antiphonal and reverberate. But nothing of new verse here clings closer to the mind than the overture of that majestic fragment from the chorus of a 'Dejaneira'.

O frivolous mind of man,
Light ignorance, and hurrying, unsure thoughts,
Though man bewails you not,
How I bewail you!

We must hope to have more of the tragedy in time; that must be a noble statue which could match this massive fragment. The story of Merope, though dramatic enough in detail, is upon the whole more of a narrative romance than a tragic subject; in Mr. Arnold's poem the deepest note is that struck by the tyrant Polyphontes, whose austere and patient figure is carved with Sophoclean skill of hand. It is a poem which Milton might have praised, an august work, of steady aim and severe success; but this of Dejaneira has in it a loftier promise and a larger chance. Higher matter of tragedy there can be none; none more intense and impressive, none fuller of keen and profound interest, none simpler and statelier; none where the weight and gravity, the sweetness and shapeliness of pure thought, could be better or closelier allied with the warmth and width of common tenderness and passion. We must all hope that the poet will keep to this clear air of the ancient heights, more natural and wholesome for the spirit than the lowlands of depression and dubiety where he has set before now a too frequent foot. This alone I find profitless and painful in his work; this occasional habit of harking back and loitering in mind among the sepulchres. Nothing is to be made by an artist out of scepticism, half-hearted or double-hearted doubts or creeds; nothing out of mere dejection and misty mental weather. Tempest or calm you may put to use, but hardly a flat fog. In not a few of his former poems, in some reprinted here, there is a sensible and stagnant influence of moist vapour from those marshes of the mind where weaker souls paddle and plunge and disappear. Above these levels the sunnier fields and fresher uplands lie wide and warm; and there the lord of the land should sit at peace among his good things. If a spirit by nature clear and high, a harmonious and a shining soul, does ever feel itself 'immured in the hot prison of the present',[46] its fit work is not to hug but break its chain; and only by its own will or weakness can it remain ill at ease in a thick and difficult air. Of such poetry I would say what Joubert, as cited by Mr. Arnold, says of all coarse and violent literature: it may be produced in any amount of supply to any excess of effect, but it is no proper matter of pure art, and 'the soul says all the while, You hurt me'.[47] Deep-reaching doubt and 'large discourse'[48] are poetical; so is faith, so are sorrow and joy; but so are not the small troubles of spirits that nibble and quibble about beliefs living or dead; so are not those sickly moods which are warmed and weakened by feeding on the sullen drugs of dejection; and the savour of this disease and its medicines is enough to deaden the fresh air of poetry. Nothing which leaves us depressed is a true work of art. We must have light though it be lightning, and air though it be storm.

Where the thought goes wrong, the verse follows after it. In Mr. Arnold's second book there was more of weak or barren matter, and more therefore of feeble or faulty metre. Rhyme is the native condition of lyric verse in English; a rhymeless lyric is a maimed thing, and halts and stammers in the delivery of its message. There are some few in the language as good as rare; but the habit or rule is bad. The fragments of his 'Antigone' and 'Dejaneira' no reader can wish other than they are; and the chorus for example in *Merope* which tells of Arcas and Callisto is a model of noble form and colour; but it does not fasten at once upon the memory like a song of Callicles, or like the 'Merman', or like any such other. To throw away the natural grace of rhyme from a modern song is a wilful abdication of half the power and half the charm of verse. It is hard to realise and hopeless to reproduce the musical force of classic metres so recondite and exquisite as the choral parts of a Greek play. Even Milton could not; though with his godlike instinct and his godlike might of hand he made a kind of strange and enormous harmony by intermixture of assonance and rhyme with irregular blank verse, as in that last Titanic chorus of Samson which utters over the fallen Philistines the trumpet-blast and thunder of its triumph. But Milton, it may be said, even if he knew them, did not obey the laws of the choral scheme, and so forfeited the legitimate condition of its music. Who then has observed those laws and obtained that success which he did not? I scarcely think that Mr. Arnold has; and if ever man was qualified for the work it is he only. I have never seen other attempts at rhymeless choral metre which were not mere amorphous abortions of misshapen prose, halting on helpless broken limbs and feet. A poet of Mr. Arnold's high station cannot of course but write in verse, and in good verse as far as the kind will allow; but that is not far enough to attain the ultimate goal, to fill up the final measure of delight. We lose something of the glory and the joy of poetry, of which he has no reason and no right to defraud us. It is in no wise a question of scholarship, or in the presence of a scholar I should be silent; as it is, I must say how inexplicable it seems to me that Mr. Arnold, of all men, should be a patron of English hexameters.[49] His own I have tried in vain to reduce by scansion into any metrical feet at all; they look like nothing on earth, and sound like anapæsts broken up and driven wrong; neither by ear nor by finger can I bring them to any reckoning. I am sure of one thing, that some of them begin with a pure and absolute anapæst; and how a hexameter can do this it passes my power to conceive. And at best what ugly bastards of verse are these self-styled hexameters! how human tongues or hands could utter or could write them except by way of burlesque improvisation I could never imagine, and never shall. Once only, to be candid—and I will for once show all possible loyalty and reverence to past authority—once only, as far as I know, in Dr. Hawtrey's[50] delicate and fluent verse, has the riddle been resolved; the verses are faultless, are English, are hexametric; but that is simply a graceful interlude of pastime, a well-played stroke in a game of skill played with language. Such as pass elsewhere for English hexameters I do hope and suppose impossible to Eton. Mr. Clough's I will not presume to be serious attempts or studies in any manner of metre; they are admirable studies in graduated prose, full of fine sound and effect. Even Mr. Kingsley's *Andromeda*, the one good poem extant in that pernicious metre, for all its spirit and splendour, for all the grace and glory and exultation of its rushing and ringing words, has not made possible the impossible thing. Nothing but loose rhymeless anapæsts can be made of the language in that way; and we hardly want these, having infinite command and resource of metre without them, and rhyme thrown in to turn the overweighted scale. I am unwilling to set my face against any doctrine or practice of a poet such as Mr. Arnold, but on this matter of metre I was moved to deliver my soul.

This is not the only example in his writings of some quality which seems to me intrusive and incoherent with his full general accuracy and clearness. These points of view and heads of theory which in my eyes seem out of perspective do indeed cohere each with the other; but hardly with his own high practice and bright intuition of the best thing. His alliance is so precious against the mailed and gowned array of the Philistines, that the least defection, the least error of movement, imperils more than his own position; a whole regiment may be misled into ruin by the general, while the heat and burden of the day[51] lie before us yet. No man has done so much to exalt and to correct men's view of the higher criticism and its office. Wherever therefore in things great or small he outruns or falls short of the immediate goal of a just judgment, the instant aim of a pure argument, it is worth while to take note of the slippery or oblique reasoning, or at least to sift and strain it, on the chance that here may be some error. 'The light of the body is the eye'; he is the eye of English criticism; and if ever for some passing purblind minute the light that is in that body be darkness, how great indeed is that darkness![52] Dark however he properly never is, but I think at times oblique or drowsy. He has smitten the Janus of Philistine worship on one face; under the other, if he has not himself burnt a pinch or two of adulterate incense, he has encouraged or allowed others to burn. At the portal by which English devotees press thickest into the temple of Dagon[53] he has stood firm as in a breach, and done good service; but he has left unguarded other points of entrance. All that is said in his essays on the religious tradition and the religious idea, as opposed to Philistine demolition or to Philistine edification, I accept and admire as truth, excellent if not absolute, and suggestive if not final; but from his own vantage ground of meditation and idea I start my objection to this inference and that. Protestantism, conservative and destructive, is the form in which the enemy has appeared to him; such in his eyes has been the banner, such the watchword under which they serve. All Philistia for him is resumed in the English Philistine; who may probably be the most noisome example in the world, but is assuredly not the only one. I do not say that marriage dissoluble only in an English divorce court is a lovely thing or a venerable; I do say that marriage indissoluble except by Papal action is not. It is irrelevant and unfair for a soldier of light to ally himself with Philistine against Philistine. From the ideal point of meditation to which he would recall us, where the pure justice and the naked beauty of thought are alone held sacred, I cannot 'find the marriage theory of Catholicism refreshing and elevating' merely because the

Protestant theory, which 'neither makes divorce impossible nor makes it decent',[54] has assumed in English law-courts a gross and hideous incarnation. What is anomalous, what is unjust, cannot surely be beautiful to purged eyes looking from 'the ideal sphere'.[55] Of course the idea of a lifelong union has its beauty and significance; so has the idea of liberty and sincerity of action. Faith is good, and freedom is good; the office of the idea is to give free play and full justice to both. The Philistines on either side would fain draw sharper and harder the lines of demarcation and division; the thinkers on neither side would fain not reject but reconcile.

Again, it is doubtless the best and most direct service that a critic can do his countrymen to strip and smite their especial errors, to point out and fence off their peculiar pitfalls; and this Mr. Arnold has done for his English not once or twice only. I doubt if he has ever assailed or advised them without due cause: in one point above all he has done them most loyal and liberal service; he has striven to purge them of the pestilence of provincial thought and tradition, of blind theory and brute opinion, of all that hereditary policy of prejudice which substitutes self-esteem for self-culture, self-worship for self-knowledge; which clogs and encrusts all powers and all motions of the mind with a hard husk of mechanical conceit. And here, heaven knows, in his dull dumb way the Briton stands ahead of all men, towers above all men in stolid and sublime solitude, a massive, stupid, inarticulate god and priest in one; his mute and majestic autolatry is a deeper and more radical religion than the self-love of other nations, the more vocal vanities of France or America. In the stone walls and iron girders of this faith our champion has done what a man may to make a breach; and the weapon was well chosen, the brand of provinciality, wherewith to stamp and mark that side of the double-faced head of Dagon which looks towards us with English features. But, to use his own term, there are two notes of provinciality perceptible, one or other, in most criticism of foreign things; error in praise and error in dispraise. He could have prescribed for the soul-sick British Philistine, 'sick of self-love',[56] no better method of cure than study and culture of the French spirit, of its flexible intelligence and critical ambition, its many-sided faith in perfection, in possible excellence and ideal growth outward and upward, and the single-hearted love of all these which goes hand in hand with that faith. Faith in light and motion is what England has not and France has; often a blind, erring, heretical faith, often perverse and fanatical, a faith which kills its prophets and stones its proto-martyrs; but in art as in politics, in literature as in ethics, an active and a living faith. To show this to English eyes and impress upon English ears its truth and its importance is to do a good work; but to pass from general doctrine to example and detail is hard and unsafe for a foreign preacher. Those who deserve gratitude at our hands deserve also candour; and I must in candour say that Mr. Arnold is not a sure guide over French ground. He does not know quite how the land lies: he turns down this declivity or stops short by that well-head, where a native guide would hardly bid one halt. With a large and fine appreciation of the beauties and capacities of the national character, with a justice and strength of insight into these which compared with an average English judgment are wonderful and admirable, he has not the eyes and the nerves of one to the manner born, the sudden and sensitive intuition of an innate instinct: he thinks right, but he feels wrong; some men are right without being reasonable, he is reasonable without being right. He sets up a rational argument to prove why France should be, and why she is, weak in poetry and strong in prose;[57] a very keen and clear argument, only the facts are all against it. Of classic verse Mr. Arnold is so much more competent to speak than I am that I dare not press the debateable question of choric metre; but of French verse I must have leave to say that he is not competent to speak. His touch has in it no pulse or play of French blood; his fine ear is deaf on that side. It would clearly be impossible to show him, to make him feel, the silent horror and wonder with which other ears receive such utterances from him as from the common Briton we expect and accept with all composure. Whether it be 'the German paste in his composition'[58] which so far thickens and deadens his subtle sense of song, I cannot say; but I can say that in that case it would be well for him to get quit of it. The cadence and impulse of harmonies in French verse are of course unlike those in English verse or Italian, and the laws which are their outgrowth are unlike too; but the one is not more sure and satisfying than the other: only there must be the right hands to play and the right ears to hear. Mr. Arnold says that a Frenchman born with the faculty or instinct of poetry finds in prose a fuller and easier expression than in verse. As justly might a French critic say this of an Englishman. In either case, the man who is a poet or nothing must be judged by his power of writing verse. If he can neither do that well nor do any other work, whatever his charm of aspiration and sentiment and sincerity may be, he slips into the second rank as surely if French as if English. Imagine that Frenchman's tone of mind, or his tone of ear, who should proclaim the inadequacy of a language which has sufficed for all the great lyric poets of France, all the copious and glorious roll from François Villon and Charles of Orleans to Victor Hugo and Théophile Gautier, but is now convicted of inaptitude to render in full the sentiments of a Maurice de Guérin! The English poet is here hopelessly at sea without oar or rudder, haven or guiding-star. He cannot even be trusted to speak of the academic poets, easier though they are of access and apprehension even to the run of Englishmen. The thin, narrow, shallow, but very real melodies of Racine are as inaudible to him as the mightier symphonies of the great school; this perhaps, as he says, is natural in a foreigner. But no such excuse will serve for the confusion of judgment which places on a level the very best man of his kind, Pope, and Boileau, the very worst. Perhaps their respective Odes on St. Cecilia's Day and the Siege of Namur may be allowed to pair off as the shamefullest two lyrical poems in the world; but compare for a moment their general work, their didactic and satirical verse! the comparison is an insult too absurd to affect the Englishman. He is the finest, Boileau the dullest craftsman of their age and school.

It is singular and significant that Mr. Arnold, himself established and acknowledged as a poet standing in the first rank among his own people, has chosen for special praise and patronage men who have tried their hands at his work and failed, men who have fallen back baffled from the cliff-side he has climbed. Again I cite the evidence of his French critic; who naturally feels that he has paid the French but a poor compliment in praising as their best men those who fall short of their own aim and his achievement:[59] 'Il y a quelque chose de louche, de suspect, dans les louanges que prodigue aux poëtes manqués un poëte réussi. Or, parmi tous les nôtres c'est à M. Sainte-Beuve, poëte manqué dont le temps a fait un critique réussi, que le poëte anglais adresse son hommage respectueux. Il a eu mille fois raison d'étudier, d'apprécier, de louer cet illustre écrivain; il n'a peut-être pas eu tort de le suivre les yeux fermés lorsqu'il s'envole à tire d'ailes dans les nuages du paradoxe, de le croire sur parole quand il affirme qu'on peut être grand poëte tout en échouant dans le champ poétique: pour moi, je préfere, soit dit en passant, les peintres qui sachent peindre, les médecins qui sachent guérir, les poëtes qui font des vers. Passons-lui ces spécialités; ce n'est pas une raison d'affirmer qu'il ne saurait être en France de meilleurs poëtes que ces prosateurs, de plus forts travailleurs que ces lutteurs étiques, que ces génies tronqués. Quand on dénonce chez autrui les jugements saugrenus,[60] les bêtises réciproques de l'esprit insulaire et provincial, il faudrait se garder par exemple de ranger au niveau des grands poëtes les talents délicats, de prendre pour des Keats les Maurice de Guérin, pauvres belles âmes étiolées, douces et frêles petites fleurs effeuillées en pleine éclosion. Ces roses pâles, ces pousses maladives, ont bien leur charme et leur parfum, valent bien la peine qu'on les arrose et les recueille; mais on ne tresse point avec celles-là les grandes couronnes poétiques.' [There is something dubious, something suspect, in the praises that a successful poet lavishes upon inferior poets. Now, among all our own it is to M. Sainte-Beuve, an unsuccessful poet of whom time has made a successful critic, that the English poet addresses his respectful homage. He was right a thousand times over to study, to appreciate, to praise this illustrious writer; perhaps he was not wrong to follow him blindly when he soars into the clouds of paradox, to accept his word when he affirms that one can be a great poet even when failing in the poetic terrain. As for me, I prefer, if I may say so in passing, the painters who know how to paint, the physicians who know how to cure, the poets who compose poetry. Let us allow him these specialties: that is not a reason for affirming that in France there could not be better poets than these writers of prose, stronger workmen than these lean wrestlers, than these mutilated geniuses. When one denounces absurd judgments by others, the reciprocal stupidity of the insular and the provincial spirit, one ought to guard against, for example, putting delicate talents on a level with great poets, taking for Keatses the Maurice de Guérins—poor lonely sickly souls, sweet and fragile little flowers defoliated in full bloom. These pale roses, these puny shoots, certainly have their charm and their fragrance, and are surely worth watering and collecting; but one does not by any means weave with them the great poetic coronals.]

The gentle pupil of Lamennais[61] is to Mr. Arnold what the lesser celandine was to Wordsworth: he has unearthed a new favourite, and must have some three or four who will love his little flower. It were churlish and foolish to refuse; the small petals are fresh and dewy, the slim stem bends and sways with a sylvan grace. But it is something too much to hold up a bit of pilewort as the rose of Sharon; it provokes one to deny the poor blossom a place among flowers at all: it is indecorous and ludicrous. 'The Centaur' is really so fine and graceful a little study, there are really such delicate and distinctive touches of expression and feeling, such traces of a bright clear sense of beauty and charm and meaning in nature, that it was but just, when the man was well dead and could get no good of it and no harm, to praise him without grudging and pick up his leavings as a windfall. A place in the cabinet of M. Sainte-Beuve was no more than his desert. But the place which Mr. Arnold assigns him is reserved for men far other than this tender dreamer: five minutes of their life outweigh five centuries of such lives as his; one breath of the common air of their spirit would burn up the little tremulous soul as with fire. No tender Semele, but the queen of heaven alone, can face and enjoy the lightning of heaven.[62] Of the contact of mortal and immortal, ashes are the only fruits. In Keats there was something of the spirit and breath of the world, of the divine life of things; in Guérin there was hardly a soft breathless pulse of fluttering sympathy; here was the *anima mundi*, made flesh once more in the body of a divine interpreter such as all great poets must be after their kind; there was the *animula vagula*, *blandula*,[63] of a tentative, sensitive, impressible nature; full of little native pieties and sincere little sensibilities, amiable and laudable enough. But the demigods of our kind are not cast in such clay as that. M. Sainte-Beuve knew better than Mr. Arnold what was the rank and what the kindred of their foster-child when he called him a latter-day Lakist. If we must needs find him kinsmen among English poets, he may take his stand as a subordinate in the school of Gray[64] or the household of Cowper. With them he had some good things in common; his letters, if less worth reading than the best of theirs, have the same frank delicacy and gentle play of personal sentiment applied to the landscape or the hearthside, and couched sometimes in choice and excellent words. But Keats, of all men born the ablest to hold his own with nature, and translate her gods into verbal incarnation; Keats, who was at once the lyrist and the lyre of that nature, the priest and the altar of those gods; more than all other poets receptive and passive of her influences and forces, and more than all other poets able and active to turn them all to a divine use, to transfigure them without transformation, to attune all colours and attemper all harmonies; whose power upon these things, whose gift of transfusion and expression, places him apart from all in his sovereign command of nature, able to do for nature what in his own day Shelley could not achieve nor Wordsworth attempt; above all Greece and all Italy and all England in his own line and field of work; to push forward as a competitor with him in that especial field of work where all the giants and all the gods of art would fail to stand against him for an hour, a man who in his own craft could not use the tools that lay ready to his hand—who was nothing (it seems) if not a poet, and could not as much as prove himself a poet by writing passable verse at all; this is a madness of mistake explicable and excusable only as the error of a foreign and provincial judgment. Any stanza of 'Thyrsis', any fragment of 'Callicles', would outweigh in point of 'natural magic'[65] all Guérin's work, even were his thoughts clothed in the beauty of verse instead of the prettiness of prose; to weigh against it the entire work of Keats, or any such single poem as the 'Ode to Psyche' or that 'on a Grecian Urn'—poems which for perfect apprehension and execution of all attainable in their own sphere would weigh down all the world of poetry—is inexpressibly impossible.

Sweeping aside all this accumulated panegyric, we may discern the modest attraction of Guérin's little plot of ground with its borders of crocus and snowdrop; though the gardeners have done their best to kill them with hothouse fumes and water-pipes and bell-glasses. As to his first posthumous patroness—he belongs to the breed of those suckling poets who live on patronage premature even when posthumous—I must say with another critic, 'Madame Sand n'est vraiment pas heureuse en poëtes';[66] great and excellent as she is, their contact is not good for her. Assuredly the one aspiration of Guérin, his one desire that 'a stronger soul would bow down to his weaker spirit',[67] has since his death been somewhat too much fulfilled. A niche in the Sainte-Beuve collection is his due; but not the homage of George Sand and Matthew Arnold. His sister and he had in effect a certain distinction, they had graceful tastes and tunable minds: without distinction there cannot be genius, but there cannot be genius with nothing else; a man cannot live on air because he cannot live without it. Mr. Arnold would set them as stars in heaven, *lucida sidera*;[68] their little lights will hardly burn the night out, but meantime they shine well enough for children to watch them twinkle and 'wonder what they are'. Without a glimpse of genius, without more light or strength of spirit than many others unknown, Mlle. de Guérin shows always a beautiful and admirable soul; her diary and her letters have more than usual of the lovely and loving qualities of good women, true sisters and gentle wives, faithful and fervent and worthy to receive again the lavish love they give; they never would come forward, they need never be thrust forward, as genius or as saint. The immortal women in either kind—St. Theresa, St. Catherine, Vittoria Colonna, Mrs. Browning, Miss Christina Rossetti—belong to a different world and scheme of things. With one verse or one word of theirs any one of these could have absorbed and consumed her as a sunbeam of the fiery heaven a dewdrop of the dawning earth.[69] Nor, to repass for an instant from the personal to the religious question started from this cover by Mr. Arnold, is it just or rational to oppose to her delicate provincial piety the coarsest and ugliest form of English faith. There are graceful as well as loathsome forms of Protestantism, loathsome as well as graceful forms of Catholicism: probably the balance is about even. The Christ of Clapham is an ungracious god enough; the time is not fruitful of gods in any degree adorable; but the Christ of Montrouge? Exeter Hall is not a wise or lovely oracle; but what of Saint-Acheul? Is there any more of grace, of light, of culture or sweetness, under the banner of M. Veuillot than on the staff of the *Record*? There lies the question; not between Languedoc and Margate.[70] Against the best of one creed it is but fair to set the best of another, against the worst the worst. As to culture, sanity, power of grasp and reception, Mlle. de Guérin hesitating at the brink of Hugo is assuredly as pitiable as any Puritan shuddering on the verge of Shakespeare.

Again, Mr. Arnold has a fond faith in the French Academy and in the *Revue des Deux Mondes* which is nothing short of pathetic; he seems actually to take them at their own valuation. The too outspoken critic before cited ventures to express in ribald phrase his wonder that such a pair of 'hoarse and haggard old temptresses' (*vieilles tentatrices hâves et rauques*) should play the part of Delilah to the scourger of Philistines. Not, as he adds, that he would impugn the venerable maiden reputation of their hoary hairs; but such as they are, 'ces étranges séductrices ont failli couper de leurs ciseaux émoussés les cheveux au Samson anglais. Déjà son engouement a manqué l'aveugler. Aux yeux de M. Arnold, l'amour a refait à l'Académie une virginité; il est tout prêt à épouser sa Marion,[71] à prôner ses quelques appas émérites, à faire courber toutes les têtes anglaises devant cette Dulcinée à quarante.[72] Il est l'amant fougueux du bon sens, l'apôtre échauffé de la froide raison, l'avocat furibond du goût sain.' [These strange seductresses have almost cut off the hair of the English Samson with their dull shears. Already his infatuation has nearly blinded him. In Mr Arnold's eyes, love has restored a kind of virginity to the Academy; he is quite ready to espouse his Marion, to extol her few venerable charms, to make all the English heads bow down to that Dulcinea with forty members. He is the passionate lover of good sense, the inflamed apostle of cold reason, the raging advocate of sound taste.] This is not a fair or clear judgment; it is indigested and violent and deformed in expression;

but it shows as in a cracked and blurred mirror the reflection thrown upon other minds by Mr. Arnold's act of homage in the outer courts of the Philistine temple: for thither he has unwittingly turned, and there has bent his knee, as no Frenchman could have done who was not a Philistine born and baptised and branded to the bone with the signet of the sons of Dagon. We may grant that the real office of an Academy should be—what the nominal office of this Academy is—culture and perfection of intelligence, elevation of the general standard of work, the average of mind and taste and sense which precludes absurdity or aberration and ensures something of care and conscience among the craftsmen of literature. Greater work an ideal Academy could hardly undertake, for greater work would require the vivid and personal advent of genius; and that, I presume, it could hardly undertake to supply. But has the actual Academy done this? Whom has it controlled, whom has it impelled, who but for such influence would either have gone wrong or failed to go right? whom at least among men really memorable and precious? Has it constantly done homage to the best? has it constantly rejected or rebuked the worst? Is it to the Academy that we owe the sound judgment, taste, temperance of the French prose classics whom Mr. Arnold eloquently extols? Did not the great Richelieu, its founder, set in motion the still virgin machinery of his engine against the greater Corneille? What was Molière in its eyes? and what was not Boileau? Where now are its great men, in an age for France so fruitful of literary greatness? Does it include one of high and fine genius besides Mérimée? and do the rest of the sacred forty respect in him the official antiquary or the faultless writer on whose dawn Goethe looked out and prophesied overmuch? There are names indeed still greater on its roll, but you do not see appended to them the academic title. Once for all, waiving its mere theories and reserving its mere pretensions, let us inquire if in effect it now does, if it ever has done, if it ever will do, any real and good service whatever to pure literature? The advice which Mr. Arnold gives by implication to his English audience while preaching on the text of academies is precious and necessary in itself, if the mass of English literature now current or floating is ever to be in any measure elevated or purified; but the selection of text is merely fantastic, the process of deduction vicious and baseless. This double impression was made on me by the lecture when I heard it delivered at Oxford; I have read it since more than once, and the impression is strengthened and deepened. It is possible to start from some incongruous or ignorant assumption and yet proceed to speak words of truth and soberness; the sermon may be useful and noble though the text be strained and misapplied. For the *Revue des Deux Mondes* I have as earnest a respect as Mr. Arnold; so far from regarding it with the eyes of irreverence and ribaldry, as an old lady of pleasure, a Delilah of dangerously gay repute, the ideas of pleasure or gaiety are the last I should associate with a name so justly venerated, a fame so sound and round and solid. Rather would I regard it, as the author of *Mademoiselle de Maupin* used to regard virtue in the days which found him unambitious of academic eminence, with such eyes as turn towards a fond and watchful grandmother.[73] It is dangerous to ruffle the robe of that dowager. But I cannot regard her bosom as a safe pillow for the yet unshorn head of a Nazarite champion. Too many of the uncircumcised Philistines lie in wait for him slumbering in the lap of M. Buloz.[74] Are there not giants among them, and the sons of the old giant, all of them children of uncircumcision? and the least of these has twice the thews and seven times the wits of the heavy-headed horny-eyed English Philistine. Some of them there are that sleep with their father Goliath, and some abide to this day; and the acts of them past and present, and all that they did, and their might, are they not written in the books of the *Revue des Deux Mondes*? There is M. Gustave Planche,[75] the staff of whose spear was so very like a weaver's beam; there is M. Armand de Pontmartin,[76] a man of great moral stature, having on every hand six fingers to fight with, if haply he may give the flesh of poets to the fowls of the air and to the beasts of the field;[77] there is M. Louis Etienne, who lately laid lance in rest against me unoffending in championship of the upper powers.[78] Since the time of Goliath it has been a holy habit and tradition with the Philistines to curse 'by their gods'—which indeed seems the chief utility of those divine beings.

The comparative culture and relative urbanity of responsible criticism—qualities due to no prescription of academic authority, but in part to natural sense and self-respect, in part to the code of habitual honour which rather impels than compels a man to avow his words and his works—these qualities, which preserve from mere contempt even the Philistines of French literature when we turn from them to their English fellow-soldiers, have I suspect blinded Mr. Arnold to the real colours under which they also serve. As yet however they have not made a prey of him; Delilah has merely woven the seven locks of the champion's head with the web and fastened it with the pin; he has but to awake out of his sleep and go away with the pin of the beam and with the web.[79] But next time he goes to Gaza and sees there the Academy he must beware of going in unto that siren, or in the morning he may find the gates too heavy to carry off. We may trust indeed never to find him there eyeless at the mill with slaves;[80] but it is no good sign that he should ever be blind of this eye or deaf of that ear—blind to infirmities on this side, or deaf to harmonies on that. I write not as a disciple of the dishevelled school, *romantique à tous crins*;[81] all such false and foolish catchwords as the names of classic and romantic I repudiate as senseless, and revere form or harmony as the high one law of all art. It is because, both as poet and critic, Mr. Arnold has done the service he has in the front rank of an army which finds among us few enough of able recruits, that I grudge in him the least appearance of praise or dispraise unworthy of his rank and office. Otherwise he would be as welcome for me as another Englishman to deny the power and variety, the supple sweetness and the superb resources of French verse in its depths and heights of song; as welcome to ignore the higher and enhance the minor merits of a foreign literature; to mistake for the causes the effects of these minor merits, which in their turn become (as in this case of the Academy) causes of grave error and defect, weakening where they should strengthen the hands and eyes they have in training. But in a child and champion of the light the least obliquity or obscurity of vision is to be noted as dangerous. If to any one these seem things of minor moment, to a poet such as he is they cannot; to him they must be more serious than to another. We owe him too much to keep silence here, though we might allow as harmless such graceful errors of pastime or paradox as the faith in Oxford which will not allow that she has ever 'given herself to the Philistines';[82] the beauty of the valley of Sorek[83] has surely blinded him to the nation and nature of the Gazites and Ascalonites who have dwelt there now and again as surely as have many of their betters. Both here and in the Academy there may be a profession, a tradition of culture, of sweetness, urbanity, loyalty to the light; but where, we may too often have had to ask, are the things themselves? By their fruits ye shall know them;[84] and what are these? In them both, if not of them, there may be good men and great; have such been always their leaders? or were ever such their types?

Not here, O Apollo!
   Are haunts meet for thee;
But where Helicon breaks down
   In cliff to the sea.[85]

There, and not in the academies or the market-places of the Philistines, for peace or war; there, where all airs are full of the breath and all fields of the feet of the gods; where the sea-wind that first waved the wet hair of Venus moves now only the ripples that remember her rising limbs; where the Muses are, and their mother. There is his place, who in such a place long since found Circe feasting and heard Apollo play; there, below the upper glens and wellsprings of the Centaurs, above the scooped sea-shelves and flushing sands of the Sirens.[86] Whatever now he say or do, he has been and will remain to us a lover and a giver of light; unwittingly, by impulse, for pure love of it; and such lead further and lighten otherwise than they know. All conscious help or guidance serves us less than unconscious leadership. In his best words there is often a craft and a charm; but in his best work there is always rest, and air, and a high relief; it satisfies, enlarges, refreshes with its cool full breath and serenity. On some men's nerves the temperature strikes somewhat cold; there are lungs that cannot breathe but in the air of a hothouse or a hospital. There is not much indeed of heat or flame in the Vestal or lunar light that shines from this hearth; but it does not burn down. His poetry is a pure temple, a white flower of marble, unfretted without by intricate and grotesque traceries, unvexed within by fumes of shaken censers or intoning of hoarse choristers; large and clear and cool, with many chapels in it and outer courts, full of quiet and of music. In the plainest air played here there is a sound of sincerity and skill; as in one little '*Requiescat*', which without show of beauty or any thought or fancy leaves long upon the ear an impressure of simple, of earnest, of weary melody, wound up into a sense of rest. We do not always want to bathe our spirit in overflowing waters or flaming fires of imagination; pathos and passion and aspiration and desire are not the only springs we seek for song. Sorrows and joys of thought or sense meet us here in white raiment and wearing maiden crowns. In each court or chapel there is a fresh fragrance of early mountain flowers which bring with them the wind and the sun and a sense of space and growth, all of them born in high places, washed and waved by upper airs and rains. Into each alike there falls on us as we turn a conscience of calm beauty, of cool and noble repose, of majestic work under melodious and lofty laws; we feel and accept the quiet sovereignties of happy harmony and loyal form, whose service for the artist is perfect freedom: it is good for us to be here.[87] Nor are all these either of modern structure or of Greek; here is an Asiatic court, a Scandinavian there. And everywhere is the one ruling and royal quality of classic work, an assured and equal excellence of touch. Whether for Balder dead and the weeping gods in Asgard, or for the thought-sick heart-sore king of a weary land far east,[88] blinded and vexed in spirit with the piteous pains and wrongs of other men, the same good care and wise charm of right words are used to give speed of wing and sureness of foot to the ministering verse. The stormy northern world of water and air and iron and snow, the mystic oppression of eastern light and cruel colour in fiery continents and cities full of sickness and splendour and troubled tyrannies, alike yield up to him their spirit and their secret, to be rendered again in just and full expression. These are the trophies of his work and the gifts of his hand; through these and such as these things, his high and distinct seat is assured to him among English poets.

NOTES

1 Cf. 1 Cor. 13: 1: 'Though I speak with the tongues of men and of angels. . . .'

2 A question which I still regret should be yet unanswered in its favour (1875). (ACS)

Arnold reprinted 'The New Sirens' in *Macmillan's Magazine* for December 1876, with a note explaining that he did so because of 'the regrets of a most distinguished mourner, Mr. Swinburne'. See C. B. Tinker and H. F. Lowry, *The Poetry of Matthew Arnold: A Commentary* (London and New York, 1940), 45–6.

3 Cf. *Measure for Measure*, II, i: 'I hope here be truths.'

4 Probably based on an indistinct memory of 'A French Eton', in which Arnold says that a student in a French school remarked 'with the amiability of his race . . . (God forgive him!) that he was well acquainted with my poems'.

5 Cf. Isaiah 32: 2.

6 From Arnold's essay on Marcus Aurelius.

7 It has since been replaced, with the final stanza wholly rewritten. For its recovery I believe that I may take some credit to myself, and claim in consequence some thanks from all serious students of contemporary poetry. (ACS)

In 1877 Arnold substituted the earlier version of the last stanza of '*In Utrumque Paratus*' for the 'final stanza wholly rewritten'.

8 A letter from Arnold to Swinburne (Lang, 269–70) shows that he had guessed that the words assigned to 'a French critic' were composed by Swinburne. A translation in square brackets follows the passage in French.

9 This is a strange and sad instance of the ignorance and perversity as foreign to Englishmen as they are natural to foreigners. Any one could have answered him, and at any length. Envy doubtless as well as error must have inspired this blasphemy against the Constitution once delivered to the saints—that august result of a plenary inspiration above the reach of human wisdom, sent down direct from heaven, and vouchsafed alone to this chosen nation, this peculiar people; to which, as to Tyre or Jerusalem in time past, the Supreme Powers have said by the sweet voices of their representative elect—elect of gods and men—'Thou sealest up the sum; full of wisdom, and perfect in beauty.' (ACS)

The quotation is from Ezek. 28: 12.

10 Allusions to Browning's 'A Death in the Desert', the 'Epilogue' to *Dramatis Personae*, and 'Gold Hair'. The last poem refers to Bishop J. W. Colenso, whose analysis of early parts of the Bible was regarded as heretical.

11 Probably Swinburne recalls Pascal's '*deux abimes de l'infini et du néant*', 'the two abysses of the infinite and of nothingness' (*Pensées*, 72).

12 Far better than in the long literal version of Omar Khayyám which is all that the French language can show, may the soul and spirit of his thought be tasted in that most exquisite English translation, sovereignly faultless in form and colour of verse, which gives to those ignorant of the East a relish of the treasure and a delight in the beauty of its wisdom. (ACS)

13 There are varieties of opinion in this world; and the British critic's fond faith in the British thinker will not soon be shaken by the adverse verdict of any French heretic. Witness the words of a writer whom I once fell in with, heaven knows where; who, being far above the shallow errors of foolish 'Greeks' and puerile 'pagans', takes occasion to admonish their disciples that '*our* philosophers and poets will tell you that they have got far beyond *this* stage. The riddles *they* have to unravel involve finer issues' (and among these perhaps they might deign to expound what manner of thing may be the involution of an issue); no doubt, in a word, but they are the people, and wisdom shall die with them. They may tell us so, certainly; thought and speech are free, and for aught I know they may be fully capable of the assertion. But it is for us to choose what amount of belief it may please us to accord them. (ACS)

'They are the people . . . them'. Cf. Job 12: 2.

14 *Empedocles on Etna*, I, ii, 111. Fifteen succeeding quotations not otherwise identified are also from *Empedocles*.

15 I take leave to forge this word, because 'self-sufficingness' is a compound of too barbaric sound, and 'self-sufficiency' has fallen into a term of reproach. Archbishop Trench has pointed out how and why a word which to the ancient Greek signified a noble virtue came to signify to the modern Christian the base vice of presumption. I do not see that

human language has gained by this change of meaning, or that the later mood of mind which dictated this debasement of the word is at all in advance of the older, or indicative of any spiritual improvement; rather the alteration seems to me a loss and a discredit, and the tone of thought which made the quality venerable more sound and wise than that which declares it vile. (ACS)

For 'self-sufficiency' see the index to Richard Chenevix Trench's *On the Study of Words*.

16 Sophocles, *Oedipus at Colonus*, ll. 670–3: 'Where the nightingale, a constant guest, trills her clear note in the covert of green glades' (tr. Sir Richard C. Jebb).

17 *Ibid.*, ll. 691–3: 'Nor hath the Muses' choir abhorred this place, nor Aphrodite of the golden rein' (tr. Jebb).

18 English might have seemed a 'Hyperborean dialect' (of the far north) to the Greeks. The satyr Marsyas was flayed alive by Apollo after he had challenged the god to a contest with the flute and had been defeated.

19 Cf. Gen. 1:2.

20 'We should have been made to feel the setting, the attire, the breathable milieu of that clouded soul, of that wearied spirit.'

21 *Hamlet*, I, v, 125.

22 'Heine's Grave', ll. 115ff.

23 From *Empedocles on Etna*, ii, 242–3.

24 Shelley, 'Peter Bell the Third', VI, xxxii, 5 and 1.

25 The allusion is to Judges 16: 21; 'Agonistes' may recall Milton's *Samson Agonistes*.

26 Swinburne thinks of Wordsworth, whose home was Rydal Mount and who was a friend and neighbour of the Arnolds at Fox Howe, as Arnold's teacher. He regards Dr Thomas Arnold, the famous headmaster of Rugby, as an influence making for Philistinism, though it was the son who popularized 'Philistine' as a term for an uncultivated member of the middle class. Hence 'David the son of Goliath' for Matthew Arnold. In chapter 3 of *Culture and Anarchy* Arnold comments: '. . . I myself am properly a Philistine,—Mr Swinburne would add, the son of a Philistine.'

27 Cf. 2 Sam. 1:20.

28 Judges 11 and 12.

29 Cf. Psalm 144: 1.

30 Acts 22: 3.

31 'Memorial Verses.'

32 'Resignation', l. 195.

33 'The Buried Life', ll. 74–6.

34 Cf. Wordsworth's *Excursion*, i, 79: 'The vision and the faculty divine.'

35 This was a poor young Scotchman who may be remembered as having sought and found help and patronage at the hands first of Mr. Dobell

and afterwards of Lord Houghton. In some of his sonnets there are touches of sweet and sincere emotion; but the most remarkable points in his poor little book, and those which should be most memorable to other small poets of his kind (if at least the race of them were capable of profiting by any such lesson), are first the direct and seemingly unconscious transference of some of the best-known lines or phrases from such obscure authors as Shakespeare and Wordsworth into the somewhat narrow and barren field of his own verse, and secondly the incredible candour of expression given in his correspondence to such flatulent ambition and such hysterical self-esteem as the author of *Balder* must have regarded, I should think, with a sorrowful sense of amusement. I may add that the poor boy's name was here cited with no desire to confer upon it any undeserved notoriety for better or for worse, and assuredly with no unkindlier feeling than pity for his poor little memory, but simply as conveying the most apt and the most flagrant as well as the most recent instance I happened to remember of the piteous and grievous harm done by false teaching and groundless encouragement to spirits not strong enough to know their own weakness. It was a kindly but uncritical reference in Mr. Arnold's kindly but uncritical essay on Maurice de Guérin—an essay of which I have said a few words further on—that upon this occasion for once recalled the name to my mind, and supplied me with the illustration required. (ACS)

Arnold's essay 'Maurice de Guérin' mentions David Gray as 'another youth of genius, whose name . . . Lord Houghton has so gracefully written in the history of English poetry'.

36 Job 15:2.

37 'The Good Shepherd with the Kid.'

38 Now called 'The Better Part'. In the *Fortnightly Review* Swinburne refers to the earlier title: 'headed (not happily) "Anti-Desperation".'

39 From *Empedocles on Etna*, ii, 447–8.

40 'Lycidas', l. 14.

41 Cf. Isaiah 33: 17.

42 George Chapman, 'To His Loving Friend, Master John Fletcher' (verses prefixed to *The Faithful Shepherdess*), ll. 21–4.

43 Among these the stanzas on the advent of Christianity, of 'the Mother with the Child', and their enduring life while only faith in them endured, recall the like passage, more thoughtful and fruitful still, in that wise and noble poem, Mr. W. B. Scott's 'Year of the World'; a poem to whose great qualities and affluent beauties of letter and of spirit the requisite and certain justice of time remains hitherto a debt unpaid. Its author must divide with Mr. Arnold the palm of intellectual or philosophic poetry, the highest achieved in England since Wordsworth, and in many things of moment higher than his. (ACS)

44 'Love.'

45 'V. To Marguerite. Continued' in the group called 'Switzerland', l. 1.

46 'Growing Old', ll. 23–4.
47 From Arnold's essay on Joubert.
48 *Hamlet*, IV, iv, 36.
49 Especially in *On Translating Homer*.
50 Edward Craven Hawtrey (1789–1862), headmaster and later provost of Eton, published 'Two Translations from Homer in English Hexameters', praised by Arnold, and used the metre in translations from German poets.
51 Cf. Matt. 20: 12.
52 Matt. 6: 22–3.
53 I Chron. 10: 10. Dagon was the god of the Philistines, whose temple at Gaza Samson destroyed.
54 From 'The Function of Criticism at the Present Time'.
55 *Ibid.*
56 *Twelfth Night*, I, v, 97.
57 In 'The Literary Influence of Academies'.
58 From Arnold's 'Heinrich Heine': 'After the rhythm, to us, at any rate, with the German paste in our composition. . . .'
59 See note 8.
60 In his essay on Joubert, Arnold explains that *saugrenu* 'means something like *impudently absurd*'.
61 H. F. R. de Lamennais (1782–1854), influential priest whose belief that Catholicism and democracy would save society finally led to his severance of church ties and championing of revolutionary change.
62 Semele, beloved by Zeus, was induced by the jealous Hera to ask her lover to appear in full Olympian panoply, with the result that Semele was reduced to ashes.
63 The *anima mundi*, 'the soul of the world', is contrasted with the '*animula vagula, blandula*'—words which begin the Emperor Hadrian's 'dying address to his soul', a poem which Byron paraphrased thus:

> Ah! gentle, fleeting, wav'ring sprite,
> Friend and associate of this clay!
> To what unknown region borne,
> Wilt thou now wing thy distant flight?
> No more with wonted humour gay,
> But pallid, cheerless, and forlorn.

64 I am here reminded to ask in passing how Mr. Arnold, who says of Gray that he never used the popular metre of his century, came to forget his admirable fragment of a didactic poem in the ten-syllable couplet; and tempted, while on this ground, to appeal against the judgment which ranks him as a poet above Collins, the man of all his age, it seems to me, who had most in him of the pure and high and durable spirit of poetry. The overture of his Ode to Liberty is worthy of

Coleridge or Shelley; Gray's best ode by its side is somewhat hard and thin. (ACS)

65 Arnold's phrase, used in 'Maurice de Guérin' and elsewhere.

66 'Madame Sand is not really fortunate in her choice of poets.'

67 The English equivalent of a passage quoted in Sainte-Beuve's review of Guérin's *Œuvres* (1 October 1860 in the *Causeries du Lundi*, third edition, xv, 29).

68 Horace, *Carm.*, I, iii, 2, 'clear stars'; the Latin phrase, used of the Guérins, comes at the end of Arnold's essay on Eugénie de Guérin, Maurice's sister.

69 If you would see the note of distinction between religious genius and religious talent, compare with any of Mlle. de Guérin's idyllic effusions of gracious piety, fresh and sweet in their small way as the dusk and the dew, the great new-year hymn of Miss Rossetti,

Passing away, saith the world, passing away,

so much the noblest of sacred poems in our language that there is none which comes near it enough to stand second; a hymn touched as with the fire and bathed as in the light of sunbeams, tuned as to chords and cadences of refluent sea-music beyond reach of harp and organ, large echoes of the serene and sonorous tides of heaven. (ACS)

70 Arnold mentions Margate ('that brick-and-mortar image of English Protestantism') to point a contrast with Languedoc in the country of Eugénie de Guérin. More than once in *Essays in Criticism* he refers to Exeter Hall, where the noted Baptist minister C. H. Spurgeon, for example, preached, and with it Swinburne associates Saint-Acheul, a suburb of Amiens, the site of an ancient abbey and later of a Jesuit college. In 'The Function of Criticism at the Present Time' Arnold calls the *Record* 'the Evangelical hyena', with which Swinburne pairs the work of Louis Veuillot, a French journalist known for his extreme ultramontane views and often denounced by Victor Hugo. Clapham, in south-west London, which was associated with certain Evangelical leaders, suggests a contrast with Montrouge, in the southern outskirts of Paris.

71 Marion, the name of the heroine of the Old French *Jeu de Robin et Marion* who resisted the advances of a knight, came to be used in French as the common name for a girl, sometimes one of doubtful virginity.

72 Dulcinea del Toboso, championed by Don Quixote as his ideal, of course owed her charms to his imagination. The phrase '*à quarante*' refers to the fact that the French Academy has forty members.

73 From a statement in Gautier's preface to *Mademoiselle de Maupin*.

74 Editor of the *Revue des Deux Mondes* from 1831 to 1877.

75 A French literary critic (1808–57) associated with Buloz. With Swinburne's addition of 'very', what follows is from 2 Samuel 21: 19.

76 A critic (1811–90) who attacked most of the contemporary French authors.

77 Cf. 2 Samuel 21: 20: 'And there was yet a battle in Gath, where was a man of great stature, that had on every hand six fingers . . .; Gen. 6:7 and other passages: 'fowls of the air'; Jer. 12:9: 'beasts of the field.'

78 He contributed to the *Revue des Deux Mondes* for 15 May 1867 an article on Swinburne's paganism.

79 Judges 16: 14.

80 Judges 16: 3, 21.

81 'Romantic with flowing mane and tail'—zealously romantic.

82 From Arnold's preface to *Essays in Criticism.*

83 Judges 16: 4.

84 Matt. 7: 20.

85 From *Empedocles on Etna*, ii, 421–4.

86 Reminiscent of 'The Strayed Reveller' and 'The New Sirens'.

87 *The Book of Common Prayer*, 'A Collect for Peace'; Matt. 17: 4.

88 Allusions to 'Balder Dead' and 'The Sick King in Bokhara'.

4 William Blake
1868

In his dedication of *William Blake* to his friend W. M. Rossetti, Swinburne explains: 'To me at least the subject before long seemed too expansive for an article; and in the leisure of months, and in the intervals of my natural work, the first slight study became little by little an elaborate essay. I found so much unsaid, so much unseen, that a question soon rose before me of simple alternatives: to do nothing, or to do much. I chose the latter; and you, who have done more than I to serve and to exalt the memory of Blake, must know better how much remains undone.' As early as October 1863 Swinburne had decided to review Alexander Gilchrist's biography of Blake. He was encouraged not only by W. M. Rossetti but also by D. G. Rossetti, William Michael's brother, the poet-painter who was also a Blake enthusiast, who owned a valuable Blake manuscript, and who was a friend of the Gilchrists. Study and research led Swinburne to reconsider his original plan. During his visit to Florence in 1864 he gathered information from Seymour Kirkup, Blake's friend. Early in 1865 he was ready for Moxon and Company to publish his book, but after the outcry over *Poems and Ballads* (1866) that company refused to continue its publication; publication rights for *William Blake* also were transferred to Hotten. Swinburne decided upon a number of changes in what he had written of Blake, and it was not until August 1868 that the book appeared.

William Blake retains traces of its origin as a review, on some points supplementing Gilchrist's *Life* but dealing mainly with aspects of Blake that Gilchrist had neglected. In writing of Blake's 'Prophetic Books' Swinburne was a bold pioneer, interpreting Blake's outlook with insight. Occasionally he digressed to discuss topics that were timely, such as '*L'art pour l'art*' and Walt Whitman. Apart from *Notes on Poems and Reviews*, which explained some of his own poems, the book contains more extended 'explications' than

Swinburne's other critical works. Not merely because Blake has been fashionable in recent years but because of its intrinsic merits, *William Blake* has been considered by some critics to be Swinburne's best longer prose work.

Letters

These letters bear upon them the common stamp of all Blake's doings and writings; the fiery and lyrical tone of mind and speech, the passionate singleness of aim, the heat and flame of faith in himself, the violence of mere words, the lust of paradox, the loud and angry habits of expression which abound in his critical or didactic work, are not here missing; neither are clear indications wanting of his noblest qualities; the great love of great things, the great scorn of small men, the strong tenderness of heart, the tender strength of spirit, which won for him honour from all that were honourable. Ready even in a too fervent manner to accept, to praise, to believe in worth and return thanks for it, he will have no man or thing impede or divert him, either for love's sake or hate's. Small friends with feeble counsels to suggest must learn to suppress their small feelings and graceful regrets, or be cleared out of his way with all their powers to help or hinder: lucky if they get off without some label of epigram on the forehead or sting of epigram in the flesh. Upon Hayley,[1] as we may see by collation of Blake's note-book with his letters, the lash fell at last, after long toleration of things intolerable, after 'great objections to my doing anything but the mere drudgery of business' (as for instance engraving illustrations to Hayley's poems designed by Flaxman's sister—not by his wife, as stated at p. 171 of the *Life* by some momentary slip of a most careful pen), 'and intimations that if I do not confine myself to this I shall not live. This,' adds Blake, 'has always pursued me. You will understand by this the source of all my uneasiness. This from Johnson and Fuseli brought me down here, and this from Mr. H. will bring me back again.' In a sharper mood than this, he appended to the decent skirts of Mr. Hayley one of the best burlesque epigrams in the language:

> Of Hayley's birth this was the happy lot:
> His mother on his father him begot.

With this couplet tied to his tail, the ghost of Hayley may perhaps run further than his own strength of wind or speed of foot would naturally have carried him: with this hook in his nose, he may be led by 'his good Blake' some way towards the temple of memory.

What is most to be regretted in these letters is the wonderful tone of assertion respecting the writer's own pictures and those of the great Italian schools. This it would be difficult enough to explain, dishonest to overlook, easy to ridicule, and unprofitable to rebuke. All that need be said of this singular habit of Blake's has been said with admirable clearness and fairness in the prefatory note to the prose selections in Vol. II. Higher authority than the writer's of that note no man can have or can require. And as Blake's artistic heresies are in fact mere accidents—the illegitimate growth of chance and circumstance—we may be content to leave them wholly to the practical judgment and the wise charity of such artists as are qualified to pass sentence upon the achievements and the shortcomings of this great artist. Their praise can alone be thoroughly worth having; their blame can alone be of any significance: and in no other hands than theirs may we safely leave the memory and the glory of a fellow-labourer so illustrious as Blake.

Other points and shades of character not less singular it is essential here to take notice of. These are not matters of accident, like the errors of opinion or perversities of expression which may distort or disfigure the notes and studies on purely artistic matters; they compose the vital element and working condition of Blake's talent. From the fifth to the tenth letter especially, it becomes evident that the writer was passing through strange struggles of spirit and passionate stages of faith. As early as the fourth letter, dated almost exactly a year later than the first written on his arrival at Felpham, Blake refers in a tone of regret and perplexity to the 'abstract folly' which makes him incapable of direct practical work, though not of earnest and continuous labour. This action of the nerves or of the mind he was plainly unable to regulate or modify. It hurries him while yet at work into 'lands of abstraction'; he 'takes the world with him in his flight'. Distress he knows would make the world heavier to him, which seems now 'lighter than a ball of wool rolled by the wind'; and this distress material philosophies or methodical regulations would 'prescribe as a medicinal potion' for a mind impaired or diseased merely by the animal superflux of spirits and childlike excess of spiritual health. But this medicine the strange and strong faculty of faith innate in the man precludes him from taking. Physical distress 'is his mock and scorn; mental no man can give; and if Heaven inflicts it, all such distress is a mercy'. It is not easy, but it is requisite, to realise the perpetual freshness and fulness of belief, the inalterable vigour and fervour of spirit with which Blake, heretic and mystic as he may have been, worshipped and worked; by which he was throughout life possessed and pursued. Above all gods or dæmons of creation and division, he beheld by faith in a perfect man a supreme God. 'Though I have been very unhappy, I am so no longer. I am again emerged into the light of day; I still (and shall to eternity) embrace Christianity, and adore Him who is the express image of God.' In the light of his especial faith all visible things were fused into the intense heat and sharpened into the keen outline of vision. He walked and laboured under other heavens, on another earth, than the earth and the heaven of material life:

> With a blue sky spread over with wings,
> And a mild sun that mounts and sings;
> With trees and fields full of fairy elves
> And little devils who fight for themselves;
> With angels planted in hawthorn bowers,
> And God Himself in the passing hours.[2]

All this was not a mere matter of creed or opinion, much less of decoration or ornament to his work. It was, as we said, his element of life, inhaled at every breath with the common air, mixed into his veins with their natural blood. It was an element almost painfully tangible and actual; an absolute medium or state of existence, inevitable, inexplicable, insuperable. To him the veil of outer things seemed always to tremble with some breath behind it: seemed at times to be rent in sunder with clamour and sudden lightning. All the void of earth and air seemed to quiver with the passage of sentient wings and palpitate under the pressure of conscious feet. Flowers and weeds, stars and stones, spoke with articulate lips and gazed with living eyes. Hands were stretched towards him from beyond the darkness of material nature, to tempt or to support, to guide or to restrain. His hardest facts were the vaguest allegories of other men. To him all symbolic things were literal, all literal things symbolic. About his path and about his bed, around his ears and under his eyes, an infinite play of spiritual life seethed and swarmed or shone and sang. Spirits imprisoned in the husk and shell of earth consoled or menaced him. Every leaf bore a growth of angels; the pulse of every minute sounded as the falling foot of God; under the rank raiment of weeds, in the drifting down of thistles, strange faces frowned and white hair fluttered; tempters and allies, wraiths of the living and phantoms of the dead, crowded and made populous the winds that blew about him, the fields and hills over which he gazed. Even upon earth his vision was 'twofold always';[3] singleness of vision he scorned and feared as the sign of mechanical intellect, of talent that walks while the soul sleeps, with the mere activity of a blind somnambulism. It was fourfold in the intervals of keenest inspiration and subtlest rapture; threefold in the paradise of dreams lying between earth and heaven, lulled by lighter airs and lit by fainter stars; a land of night and moonlight, spectral and serene. These strange divisions of spirit and world according to some dim and mythologic hierarchy were with Blake matters at once serious and commonplace. The worlds of Beulah and Jerusalem, the existence of Los god of Time and Enitharmon goddess of Space, the fallen manhood of Theotormon, the imprisoned womanhood of Oothoon, were more to him even than significant names; to the reader they must needs seem less. This monstrous nomenclature, this jargon of miscreated things in chaos, rose as by nature to his lips, flowed from them as by instinct. Time, an incarnate spirit clothed with fire, stands before him in the sun's likeness; he is threatened with poverty, tempted to make himself friends of this world; and makes answer as though to a human tempter:

> My hands are laboured day and night
> And rest comes never in my sight;
> My wife has no indulgence given
> Except what comes to her from heaven;
> We eat little, we drink less;
> This earth breeds not our happiness.[4]

He beheld, he says, Time and Space as they were eternally, not as they are seen upon earth; he saw nothing as man sees: his hopes and fears were alien from all men's; and upon him and his the light of prosperous days and the terrors of troubled time had no power.

> When I had my defiance given
> The sun stood trembling in heaven;
> The moon, that glowed remote below,
> Became leprous and white as snow;
> And every soul of man on the earth
> Felt affliction and sorrow and sickness and dearth.[5]

In all this we may see on one side the reflection and refraction of outer things, on the other side the projection of his own mind, the effusion of his individual nature, throughout the hardest and remotest alien matter. Strangely severed from other men, he was, or he conceived himself, more strangely interwoven with them. The light of his spiritual weapons, the sound of his spiritual warfare, was seen, he believed, and was heard in faint resonance and far reverberation among men who knew not what such sights and sounds might mean. If, worsted in this 'mental fight', he should let 'his sword sleep in his hand',[6] or 'refuse to do spiritual acts because of natural fears and natural desires',[7] the world would be the poorer for his defection, and himself 'called the base Judas who betrays his friend'.[8] Fear of this rebuke shook and wasted him day and night; he was rent in sunder with pangs of terror and travail. Heaven was full of the dead, coming to witness against him with blood-shedding and with shedding of tears:

> The sun was hot
> With the bows of my mind and with arrows of thought.[9]

In this spirit he wrought at his day's work, seeing everywhere the image of his own mood, the presence of foes and friends. Nothing to him was neutral; nothing without significance. The labour and strife of soul in which he lived was a thing as earnest as any bodily warfare. Such struggles of spirit in poets or artists have been too often made the subject of public study; nay, too often the theme of chaotic versifiers. A theme more utterly improper it is of course impossible to devise. It is just that a workman should see all sides of his work, and labour with all his might of mind and dexterity of hand to make it great and perfect; but to use up the details of the process as crude material for cruder verse—to invite spectators as to the opening of a temple, and show them the unbaked bricks and untempered mortar—to expose with immodest violence and impotent satisfaction the long revolting labours of mental abortion—this no artist will ever attempt, no craftsman ever so perform as to escape ridicule. It is useless for those who can carve no statue worth the chiselling to exhibit instead six feet or nine feet of shapeless plaster or fragmentary stucco, and bid us see what sculptors work with; no man will accept that in lieu of the statue. Not less futile and not less indecent is it for those who can give expression to no great poem to disgorge masses of raw incoherent verse on the subject of verse-making: to offer, in place of a poem ready wrought out, some chaotic and convulsive story about the way in which a poet works, or does not work.

To Blake the whole thing was too grave for any such exposure of spiritual nudity. In these letters he records the result of his 'sore travail';[10] in these verses he commemorates the manner of his work 'under the direction of messengers from heaven daily and nightly, not without trouble or care';[11] but he writes in private and by pure instinct; he speaks only by the impulse of confidence, in the ardour of faith. What he has to say is said with the simple and abstract rapture of apostles or prophets; not with the laborious impertinence and vain obtrusion of tortuous analysis. For such heavy play with gossamer and straws his nature was too earnest and his genius too exalted. This is the mood in which he looks over what work he has done or has to do: and in his lips the strange scriptural language used has the sincerity of pure fire. 'I see the face of my Heavenly Father; He lays His hand upon my head, and gives a blessing to all my work. Why should I be troubled? why should my heart and flesh cry out? I will go on in the strength of the Lord; through hell will I sing forth His praises; that the dragons of the deep may praise Him, and that those who dwell in darkness and in the sea-coasts may be gathered into His kingdom.'[12] So did he esteem of art, which indeed is not a light thing; nor is it wholly unimportant to men that they should have one capable artist more or less among them. How it may fare with artisans (be they never so pretentious) is a matter of sufficiently small moment. One blessing there assuredly was upon all Blake's work; the infinite blessing of life; the fervour of vital blood.

Lyrical Poems

First then for the *Songs of Innocence and Experience*.[1] These at a first naming recall only that incomparable charm of form in which they first came out clothed, and hence vex the souls of men with regretful comparison. For here by hard necessity we miss the lovely and luminous setting of designs, which makes the *Songs* precious and pleasurable to those who know or care for little else of the master's doing; the infinite delight of those drawings, sweeter to see than music to hear, where herb and stem break into grace of shape and blossom of form, and the branch-work is full of little flames and flowers, catching as it were from the verse enclosed the fragrant heat and delicate sound they seem to give back; where colour lapses into light and light assumes feature in colour. If elsewhere the artist's strange strength of thought and hand is more visible, nowhere is there such pure sweetness and singleness of design in his work. All the tremulous and tender splendour of spring is mixed into the written word and coloured draught; every page has the smell of April. Over all things given, the sleep of flocks and the growth of leaves, the laughter in dividing lips of flowers and the music at the moulded mouth of the flute-player, there is cast a pure fine veil of light, softer than sleep and keener than sunshine. The sweetness of sky and leaf, of grass and water—the bright light life of bird and child and beast—is so to speak kept fresh by some graver sense of faithful and mysterious love, explained and vivified by a conscience and purpose in the artist's hand and mind. Such a fiery outbreak of spring, such an insurrection of fierce floral life and radiant riot of childish power and pleasure, no poet or painter ever gave before: such lustre of green leaves and flushed limbs, kindled cloud and fervent fleece, was never wrought into speech or shape. Nevertheless this decorative work is after all the mere husk and shell of the *Songs*. These also, we may notice, have to some extent shared the comparative popularity of the designs which serve as framework to them. They have absolutely achieved the dignity of a reprint; have had a chance before now of swimming for life; whereas most of Blake's offspring have been thrown into Lethe bound hand and foot, without hope of ever striking out in one fair effort. Perhaps on some accounts this preference has been not unreasonable. What was written for children can hardly offend men; and the obscurities and audacities of the prophet would here have been clearly out of place. It is indeed some relief to a neophyte serving in the outer courts of such an intricate and cloudly temple, to come upon this little side-chapel set about with the simplest wreaths and smelling of the fields rather than incense, where all the singing is done by clear children's voices to the briefest and least complex tunes. Not at first without a sense of release does the human mind get quit for a little of the clouds of Urizen, the fires of Orc, and all the Titanic apparatus of prophecy. And these poems are really unequalled in their kind. Such verse was never written for children since verse-writing began. Only in a few of those faultless fragments of childish rhyme which float without name or form upon the memories of men shall we find such a pure clear cadence of verse, such rapid ring and flow of lyric laughter, such sweet and direct choice of the just word and figure, such an impeccable simplicity; nowhere but here such a tender wisdom of holiness, such a light and perfume of innocence. Nothing like this was ever written on that text of the lion and the lamb; no such heaven of sinless animal life was ever conceived so intensely and sweetly.

And there the lion's ruddy eyes
Shall flow with tears of gold,
And pitying the tender cries,
And walking round the fold,
Saying *Wrath by His meekness*
And by His health sickness
Is driven away
From our immortal day.
And now beside thee, bleating lamb,
I can lie down and sleep,
Or think on Him who bore thy name,
Graze after thee, and weep.

The leap and fall of the verse is so perfect as to make it a fit garment and covering for the profound tenderness of faith and soft strength of innocent impulse embodied in it. But the whole of this hymn of 'Night' is wholly beautiful; being perhaps one of the two poems of loftiest loveliness among all the *Songs of Innocence.* The other is that called 'The Little Black Boy'; a poem especially exquisite for its noble forbearance from vulgar pathos and achievement of the highest and most poignant sweetness of speech and sense; in which the poet's mysticism is baptized with pure water and taught to speak as from faultless lips of children, to such effect as this.

And we are put on earth a little space
That we may learn to bear the beams of love ;
And these black bodies and this sunburnt face
Are like a cloud and like a shady grove.

Other poems of a very perfect beauty are those of 'The Piper', 'The Lamb', 'The Chimney-sweeper', and 'The two-days-old Baby'; all, for the music in them, more like the notes of birds caught up and given back than the modulated measure of human verse. One cannot say, being so slight and seemingly wrong in metrical form, how they come to be so absolutely right; but right even in point of verses and words they assuredly are. Add fuller formal completion of rhyme and rhythm to that song of 'Infant Joy', and you have broken up the soft birdlike perfection of clear light sound which gives it beauty; the little bodily melody of soulless and painless laughter.

Against all articulate authority we do however class several of the *Songs of Experience* higher for the great qualities of verse than anything in the earlier division of these poems. If the *Songs of Innocence* have the shape and smell of leaves or buds, these have in them the light and sound of fire or the sea. Entering among them, a fresher savour and a larger breath strikes one upon the lips and forehead. In the first part we are shown who they are who have or who deserve the gift of spiritual sight: in the second, what things there are for them to see when that gift has been given. Innocence, the quality of beasts and children, has the keenest eyes; and such eyes alone can discern and interpret the actual mysteries of experience. It is natural that this second part, dealing as it does with such things as underlie the outer forms of the first part, should rise higher and dive deeper in point of mere words. These give the distilled perfume and extracted blood of the veins in the rose-leaf, the sharp, liquid, intense spirit crushed out of the broken kernel in the fruit. The last of the *Songs of Innocence* is a prelude to these poems; in it the poet summons to judgment the young and single-spirited, that by right of the natural impulse of delight in them they may give sentence against the preachers of convention and assumption; and in the first poem of the second series he, by the same 'voice of the bard',[2] calls upon earth herself, the mother of all these, to arise and become free: since upon her limbs also are bound the fetters, and upon her forehead also has fallen the shadow, of a jealous law: from which nevertheless, by faithful following of instinct and divine liberal impulse, earth and man shall obtain deliverance.

Hear the voice of the bard!
  Who present, past, and future sees:
Whose ears have heard
The ancient Word
  That walked among the silent trees:
Calling the lapsèd soul
  And weeping in the evening dew;
That might control
The starry pole
  And fallen fallen light renew!

If they will hear the Word, earth and the dwellers upon earth shall be made again as little children; shall regain the strong simplicity of eye and hand proper to the pure and single of heart; and for them inspiration shall do the work of innocence; let them but once abjure the doctrine by which comes sin and the law by which comes prohibition. Therefore must the appeal be made; that the blind may see and the deaf hear,[3] and the unity of body and spirit be made manifest in perfect freedom: and that to the innocent even the liberty of 'sin' may be conceded. For if the soul suffer by the body's doing, are not both degraded? and if the body be oppressed for the soul's sake, are not both the losers?

O Earth, O Earth, return!
  Arise from out the dewy grass!
Night is worn,
And the morn
  Rises from the slumberous mass.
Turn away no more;
  Why wilt thou turn away?
The starry shore,
The watery floor,
  Are given thee till the break of day.[4]

For so long, during the night of law and oppression of material form, the divine evidences hidden under sky and sea are left her; even 'till the break of day'. Will she not get quit of this spiritual bondage to the heavy body of things, to the encumbrance of deaf clay and blind vegetation, before the light comes that shall redeem and reveal? But the earth, being yet in subjection to the creator of men, the jealous God who divided nature against herself—father of woman and man, legislator of sex and race—makes blind and bitter answer as in sleep, 'her locks covered with grey despair'.[5]

Prisoned on this watery shore,
  Starry Jealousy does keep my den;
Cold and hoar,
Weeping o'er,
  I hear the father of the ancient men.

Thus, in the poet's mind, Nature and Religion are the two fetters of life, one on the right wrist, the other on the left; an obscure material force on this hand, and on that a mournful imperious law: the law of divine jealousy, the government of a God who weeps over his creature and subject with unprofitable tears, and rules by forbidding and dividing: the 'Urizen' of the 'Prophetic Books', clothed with the coldness and the grief of remote sky and jealous cloud. Here as always, the cry is as much for light as for licence, the appeal not more against prohibition than against obscurity.

Can the sower sow by night,
Or the ploughman in darkness plough?[6]

In the *Songs of Innocence* there is no such glory of metre or sonorous beauty of lyrical work as here. No possible effect of verse can be finer in a great brief way than that given in the second and last stanzas of the first part of this poem. It recalls within one's ear the long relapse of recoiling water and wash of the refluent wave; in the third and fourth lines sinking suppressed as with equal pulses and soft sobbing noise of ebb, to climb again in the fifth line with a rapid clamour of ripples and strong ensuing strain of weightier sound, lifted with the lift of the running and ringing sea.

Here also is that most famous of Blake's lyrics, 'The Tiger'; a poem beyond praise for its fervent beauty and vigour of music. It appears by the MS. that this was written with some pains; the cancels and various readings bear marks of frequent rehandling. One of the latter is worth transcription for its own excellence and also in proof of the artist's real care for details, which his rapid instinctive way of work has induced some to disbelieve in.

> Burnt in distant deeps or skies
> The cruel fire of thine eyes?
> Could heart descend or wings aspire?[7]
> What the hand dare seize the fire?

Nor has Blake left us anything of more profound and perfect value than 'The Human Abstract'; a little mythical vision of the growth of error; through soft sophistries of pity and faith, subtle humility of abstinence and fear, under which the pure simple nature lies corrupted and strangled; through selfish loves which prepare a way for cruelty, and cruelty that works by spiritual abasement and awe.

> Soon spreads the dismal shade
> Of Mystery over his head;
> And the caterpillar and fly
> Feed on the Mystery.
>
> And it bears the fruit of Deceit,
> Ruddy and sweet to eat;
> And the raven his nest has made
> In the thickest shade.

Under the shadow of this tree of mystery,[8] rooted in artificial belief, all the meaner kind of devouring things take shelter and eat of the fruit of its branches; the sweet poison of false faith, painted on its outer husk with the likeness of all things noble and desirable; and in the deepest implication of barren branch and deadly leaf, the bird of death, with priests for worshippers ('the priests of the raven of dawn', loud of lip and hoarse of throat until the light of day have risen), finds house and resting-place. Only in the 'miscreative brain' of fallen men can such a thing strike its tortuous root and bring forth its fatal flower; nowhere else in all nature can the tyrants of divided matter and moral law, 'Gods of the earth and sea', find soil that will bear such fruit.

Nowhere has Blake set forth his spiritual creed more clearly and earnestly than in the last of the *Songs of Experience*. 'Tirzah', in his mythology, represents the mere separate and human nature, mother of the perishing body and daughter of the 'religion' which occupies itself with laying down laws for the flesh; which, while pretending (and that in all good faith) to despise the body and bring it into subjection as with control of bit and bridle, does implicitly overrate its power upon the soul for evil or good, and thus falls foul of fact on all sides by assuming that spirit and flesh are twain, and that things pleasant and good for the one can properly be loathsome or poisonous to the other. This 'religion' or 'moral law', the inexplicable prophet has chosen to baptize under the singular type of 'Rahab'—the 'harlot virgin-mother', impure by dint of chastity and forbearance from such things as are pure to the pure of heart: for in this creed the one thing unclean is the belief in uncleanness, the one thing forbidden is to believe in the existence of forbidden things. Of this mystical mother and her daughter we shall have to take some further account when once fairly afloat on those windy waters of prophecy through which all who would know Blake to any purpose must be content to steer with such pilotage as they can get. For the present it will be enough to note how eager and how direct is the appeal here made against any rule or reasoning based on reference to the mere sexual and external nature of man—the nature made for ephemeral life and speedy death, kept alive 'to work and weep' only through that mercy which 'changed death into sleep'; how intense the reliance on redemption from such a law by the grace of imaginative insight and spiritual freedom, typified in 'the death of Jesus'. Nor are any of these poems finer in structure or nobler in metrical form.

The Prophetic Books

Before entering upon any system of remark or comment on the 'Prophetic Books', we may set down in as few and distinct words as possible the reasons which make this a thing seriously worth doing; nay, even requisite to be done, if we would know rather the actual facts of the man's nature than the circumstances and accidents of his life. Now, first of all, we are to recollect that Blake himself regarded these works as his greatest, and as containing the sum of his achieved ambitions and fulfilled desires: as in effect inspired matter, of absolute imaginative truth and eternal import. We shall not again pause to rebut the familiar cry of response, to the effect that he was mad and not accountable for the uttermost madness of error. It must be enough to reply here that he was by no means mad, in any sense that would authorize us in rejecting his own judgment of his own aims and powers on a plea which would be held insufficient in another man's case. Let all readers and all critics get rid of that notion for good—clear their minds of it utterly and with all haste; let them know and remember, having once been told it, that in these strangest of all written books there is purpose as well as power, meaning as well as mystery. Doubtless, nothing quite like them was ever pitched out headlong into the world as they were. The confusion, the clamour, the jar of words that half suffice and thoughts that half exist—all these and other more absolutely offensive qualities—audacity, monotony, bombast, obscure play of licence and tortuous growth of fancy—cannot quench or even wholly conceal the living purport and the imperishable beauty which are here latent.

And secondly we are to recollect this; that these books are not each a set of designs with a text made by order to match, but are each a poem composed for its own sake and with its own aim, having illustrations arranged by way of frame or appended by way of ornament. On all grounds, therefore, and for all serious purpose, such notices as some of those given in this biography are actually worse than worthless. Better have done nothing than have done this and no more. All the criticism included as to the illustrative parts merely, is final and faultless, nothing missed and nothing wrong; this could not have been otherwise, the work having fallen under hands and eyes of practical taste and trained to actual knowledge, and the assertions being therefore issued by authority. So much otherwise has it fared with the books themselves, that (we are compelled in this case to say it) the clothes are all right and the body is all wrong. Passing from some phrase of high and accurate eulogy to the raw ragged extracts here torn away and held up with the unhealed scars of mutilation fresh and red upon them, what is any human student to think of the poet or his praisers? what, of the assertion of his vindicated sanity with such appalling counterproof thrust under one's eyes? In a word, it must be said of these notices of Blake's 'Prophetic Books'[1] (except perhaps that insufficient but painstaking and well-meant chapter on *The Marriage of Heaven and Hell*) that what has been done should not have been done, and what should have been done has not been done.

Not that the thing was easy to do. If any one would realize to himself for ever a material notion of chaos, let him take a blind header into the midst of the whirling foam and rolling weed of this sea of words. Indeed the sound and savour of these prophecies constantly recall some such idea or some such memory. This poetry has the huge various monotonies, the fervent and fluent colours, the vast limits, the fresh sonorous strength, the certain confusion and tumultuous law, the sense of windy and weltering space, the intense refraction of shadow or light, the crowded life and inanimate intricacy, the patience and the passion of the sea. By no manner of argument or analysis will one be made able to look back or forward with pure confidence and comprehension. Only there are laws, strange as it must sound, by which the work is done and against which it never sins. The biographer once attempts to settle the matter by asserting that Blake was given to contradict himself, by mere impulse if not by brute instinct, to such an extent that consistency is in no sense to be sought for or believed in throughout these works of his: and quotes, by way of ratifying this quite false notion, a noble sentence from the 'Proverbs of Hell',[2] aimed by Blake with all his force against that obstinate adherence to one external opinion which closes and hardens the spirit against all further message from the new-grown feelings or inspiration from the altering circumstances of a man. Never was there an error more grave or more complete than this. The expression shifts perpetually, the types blunder into new forms, the meaning tumbles into new types; the purpose remains, and the faith keeps its hold.

There are certain errors and eccentricities of manner and matter alike common to nearly all these books, and distinctly referable to the character and training of the man. Not educated in any regular or rational way, and by nature of an eagerly susceptible and intensely adhesive mind, in which the lyrical faculty had gained and kept a preponderance over all others visible in every scrap of his work, he had saturated his thoughts and kindled his senses with a passionate study of the forms of the Bible as translated into English, till his fancy caught a feverish contagion and his ear derived a delirious excitement from the mere sound and shape of the written words and verses.

Hence the quaint and fervent imitation of style, the reproduction of peculiarities which to most men are meaningless when divested of their old sense or invested with a new. Hence the bewildering catalogues, genealogies, and divisions which (especially in such later books as the *Jerusalem*) seem at first invented only to strike any miserable reader with furious or lachrymose lunacy. Hence, though heaven knows by no fault of the originals, the insane cosmogony, blatant mythology, and sonorous aberration of thoughts and theories. Hence also much of the special force and supreme occasional loveliness or grandeur in expression. Conceive a man incomparably gifted as to the spiritual side of art, prone beyond all measure to the lyrical form of work, incredibly contemptuous of all things and people dissimilar to himself, of an intensely sensitive imagination and intolerant habit of faith, with a passionate power of peculiar belief, taking with all his might of mental nerve and strain of excitable spirit to a perusal and reperusal of such books as Job and Ezekiel. Observe too that his tone of mind was as far from being critical as from being orthodox. Thus his ecstasy of study was neither on the one side tempered and watered down by faith in established forms and external creeds, nor on the other side modified and directed by analytic judgment and the lust of facts. To Blake either form of mind was alike hateful. Like the Moses of Rabbinical tradition, he was 'drunken with the kisses of the lips of God'. Rational deism and clerical religion were to him two equally abhorrent incarnations of the same evil spirit, appearing now as negation and now as restriction. He wanted supremacy of freedom with intensity of faith. Hence he was properly neither Christian nor infidel: he was emphatically a heretic. Such men, according to the temper of the times, are burnt as demoniacs or pitied as lunatics. He believed in redemption by Christ, and in the incarnation of Satan as Jehovah. He believed that by self-sacrifice the soul should attain freedom and victorious deliverance from bodily bondage and sexual servitude; and also that the extremest fullness of indulgence in such desire and such delight as the senses can aim at or attain was absolutely good, eternally just, and universally requisite. These opinions, and stranger than these, he put forth in the cloudiest style, the wilfullest humour, and the stormiest excitement. No wonder the world let his books drift without caring to inquire what gold or jewels might be washed up as waifs from the dregs of churned foam and subsiding surf. He was the very man for fire and faggot; a mediæval inquisitor would have had no more doubt about him than a materialist or 'theophilanthropist' of his own day or of ours.

A wish is expressed in the *Life* that we could accompany the old man who appears entering an open door, star in hand, at the beginning of the *Jerusalem*, and thread by his light those infinite dark passages and labyrinthine catacombs of invention or thought. In default of that desirable possibility, let us make such way as we can for ourselves into this submarine world, along its slippery and unpaven ways, under its roof of hollow sound and tumbling storm.

We shall see, while above us
The waves roar and whirl,
A ceiling of amber,
A pavement of pearl.[3]

At the entrance of the labyrinth we are met by huge mythologic figures, created of fire and cloud. Titans of monstrous form and yet more monstrous name obstruct the ways; sickness or sleep never formed such savage abstractions, such fierce vanities of vision as these: office and speech they seem at first to have none: but to strike or clutch at the void of air with feeble fingers, to babble with vast lax lips a dialect barren of all but noise, loud and loose as the wind. Slowly they grow into something of shape, assume some foggy feature and indefinite colour: word by word the fluctuating noise condenses into music, the floating music divides into audible notes and scales. The sound which at first was as the mere collision of cloud with cloud is now the recognizable voice of god or dæmon. Chaos is cloven into separate elements; air divides from water, and earth releases fire. Upon each of these the prophet, as it were, lays hand, compelling the thing into shape and speech, constraining the abstract to do service as a man might. These and such as these make up the personal staff or executive body of his prophecies. But it would be waste of time to conjecture how or why he came to inflict upon them such incredible names. These hapless energies and agencies are not simply cast into the house of allegoric bondage, and set to make bricks without straw, to construct symbols without reason; but find themselves baptized with muddy water and fitful fire, by names inconceivable, into a church full of storm and vapour; regenerated with a vengeance, but disembodied and disfigured in their resurrection. Space fell into sleep, and awoke as Enitharmon: Time suffered eclipse, and came forth as Los. The Christ or Prometheus of this faith is Orc or Fuzon; Urizen takes the place of 'Jehovah, Jove, or Lord'.[4] Hardly in such chaotic sounds can one discern the slightest element of reason gone mad, the narrowest channel of derivation run dry. In this last word, one of incessant recurrence, there seems to flicker a thin reminiscence of such names as Uranus, Uriel, and perhaps Urien; for the deity has a diabolic savour in him, and Blake was not incapable of mixing the Hellenic, the Miltonic, and the Celtic mythologies into one drugged and adulterated compound. He had read much and blindly; he had no leaning to verbal accuracy, and never acquired any faculty of comparison. Any sound that in the dimmest way suggested to him a notion of hell or heaven, of passion or power, was significant enough to adopt and register. Commentary was impossible to him: if his work could not be apprehended or enjoyed by an instinct of inspiration like his own, it was lost labour to dissect or expound; and here, if ever, translation would have been treason. He took the visions as they came; he let the words lie as they fell. These barbarous and blundering names are not always without a certain kind of melody and an uncertain sort of meaning. Such as they are, they must be endured; or the whole affair must be tossed aside and thrown up. Over these clamorous kingdoms of speech and dream some few ruling forces of supreme discord preside: and chiefly the lord of the world of man; Urizen, God of cloud and star, 'Father of jealousy', clothed with a splendour of shadow, strong and sad and cruel; his planet faintly glimmers and slowly revolves, a horror in heaven; the night is a part of his thought, rain and wind are in the passage of his feet; sorrow is in all his works; he is the maker of mortal things, of the elements and sexes; in him are incarnate that jealousy which the Hebrews acknowledged and that envy which the Greeks recognized in the divine nature; in his worship faith remains one with fear. Star and cloud, the types of mystery and distance, of cold alienation and heavenly jealousy, belong of right to the God who grudges and forbids: even as the spirit of revolt is made manifest in fiery incarnation—pure prolific fire, 'the cold loins of Urizen dividing'. These two symbols of 'cruel fear', or 'starry jealousy' in the divine tyrant, of ardent love or creative lust in the rebellious saviour of man, pervade the mystical writings of Blake. Orc, the man-child, with hair and flesh like fire, son of Space and Time, a terror and a wonder from the hour of his birth, containing within himself the likeness of all passions and appetites of men, is cast out from before the face of heaven; and falling upon earth, a stronger Vulcan or Satan, fills with his fire the narrowed foreheads and the darkened eyes of all that dwell thereon; imprisoned often and fed from vessels of iron with barren food and bitter drink,[5] a wanderer or a captive upon earth, he shall rise again when his fire has spread through all lands to inflame and to infect with a strong contagion the spirit and the sense of man, and shall prevail against the law and the commandments of his enemy. This endless myth of oppression and redemption, of revelation and revolt, runs through many forms and spills itself by strange straits and byways among the sands and shallows of prophetic speech. But in these books there is not the substantial coherence of form and reasonable unity of principle which bring within scope of apprehension even the wildest myths grown out of unconscious idealism and impulsive tradition. A single man's work, however exclusively he may look to inspiration for motive and material, must always want the breadth and variety of meaning, the supple beauty of symbol, the infectious intensity of satisfied belief, which grow out of creeds and fables native to the spirit of a nation, yet peculiar to no man or sect, common yet sacred, not invented or constructed, but found growing and kept fresh with faith. But for all the dimness and violence of expression which pervert and darken the mythology of these attempts at gospel, they have qualities great enough to be worth finding out. Only let none conceive that each separate figure in the swarming and noisy life of this populous dæmonic creation has individual meaning and vitality. Blake was often taken off his feet by the strong currents of fancy, and indulged, like a child during its first humour of invention, in wild byplay and erratic excesses of simple sound; often lost his way in a maze of wind-music, and transcribed as it were with eyes closed and open ears the notes caught by chance as they drifted across the dream of his subdued senses. Alternating between lyrical invention and gigantic allegory, it is hard to catch and hold him down to any form or plan. At one time we have mere music, chains of ringing names, scattered jewels of sound without a thread, tortuous network of harmonies without a clue; and again we have passages, not always unworthy of an Æschylean chorus, full of fate and fear; words that are strained wellnigh in sunder by strong significance and earnest passion; words that deal greatly with great things, that strike deep and hold fast; each inclusive of some fierce apocalypse or suggestive of some obscure evangel. Now the matter in hand is touched with something of an epic style; the narrative and characters lose half their hidden sense, and the reciter passes from the prophetic tripod to the seat of a common singer; mere names, perhaps not even musical to other ears than his, allure and divert him; he plays with stately cadences, and lets the wind of swift or slow declamation steer him whither it will. Now again he falls with renewed might of will to his purpose; and his grand lyrical gift becomes an instrument not sonorous merely but vocal and articulate. To readers who can but once take their stand for a minute on the writer's footing, look for a little with his eyes and listen with his ears, even the more incoherent cadences will become not undelightful; something of his pleasure, with something of his perception, will pass into them; and understanding once the main gist of the whole fitful and high-strung tune, they will tolerate, where they cannot enjoy, the strange diversities and discords which intervene.

Among many notable eccentricities we have touched upon but two as yet; the huge windy mythology of elemental dæmons, and the capricious passion for catalogues of random names, which make obscure and hideous so much of these books. Akin to these is the habit of seeing or assuming in things inanimate or in the several limbs and divisions of one thing, separate forms of active and symbolic life. This, like many other of Blake's habits, grows and swells enormously by progressive indulgence. At first, as in *Thel*, clouds and flowers, clods and creeping things, are given speech and sense; the degree of symbolism is already excessive, owing to the strength of expression and directness of dramatic vision peculiar to Blake; but in later books everything is given a soul to feel and a tongue to speak; the very members of the body become spirits, each a type of some spiritual state. Again, in the prophecies of *Europe* and *America*, there is more fable and less allegory, more overflow of lyrical invention, more of the divine babble which sometimes takes the place of earthly speech or sense, more vague emotion with less of reducible and amenable quality than in almost any of these poems. In others, a habit of mapping out and marking down the lines of his chaotic and Titanic scenery has added to Blake's other singularities of manner this above all, that side by side with the jumbled worlds of Tharmas and Urthona, the whirling skies and plunging planets of Ololon and Beulah, the breathless student of prophecy encounters places and names absurdly familiar; London streets and suburbs make up part of the mystic antediluvian world; Fulham and Lambeth, Kentish Town and Poland Street, cross the courses and break the metres of the stars. This apparent madness of final absurdity has also its root in the deepest and soundest part of Blake's mind and faith. In the meanest place as in the meanest man he beheld the hidden spirit and significance of which the flesh or the building is but a type. If continents have a soul, shall suburbs or lanes have less? where life is, shall not the spirit of life be there also? Europe and America are vital and significant; we mean by all names somewhat more than we know of; for where there is anything visible or conceivable, there is also some invisible and inconceivable thing. This is but the rough grotesque result of the tenet that matter apart from spirit is non-existent. Launched once upon that theory, Blake never thought it worth while to shorten sail or tack about for fear of any rock or shoal. It is inadequate and even inaccurate to say that he allotted to each place as to each world a presiding dæmon or deity. He averred implicitly or directly, that each had a soul or spirit, the quintessence of its natural life, capable of change but not of death; and that of this soul the visible externals, though a native and actual part, were only a part, inseparable as yet but incomplete. Thus whenever, to his misfortune and ours, he stumbles upon the proper names of terrene men and things, he uses these names as signifying not the sensual form or body but the spirit which he supposed to animate these, to speak in them and work through them. In *America* the names of liberators, in *Jerusalem* the names of provinces, have no separate local or mundane sense whatever; throughout the prophecies 'Albion' is the mythical and typical fatherland of human life, much what the East might seem to other men: and by way of making this type actual and prominent enough, Blake seizes upon all possible divisions of the modern visible England in town or country, and turns them in his loose symbolic way into minor powers and serving spirits. That he was wholly unconscious of the intolerably laughable effect we need not believe. He had all the delight in laying snares and giving offence, which is proper to his kind. He had all the confidence in his own power and right to do such things and to get over the doing of them which accompanies in such men the subtle humour of scandalizing. And unfortunately he had not by training, perhaps not by nature, the conscience which would have reminded him that whether or not an artist may allowably play with all other things in heaven and earth, one thing he must certainly not play with; the material forms of art: that levity and violence are here prohibited under grave penalties. Allowing however for this, we may notice that in the wildest passages of these books Blake merely carries into strange places or throws into strange shapes such final theories as in the dialect of calmer and smaller men have been accounted not unreasonable.

NOTES

Letters

1 William Hayley (1745–1820), mediocre poet and friend of Blake and Cowper.
2 In Letter 23, *Poetry and Prose of William Blake*, ed. Geoffrey Keynes (1927), containing the poem 'With happiness stretch'd across the hills'.
3 *Ibid.*, l. 87.
4 *Ibid.*, ll. 59ff.
5 *Ibid.*, ll. 71ff.
6 From the last stanza of the poem in the preface to *Milton.*
7 Letter 21.
8 *Ibid.*
9 In Letter 23, ll. 77–8 of the poem.
10 Letter 25.
11 Letter 21.
12 Letter 25.

Lyrical Poems

1 Originally *Songs of Innocence* (1789), *Songs of Experience* (1794).
2 'Introduction' to *Songs of Experience.*
3 Cf. Luke 7: 22.
4 See note 2.
5 'Earth's Answer', l. 5.
6 Cf. *ibid.*, ll. 18–20.
7 Could God bring down his heart to the making of a thing so deadly and strong? or could any lesser dæmonic force of nature take to itself wings and fly high enough to assume power equal to such a creation? Could spiritual force so far descend or material force so far aspire? Or, when the very stars, and all the armed children of heaven, the 'helmed cherubim' that guide and the 'sworded seraphim' that guard their several planets, wept for pity and fear at sight of this new force of monstrous matter seen in the deepest night as a fire of menace to man—

Did he smile his work to see?
Did he who made the lamb make thee?

We may add another cancelled reading to show how delicately the poem has been perfected; although by an oversight of the writer's most copies hitherto have retained some trace of the rough first draught, neglecting in one line a change necessary to save the sense as well as to complete the sentence.

And when thy heart began to beat,
What dread hand and what dread feet

Could fetch it from the furnace deep
And in thy horrid ribs dare steep?
In what clay and in what mould
Were thine eyes of fury rolled?

Having cancelled this stanza or sketched ghost of a stanza, Blake in his hurry of rejection did not at once remember to alter the last line of the preceding one; leaving thus a stone of some size and slipperiness for editorial feet to trip upon, until the recovery of that nobler reading—

What dread hand *framed thy* dread feet?

Nor was this little 'rock of offence' cleared from the channel of the poem even by the editor of 1827, who was yet not afraid of laying hand upon the text. So grave a flaw in so short and so great a lyric was well worth the pains of removing and is yet worth the pains of accounting for; on which ground this note must be of value to all who take in verse with eye and ear instead of touching it merely with eyelash and finger-tip in the manner of sand-blind students. (ACS)

'Rock of offence' is from Isaiah 8: 14.

8 Compare the passage in *Ahania* where the growth of it is defined; rooted in the rock of separation, watered with the tears of a jealous God, shot up from sparks and fallen germs of material seed; being after all a growth of mere error, and vegetable (not spiritual) life; the topmost stem of it made into a cross whereon to nail the dead redeemer and friend of men. (ACS)

The Prophetic Books

1 It should not be overlooked that this part of his work was left unfinished, all but untouched, by the author of the *Life*. Without as long a study and as deep a sympathy as his, it would seem to any follower, however able and zealous, the most toilsome as well as the most sterile part of the task in hand. The fault therefore lies with chance or fate alone. Less than I have said above could not here be said; and more need not be. I was bound at starting to register my protest against the contempt and condemnation which these books have incurred, thinking them as I do not unworthy the trouble of commentary; but no word was designed to depreciate the careful and admirable labour which has completed a monument cut short with the life of the sculptor, joined now in death to the dead whom he honoured. (ACS)

2 In *The Marriage of Heaven and Hell.*

3 Matthew Arnold, 'The Forsaken Merman', ll. 116–9.

4 Alexander Pope, 'Universal Prayer', l. 4.

5 Something like this may be found in a passage of Werner translated by

Mr. Carlyle, but mixed with much of meaner matter, and debased by a feebleness and a certain spiritual petulance proper to a man so much inferior. The German mystic, though ingenious and laborious, is also tepid, pretentious, insecure; half terrified at his own timid audacities, half choked by the fumes of his own alembic. He labours within a limit, not fixed indeed, but never expansive; narrowing always at one point as it widens at another: his work is weak in the head and the spine; he ventures with half a heart and strikes with half a hand; throughout his myth of Phosphorus he goes halting and hinting; not ungracefully, nay with a real sense of beauty, but never like a man braced up for the work requisite; he labours under a dull devotion and a cloudy capacity. Above all, he can neither speak nor do well, being no artist or prophet; and so makes but a poor preacher or essayist. The light he shows is thick and weak; Blake's light, be it meteor or star, rises with the heat and radiance of fire or the morning. (ACS)

5 Michelangelo
1868, 1875

At the beginning of his 'Notes on Designs of the Old Masters at Florence', from which the following passage is extracted, Swinburne explains that during his visit to the Italian city in the spring of 1864 he had spent many days studying the Uffizi collections, including 'one precious division . . . unregistered. . . . The huge mass of original designs, in pencil or ink or chalk, swept together by Vasari and others, had then been but recently unearthed and partially assorted.' His description of Michelangelo's work may recall Pater's imaginative essay on Leonardo da Vinci, whose designs Swinburne also discussed, but has any literary critic besides Hazlitt rivalled Swinburne in understanding and imaginative description of pictorial art?

'Notes on Designs of the Old Masters at Florence' originally appeared in the *Fortnightly Review* for July 1868 and was reprinted in *Essays and Studies* (1875).

Here, as in his own palace and wherever in Florence the shadow of his supreme presence has fallen and the mark of his divine hand been set, the work of Michel Angelo for a time effaces all thought of other men or gods. Before the majesty of his imperious advent the lesser kings of time seem as it were men bidden to rise up from their thrones, to cover their faces and come down. Not gratitude, not delight, not sympathy, is the first sense excited in one suddenly confronted with his designs; fear rather, oppressive reverence, and well-nigh intolerable adoration. Their tragic beauty, their inexplicable strength and wealth of thought, their terrible and exquisite significance, all the powers they unveil and all the mysteries they reserve, all their suggestions and all their suppressions, are at first adorable merely. Delightful beyond words they become in time, as the subtler and weightier work of Æschylus or Shakespeare; but like these they first fill and exalt the mind with a strange and violent pleasure which is the highest mood of worship; reverence intensified to the last endurable degree. The mind, if then it enjoys at all or wonders at all, knows little of its own wonder or its own enjoyment; the air and light about it is too fine and pure to breathe or bear. The least thought of these men has in it something intricate and enormous, faultless as the formal work of their triumphant art must be. All mysteries of good and evil, all wonders of life and death, lie in their hands or at their feet. They have known the causes of things, and are not too happy. The fatal labour of the world, the clamour and hunger of the open-mouthed all-summoning grave, all fears and hopes of ephemeral men, are indeed made subject to them, and trodden by them underfoot; but the sorrow and strangeness of things are not lessened because to one or two their secret springs have been laid bare and the courses of their tides made known; refluent evil and good, alternate grief and joy, life inextricable from death, change inevitable and insuperable fate. Of the three, Michel Angelo is saddest; on his, the most various genius of the three, the weight of things lies heaviest. Glad or sad as the days of his actual life may have been, his work in the fullness of its might and beauty has most often a mournful meaning, some grave and subtle sorrow latent under all its life. Here in one design is the likeness of perishable pleasure; Vain Delight with all her children; one taller boy has drawn off a reverted and bearded mask, on which another lays hold with one hand, fingering it as with lust or curiosity; his other hand holds to the mother's knee; behind her a third child lurks and cowers; she, with a hard broad smile of dull pleasure, feeds her eyes on the sight of her own face in a hand-mirror. Fear and levity, cruelty and mystery, make up their mirth; evil seems to impend over all these joyous heads, to hide behind all these laughing features: they are things too light for hell, too low for heaven; bubbles of the earth, brilliant and transient and poisonous, blown out of unclean foam by the breath of meaner spirits, to glitter and quiver for a little under the beams of a mortal sun. Cruel and curious and ignorant, all their faces are full of mean beauty and shallow delight. Hard by, a troop of Loves haul after them, with mocking mouths and straining arms, a live human mask, a hollow face shorn off from the head, old and grim and sad, worn through and through with pain and time, from the vexed forehead to the sharp chin which grates against the ground; the eyes and lips full of suffering, sardonic and helpless; the face of one knowing his own fate, who has resigned himself sadly and scornfully to the violence of base and light desires; the grave and great features all hardened into suffering and self-contempt.

But in one separate head there is more tragic attraction than in these: a woman's, three times studied, with divine and subtle care; sketched and re-sketched in youth and age, beautiful always beyond desire and cruel beyond words; fairer than heaven and more terrible than hell; pale with pride and weary with wrong-doing; a silent anger against God and man burns, white and repressed, through her clear features. In one drawing she wears a head-dress of eastern fashion rather than western, but in effect made out of the artist's mind only; plaited in the likeness of closely-welded scales as of a chrysalid serpent, raised and waved and rounded in the likeness of a sea-shell. In some inexplicable way all her ornaments seem to partake of her fatal nature, to bear upon them her brand of beauty fresh from hell; and this through no vulgar machinery of symbolism, no serpentine or otherwise bestial emblem: the bracelets and rings are innocent enough in shape and workmanship; but in touching her flesh they have become infected with deadly and malignant meaning. Broad bracelets divide the shapely splendour of her arms; over the nakedness of her firm and luminous breasts, just below the neck, there is passed a band as of metal. Her eyes are full of proud and passionless lust after gold and blood; her hair, close and curled, seems ready to shudder in sunder and divide into snakes. Her throat, full and fresh, round and hard to the eye as her bosom and arms, is erect and stately, the head set firm on it without any droop or lift of the chin; her mouth crueller than a tiger's, colder than a snake's, and beautiful beyond a woman's. She is the deadlier Venus incarnate;

> *πολλὴ μὲν ἐν θεοῖσι κοὐκ ἀνώνυμος*
> *θεά·*[1]

for upon earth also many names might be found for her: Lamia re-transformed, invested now with a fuller beauty, but divested of all feminine attributes not native to the snake—a Lamia loveless and unassailable by the sophist, readier to drain life out of her lover than to fade for his sake at his side; or the Persian Amestris,[2] watching the only breasts on earth more beautiful than her own cut off from her rival's living bosom; or Cleopatra, not dying but turning serpent under the serpent's bite; or that queen of the extreme East who with her husband marked every day as it went by some device of a new and wonderful cruelty.[3] In one design, where the cruel and timid face of a king rises behind her, this crowned and cowering head might stand for Ahab's, and hers for that of Jezebel.[4] Another study is in red chalk; in this the only ornaments are ear-rings. In a third, the serpentine hair is drawn up into a tuft at the crown with two ringlets hanging, heavy and deadly as small tired snakes. There is a drawing in the furthest room at the Buonarroti Palace which recalls and almost reproduces the design of these three. Here also the electric hair, which looks as though it would hiss and glitter with sparks if once touched, is wound up to a tuft with serpentine plaits and involutions; all that remains of it unbound falls in one curl, shaping itself into a snake's likeness as it unwinds, right against a living snake held to the breast and throat. This is rightly registered as a study for Cleopatra; but notice has not yet been accorded to the subtle and sublime idea which transforms her death by the aspic's bite into a meeting of serpents which recognise and embrace, an encounter between the woman and the worm of Nile, almost as though this match for death were a monstrous love-match, or such a mystic marriage as that painted in the loveliest passage of *Salammbô*,[5] between the maiden body and the scaly coils of the serpent and the priestess alike made sacred to the moon; so closely do the snake and the queen of snakes caress and cling. Of this idea Shakespeare also had a vague and great glimpse when he made Antony 'murmur, "Where's my serpent of old Nile?"'[6] mixing a foretaste of her death with the full sweet savour of her supple and amorous 'pride of life'.[7] For what indeed is lovelier or more luxuriously loving than a strong and graceful snake of the nobler kind?

After this the merely terrible designs of Michel Angelo are shorn of half their horror; even the single face as of one suddenly caught and suddenly released from hell, with wild drapery blown behind it by a wind not of this world, strikes upon the sight and memory of a student less deeply and sharply. Certain of his slight and swift studies for damned souls and devils—designs probably for the final work in which he has embodied and made immortal the dream of a great and righteous judgment between soul and soul—resemble much at first sight, and more on longer inspection, the similar studies and designs of Blake. One devil indeed recalls at once the famous 'ghost of a flea',[8] having much of the same dull and liquorish violence of expression. Other sketches in the small chamber of his palace bring also to mind his great English disciple: the angry angel poised as in fierce descent; the falling figure with drawn-up legs, splendidly and violently designed; the reverted head showing teeth and nostrils: the group of two old men in hell; one looks up howling, with level face; one looks down with lips drawn back. Nothing can surpass the fixed and savage agony of his face, immutable and imperishable. In this same room are other studies worth record: a Virgin and Child, unfinished, but of supreme strength and beauty; the child fully drawn, with small strong limbs outlined in faint red, rounded and magnificent; soft vigorous arms, and hands that press and cling. There is a design of a covered head, looking down; mournful, with nervous mouth, with clear and deep-set eyes; the nostril strong and curved. Another head, older, with thicker lips, is drawn by it in the same attitude.

Beside the Jezebel or Amestris of the Uffizi there is a figure of Fortune, with a face of cold exaltation and high clear beauty; strong wings expand behind her, or shadows rather of vast and veiled plumes; below her the wheel seems to pause, as in a lull of the perpetual race. This design was evidently the sketch out of which the picture of Fortune in the Corsini Palace was elaborated by some pupil of the master's. In that picture, as in the Venus and Cupid with mystic furniture of melancholy masks and emblems in the background, lodged now in the last Tuscan chamber but one of the Uffizi, the meaner hand of the executive workman has failed to erase or overlay the great and fruitful thought of that divine mind in which their first conceptions lay and gathered form. The strong and laughing God treading with a vigorous wantonness the fair flesh of his mother; the goddess languid and effused like a broad-blown flower, her soft bright side pressed hard under his foot and nestling heel, her large arm lifted to wrest the arrow from his hand, with a lazy and angry mirth; and at her feet the shelves full of masks, sad inverted faces, heads of men overset, blind strings of broken puppets forgotten where they fell; all these are as clearly the device of Michel Angelo's great sad mind as the handiwork is clearly none of his. Near the sketch of Fortune is a strange figure, probably worked up into some later design. A youth with reverted head, wearing furry drapery with plumy fringes, has one leg drawn up and resting on a step; the face, as it looks back, is laughing with fear; the hysterical horror of some unseen thing is branded into the very life of its fair features. This violent laugh as of a child scared into madness subjects the whole figure, brilliant and supple in youth as it seems, to the transformation of terror. Upon this design also much tragic conjecture of allegory or story might be spent, and wasted.

NOTES

1 Euripides, *Hippolytus*, ll. 1–2: 'Great in the sight of mortals, and not without a name am I, the goddess' (tr. T. A. Buckley).
2 The wife of Xerxes; her story is told by Herodotus near the end of Book ix of his history.
3 As Mr John S. Mayfield has discovered, the queen of Kié, the last emperor of the Hia dynasty in China, overthrown in 1766 B.C. Swinburne learned of the cruelties of the royal couple from a note in the Marquis de Sade's *Justine*.
4 See I Kings 21: 5–25.
5 In chapter 10 of Flaubert's novel.
6 *Antony and Cleopatra*, I, v, 25.
7 I John 2: 16.
8 A picture by Blake. See Alexander Gilchrist's *Life of William Blake*, the last paragraph of chapter 28.

6 Rossetti's pictures
1868, 1875

'Notes on Some Pictures of 1868', the title used in *Essays and Studies* (1875), from which the passage below is taken, was reprinted, with some omissions, from Part II of *Notes on the Royal Academy Exhibition, 1868*, Part I having been written by William Michael Rossetti. In reprinting the original text, Swinburne omitted 'English' before 'painter' in the third sentence below, probably to strengthen the statement but perhaps also because D. G. Rossetti was of partly Italian extraction. He omitted three other passages, in each of which he quotes from a sonnet by Rossetti illustrative of a picture—'Lady Lilith' ('words inscribed on the frame of the picture'), 'Sibylla Palmifera', and 'Venus Verticordia'. Another paper in *Essays and Studies* was a perceptive and friendly appreciation of Rossetti's poems.

It is well known that the painter of whom I now propose to speak has never suffered exclusion or acceptance at the hand of any academy. To such acceptance or such rejection all other men of any note have been and may be liable. It is not less well known that his work must always hold its place as second in significance and value to no work done by any painter of his time. Among the many great works of Mr. D. G. Rossetti, I know of none greater than his two latest. These are types of sensual beauty and spiritual, the siren and the sibyl. The one is a woman of the type of Adam's first wife; she is a living Lilith, with ample splendour of redundant hair;

> She excels
> All women in the magic of her locks;
> And when she winds them round a young man's neck
> She will not ever set him free again.[1]

Clothed in soft white garments, she draws out through a comb the heavy mass of hair like thick spun gold to fullest length; her head leans back half sleepily, superb and satiate with its own beauty; the eyes are languid, without love in them or hate; the sweet luxurious mouth has the patience of pleasure fulfilled and complete, the warm repose of passion sure of its delight. Outside, as seen in the glimmering mirror, there is full summer; the deep and glowing leaves have drunk in the whole strength of the sun. The sleepy splendour of the picture is a fit raiment for the idea incarnate of faultless fleshly beauty and peril of pleasure unavoidable. For this serene and sublime sorceress there is no life but of the body; with spirit (if spirit there be) she can dispense. Were it worth her while for any word to divide those terrible tender lips, she too might say with the hero of the most perfect and exquisite book of modern times—*Mademoiselle de Maupin*—'*Je trouve la terre aussi belle que le ciel, et je pense que la correction de la forme est la vertu.*'[2] Of evil desire or evil impulse she has nothing; and nothing of good. She is indifferent, equable, magnetic; she charms and draws down the souls of men by pure force of absorption, in no wise wilful or malignant; outside herself she cannot live, she cannot even see: and because of this she attracts and subdues all men at once in body and in spirit. Beyond the mirror she cares not to look, and could not.

Ma mia suora Rahel mai non si smaga
Dal suo miraglio, e siede tutto 'l giorno.[3]

So, rapt in no spiritual contemplation, she will sit to all time, passive and perfect: the outer light of a sweet spring day flooding and filling the massive gold of her hair. By the reflection in a deep mirror of fervent foliage from without, the chief chord of stronger colour is touched in this picture; next in brilliance and force of relief is the heap of curling and tumbling hair on which the sunshine strikes; the face and head of the siren are withdrawn from the full stroke of the light.

The other picture gives the type opposite to this; a head of serene and spiritual beauty, severe and tender, with full and heavy hair falling straight in grave sweet lines, not, like Lilith's, exuberant of curl and coil; with carven column of throat, solid and round and flawless as living ivory; with still and sacred eyes and pure calm lips; an imperial votaress truly, in maiden meditation:[4] yet as true and tangible a woman of mortal mould, as ripe and firm of flesh as her softer and splendid sister. The mystic emblems in the background show her power upon love and death to make them loyal servants to the law of her lofty and solemn spirit. Behind this figure of the ideal and inaccessible beauty, an inlaid wall of alternate alabaster and black marble bears inwrought on its upper part the rival twin emblems of love and death, over the bare carven skull poppies impend, and roses over the sweet head with bound blind eyes: in her hand is the palm-branch, a sceptre of peace and of power.[5] The cadence of colour is splendid and simple, a double trinity of green and red, the dim red robe, the deep red poppies, the soft red roses; and again the green veil wound about with wild flowers, the green down of poppy-leaves, the sharper green of rose-leaves.

An unfinished picture of Beatrice (the *Beata Beatrix* of the *Vita Nuova*), a little before death, is perhaps the noblest of Mr. Rossetti's many studies after Dante. This work is wholly symbolic and ideal; a strange bird flown earthward from heaven brings her in its beak a full-blown poppy, the funereal flower of sleep. Her beautiful head lies back, sad and sweet, with fast-shut eyes in a death-like trance that is not death; over it the shadow of death seems to impend, making sombre the splendour of her ample hair and tender faultless features. Beyond her the city and the bridged river are seen as from far, dim and veiled with misty lights as though already 'sitting alone, made as a widow'.[6] Love, on one side, comes bearing in his hand a heart in flames, having his eyes bent upon Dante's; on the other side is Dante, looking sadly across the way towards Love. In this picture the light is subdued and soft, touching tenderly from behind the edges of Beatrice's hair and raiment; in the others there is a full fervour of daylight.

The great picture of Venus Verticordia[7] has now been in great measure recast; the head is of a diviner type of beauty; golden butterflies hover about the halo of her hair, alight upon the apple or the arrow in her hands; her face has the sweet supremacy of a beauty imperial and immortal; her glorious bosom seems to exult and expand as the roses on each side of it. The painting of leaf and fruit and flower in this picture is beyond my praise or any man's; but of one thing I will here take note; the flash of green brilliance from the upper leaves of the trellis against the sombre green of the trees behind.

Another work, as yet incomplete, is a study of La Pia; she is seen looking forth from the ramparts of her lord's castle, over the fatal lands without; her pallid splendid face hangs a little forward, wan and white against the mass of dark deep hair; under her hands is a work of embroidery, hanging still on the frame unfinished; just touched by the weak weary hands, it trails forward across the lap of her pale green raiment, into the foreground of the picture. In her eyes is a strange look of wonder and sorrow and fatigue, without fear and without pain, as though she were even now looking beyond earth into the soft and sad air of purgatory: she presses the deadly marriage-ring into the flesh of her finger, so deep that the soft skin is bloodless and blanched from the intense imprint of it.[8]

Two other studies, as yet only sketched, give promise of no less beauty; the subject of one was long since handled by the artist in a slighter manner. It also is taken from the *Vita Nuova*; Dante in a dream beholding Beatrice dead, tended by handmaidens, and Love, with bow and dart in hand, in act to kiss her beautiful dead mouth. The other is a design of Perseus showing to Andromeda the severed head of Medusa, reflected in water; an old and well-worn subject, but renewed and reinformed with life by the vital genius of the artist. In the Pompeian picture we see the lovers at halt beside a stream, on their homeward way; here we see them in their house, bending over the central cistern or impluvium of the main court. The design is wonderful for grace and force; the picture will assuredly be one of the painter's greatest.

NOTES

1 Shelley's 'Scenes from the *Faust* of Goethe', ii, 319ff.

2 'I find earth as beautiful as heaven, and I think correctness of form is virtue.'

3 'But my sister Rachel never turns from her mirror, and sits all day.' Rachel's activity (*Purgatorio*, xxvii, 104–5) is a symbol of contemplation.

4 Cf. *A Midsummer-Night's Dream*, II, i, 163–4:

> And the imperial votaress passed on,
> In maiden meditation, fancy-free.

5 The picture is called 'Sibylla Palmifera'.

6 In his *Vita Nuova* (section xxxi) Dante likens Florence after the death of Beatrice to a widow, recalling the Lamentations of Jeremiah, i, I: 'How doth the city sit solitary . . .! how is she become as a widow!'

7 'Changer of Hearts.'

8 La Pia, Pia de' Tolomei, tells Dante (*Purgatorio*, v): 'Siena made me, Maremma unmade; that he knows who ringed my finger with his gem.' Her husband, wishing to marry another woman, had become her murderer.

7 Coleridge
1869, 1875

'Coleridge', in *Essays and Studies* (1875), had been published as the introduction to Swinburne's *Christabel and the Lyrical and Imaginative Poems of S. T. Coleridge* (1869). Changes in phraseology and punctuation were few and slight.

The great man of whom I am about to speak seems to me a figure more utterly companionless, more incomparable with others, than any of his kind. Receptive at once and communicative of many influences, he has received from none and to none did he communicate any of those which mark him as a man memorable to all students of men. What he learnt and what he taught are not the precious things in him. He has founded no school of poetry, as Wordsworth has, or Byron, or Tennyson; happy in this, that he has escaped the plague of pupils and parodists. Has he founded a school of philosophy? He has helped men to think; he has touched their thought with passing colours of his own thought; but has he moved and moulded it into new and durable shapes? Others may judge better of this than I, but to me, set beside the deep direct work of those thinkers who have actual power to break down and build up thought, to construct faith or destroy it, his work seems not as theirs is. And yet how very few are even the great names we could not better afford to spare, would not gladlier miss from the roll of 'famous men and our fathers that were before us'.[1] Of his best verses I venture to affirm that the world has nothing like them, and can never have: that they are of the highest kind, and of their own. They are jewels of the diamond's price, flowers of the rose's rank, but unlike any rose or diamond known. In all times there have been gods that alighted and giants that appeared on earth; the ranks of great men are properly divisible, not into thinkers and workers, but into Titans and Olympians. Sometimes a supreme poet is both at once: such above all men is Æschylus; so also Dante, Michel Angelo, Shakespeare, Milton, Goethe, Hugo, are gods at once and giants; they have the lightning as well as the light of the world, and in hell they have command as in heaven; they can see in the night as by day. As godlike as these, even as the divinest of them, a poet such as Coleridge needs not the thews and organs of any Titan to make him greater. Judged by the justice of other men, he is assailable and condemnable on several sides; his good work is the scantiest in quantity ever done by a man so famous in so long a life; and much of his work is bad. His genius is fluctuant and moonstruck as the sea is, and yet his mind is not, what he described Shakespeare's to be, 'an oceanic mind'. His plea against all accusers must be that of Shakespeare, a plea unanswerable:

> I am that I am; and they that level
> At my abuses reckon up their own.[2]

'I am that I am'; it is the only solid and durable reply to any impertinence of praise or blame. We hear too much and too often of circumstances or accidents which extenuate this thing or qualify that; and such, no doubt, there always may be; but usually—at least it seems so to me—we get out of each man what he has in him to give. Probably at no other time, under no other conditions, would Coleridge for example have done better work or more. His flaws and failures are as much ingrained in him as his powers and achievements.

For from the very first the two sides of his mind are visible and palpable. Among all verses of boys who were to grow up great, I remember none so perfect, so sweet and deep in sense and sound, as those which he is said to have written at school, headed 'Time, Real and Imaginary'. And following hard on these come a score or two of 'poems' each more feeble and more flatulent than the last. Over these and the like I shall pass with all due speed, being undesirous to trouble myself or any possible reader with the question whether 'Religious Musings' be more damnable than 'Lines to a Young Ass', or less damnable. Even when clear of these brambles, his genius walked for some time over much waste ground with irregular and unsure steps. Some poems, touched with exquisite grace, with clear and pure harmony, are tainted with somewhat of feeble and sickly which impairs our relish; 'Lewti' for instance, an early sample of his admirable melody, of tender colour and dim grace as of clouds, but effeminate in build, loose-hung, weak of eye and foot. Yet nothing of more precious and rare sweetness exists in verse than that stanza of the swans disturbed. His style indeed was a plant of strangely slow growth, but perfect and wonderful in its final flower. Even in the famous verses called 'Love' he has not attained to that strength and solidity of beauty which was his special gift at last. For melody rather than for harmony it is perfect; but in this œnomel there is as yet more of honey than of wine.

Coleridge was the reverse of Antæus;[3] the contact of earth took all strength out of him. He could not handle to much purpose any practical creed; his political verse is most often weak of foot and hoarse of accent. There is a graceful Asiatic legend cited by his friend Southey of 'the footless birds of Paradise' who have only wings to sustain them, and live their lives out in a perpetual flight through the clearest air of heaven. Ancient naturalists, Cardan and Aldrovandus,[4] had much dispute and dissertation as to the real or possible existence of these birds, as to whether the female did in effect lay her eggs in a hollow of the male's back, designed by nature to that end; whether they could indeed live on falling dew; and so forth. These questions we may presume to be decided; but it is clear and certain enough that men have been found to live in much this fashion. Such a footless bird of Paradise was Coleridge; and had his wings always held out it had been well for him and us. Unhappily this winged and footless creature would perforce too often furl his wings in mid air and try his footing on earth, where his gait was like a swan's on shore.

Of his flight and his song when in the fit element, it is hard to speak at all, hopeless to speak adequately. It is natural that there should be nothing like them discoverable in any human work; natural that his poetry at its highest should be, as it is, beyond all praise and all words of men. He who can define it could 'unweave a rainbow';[5] he who could praise it aright would be such another as the poet. The *Christabel*, the 'Kubla Khan', with one or two more, are outside all law and jurisdiction of ours. When it has been said that such melodies were never heard, such dreams never dreamed, such speech never spoken, the chief thing remains unsaid, and unspeakable. There is a charm upon these poems which can only be felt in silent submission of wonder. Any separate line has its own heavenly beauty, but to cite separate lines is intolerable. They are to be received in a rapture of silence; such a silence as Chapman describes; silence like a god 'peaceful and young', which

Left so free mine ears,
That I might hear the music of the spheres,
And all the angels singing out of heaven.[6]

More amenable to our judgment, and susceptible of a more definite admiration, the *Ancient Mariner*, and the few other poems cast in something of a ballad type which we may rank around or below it, belong to another class. The chief of these is so well known that it needs no fresh comment. Only I will say that to some it may seem as though this great sea-piece might have had more in it of the air and savour of the sea. Perhaps it is none the worse; and indeed any one speaking of so great and famous a poem must feel and know that it cannot but be right, although he or another may think it would be better if this were retrenched or that appended. And this poem is beyond question one of the supreme triumphs of poetry. Witness the men who brought batteries to bear on it right and left. Literally: for one critic said that the 'moral sentiment'[7] had impaired the imaginative excellence; another, that it failed and fell through for want of a moral foothold upon facts.[8] Remembering these things, I am reluctant to proceed—but desirous to praise, as I best may. Though I doubt if it be worth while, seeing how the *Ancient Mariner*—praised or dispraised—lives and is like to live for the delight equally of young boys and old men; and seeing also that the last critic cited was no less a man than Hazlitt. It is fortunate—among many misfortunes—that for Coleridge no warning word was needed against the shriek of the press-gang from this side or that. He stooped once or twice to spurn them; but he knew that he stooped. His intense and overwrought abstraction from things of the day or hour did him no ill service here.

The *Ancient Mariner* has doubtless more of breadth and space, more of material force and motion, than anything else of the poet's. And the tenderness of sentiment which touches with significant colour the pure white imagination is here no longer morbid or languid, as in the earlier poems of feeling and emotion. It is soft and piteous enough, but womanly rather than effeminate; and thus serves indeed to set off the strange splendours and boundless beauties of the story. For the execution, I presume no human eye is too dull to see how perfect it is, and how high in kind of perfection. Here is not the speckless and elaborate finish which shows everywhere the fresh rasp of file or chisel on its smooth and spruce excellence; this is faultless after the fashion of a flower or a tree. Thus it has grown: not thus has it been carved.

Nevertheless, were we compelled to the choice, I for one would rather preserve 'Kubla Khan' and *Christabel* than any other of Coleridge's poems. It is more conceivable that another man should be born capable of writing the *Ancient Mariner* than one capable of writing these. The former is perhaps the most wonderful of all poems. In reading it we seem rapt into that paradise revealed to Swedenborg, where music and colour and perfume were one, where you could hear the hues and see the harmonies of heaven. For absolute melody and splendour it were hardly rash to call it the first poem in the language. An exquisite instinct married to a subtle science of verse has made it the supreme model of music in our language, a model unapproachable except by Shelley. All the elements that compose the perfect form of English metre, as limbs and veins and features a beautiful body of man, were more familiar, more subject as it were, to this great poet than to any other. How, for instance, no less than rhyme, assonance and alliteration are forces, requisite components of high and ample harmony, witness once for all the divine passage[9] which begins—

Five miles meandering with a mazy motion, &c.

All these least details and delicacies of work are worth notice when the result of them is so transcendent. Every line of the poem might be subjected to the like scrutiny, but the student would be none the nearer to the master's secret. The spirit, the odour in it, the cloven tongue of fire that rests upon its forehead,[10] is a thing neither explicable nor communicable.

Of all Coleridge's poems the loveliest is assuredly *Christabel.* It is not so vast in scope and reach of imagination as the *Ancient Mariner*; it is not so miraculous as 'Kubla Khan'; but for simple charm of inner and outer sweetness it is unequalled by either. The very terror and mystery of magical evil is imbued with this sweetness; the witch has no less of it than the maiden; their contact has in it nothing dissonant or disfiguring, nothing to jar or to deface the beauty and harmony of the whole imagination. As for the melody, here again it is incomparable with any other poet's. Shelley indeed comes nearest; but for purity and volume of music Shelley is to Coleridge as a lark to a nightingale; his song heaven-high and clear as heaven, but the other's more rich and weighty, more passionately various, and warmer in effusion of sound.[11] On the other hand, the nobler nature, the clearer spirit of Shelley, fills his verse with a divine force of meaning, which Coleridge, who had it not in him, could not affect to give. That sensuous fluctuation of soul, that floating fervour of fancy, whence his poetry rose as from a shifting sea, in faultless completion of form and charm, had absorbed—if indeed there were any to absorb—all emotion of love or faith, all heroic beauty of moral passion, all inner and outer life of the only kind possible to such other poets as Dante or Shelley, Milton or Hugo. This is neither blameable nor regrettable; none of these could have done his work; nor could he have done it had he been in any way other or better than he was. Neither, for that matter, could we have had a *Hamlet* or a *Faust* from any of these, the poets of moral faith and passion, any more than a *Divina Commedia* from Shakespeare, a *Prometheus Unbound* from Goethe. Let us give thanks for each after their kind to nature and the fates.

Alike by his powers and his impotences, by his capacity and his defect, Coleridge was inapt for dramatic poetry. It were no discredit to have fallen short of Shelley on this side, to be overcome by him who has written the one great English play of modern times; but here the very comparison would seem a jest. There is little worth praise or worth memory in the *Remorse* except such casual fragments of noble verse as may readily be detached from the loose and friable stuff in which they lie imbedded. In the scene of the incantation, in the scene of the dungeon, there are two such pure and precious fragments of gold. In the part of Alhadra there are lofty and sonorous interludes of declamation and reflection. The characters are flat and shallow; the plot is at once languid, violent, and heavy. To touch the string of the spirit, thread the weft of evil and good, feel out the way of the soul through dark places of thought and rough places of action, was not given to this the sweetest dreamer of dreams. In *Zapolya* there are no such patches of imperial purple sewn on, but there is more of air and motion; little enough indeed of high dramatic quality, but a native grace and ease which give it something of the charm of life. In this lighter and more rapid work, the song of Glycine[12] flashes out like a visible sunbeam; it is one of the brightest bits of music ever done into words.

The finest of Coleridge's odes is beyond all doubt the 'Ode to France'. Shelley declared it the finest of modern times, and justly, until himself and Keats had written up to it at least. It were profitless now to discuss whether it should take or yield precedence when weighed with the 'Ode to Liberty' or the 'Ode to Naples'. There is in it a noble and loyal love of freedom, though less fiery at once and less firm than Shelley's, as it proved in the end less durable and deep. The prelude is magnificent in music, and in sentiment and emotion far above any other of his poems; nor are the last notes inadequate to this majestic overture. Equal in force and sweetness of style, the 'Ode on Dejection' ranks next in my mind to this one; some may prefer its vaguer harmonies and sunset colours to the statelier movement, the more august and solemn passion of the earlier ode.[13]

It is noticeable that only his supreme gift of lyrical power could sustain Coleridge on political ground. His attempts of the kind in blank verse are poor indeed:—

> Untimely breathings, sick and short assays.[14]

Compare the nerveless and hysterical verses headed 'Fears in Solitude' (exquisite as is the overture, faultless in tone and colour, and worthy of a better sequel) with the majestic and masculine sonnet of Wordsworth, written at the same time on the same subject: the lesser poet—for, great as he is, I at least cannot hold Wordsworth, though so much the stronger and more admirable man, equal to Coleridge as mere poet—speaks with a calm force of thought and resolution; Coleridge wails, appeals, deprecates, objurgates in a flaccid and querulous fashion without heart or spirit. This debility of mind and manner is set off in strong relief by the loveliness of landscape touches in the same poem. The eclogue of 'Fire, Famine, and Slaughter', being lyrical, is worthier of a great name; it has force and motion enough to keep it alive yet and fresh, impeded and trammelled though it usually be by the somewhat vain and verbose eloquence of a needlessly 'Apologetic Preface'. Blank verse Coleridge could never handle with the security of conscious skill and a trained strength; it grows in his hands too facile and feeble to carry the due weight or accomplish the due work. I have not found any of his poems in this metre retouched and reinvigorated as a few have been among his others. One such alteration is memorable to all students of his art; the excision from the *Ancient Mariner* of a stanza (eleventh of the Third Part) which described the Death-mate of the Spectre-Woman, his bones foul with leprous scurf and green corruption of the grave, in contrast to the red lips and yellow locks of the fearfuller Nightmare Life-in-Death. Keats in like manner cut off from the 'Ode on Melancholy' a first stanza preserved for us by his biographer, who has duly noted the delicate justice of instinct implied by this rejection of all ghastly and violent images, however noble and impressive in their violence and ghastliness, from a poem full only of the subtle sorrow born of beauty. The same keen and tender sense of right made Coleridge reject from his work the horrors while retaining the terrors of death. But of his studies in blank verse he seems to have taken no such care. They remain mostly in a hybrid or an embryonic state, with birthmarks on them of debility or malformation. Two of these indeed have a charm of their own, not shallow or transient: the 'Nightingale' and 'Frost at Midnight'. In colour they are perfect, and not (as usual) too effusive and ebullient in style. Others, especially some of the domestic or religious sort, are offensive and grievous to the human sense on that score. Coleridge had doubtless a sincere belief in his own sincerity of belief, a true feeling of his own truth of feeling; but he leaves with us too often an unpleasant sense or taste—as it were a tepid dilution of sentiment, a rancid unction of piety. A singular book published in 1835 without author's name—the work, as I find, of a Mr. Alsop, long after to be advertised for on public placards as an accomplice in the enterprise which clouded the fiery fame and closed the heroic life of Felice Orsini[15]—gives further samples of this in *Letters, Conversations and Recollections*; samples that we might well have spared.[16] A selection from his notes and remains, from his correspondence and the records of his *Table-Talk*, even from such books as Cottle's and this anonymous disciple's, would be of real interest and value, if well edited, sifted and weeded of tares and chaff. The rare fragments of work done or speech spoken in his latter years are often fragments of gold beyond price. His plastic power and flexible charm of verse, though shown only in short flashes of song, lose nothing of the old freshness and life. To the end he was the same whose 'sovereign sway and masterdom'[17] of music could make sweet and strong even the feeble and tuneless form of metre called hexameters in English; if form of metre that may be called which has neither metre nor form. But the majestic rush and roll of that irregular anapæstic measure used once or twice by this supreme master of them all, no student can follow without an exultation of enjoyment. The 'Hymn to the Earth' has a sonorous and oceanic strength of harmony, a grace and a glory of life, which fill the sense with a vigorous delight. Of such later work as the divine verses on 'Youth and Age', 'The Garden of Boccaccio', sun-bright and honey-sweet, 'Work without Hope' (what more could be left to hope for when the man could already do such work?)—of these, and of how many more! what can be said but that they are perfect, flawless, priceless? Nor did his most delicate and profound power of criticism ever fail him or fall off. To the perfection of that rare faculty there were but two things wanting: self-command and the natural cunning of words which has made many lesser men as strong as he was weak in the matter of verbal emendation. In that line of labour his hand was unsure and infirm. Want of self-command, again, left him often to the mercy of a caprice which swept him through tangled and tortuous ways of thought, through brakes and byways of fancy, where the solid subject in hand was either utterly lost and thrown over, or so transmuted and transfigured that any recognition of it was as hopeless as any profit. In an essay well worth translating out of jargon into some human language, he speaks of 'the holy jungle of transcendental metaphysics'.[18] Out of that holy and pestilential jungle he emerged but too rarely into sunlight and clear air. It is not depth of thought which makes obscure to others the work of a thinker; real and offensive obscurity comes merely of inadequate thought embodied in inadequate language. What is clearly comprehended or conceived, what is duly thought and wrought out, must find for itself and seize upon the clearest and fullest expression. That grave and deep matter should be treated with the fluency and facility proper to light and slight things, no fool is foolish enough to desire: but we may at least demand that whatever of message a speaker may have for us be delivered without impediment of speech. A style that stammers and rambles and stumbles, that stagnates here, and there overflows into waste marsh relieved only by thick patches of powdery bulrush and such bright flowerage of barren blossom as is bred of the fogs and the fens—such a style gives no warrant of depth or soundness in the matter thus arrayed and set forth. What grains of truth or seeds of error were borne this way or that on the perpetual tide of talk concerning 'subject and object', 'reason and understanding', those who can or who care may at their leisure determine with the due precision. If to the man's critical and philosophic faculty there had been added a formative power as perfect as was added to his poetic faculty, the fruit might possibly have been wellnigh as precious after its kind. As it is, we must judge of his poetic faculty by what is accomplished; of the other we must judge, not by what is accomplished, but by what is suggested. And the value of this is sometimes[19] great, though the value of that be generally small: so great indeed that we cannot weigh or measure its influence and its work.

Our study and our estimate of Coleridge cannot now be discoloured or misguided by the attraction or repulsion to which all contemporary students or judges of a great man's work cannot but be more or less liable. Few men, I suppose, ever inspired more of either feeling than he in his time did. To us his moral or social qualities, his opinion on this matter and his action in that, are nothing except in so far as they affect the work done, the inheritance bequeathed us. With all fit admiration and gratitude for the splendid fragments so bequeathed of a critical and philosophic sort, I doubt his being remembered, except by a small body of his elect, as other than a poet. His genius was so great, and in its greatness so many-sided, that for some studious disciples of the rarer kind he will doubtless, seen from any possible point of view, have always something about him of the old magnetism and magic. The ardour, delicacy, energy of his intellect, his resolute desire to get at the roots of things and deeper yet, if deeper might be, will always enchant and attract all spirits of like mould and temper. But as a poet his place is indisputable. It is high among the highest of all time. An age that should forget or neglect him might neglect or forget any poet that ever lived. At least, any poet whom it did remember such an age would remember as something other than a poet; it would prize and praise in him, not the absolute and distinctive quality, but something empirical or accidental. That may be said of this one which can hardly be said of any but the greatest among men; that come what may to the world in course of time, it will never see his place filled. Other and stronger men, with fuller control and concentration of genius, may do more service, may bear more fruit; but such as his was they will not have in them to give. The highest lyric work is either passionate or imaginative; of passion Coleridge's has nothing; but for height and perfection of imaginative quality he is the greatest of lyric poets. This was his special power, and this is his special praise.

NOTES

1 Ecclesiasticus 44: 1, as in *The Book of Common Prayer.*
2 Cf. Shakespeare, Sonnet 121, ll. 9–10.
3 Mythical giant, son of Poseidon and Gaea, whose strength as a wrestler depended on his contact with his mother Earth.
4 Jerome Cardan, or Girolamo Cardano (1501–76), Italian physician, scientist, and philosopher; Ulisse Aldrovandi (1522–1605), Italian naturalist.
5 Keats, 'Lamia', ii, 237.
6 *Euthymiæ Raptus; The Tears of Peace* (1609). (ACS)
7 Coleridge's *Table Talk*, 31 May 1830, mentions Mrs Barbauld's opinion that the poem has no moral. Coleridge himself thought the 'moral sentiment' expressed too openly.
8 Swinburne seems to have thought that Hazlitt's 'On the Living Poets' implies such a judgment.

9 Witness also the matchless fragments of metrical criticism in Coleridge's *Remains*, which prove with what care and relish the most sweet and perfect melodist among all our poets would set himself to examine and explain the alternations and sequences of sound in the noblest verse of others. (ACS)

10 Acts 2: 3.

11 From this general rule I except of course the transcendent antiphonal music which winds up the *Prometheus* of Shelley, and should perhaps except also the 'Ode to the West Wind', and the close of the 'Ode to Naples'. Against *Christabel* it would for example be fairer to set 'The Sensitive Plant' for comparison of harmonies. (ACS)

12 See p. 183, n. 4.

13 Some time later, when France, already stripped of freedom and violated by treason, was openly paraded in her prostitution to the first Buonaparte, Coleridge published his 'Ode to Tranquillity', beginning with two stanzas since retrenched. Having unearthed them in the *Annual Register* for 1801 (vol. xliii, p. 525), I set them down here as better worth saving than most of his political verse: [quotes two stanzas.] (ACS)

14 Shakespeare's *Lucrece*, l. 1720.

15 Thomas Allsop, friend and disciple of Coleridge, was suspected of more than sympathy with Felice Orsini, the Italian revolutionary who was executed in 1858 for having attempted to assassinate Napoleon III as the 'great obstacle to Italian independence'. In the earlier form of his essay, Swinburne assigned Allsop's book to 'some female follower'.

16 It contains however among others one elaborate letter of some interest and significance, in which Coleridge, not without a tone of contempt, falls foul of the orthodox vulgarity of Wordsworth's theism ('what Hartley,' his son, I presume, 'calls the popping in of the old man with a beard') in a fashion showing how far apart his own theosophic mysticism, though never so daintily dressed up in cast church-clothes, had drifted from the more clear and rigid views of a harder and sounder mind. (ACS)

17 *Macbeth*, I, v, 71.

18 'On the Prometheus of Æschylus: An Essay. . . . Read at the Royal Society of Literature, May 18, 1825.'

19 This qualification did not appear in the original essay.

8 On choice of subjects
1872, 1875

The following selection, defining Swinburne's attitude towards '*l'art pour l'art*' and the question of whether subjects should be chosen from ancient or modern life, is from his essay on Hugo's *L'Année terrible*, in the *Fortnightly Review* for September 1872 and in *Essays and Studies* (1875). Swinburne's opinions on 'art for art's sake' have been discussed in the Introduction, section III. In his preface of 1853 (later republished as 'Poetry and the Classics') Matthew Arnold had defended the choice of subjects from ancient life: poetry concerns 'the great primary human affections', which are 'independent of time', so that 'the modernness or antiquity of an action . . . has nothing to do with its fitness for poetical representation; this depends upon its inherent qualities.' In *Aurora Leigh* (1857), Mrs Browning, on the other hand, urged the claims of modern life as being superior to those of earlier periods, as Walt Whitman often did. Swinburne addresses himself particularly to points of view expressed by Mrs Browning and Whitman, quoting from both.

A poem having in it any element of greatness is likely to arouse many questions with regard to the poetic art in general, and certain in that case to illustrate them with fresh lights of its own. This of Victor Hugo's at once suggests two points of frequent and fruitless debate between critics of the higher kind. The first, whether poetry and politics are irreconcilable or not; the second, whether art should prefer to deal with things immediate or with things remote. Upon both sides of either question it seems to me that even wise men have ere now been led from errors of theory to errors of decision. The well-known formula of art for art's sake, opposed as it has ever been to the practice of the poet who was so long credited with its authorship,[1] has like other doctrines a true side to it and an untrue. Taken as an affirmative, it is a precious and everlasting truth. No work of art has any worth or life in it that is not done on the absolute terms of art; that is not before all things and above all things a work of positive excellence as judged by the laws of the special art to whose laws it is amenable. If the rules and conditions of that art be not observed, or if the work done be not great and perfect enough to rank among its triumphs, the poem, picture, statue, is a failure irredeemable and inexcusable by any show or any proof of high purpose and noble meaning. The rule of art is not the rule of morals; in morals the action is judged by the intention, the doer is applauded, excused, or condemned, according to the motive which induced his deed; in art, the one question is not what you mean but what you do. Therefore, as I have said elsewhere,[2] the one primary requisite of art is artistic worth; 'art for art's sake first, and then all things shall be added to her—or if not, it is a matter of quite secondary importance; but from him that has not this one indispensable quality of the artist, shall be taken away even that which he has; whatever merit of aspiration, sentiment, sincerity, he may naturally possess, admirable and serviceable as in other lines of work it might have been and yet may be, is here unprofitable and unpraiseworthy.' Thus far we are at one with the preachers of 'art for art'; we prefer for example Goethe to Körner and Sappho to Tyrtæus;[3] we would give many patriots for one artist, considering that civic virtue is more easily to be had than lyric genius, and that the hoarse monotony of verse lowered to the level of a Spartan understanding, however commendable such verse may be for the doctrine delivered and the duty inculcated upon all good citizens, is of less than no value to art, while there is a value beyond price and beyond thought in the Lesbian music which spends itself upon the record of fleshly fever and amorous malady. We admit then that the worth of a poem has properly nothing to do with its moral meaning or design; that the praise of a Cæsar as sung by Virgil, of a Stuart as sung by Dryden, is preferable to the most magnanimous invective against tyranny which love of country and of liberty could wring from a Bavius or a Settle;[4] but on the other hand we refuse to admit that art of the highest kind may not ally itself with moral or religious passion, with the ethics or the politics of a nation or an age. It does not detract from the poetic supremacy of Æschylus and of Dante, of Milton and of Shelley, that they should have been pleased to put their art to such use; nor does it detract from the sovereign greatness of other poets that they should have had no note of song for any such theme. In a word, the doctrine of art for art is true in the positive sense, false in the negative; sound as an affirmation, unsound as a prohibition. If it be not true that the only absolute duty of art is the duty she owes to herself, then must art be dependent on the alien conditions of subject and of aim; whereas she is dependent on herself alone, and on nothing above her or beneath; by her own law she must stand or fall, and to that alone she is responsible; by no other law can any work of art be condemned, by no other plea can it be saved. But while we refuse to any artist on any plea the license to infringe in the least article the letter of this law, to overlook or overpass it in the pursuit of any foreign purpose, we do not refuse to him the liberty of bringing within the range of it any subject that under these conditions may be so brought and included within his proper scope of work. This liberty the men who take 'art for art' as their motto, using the words in an exclusive sense, would refuse to concede; they see with perfect clearness and accuracy that art can never be a 'handmaid' of any 'lord', as the moralist, pietist, or politician would fain have her be; and therefore they will not allow that she can properly be even so much as an ally of anything else. So on the one side we have the judges who judge of art by her capacity to serve some other good end than the production of good work; these would leave us for instance *King John*, but would assuredly deprive us of *As You Like It*; the national devotion and patriotic fire of *King Henry V* would suffice in their estimation to set it far above the sceptic and inconclusive meditations of *Hamlet*, the pointless and aimless beauty of *A Midsummer Night's Dream*. On the other side we have the judges who would ostracise every artist found guilty of a moral sense, of the political faith or the religious emotion of patriots and heroes; whose theory would raze the *Persæ* from the scroll of Æschylus, and leave us nothing of Dante but the *Vita Nuova*, of Milton but the 'Allegro' and 'Penseroso', of Shelley but the 'Skylark' and 'The Cloud'. In consistency the one order of fanatics would expel from the poetic commonwealth such citizens as Coleridge and Keats, the other would disfranchise such as Burns and Byron. The simple truth is that the question at issue between them is that illustrated by the old child's parable of the gold and silver shield. Art is one, but the service of art is diverse. It is equally foolish to demand of a Goethe, a Keats, or a Coleridge, the proper and natural work of a Dante, a Milton, or a Shelley, as to invert the demand; to arraign the *Divina Commedia* in the name of *Faust*, the Sonnet on the Massacres in Piedmont in the name of the 'Ode on a Grecian Urn', or the 'Ode to Liberty' in the name of 'Kubla Khan'. I know nothing stranger in the history of criticism than the perversity even of eminent and exquisite critics in persistent condemnation of one great artist for his deficiency in the qualities of another. It is not that critics of the higher kind expect to gather grapes of thorns or figs of thistles;[5] but they are too frequently surprised and indignant that they cannot find grapes on a fig-tree or figs on a vine. M. Auguste Vacquerie has remarked before me on this unreasonable expectation and consequent irritation of the critical mind, with his usual bright and swift sense of the truth[6]—a quality which we are sure to find when a good artist has occasion to speak of his own art and the theories current with respect to it. In this matter proscription and prescription are alike unavailing; it is equally futile to bid an artist forego the natural bent of his genius or to bid him assume the natural office of another. If the spirit or genius proper to himself move him for instance to write political poetry, he will write it; if it bid him abstain from any such theme and write only on personal or ideal subjects, then also he will obey; or if ever he attempt to force his genius into unnatural service, constrain it to some alien duty, the most praiseworthy purpose imaginable will not suffice to put life or worth into the work so done. Art knows nothing of choice between the two kinds or preference of the one to the other; she asks only that the artist shall 'follow his star'[7] with the faith and the fervour of Dante, whether it lead him on a path like or unlike the way of Dante's work; the ministers of either tribe, the savours of either sacrifice, are equally excellent in her sight.

The question whether past or present afford the highest matter for high poetry and offer the noblest reward to the noble workman has been as loudly and as long debated, but is really less debateable on any rational ground than the question of the end and aim of art. It is but lost labour that the champions on one side summon us to renounce the present and all its works, and return to bathe our spirits in the purer air and living springs of the past; it is but waste of breath for the champions of the other party to bid us break the yoke and cast off the bondage of that past, leave the dead to bury their dead,[8] and turn from the dust and rottenness of old-world themes, epic or romantic, classical or feudal, to face the age wherein we live and move and have our being, to send forth our souls and songs in search of the wonderful and doubtful future. Art knows nothing of time; for her there is but one tense, and all ages in her sight are alike present; there is nothing old in her sight, and nothing new. It is true, as the one side urges, that she fears not to face the actual aspect of the hour, to handle if it please her the immediate matters of the day; it is true, as the other side insists, that she is free to go back when she will to the very beginnings of tradition and fetch her subject from the furthest of ancient days; she cannot be vulgarised by the touch of the present or deadened by the contact of the past. In vain, for instance, do the first poetess of England and the first poet of America[9] agree to urge upon their fellows or their followers the duty of confronting and expressing the spirit and the secret of their own time, its meaning and its need; such work is worthy of a poet, but no worthier than any other work that has in it the principle of life. And a poem of the past, if otherwise as good, has in it as much of this principle as a poem of the present. If a poem cast in the mould of classic or feudal times, of Greek drama or mediæval romance, be lifeless and worthless, it is not because the subject or the form was ancient, but because the poet was inadequate to his task, incompetent to do better than a flat and feeble imitation; had he been able to fill the old types of art with new blood and breath, the remoteness of subject and the antiquity of form would in no wise have impaired the worth and reality of his work; he would have brought close to us the far-off loveliness and renewed for us the ancient life of his models, not by mechanical and servile transcript as of a copying clerk, but by loving and reverent emulation as of an original fellow-craftsman. No form is obsolete, no subject out of date, if the right man be there to rehandle it. To the question 'Can these bones live?' there is but one answer;[10] if the spirit and breath of art be breathed upon them indeed, and the voice prophesying upon them be indeed the voice of a prophet, then assuredly will the bones 'come together, bone to his bone'; and the sinews and the flesh will come up upon them, and the skin cover them above, and the breath come into them, and they will live. For art is very life itself, and knows nothing of death; she is absolute truth, and takes no care of fact; she sees that Achilles and Ulysses are even now more actual by far than Wellington and Talleyrand; not merely more noble and more interesting as types and figures, but more positive and real; and thus it is (as Victor Hugo has himself so finely instanced it) 'that Trimalchio is alive, while the late M. Romieu is dead'.[11] Vain as is the warning of certain critics to beware of the present and abstain from its immediate vulgarities and realities, not less vain, however nobly meant or nobly worded, is the counter admonition to 'mistrust the poet' who 'trundles back his soul' some centuries to sing of chiefs and ladies 'as dead as must be, for the greater part, the poems made on their heroic bones';[12] for if he be a poet indeed, these will at once be reclothed with instant flesh and reinspired with immediate breath, as present and as true, as palpable and as precious, as anything most near and real; and if the heroic bones be still flesh-less and the heroic poems lifeless, the fault is not in the bones but in the poems, not in the theme but in the singer. As vain it is, not indeed to invite the muse to new spheres and fresher fields whither also she will surely and gladly come, but to bid her 'migrate from Greece and Ionia, cross out those immensely overpaid accounts, that matter of Troy, and Achilles' wrath, and Æneas', Odysseus' wanderings';[13] forsake her temples and castles of old for the new quarters which doubtless also suit her well and make her welcome; for neither epic nor romance of chivalrous quest or classic war is obsolete yet, or ever can be; there is nothing in the past extinct; no scroll is 'closed for ever', no legend or vision of Hellenic or feudal faith 'dissolved utterly like an exhalation': all that ever had life in it has life in it for ever; those themes only are dead which never were other than dead. 'She has left them all, and is here'; so the prophet of the new world vaunts himself in vain; she is there indeed, as he says, 'by thud of machinery and shrill steam-whistle undismayed—smiling and pleased, with palpable intent to stay'; but she has not needed for that to leave her old abodes; she is not a dependent creature of time or place, 'servile to all the skiey influences';[14] she need not climb mountains or cross seas to bestow on all nations at once the light of her countenance; she is omnipresent and eternal, and forsakes neither Athens nor Jerusalem, Camelot nor Troy, Argonaut nor Crusader, to dwell as she does with equal good-will among modern appliances in London and New York. All times and all places are one to her; the stuff she deals with is eternal, and eternally the same; no time or theme is inapt for her, no past or present preferable.

NOTES

1 Swinburne was familiar with Victor Hugo's belief, expressed in *William Shakespeare* (1864), that he had given currency to the phrase '*l'art pour l'art*' without accepting the principle as usually understood. The persistence with which critics tended to attribute acceptance of the principle to Hugo had been discussed by Auguste Vacquerie in *Profils et Grimaces* (Paris, 1856), '*L'art pour l'art*', 244–7.

2 In *William Blake*, though the quotation that follows is not exact.

3 Karl Theodor Körner (1791–1813), 'the German Tyrtæus', and Tyrtæus (*fl. c.* 630 B.C.) both wrote patriotic but mediocre verse.

4 Bavius, a contemporary of Horace and Vergil, and Elkanah Settle (1648–1724), a poet and dramatist known to Dryden, also obvious types of mediocrity. (In the *Fortnightly Review* Swinburne named Shadwell rather than Settle.)

5 Matt. 7: 16.

6 Especially in '*Tas de Critiques*' in *Profils et Grimaces*, 141–54.

7 Brunetto Latini to Dante: 'If you follow your star, you cannot fail to reach the glorious port' (*Inferno*, xv, 55–6).

8 Matt. 8: 22, Luke 9: 60.

9 Mrs Browning and Walt Whitman.

10 For the question and answer cf. Ezek. 37: 3–7.

11 In *William Shakespeare*, part two, '*L'Œuvre*'. Trimalchio is a character in Petronius's *Satyricon*. Auguste Romieu (1800–55), as other allusions by Hugo indicate, was disliked most for the anti-Republican writings that helped prepare for Napoleon III's *coup d'état*.

12 From the fifth book of Mrs Browning's *Aurora Leigh*.

13 This and the next four quotations are from Whitman's 'Song of the Exposition'.

14 *Measure for Measure*, III, i, 9.

9 Hugo's poems

1872, 1875

Victor Hugo was the object of Swinburne's lifelong devotion. Swinburne's early contributions to the *Spectator* included reviews of Parts II–V of *Les Miserables*, but it is now known that he did not write the review of Part I in the *Spectator* of 12 April 1862 (reprinted in the Bonchurch Edition, xiii, 151–8) or 'Victor Hugo's Philosophy' in the *Spectator* for 25 October 1862 (reprinted in the Bonchurch Edition, xiii, 180–8). (See Introduction, note 6.) The Bonchurch Edition of Swinburne is also somewhat misleading in that it groups with *A Study of Victor Hugo* (1886) material that appeared in *Essays and Studies* (1875) and *Studies in Prose and Poetry* (1894). The passage that follows (see the headnote for No. 8), briefly characterizing several of Hugo's volumes, is at least a remarkable *tour de force*.

But whether or not there be reason in the objection that even such great works as *Marion de Lorme* and *Ruy Blas* are comparatively discoloured by this moral earnestness and strenuous preference of good to evil, or that besides this alleged distortion and diversion of art from its proper line of work, too much has been sacrificed or at least subordinated to the study of stage surprises conveyed in a constant succession of galvanic shocks, as though to atone for neglect or violation of dramatic duty and the inner law of artistic growth and poetic propriety by excess of outward and theatrical observance of effect; whether or not these and such-like deductions may be made from the fame of this great poet as dramatist or as novelist, in such a book as that now before us this quality is glorious only and dangerous no more. The partisanship which is the imperfection of a play is the perfection of a war-song or other national lyric, be it of lamentation, of exhortation, or of triumph. This book of song takes its place beyond question beside the greatest on that lyric list which reaches from the

Odes et Ballades to the *Chansons des Rues et des Bois*; such a list of labours and triumphs as what other lyrist can show? First come the clear boyish notes of prelude, songs of earliest faith and fancy, royalist and romantic; then the brilliant vivid ballads, full already of supple harmonies and potent masteries of music, of passion and sentiment, force and grace; then the auroral resonance and radiance of the luminous *Orientales*, the high and tender cadences of the *Feuilles d'Automne*, the floating and changing melodies of the *Chants du Crépuscule*, the fervent and intimate echoes of the *Voix Intérieures*, the ardent and subtle refractions of *Les Rayons et les Ombres*; each in especial of these two latter books of song crowned by one of the most perfect lyrics in all the world of art for sweetness and sublimity—the former by those stanzas on the sound of the unseen sea by night, which have in them the very heart and mystery of darkness, the very music and the very passion of wave and wind; the other by that most wonderful and adorable poem in which all the sweet and bitter madness of love strong as death is distilled into deathless speech, the little lyric tragedy of Gastibelza:[1] next, after many silent or at least songless years, the pealing thunders and blasting sunbeams of the *Châtiments*: then a work yet wider and higher and deeper than all these, the marvellous roll of the *Contemplations*, having in it all the stored and secret treasures of youth and age, of thought and faith, of love and sorrow, of life and death; with the mystery of the stars and the sepulchres above them and beneath: then the terrible and splendid chronicle of human evil and good, the epic and lyric *Légende des Siècles*, with its infinite variety of action and passion infernal and divine: then the subtle and full-throated carols of vigorous and various fancy built up in symmetrical modulation of elaborate symphonies by vision or by memory among the woods and streets:[2] and now the sorrowful and stormy notes of the giant organ whose keys are the months of this *Année Terrible*. And all these make up but one division of the work of one man's life: and we know that in the yet unsounded depth of his fathomless genius, as in the sunless treasure-houses of the sea, there are still jewels of what price we know not that must in their turn see light and give light. For these we have a prayer to put up that the gift of them may not be long delayed. There are few delights in any life so high and rare as the subtle and strong delight of sovereign art and poetry; there are none more pure and more sublime. To have read the greatest works of any great poet, to have beheld or heard the greatest works of any great painter or musician, is a possession added to the best things of life. As we pity ourselves for the loss of poems and pictures which have perished, and left of Sappho but a fragment and of Zeuxis but a name, so are we inclined to pity the dead who died too soon to enjoy the great works that we have enjoyed. At each new glory that 'swims into our ken'[3] we surely feel that it is something to have lived to see this too rise. Those who might have had such an addition to the good things of their life, and were defrauded of it by delay, have reason to utter from the shades their ghostly complaint and reproach against the giver who withheld his gift from the world till they had passed out of it, and so made their lives less by one good thing, and that good thing a pleasure of great price. We know that our greatest poet living has kept back for many years some samples of his work; and much as he has given, we are but the more impelled by consideration of that imperial munificence to desire and demand its perfect consummation. Let us not have to wait longer than must needs be for the gift of our promised treasures; for the completion of that social and historic trilogy which has yet two parts to accomplish; for the plays whose names are now to us as the names of the lost plays of Æschylus, for the poems which are as the lost poems of Pindar; for the light and sustenance, the glory and the joy, which the world has yet to expect at the hands of Victor Hugo.

NOTES

1 XXII, '*Guitare*'.
2 *Les Chansons des rues et des bois.*
3 Keats, 'On First Looking into Chapman's Homer', l. 10.

10 Browning's 'obscurity'

1875

The charge of obscurity was one that for long weighed against appreciation of Browning's poetic achievement. Swinburne thought his 'excursus on Browning' in *George Chapman* (1875) 'the truest criticism, and most to the point, that has appeared on the subject' and hoped that it would attract the notice of reviewers (Lang, iii, 2), as it did. It evoked from Browning a generous letter, to which Swinburne replied, also generously (Lang, iii, 18–19, 19–20).

The charge of obscurity is perhaps of all charges the likeliest to impair the fame or to imperil the success of a rising or an established poet. It is as often misapplied by hasty or ignorant criticism as any other on the roll of accusations; and was never misapplied more persistently and perversely than to an eminent writer of our own time. The difficulty found by many in certain of Mr. Browning's works arises from a quality the very reverse of that which produces obscurity properly so called. Obscurity is the natural product of turbid forces and confused ideas; of a feeble and clouded or of a vigorous but unfixed and chaotic intellect. Such a poet as Lord Brooke,[1] for example—and I take George Chapman and Fulke Greville to be of all English poets the two most genuinely obscure in style upon whose works I have ever adventured to embark in search of treasure hidden beneath the dark gulfs and crossing currents of their rocky and weedy waters, at some risk of my understanding being swept away by the groundswell—such a poet, overcharged with overflowing thoughts, is not sufficiently possessed by any one leading idea, or attracted towards any one central point, to see with decision the proper end and use with resolution the proper instruments of his design. Now if there is any great quality more perceptible than another in Mr. Browning's intellect it is his decisive and incisive faculty of thought, his sureness and intensity of perception, his rapid and trenchant resolution of aim. To charge him with obscurity is about as accurate as to call Lynceus[2] purblind or complain of the sluggish action of the telegraphic wire. He is something too much the reverse of obscure; he is too brilliant and subtle for the ready reader of a ready writer to follow with any certainty the track of an intelligence which moves with such incessant rapidity, or even to realize with what spider-like swiftness and sagacity his building spirit leaps and lightens to and fro and backward and forward as it lives along the animated line of its labour, springs from thread to thread and darts from centre to circumference of the glittering and quivering web of living thought woven from the inexhaustible stores of his perception and kindled from the inexhaustible fire of his imagination. He never thinks but at full speed; and the rate of his thought is to that of another man's as the speed of a railway to that of a waggon or the speed of a telegraph to that of a railway. It is hopeless to enjoy the charm or to apprehend the gist of his writings except with a mind thoroughly alert, an attention awake at all points, a spirit open and ready to be kindled by the contact of the writer's. To do justice to any book which deserves any other sort of justice than that of the fire or the wastepaper basket, it is necessary to read it in the fit frame of mind; and the proper mood in which to study for the first time a book of Mr. Browning's is the freshest, clearest, most active mood of the mind in its brightest and keenest hours of work. Read at such a time, and not 'with half-shut eyes falling asleep in a half-dream',[3] it will be found (in Chapman's phrase) 'pervial' enough to any but a sluggish or a sandblind eye; but at no time and in no mood will a really obscure writer be found other than obscure. The difference between the two is the difference between smoke and lightning; and it is far more difficult to pitch the tone of your thought in harmony with that of a foggy thinker, than with that of one whose thought is electric in its motion. To the latter we have but to come with an open and pliant spirit, untired and undisturbed by the work or the idleness of the day, and we cannot but receive a vivid and active pleasure in following the swift and fine radiations, the subtle play and keen vibration of its sleepless fires; and the more steadily we trace their course the more surely do we see that these forked flashes of fancy and changing lights of thought move unerringly around one centre, and strike straight in the end to one point. Only random thinking and random writing produce obscurity; and these are the radical faults of Chapman's style of poetry. We find no obscurity in the lightning, whether it play about the heights of metaphysical speculation or the depths of character and motive; the mind derives as much of vigorous enjoyment from the study by such light of the one as of the other. The action of so bright and swift a spirit gives insight as it were to the eyes and wings to the feet of our own; the reader's apprehension takes fire from the writer's, and he catches from a subtler and more active mind the infection of spiritual interest; so that any candid and clear-headed student finds himself able to follow for the time in fancy the lead of such a thinker with equal satisfaction on any course of thought or argument; when he sets himself to refute Renan through the dying lips of St. John[4] or to try conclusions with Strauss in his own person,[5] and when he flashes at once the whole force of his illumination full upon the inmost thought and mind of the most infamous criminal, a Guido Franceschini or a Louis Bonaparte,[6] compelling the black and obscene abyss of such a spirit to yield up at last the secret of its profoundest sophistries, and let forth the serpent of a soul that lies coiled under the most intricate and supple reasonings of self-justified and self-conscious crime. And thanks to this very quality of vivid spiritual illumination, we are able to see by the light of the author's mind without being compelled to see with his eyes, or with the eyes of the living mask which he assumes for his momentary impersonation of saint or sophist, philosopher or malefactor; without accepting one conclusion, conceding one point, or condoning one crime. It is evident that to produce any such effect requires above all things brightness and decision as well as subtlety and pliancy of genius; and this is the supreme gift and distinctive faculty of Mr. Browning's mind. If indeed there be ever any likelihood of error in his exquisite analysis, he will doubtless be found to err rather through excess of light than through any touch of darkness; we may doubt, not without a sense that the fittest mood of criticism might be that of a self-distrustful confidence in the deeper intuition of his finer and more perfect knowledge, whether the perception of good or evil would actually be so acute in the mind of the supposed reasoner; whether for instance a veritable household assassin, a veritable saviour of society or other incarnation of moral pestilence, would in effect see so clearly and so far, with whatever perversion or distortion of view, into the recesses of the pit of hell wherein he lives and moves and has his being; recognising with quick and delicate apprehension what points of vantage he must strive to gain, what outposts of self-defence he may hope to guard, in the explanation and vindication of the motive forces of his nature and the latent mainspring of his deeds. This fineness of intellect and dramatic sympathy which is ever on the watch to anticipate and answer the unspoken imputations and prepossessions of his hearer, the very movements of his mind, the very action of his instincts, is perhaps a quality hardly compatible with a nature which we might rather suppose, judging from public evidence and historic indication, to be sluggish and short-sighted, 'a sly slow thing with circumspective eye'[7] that can see but a little way immediately around it, but neither before it nor behind, above it nor beneath; and whose introspection, if ever that eye were turned inward, would probably be turbid, vacillating, cloudy and uncertain as the action of a spirit incapable of self-knowledge but not incapable of self-distrust, timid and impenitent, abased and unabashed, remorseless but not resolute, shameless but not fearless. If such be in reality the public traitor and murderer of a nation, we may fairly infer that his humbler but not viler counterpart in private life will be unlikely to exhibit a finer quality of mind or a clearer faculty of reason. But this is a question of realism which in no wise affects the spiritual value and interest of such work as Mr. Browning's. What is important for our present purpose is to observe that this work of exposition by soliloquy and apology by analysis can only be accomplished or undertaken by the genius of a great special pleader, able to fling himself with all his heart and all his brain, with all the force of his intellect and all the strength of his imagination, into the assumed part of his client; to concentrate on the cause in hand his whole power of illustration and illumination, and bring to bear upon one point at once all the rays of his thought in one focus. Apart from his gift of moral imagination, Mr. Browning has in the supreme degree the qualities of a great debater or an eminent leading counsel; his finest reasoning has in its expression and development something of the ardour of personal energy and active interest which inflames the argument of a public speaker; we feel, without the reverse regret of Pope,[8] how many a firstrate barrister or parliamentary tactician has been lost in this poet. The enjoyment that his best and most characteristic work affords us is doubtless far other than the delight we derive from the purest and highest forms of lyric or dramatic art; there is a radical difference between the analyst and the dramatist, the pleader and the prophet. It would be clearly impossible for the subtle tongue which can undertake at once the apology and the anatomy of such motives as may be assumed to impel or to support a 'Prince Hohenstiel-Schwangau' on his ways of thought and action, ever to be touched with the fire which turns to a sword or to a scourge the tongue of a poet to whom it is given to utter as from Patmos or from Sinai the word that fills all the heaven of song with the lightnings and thunders of chastisement.[9] But in place of lyric rapture or dramatic action we may profitably enjoy the unique and incomparable genius of analysis which gives to these special pleadings such marvellous life and interest as no other workman in that kind was ever or will ever again be able to give; we may pursue with the same sense of strenuous delight in a new exercise of intellect and interest the slender and luminous threads of speculation wound up into a clue with so fine a skill and such happy sleight of hand in *Fifine at the Fair* or the sixth book of *Sordello*, where the subtle secret of spiritual weakness in a soul of too various powers and too restless refinement is laid bare with such cunning strength of touch, condemned and consoled with such far-sighted compassion and regret.

This last-named poem has been held especially liable to the charge which we have seen to be especially inapplicable to the general work of its author; but although the manner of its construction should not seem defensible, as to me I may confess that it does not, it would be an utter misuse of terms to find in obscurity of thought or language the cause of this perceptible defect. The point of difference was accurately touched by the exquisite critical genius of Coleridge when he defined the style of Persius as 'hard—not obscure':[10] for this is equally true in the main of the style of *Sordello*; only the hard metal is of a different quality and temper, as the intellect of the English thinker is far wider in its reach, far subtler in its action and its aim, than that of the Roman stoic. The error, if I may take on myself to indicate what I conceive to be the error, of style in *Sordello* is two-fold; it is a composite style, an amalgam of irreconcilable materials that naturally refuse to coalesce; and, like a few of the author's minor poems, it is written at least partially in shorthand, which a casual reader is likely to mistake for cipher, and to complain accordingly that the key should be withheld from him. A curious light is thrown on the method of its composition by the avowal put forth in the dedication of a reissue of this poem, that since its first adventure on publicity the writer had added and had cancelled a notable amount of illustrative or explanatory matter, preferring ultimately to leave his work such a poem as the few must like, rather than such as the many might. Against this decision no one has a right to appeal; and there is doubtless much in the work as it stands that all imaginative thinkers and capable students of poetry most assuredly must regard with much more than mere liking; but when the reader is further invited to observe that the sole aim kept in sight, the sole object of interest pursued by the author, was the inner study of an individual mind, the occult psychology of a single soul, the personal pathology of a special intelligence, he has a right to suggest that in that case there is too much, and in any other case there is not enough, of external illustration and the byplay of alien actions and passions which now serve only to perplex the scheme they ought to explain. If it was the author's purpose to give to his philosophic poem a background of historic action, to relieve against the broad mass and movement of outer life the solitary process of that inward and spiritual tragedy which was the main occupation of his mind and art, to set the picture of a human spirit in the frame of circumstances within which it may actually have been environed and beset with offers of help, with threats and temptations, doubts and prospects and chances of the day it had on earth,—if this was his purpose, then surely there is not here enough of such relief to illustrate a design which there is more than enough of it to confuse. But if, as we are now obliged to assume, the author's purpose was studiously and strenuously to restrict within the limits of inner spiritual study the interest and the motive of his work, to concentrate our attention with his own upon the growth and the fortune, the triumph and the failure, the light and the darkness of this one human spirit, the soul of a man of genius fallen upon evil days[11] and elect for great occasions and begirt with strange perplexities, then surely there is here far too much of external distraction and diversion for the reader's mind even to apprehend the issue, much less to comprehend the process, of this inner tragic action. The poem, in short, is like a picture in which the background runs into the foreground, the figures and the landscape confound each other for want of space and proportion, and there is no middle distance discernible at all. It is but a natural corollary to this general error that the body like the spirit of the poem, its form not less than its thought, should halt between two or three diverse ways, and that the style should too often come to the ground between two stools or more; being as it is neither a dramatic nor a narrative style, neither personal nor impersonal, neither lyric nor historic, but at once too much of all these and not enough of any. The result may be to the hasty reader no less repellent than the result of obscurity in thought or in style; but from identity of effect we are not to infer an identity of cause.

The best parts of this poem also belong in substance always and sometimes in form to the class of monodramas or soliloquies of the spirit; a form to which the analytic genius of Mr. Browning leads him ever as by instinct to return, and in which alone it finds play for its especial faculties and security against its especial liabilities to error and confusion of styles; a security for want of which his lyric and dramatic writing is apt to be neither dramatic nor lyrical, simply because of the writer's natural and inevitable tendency to analysis, which, by the nature of things as well as by the laws of art, can only explain and express itself either through the method of direct exposition or in the form of elaborate mental monologue. The whole argument of the sixth book is monodramatic; and its counterpart is to be sought in the most dramatic and to me the most delightful passage of equal length in the poem, the magnificent soliloquy of Salinguerra in the fourth book, full of the subtle life and reality and pathos which the author, to speak truth as it seems to me, too generally fails to transfer from monologue into dialogue, to translate into the sensible action and passion of tragedy, or adequately to express in fulness and fitness of lyric form. The finest and most memorable parts of his plays not less than of his poems are almost always reducible in their essence to what I have called monodrama; and if cast into the monodramatic form common to all his later writings would have found a better if not a keener expression and left a clearer if not a deeper impression on the mind. For one example, the communing of old King Victor with himself on his return to the palace he has resigned[12] is surely far more impressive and memorable to any reader than the rest of the play where his character is exhibited in the mutual action and reaction of dialogue among characters who seem unable to say rightly what they should say except when alone or secure from interruption. Even Chapman, from whom I may be thought to have wandered somewhat far in this inquiry as to what is or is not properly definable as obscurity, has in my judgment a sounder instinct of dramatic dialogue and movement than the illustrious writer who has carved out for himself in the second period of his career a new and better way to the end appointed by nature for the exercise of his highest powers; and Chapman was certainly not remarkable among the great men of his day for the specially dramatic bent of his genius.

I have dwelt thus long on a seemingly irrelevant and discursive inquiry because I could discover no method so fit to explain the nature of the fault I cannot but find in the poet of whom I have to speak, as by contrast of his work with the work of another, upon whom this fault has been wrongly charged by the inaccurate verdict of hasty judges. In answer to these I have shown that the very essence of Mr. Browning's aim and method, as exhibited in the ripest fruits of his intelligence, is such as implies above all other things the possession of a quality the very opposite of obscurity—a faculty of spiritual illumination rapid and intense and subtle as lightning, which brings to bear upon its central object by way of direct and vivid illustration every symbol and every detail on which its light is flashed in passing. Thus in *Fifine* the illustration derived from a visionary retrospect of Venice, and in *Sordello* the superb and wonderful comparison of the mental action of a man who puts by for a season the memories in which he has indulged for a moment before turning again to the day's work, with that of a fugitive slave who thinks over in a pause of his flight and puts aside for more practical means of revenge the thought of enchantments 'sovereign to plague his enemies',[13] as he buckles himself again to the grim business of escape—these and other such illustrative passages are not more remarkable for the splendour of their imaginative quality than for the aptness of their cunning application and the direct light reflected from them on the immediate argument which is penetrated and vivified throughout by the insinuation and exploration of its radiance.

NOTES

1 Sir Fulke Greville (*c.* 1554–1628), first Baron Brooke, author of poems, plays, and a biography of Sidney.
2 A member of the Argonautic expedition, so keen-sighted that he could see through the earth.
3 Cf. Tennyson's 'The Lotus-Eaters', ll. 55–6 of the 'Choric Song'.
4 In 'A Death in the Desert'.
5 In 'Christmas Eve'.
6 In *The Ring and the Book* and 'Prince Hohenstiel-Schwangau, Saviour of Society'.
7 Adapted from Pope, *Essay on Man*, iv, 226.
8 Cf. Pope's *Dunciad*, iv, 170: 'How many Martials were in Pulteney lost.'
9 Hugo, the poet of *Les Châtiments*, containing 'chastisement' of Napoleon III; Hugo's power is compared to that of Moses or the St John of Revelation.
10 *Table Talk*, 2 September 1833.
11 Cf. *Paradise Lost*, vii, 25.
12 In *King Victor and King Charles*.
13 *Sordello*, iv, 877.

11 On Chaucer, Dante, Villon, and Spenser

1880, 1886

'Short Notes on English Poets', in *Miscellanies* (1886), from which the selection below is taken, had appeared in the *Fortnightly Review* for December 1880 as an article on W. M. Rossetti's *Lives of Famous Poets*. Swinburne's comments on Chaucer and Villon may recall the ranking of the two poets by Matthew Arnold, also in 1880 and in a sort of bird's-eye view of great poetry (as an introduction to Ward's *English Poets*), neither poet-critic having had the advantage of the systematic study that modern knowledge of Chaucer's language makes possible. Arnold found more 'high seriousness' in Villon than in Chaucer. The hypothesis that he may not have read *Troilus and Criseyde* has been supported by the discovery that the pages of that poem in a volume of his library were uncut. Swinburne had read and admired it, but his view of medieval literature was affected by his attitude towards religious faith. His interest in Villon began early and resulted in several fine translations.

Dante represents, at its best and highest, the upper class of the dark ages not less than he represents their Italy; Chaucer represents their middle class at its best and wisest, not less than he represents their England; Villon represents their lower class at its worst and its best alike, even more than he represents their France. And of these three the English middle class, being incomparably the happiest and the wisest, is indisputably, considering the common circumstances of their successive times, the least likely to have left us the highest example of all poetry then possible to men. And of their three legacies, precious and wonderful as it is, the Englishman's is accordingly the least wonderful and the least precious. The poet of the sensible and prosperous middle class in England had less to suffer and to sing than the theosophic aristocrat of Italy, or the hunted and hungry vagabond who first found articulate voice for the dumb longing and the blind love as well as for the reckless appetites and riotous agonies of the miserable and terrible multitude in whose darkness lay dormant, as in a cerecloth which was also a chrysalid, the debased and disfigured godhead which was one day to exchange the degradation of the lowest populace for the revelation of the highest people—for the world-wide apocalypse of France. The golden-tongued gallows-bird of Paris is distinguished from his two more dignified compeers by a deeper difference yet—a difference, we might say, of office and of mission no less than of genius and of gift. Dante and Chaucer are wholly and solely poets of the past or present—singers indeed for all time, but only singers of their own: Villon, in an equivocal and unconscious fashion, was a singer also of the future; he was the first modern and the last mediæval poet. He is of us, in a sense in which it cannot be said that either Chaucer or Dante is of us, or even could have been; a man of a changing and self-transforming time, not utterly held fast, though still sorely struggling, in the jaws of hell and the ages of faith.

But in happy perfection of manhood the great and fortunate Englishman almost more exceeds his great and unfortunate fellow-singers than he is exceeded by them in depth of passion and height of rapture, in ardour and intensity of vision or of sense. With the single and sublimer exception of Sophocles, he seems to me the happiest of all great poets on record; their standing type and sovereign example of noble and manly happiness. As prosperous indeed in their several ages and lines of life were Petrarca and Ariosto, Horace and Virgil; but one only of these impresses us in every lineament of his work with the same masculine power of enjoyment. And when Ariosto threw across the windy sea of glittering legend and fluctuant romance the broad summer lightnings of his large and jocund genius, the dark ages had already returned into the outer darkness where there is weeping and gnashing of teeth[1]—the tears of Dante Alighieri and the laughter of François Villon. But the wide warm harvest-field of Chaucer's husbandry was all glorious with gold of ripening sunshine while all the world beside lay in blackness and in bonds, throughout all those ages of death called ages of faith by men who can believe in nothing beyond a building or a book, outside the codified creeds of a Bible or the œcumenical structures of a Church.

Before I take my reverent leave of Chaucer, I will express in passing a slight sense of regret that Mr. Rossetti should not have added to his notice of the *Troilus and Cryseide*—a choice passage of exquisite analysis and panegyric, with every word of which I most cordially concur—some little note of applause for the Scottish poet Henryson's equally adventurous and admirable sequel to that poem.[2] For truth and power of pathetic imagination, the last meeting of Troilus with the wayside leper who once had all his heart, and played it all away at the May-game of light love, may be matched against the very best work of Chaucer: nor do I remember anything in it all so deeply and truly tragic as the doom of the transformed and disfigured traitress, who, meeting no recognition in the eyes of her old lover as he looks on her and sighs and passes, with an alms thrown sadly as to a stranger, falls back and dies in silence.

The earnest search or labour after righteousness of judgment and absolute accuracy of estimate which always, whether it may finally succeed or fail, distinguishes the critical talent of Mr. Rossetti is very happily exemplified in his analysis and summary of the aims and the claims of Spenser. His judgment or his sentiment on this matter may be said to strike a balance between the enthusiastic devotion of Scott and Southey, Ruskin and Leigh Hunt, and the wearied indifference or positive distaste of Landor. As a descendant of the great Latin race, he has naturally by way of birthright the gift which he is bound to have, an inborn sense of rule and outline which makes him instinctively aware of Spenser's shortcoming on that side, and logically averse from the luminous and fluid nebulosity of Spenser's cloudy and flowery fairyland. The lack of tangible form and line, of human flesh and breath and blood on the limbs and at the lips and in the veins of Spenser's active or passive and militant or triumphant congregation of impersonated virtues and vices, is inevitably perceptible to a scholar and evangelist of Dante, who must perforce be unconsciously inclined to measure all poets more or less after the standard of the mighty master whose missionary he was born by right at once of inheritance and of intelligence. Dante was beyond all other poets a materialist;—and this, I have heard it remarked, is of course what Blake meant to convey by the quaint apparent paradox of his essentially accurate objection to the 'atheism' (as he called it) of Dante;[3] with whom the finest forms of abstract qualities that the scholastic ingenuity of mediæval metaphysicians could devise and define became hard and sharp and rigid as tempered steel. Give Dante a moral image, he will make of it a living man: show Spenser a living man, he will make of him a moral image. It is not to the existence of allegory in Spenser that all save his fanatical admirers object; it is to the fact that this allegory, like Mrs. Malaprop's 'on the banks of the Nile',[4] is a rapacious and insatiable impostor who attracts and devours all living likenesses of men and women within reach. There is allegory also in Homer and in Dante: but prayers in Homer and qualities in Dante become vital and actual forms of living and breathing creatures. In Spenser the figure of a just man melts away into the quality of justice, the likeness of a chaste woman is dissolved into the abstraction of chastity. Nothing can be more alien from the Latin genius, with its love of clearness and definite limitation, than this indefinite and inevitable cloudiness of depiction rather than conception, which reduces the most tangible things to impalpable properties, resolves the solidest realities into smoke of perfumed metaphor from the crucible of symbolic fancy, and suffuses with Cimmerian mist[5] the hard Italian sunlight. Add to this the cloying sweetness of the Spenserian metre, with all 'its treasures of fluidity and sweet ease' (as Mr. Arnold, with his usual studious felicity of exquisite phrase, has so perfectly described it),[6] which leaves at least some readers, after a dose of a few pages, overgorged with a sense that they have been eating a whole hive's harvest of thick pressed honey by great spoonfuls, without one halfpennyworth of bread to this intolerable deal of sweet-stuff;[7] and it is easy to determine why the attraction of this noble poet, for all his luminous colour and lovely melody, the raiment of high thinking and fine feeling, is perhaps less potent than it should be over minds first nurtured on the stronger fare of Greek or Latin or Italian song. The Tarpeian Muse[8] of Spenser is not indeed crushed—there is too much vigorous and supple vitality in her lovely limbs for that—but she is heavily burdened if not sorely bruised by the ponderous and brilliant weight of allegoric shields, emblazoned with emblematic heraldry of all typic and chivalric virtues, which her poet has heaped upon her by way of signs and bucklers of her high and holy enterprise in 'fairy lands forlorn',[9] through twilight woodlands and flowery wastes of mythical and moral song. With almost equal truth he might be said to have founded and to have followed the fashion of allegorical poetry which in the next generation ran riot through the voluminous verse of his disciples till it reached its head, not even in the works of the two lesser Fletchers, but—as if the names of our dramatic Dioscuri[10] were foredoomed to poetical conjunction and unconscious fellowship on far other ways than theirs—in the limitless and lampless labyrinth of Joseph Beaumont's *Psyche*. Allegory was no doubt a powerful factor to be reckoned with in casting up the account of English poetry before Spenser; but in the allegories of his most notable precursors down to Sackville there is surely as much more of body, of tangible and palpable outline, than in his, as there is less of it in any of his followers. I cannot, therefore, but think that the great influence of Spenser on succeeding poets whose lines of work lay outside the fields of lyric and dramatic verse was far from being good as well as great. Outside those fields there was no man—unless a not very significant exception be claimed for Drayton and for Daniel as narrative chroniclers of some small and partial note—there was no man till the sundawn of Milton who could make head for a moment against that influence. The one great poet who might have done this also as well as the work he did—the yet worthier and surely far mightier work of founding the tragic stage of England—had only time to leave us a broken sample of nobler narrative and purer power than Spenser's, in the unimitated if not inimitable model of his *Hero and Leander*. And all who came after them found it easier to follow the discursive and decorative style of Spenser than the more 'simple, sensuous, and passionate'[11] manner of Marlowe.

NOTES

1 Cf. Matt. 8: 12.
2 *The Testament of Cresseid.*
3 See the passage from Crabb Robinson's diary recorded in Arthur Symons's *William Blake* (London, 1907), 262.
4 Sheridan's *The Rivals*, III, iii.
5 Book xi of the *Odyssey* describes the Cimmerians as living in 'a land of mist and cloud', at the limits of the world.
6 From Arnold's note in *On Translating Homer*: see *On the Classical Tradition*, ed. R. H. Super (Ann Arbor, 1960), i, 200 n.
7 Cf. *I Henry IV*, II, iv, 591–2: 'O monstrous! but one half-pennyworth of bread to this intolerable deal of sack!'
8 Tarpeia, the Roman maiden who opened the gates to Sabine invaders, instead of receiving the 'ornaments' on their arms promised as a reward for her treachery, was crushed by their shields.
9 Keats, 'Ode to a Nightingale', l. 70.
10 Beaumont and Fletcher are equated with the Dioscuri, the twins Castor and Pollux of ancient myth.
11 From Milton's definition of poetry in *Of Education.*

12 Collins

1880, 1886

'Collins' first appeared in Humphry Ward's *English Poets* (iii, 1880) and was included in *Miscellanies* (1886). As the polite note at the end intimates, Swinburne's estimate of Collins again suggests comparison with a judgment by Arnold. Besides adding the note, Swinburne made other minor changes. A reference to Goldsmith's verse as expressive of 'a priceless and adorable power of sweet human emotion' became 'a gentle power of human emotion', and in the final sentence about Collins 'the sweet name and the lucid memory of his genius could' was modified to 'the memory of his name and the impression of his genius can'. In both instances the critic's diction and reputation for sobriety of judgment suffered no loss. He omitted some sentences about Tennyson's revisions—stanzas excised from 'The Miller's Daughter'; the charm of the 'once revealed and long recluse "Hesperides"'; and 'the revived and reinvigorated "Lotus-Eaters"'. After his affirmation that Collins stood for 'the divine right and the godlike duty of tyrannicide' Swinburne also omitted a quotation from Browning's 'Lost Leader'.

In the reaction against that sweeping violence of indiscriminative depreciation with which the school of poets and critics usually registered as Wordsworthian, but actually founded at midnight by William Blake and fortified at sunrise by William Wordsworth, was wont for some half a century to overwhelm the poetry and criticism of the century preceding, the name which of all properly belonging to that period has incomparably the most valid and solid claim to the especial and essential praise that denotes a poet from among other men of genius has hardly yet taken by general consent the place which is unquestionably its due. Even in his own age it was the fatally foolish and uncritical fashion to couple the name of Collins with that of Gray, as though they were poets of the same order or kind. As an elegiac poet, Gray holds for all ages to come his unassailable and sovereign station; as a lyric poet, he is simply unworthy to sit at the feet of Collins. Whether it may not be a greater thing than ever was done by the greater lyrist, to have written a poem of such high perfection and such universal appeal to the tenderest and the noblest depths of human feeling as Gray's *Elegy*, is of course another and a wholly irrelevant question. But it is not a question which admits of debate at all, among men qualified to speak on such matters, that as a lyric poet Gray was not worthy to unloose the latchets of his shoes.[1] The fanfaronade and falsetto which impair the always rhetorically elaborate and sometimes genuinely sonorous notes of Gray were all but impossible to the finer touch of his precursor. In the little book of odes which dropped, a still-born immortal, from the press, and was finally burnt up even to the last procurable copy by the hands of its author in a fever-fit of angry despair, there was hardly a single false note; and there were not many less than sweet or strong. There was, above all things, a purity of music, a clarity of style, to which I know of no parallel in English verse from the death of Andrew Marvell to the birth of William Blake. Here, in the twilight which followed on the splendid sunset of Pope, was at last a poet who was content to sing out what he had in him—to sing and not to say, without a glimpse of wit or a flash of eloquence. These two valuable and admirable superfluities had for generations been regarded, not as fortuitous accessories, but as indispensable requisites, to poetic genius. Nothing so clearly shows how much finer a sense of poetry than is usually attributed to him lay radically latent, when unobscured by theories or prepossessions, in the deliberate judgment of Dr. Johnson, as his recognition in Collins of the eminent and exquisite faculty which he rightly refused to recognize in Gray. The strong-lunged and heavy-handed preacher of *The Vanity of Human Wishes* had an ear fine enough at least to distinguish the born lyric poet from him who had been made one, though self-made. His recognition of Collins had been ready and generous in his youth; it was faithful and consistent in his old age. And in both seasons he stood then, almost as he stands now, alone in the insight of his perception and the courage of his loyalty. For it needed some courage as well as some openness of mind and sureness of instinct to acknowledge as well as to appreciate a quality of merit far more alien than was the quality of Gray's best work to the merit of Pope and his scholars; among whose ranks the critic himself stood so honourably high as an ethic poet.

Strange as the paradox may sound, it must yet once again be repeated, that the first indispensable faculty of a singer is ability to sing. There was but one man in the time of Collins who had in him a note of pure lyric song, a pulse of inborn music irresistible and indubitable; and that he was that man he could not open his lips without giving positive and instant proof. Poetry was his by birthright: to the very ablest of his compeers it was never more than a christening gift. The Muse gave birth to Collins; she did but give suck to Gray. In Goldsmith's verse, again, there is a gentle power of human emotion which lay for the most part quite out of our poet's way. His range of flight was perhaps the narrowest but assuredly the highest of his generation. He could not be taught singing like a finch: but he struck straight upward for the sun like a lark. Again, he had an incomparable and infallible eye for landscape; a purity, fidelity, and simple-seeming subtlety of tone, unapproached until the more fiery but not more luminous advent of Burns. Among all English poets he has, it seems to me, the closest affinity to our great contemporary school of French landscape painters. Corot on canvas might have signed his 'Ode to Evening'; Millet might have given us some of his graver studies, and left them as he did no whit the less sweet for their softly austere and simply tender gravity. His magnificent Highland ode, so villainously defaced after his death by the most impudent interpolations on record, has much in it of Millais, and something also of Courbet when the simple genius of that star-crossed idoloclast was content with such noble and faithful use of freedom as he displayed in a picture of upland fell and tarnside copse in the curving hollow of a moor, which was once exhibited in London. Here and here only, for vigour of virile grasp and reach of possessive eyesight, Burns himself was forestalled if not excelled. Here too is a visible power, duly and tenderly subdued into subordination, of command upon human emotion and homely sympathy, less intimate than in Burns and less profound than in Wordsworth, but none the less actual and vivid, which we hardly find elsewhere in this perfect painter of still life or starlit vision. In his artistic tenderness of conscience and scrupulous self-mastery of hand he so closely resembles Lord Tennyson as once at least to provoke the same doubtful sense of jealous and admiring demur. A notable instance of this refined excess in conscience is the exquisite recast of the originally exquisite second line in the 'Ode to Evening'. But Collins may claim of us a far loftier note of praise than this: and it is one which could hardly have been sounded by the 'capacious mouth'[2] of his good and true friend Johnson. He was the first English poet, after

Milton's voice 'for the dwellers upon earth'[3] fell silent, to blow again the clarion of republican faith and freedom: to reannounce with the passion of a lyric and heroic rapture the divine right and the godlike duty of tyrannicide. And on this side of the summit of fair fame he stands loftily alone between the sunset of Milton and the sunrise of Landor. I hardly think there are much nobler verses in all English than those in which the new Alcæus, 'fancy-blest'[4] indeed, has sung the myrtle-hidden sword that rid the sunlight of the first Pisistratid. For all her evil report among men on the score of passive obedience and regiculture, Oxford has now and then turned out—in a double sense, we might say, with reference to Shelley—sons who have loved the old cause as well as any reared by the nursing mother of Milton.

There is yet another memorable bond of communion which connects the fame of Collins with that of Milton in the past and with that of Shelley in the future. Between the elegy on Edward King and the elegy on John Keats came the humbler and softer note by which Collins set the seal of a gentle consecration on the grave of the 'Druid' Thomson; a note to be as gently echoed by Wordsworth in commemoration of his own sweeter song and sadder end.[5]

The mention of Wordsworth's name reminds me of another but a casual coincidence between the fortunes of that great poet's work and of this his lyric and elegiac predecessor's. In both cases the generally accepted masterpiece of their lyric labour seems to me by no means the poem genuinely acceptable as such. Mr. Arnold, with the helpful loyalty and sound discretion of a wise disciple, has noted as much in the case of Wordsworth; it is no less demonstrable a truth in the case of Collins. As surely as, for instance, the 'Ode to Duty' is a work of greater perfection and more perfect greatness than that 'On the Intimations of Immortality', the 'Ode on the Passions' is a work of less equal elevation and purity of excellence than, for example, is the 'Ode to Evening'. Yet of course its grace and vigour, its vivid and pliant dexterity of touch, are worthy of all their inheritance of praise; and altogether it holds out admirably well to the happy and harmonious end; whereas the very 'Ode to Liberty', after an overture worthy of Milton's or of Handel's *Agonistes*, a prelude that peals as from beneath the triumphal hand of either of these demigods of music, steadily subsides through many noble but ever less and less noble verses, towards a final couplet showing not so much the flatness of failure as the prostration of collapse.

Living both in an age and after an age of critical poetry, Collins, always alien alike from the better and from the worse influences of his day, has shewn at least as plentiful a lack of critical instinct as ever did any poet on record, in his epistle to Hanmer on that worthy knight's 'inqualifiable' edition of Shakespeare. But his couplets, though incomparably inferior to Gray's, are generally spirited and competent as well as fluent and smooth.

The direct sincerity and purity of their positive and straightforward inspiration will always keep his poems fresh and sweet. He was a solitary song-bird among many more or less excellent pipers and pianists. He could put more spirit of colour into a single stroke, more breath of music into a single note, than could all the rest of his generation into all the labours of their lives. And the memory of his name and the impression of his genius can only pass away with all relics and all records of lyric poetry in England.

(This brief notice was published in the third volume of Mr. Ward's Selections from the English Poets, side by side with the admirable study in which Mr. Matthew Arnold has so powerfully advocated the claim of Gray to a higher place among these poets than he is prepared to concede to Collins. 'Something of the like merit' is all that the most distinguished of living Wordsworthians will allow him: but I am fain to believe that the verdict of Wordsworth himself would have been given on the opposite side.)

NOTES

1 Cf. Luke 3: 16.
2 Cf. John Gay, *Acis and Galatea*, II:

> Bring me a hundred reeds of decent growth
> To make a pipe for my capacious mouth.

3 Cf. Isaiah 18: 3.
4 From Collins's 'Ode to Liberty', l. 7.
5 Thomson is called 'a Druid' in 'Ode on the Death of Mr Thomson'. Wordsworth's poem is 'Remembrance of Collins'.

13 Landor
1882, 1886

Like Hugo and Mazzini, Landor had a special place in Swinburne's esteem. He procured and read all of Landor's works, including the privately printed editions, that he could find, and in 1888 wrote of his pleasure in showing some of these to Landor's grandson (Lang, v, 252). Swinburne notes in 'Landor' that a recurring fault is linked with Landor's regard for conciseness. This comment and his appreciation of the classical finish of Landor's verse and prose remind us that Swinburne's enthusiasms were not limited to those who wrote in the romantic vein and that his praise of even his idols is not often unqualified.

A contribution to the ninth edition of the *Encyclopædia Britannica* (xiv, 1882), 'Landor' was included in *Miscellanies* (1886).

Walter Savage Landor, born at Warwick, January 30, 1775, died at Florence, September 17, 1864. In the course of this long life he had won for himself such a double crown of glory in verse and in prose as has been worn by no other Englishman but Milton. And with that special object of his lifelong veneration he had likewise in common other claims upon our reverence to which no third competitor among English poets can equally pretend. He had the same constancy to the same principles, the same devotion to the same ideal of civic and heroic life; the same love, the same loyalty, the same wrath, scorn, and hatred, for the same several objects respectively; the same faith in the example and kinship to the spirit of the republican Romans, the same natural enjoyment and mastery of their tongue. Not accident merely but attraction must in any case have drawn them to enlist in the ranks and serve under the standard of the ancient Latin army of patriots and poets. But to Landor even more than to Milton the service of the Roman Muse was a natural and necessary expression of his genius, a spontaneous and just direction of its full and exuberant forces. At the age of twenty he published an eloquent vindication of her claims upon the service and devotion of modern writers —the first sketch or suggestion of a longer essay, to be published in its final form just fifty-two years later. In 1795 appeared in a small volume, 'divided into three books', *The Poems of Walter Savage Landor*, and, in pamphlet form of nineteen pages, an anonymous *Moral Epistle, respectfully dedicated to Earl Stanhope*. No poet at the age of twenty ever had more vigour of style and fluency of verse; nor perhaps has any ever shown such masterly command of epigram and satire, made vivid and vital by the purest enthusiasm and most generous indignation. Three years later appeared the first edition of the first great work which was to inscribe his name for ever among the great names in English poetry. The second edition of *Gebir* appeared in 1803, with a text corrected of grave errors and improved by magnificent additions. About the same time the whole poem was also published in a Latin form, which for might and melody of line, for power and perfection of language, must always dispute the palm of precedence with the English version. In 1808, under an impulse not less heroic than that which was afterwards to lead Byron to a glorious death in redemption of Greece and his own good fame, Landor, then aged thirty-three, left England for Spain as a volunteer to serve in the national army against Napoleon at the head of a regiment raised and supported at his sole expense. After some three months' campaigning came the affair of Cintra[1] and its disasters; 'his troop,' in the words of his biographer, 'dispersed or melted away, and he came back to England in as great a hurry as he had left it',[1] but bringing with him the honourable recollection of a brave design unselfishly attempted, and the material in his memory for the sublimest poem published in our language between the last masterpiece of Milton and the first masterpiece of Shelley—one equally worthy to stand unchallenged beside either for poetic perfection as well as moral majesty—the lofty tragedy of *Count Julian*, which appeared in 1812, without the name of its author. No comparable work is to be found in English poetry between the date of *Samson Agonistes* and the date of *Prometheus Unbound*; and with both these great works it has some points of greatness in common. The superhuman isolation of agony and endurance which encircles and exalts the hero is in each case expressed with equally appropriate magnificence of effect. The style of *Count Julian*, if somewhat deficient in dramatic ease and the fluency of natural dialogue, has such might and purity and majesty of speech as elsewhere we find only in Milton so long and so steadily sustained.

In May 1811 Landor had suddenly married Miss Julia Thuillier, with whose looks he had fallen in love at first sight in a ball-room at Bath; and in June they settled for a while at Llanthony Abbey in Wales, from whence he was worried in three years' time by the combined vexation of neighbours and tenants, lawyers and lords-lieutenant; not before much toil and money had been nobly wasted on attempts to improve the sterility of the land, to relieve the wretchedness and raise the condition of the peasantry. He left England for France at first, but after a brief residence at Tours took up his abode for three years at Como; 'and three more wandering years he passed,' says his biographer, 'between Pisa and Pistoja, before he pitched his tent in Florence in 1821.'[3] In 1824 appeared the first series of his *Imaginary Conversations*; in 1826 'the second edition, corrected and enlarged': a supplementary third volume was added in 1828; and in 1829 the second series was given to the world. Not until 1846 was a fresh instalment added, in the second volume of his collected and selected works. During the interval he had published his three other most famous and greatest books in prose: *The Citation and Examination of William Shakespeare*, 1834; *Pericles and Aspasia*, 1836; *The Pentameron*, 1837. To the last of these was originally appended *The Pentalogia*, containing five of the very finest among his shorter studies in dramatic poetry. In 1847 he published his most important Latin work, *Poemata et Inscriptiones*, comprising, with large additions, the main contents of two former volumes of idyllic, satiric, elegiac, and lyric verse; and in the same golden year of his poetic life appeared the very crown and flower of its manifold labours, *The Hellenics of Walter Savage Landor*, enlarged and completed. Twelve years later this book was reissued, with additions of more or less value, with alterations generally to be regretted, and with omissions invariably to be deplored. In 1853 he put forth *The Last Fruit off an Old Tree*, containing fresh conversations, critical and controversial essays, miscellaneous epigrams, lyrics, and occasional poems of various kind and merit, closing with *Five Scenes* on the martyrdom of Beatrice Cenci, unsurpassed even by their author himself for noble and heroic pathos, for subtle and genial, tragic and profound, ardent and compassionate insight into character, with consummate mastery of dramatic and spiritual truth. In 1856 he published *Antony and Octavius—Scenes for the Study*, twelve consecutive poems in dialogue which alone would suffice to place him high among the few great masters of historic drama. In 1858 appeared a metrical miscellany bearing the title of *Dry Sticks Fagoted by W. S. Landor*, and containing among other things graver and lighter certain epigrammatic and satirical attacks which reinvolved him in the troubles of an action for libel; and in July of the same year he returned for the last six years of his life to Italy, which he had left for England in 1835. Embittered and distracted by domestic dissensions, if brightened and relieved by the affection and veneration of friends and strangers, this final period of his troubled and splendid career came at last to a quiet end on the 17th (as aforesaid) of September, 1864. In the preceding year he had published a last volume of *Heroic Idyls, with Additional Poems*, English and Latin; the better part of them well worthy to be indeed the 'last fruit' of a genius which after a life of eighty-eight years had lost nothing of its majestic and pathetic power, its exquisite and exalted loveliness.

A complete list of Landor's writings, published or privately printed, in English, Latin, and Italian, including pamphlets, fly-sheets, and occasional newspaper correspondence on political or literary questions, it would be difficult to give anywhere and impossible to give here. From nineteen almost to ninety his intellectual and literary activity was indefatigably incessant; but, herein at least like Charles Lamb, whose cordial admiration he so cordially returned, he could not write a note of three lines which did not bear the mark of his 'Roman hand'[4] in its matchless and inimitable command of a style at once the most powerful and the purest of his age. The one charge which can ever seriously be brought and maintained against it is that of such occasional obscurity or difficulty as may arise from excessive strictness in condensation of phrase and expurgation of matter not always superfluous, and sometimes almost indispensable. His English prose and his Latin verse are perhaps more frequently and more gravely liable to this charge than either his English verse or his Latin prose. At times it is wellnigh impossible for an eye less keen and swift, a scholarship less exquisite and ready than his own, to catch the precise direction and follow the perfect course of his rapid thought and radiant utterance. This apparently studious pursuit and preference of the most terse and elliptic expression which could be found for anything he might have to say could not but occasionally make even so sovereign a master of two great languages appear 'dark with excess of light';[5] but from no former master of either tongue in prose or verse was ever the quality of real obscurity, of loose and nebulous incertitude, more utterly alien or more naturally remote. There is nothing of cloud or fog about the path on which he leads us; but we feel now and then the want of a bridge or a hand-rail; we have to leap from point to point of narrative or argument without the usual help of a connecting plank. Even in his dramatic works, where least of all it should have been found, this lack of visible connection or sequence in details of thought or action is too often a source of sensible perplexity. In his noble trilogy on the history of Giovanna Queen of Naples it is sometimes actually difficult to realize on a first reading what has happened or is happening, or how, or why, or by what agency—a defect alone sufficient, but unhappily sufficient in itself, to explain the too general ignorance of a work so rich in subtle and noble treatment of character, so sure and strong in its grasp and rendering of 'high actions and high passions',[6] so rich in humour and in pathos, so royally serene in its commanding power upon the tragic mainsprings of terror and of pity. As a poet, he may be said on the whole to stand midway between Byron and Shelley,—about as far above the former as below the latter. If we except Catullus and Simonides, it might be hard to match and it would be impossible to overmatch the flawless and blameless yet living and breathing beauty of his most perfect elegies, epigrams, or epitaphs. As truly as prettily was he likened by Leigh Hunt 'to a stormy mountain pine which should produce lilies'.[7] His passionate compassion, his bitter and burning pity for all wrongs endured in all the world, found only their natural and inevitable outlet in his lifelong defence or advocacy of tyrannicide as the last resource of baffled justice, the last discharge of heroic duty. His tender and ardent love of children, of animals, and of flowers, makes fragrant alike the pages of his writing and the records of his life. He was as surely the most gentle and generous as the most headstrong and hot-headed of heroes or of men. Nor ever was any man's best work more thoroughly imbued and informed with evidence of his noblest qualities. His loyalty and liberality of heart were as inexhaustible as his bounty and beneficence of hand. Praise and encouragement, deserved or undeserved, came yet more readily to his lips than challenge or defiance. Reviled and ridiculed by Lord Byron, he retorted on the offender living less readily and less warmly than he lamented and extolled him dead. On the noble dramatic works of his brother Robert he lavished a magnificence of sympathetic praise which his utmost self-estimate would never have exacted for his own. Age and the lapse of time could neither heighten nor lessen the fullness of this rich and ready generosity. To the poets of his own and of the next generation he was not readier to do honour than to those of a later growth, and not seldom of deserts far lower and far lesser claims than theirs. That he was not unconscious of his own, and avowed it with the frank simplicity of nobler times, is not more evident or more certain than that in comparison with his friends and fellows he was liable rather to undervalue than to overrate himself. He was a classic, and no formalist; the wide range of his just and loyal admiration had room for a genius so far from classical as Blake's. Nor in his own highest mood or method of creative as of critical work was he a classic only, in any narrow or exclusive sense of the term. On either side, immediately or hardly below his mighty masterpiece of *Pericles and Aspasia*, stand the two scarcely less beautiful and vivid studies of mediæval Italy and Shakespearean England. The very finest flower of his immortal dialogues is probably to be found in the single volume comprising only 'Imaginary Conversations of Greeks and Romans'; his utmost command of passion and pathos may be tested by its transcendent success in the distilled and concentrated tragedy of 'Tiberius and Vipsania', where for once he shows a quality more proper to romantic than classical imagination—the subtle and sublime and terrible power to enter the dark vestibule of distraction, to throw the whole force of his fancy, the whole fire of his spirit, into the 'shadowing passion'[8] (as Shakespeare calls it) of gradually imminent insanity. Yet, if this and all other studies from ancient history or legend could be subtracted from the volume of his work, enough would be left whereon to rest the foundation of a fame which time could not sensibly impair.

NOTES

1 The Convention of Cintra (1808) allowed the French army, defeated by the British and Portuguese during the Peninsular War, to return home.
2 John Forster, *Walter Savage Landor* (London, 1876), 119.
3 *Ibid.*, 191.
4 *Twelfth Night*, III, iv, 31.
5 Cf. Gray's 'Progress of Poesy', iii, 2, l. 7: 'blasted with excess of light', and Milton's *Paradise Lost*, iii, 380, 'dark with excessive bright'.
6 *Paradise Regained*, iv, 266.
7 *Lord Byron and Some of His Contemporaries* (London, 1828), 496; cited by R. H. Super, *Walter Savage Landor: A Biography* (New York, 1954), 544 n. 7.
8 *Othello*, IV, i, 41.

14 Robert Herrick
1891, 1894

'Robert Herrick' introduced the Muses' Library edition of Herrick (1891). It was reprinted in *Studies in Prose and Poetry* (1894). Swinburne measures Herrick by a criterion he often uses—for instance, in his criticism of the older dramatists—aptitude in the writing of song. The essay is a tribute to a master of song by a poet who himself wrote one of the finest songs in English ('Love laid his sleepless head').

It is singular that the first great age of English lyric poetry should have been also the one great age of English dramatic poetry; but it is hardly less singular that the lyric school should have advanced as steadily as the dramatic school declined from the promise of its dawn. Born with Marlowe, it rose at once with Shakespeare to heights inaccessible before and since and for ever, to sink through bright gradations of glorious decline to its final and beautiful sunset in Shirley; but the lyrical record that begins with the author of *Euphues* and *Endymion* grows fuller if not brighter through a whole chain of constellations, till it culminates in the crowning star of Herrick. Shakespeare's last song, the exquisite and magnificent overture to *The Two Noble Kinsmen*, is hardly so limpid in its flow, so liquid in its melody, as the two great songs in *Valentinian*;[1] but Herrick, our last poet of that incomparable age or generation, has matched them again and again. As a creative and inventive singer he surpasses all his rivals in quantity of good work; in quality of spontaneous instinct and melodious inspiration he reminds us, by frequent and flawless evidence, who, above all others, must beyond all doubt have been his first master and his first model in lyric poetry—the author of 'The Passionate Shepherd to his Love'.[2]

The last of his line, he is and will probably be always the first in rank and station of English song-writers. We have only to remember how rare it is to find a perfect song, good to read and good to sing, combining the merits of Coleridge and Shelley with the capabilities of Tommy Moore and Haynes Bayly,[3] to appreciate the unique and unapproachable excellence of Herrick. The lyrist who wished to be a butterfly, the lyrist who fled or flew to a lone vale at the hour (whatever hour it may be) 'when stars are weeping', have left behind them such stuff as may be sung, but certainly cannot be read and endured by any one with an ear for verse. The author of the Ode on France and the author of the Ode to the West Wind have left us hardly more than a song apiece which has been found fit for setting to music; and, lovely as they are, the fame of their authors does not mainly depend on the song of Glycine[4] or the song of which Leigh Hunt so justly and so critically said that Beaumont and Fletcher never wrote anything of the kind more lovely.[5] Herrick, of course, lives simply by virtue of his songs; his more ambitious or pretentious lyrics are merely magnified and prolonged and elaborated songs. Elegy or litany, epicede or epithalamium, his work is always a song-writer's; nothing more, but nothing less, than the work of the greatest song-writer—as surely as Shakespeare is the greatest dramatist—ever born of English race. The apparent or external variety of his versification is, I should suppose, incomparable; but by some happy tact or instinct he was too naturally unambitious to attempt, like Jonson, a flight in the wake of Pindar. He knew what he could not do: a rare and invaluable gift. Born a blackbird or a thrush, he did not take himself (or try) to be a nightingale.

It has often been objected that he did mistake himself for a sacred poet; and it cannot be denied that his sacred verse at its worst is as offensive as his secular verse at its worst; nor can it be denied that no severer sentence of condemnation can be passed upon any poet's work. But neither Herbert nor Crashaw could have bettered such a divinely beautiful triplet as this:—

> We see Him come, and know Him ours,
> Who with His sunshine and His showers
> Turns all the patient ground to flowers.[6]

That is worthy of Miss Rossetti herself; and praise of such work can go no higher.

But even such exquisite touches or tones of colour may be too often repeated in fainter shades or more glaring notes of assiduous and facile reiteration. The sturdy student who tackles his Herrick as a schoolboy is expected to tackle his Horace, in a spirit of pertinacious and stolid straightforwardness, will probably find himself before long so nauseated by the incessant inhalation of spices and flowers, condiments and kisses, that if a musk-rat had run over the page it could hardly be less endurable to the physical than it is to the spiritual stomach. The fantastic and the brutal blemishes which deform and deface the loveliness of his incomparable genius are hardly so damaging to his fame as his general monotony of matter and of manner. It was doubtless in order to relieve this saccharine and 'mellisonant'[7] monotony that he thought fit to intersperse these interminable droppings of natural or artificial perfume with others of the rankest and most intolerable odour; but a diet of alternate sweetmeats and emetics is for the average of eaters and drinkers no less unpalatable than unwholesome. It is useless and thankless to enlarge on such faults or such defects as it would be useless and senseless to ignore. But how to enlarge, to expatiate, to insist on the charm of Herrick at his best—a charm so incomparable and so inimitable that even English poetry can boast of nothing quite like it or worthy to be named after it—the most appreciative reader will be the slowest to affirm or imagine that he can conjecture. This, however, he will hardly fail to remark: that Herrick, like most if not all other lyric poets, is not best known by his best work. If we may judge by frequency of quotation or of reference, the ballad of the ride from Ghent to Aix is a far more popular, more generally admired and accredited specimen of Mr. Browning's work than 'The Last Ride Together', and 'The Lost Leader' than 'The Lost Mistress'. Yet the superiority of the less popular poem is in either case beyond all question or comparison:[8] in depth and in glow of spirit and of harmony, in truth and charm of thought and word, undeniable and indescribable. No two men of genius were ever more unlike than the authors of *Paracelsus* and *Hesperides*; and yet it is as true of Herrick as of Browning that his best is not always his best-known work. Everyone knows the song, 'Gather ye rosebuds while ye may'; few, I fear, by comparison, know the yet sweeter and better song, 'Ye have been fresh and green'. The general monotony of style and motive which fatigues and irritates his too persevering reader is here and there relieved by a change of key which anticipates the note of a later and very different lyric school. The brilliant simplicity and pointed grace of the three stanzas to Œnone ('What conscience, say, is it in thee') recall the lyrists of the Restoration in their cleanlier and happier mood. And in the very fine epigram headed by the words, 'Devotion makes the Deity', he has expressed for once a really high and deep thought in words of really noble and severe propriety. His 'Mad Maid's Song', again, can only be compared with Blake's, which has more of passionate imagination if less of pathetic sincerity.

NOTES

1 A play by John Fletcher.
2 Christopher Marlowe.
3 Once regarded as 'next to Moore, the most successful song-writer of our age', the author of 'I'd be a butterfly'. Thomas Moore (1779–1852) wrote better lyrics than the one referred to.
4 In Coleridge's *Zapolya*, Part II, II, i.
5 Hunt's comment, in his selections from Shelley in *Imagination and Fancy*, concerns Shelley's 'Music, when soft voices die'.
6 'A Christmas Caroll, Sung to the King in the Presence at White-Hall', ll. 22–4.
7 'Sweet-sounding', used by Thomas Randolph in *Amyntas*, V, iv.
8 The colon is used in the Muses' Library edition; *Studies in Prose and Poetry* has a semicolon.

Fiction

15 The Brontës

1877

On 26 September 1877 Swinburne wrote: 'From the first hour when as a schoolboy I read *Jane Eyre* and *Wuthering Heights* I have always retained the first intense desire I felt then to know . . . about the two women who wrote them' (Lang, iv, 21). Letters by Charlotte Brontë, supplying new biographical information, had recently been published. *A Note on Charlotte Brontë*, which contained the extracts below, was begun with the thought that it could be an article for the *Athenaeum*; as in similar instances, it grew too bulky. In May 1877 Swinburne wrote of it as 'my most serious and principal work of this winter—indeed, for the last six months' (Lang, iv, 2). Review copies were sent out before 1 September. The book was reissued in 1894.

Swinburne emphasized a contrast between Charlotte Brontë and George Eliot partly because of the vogue of the latter and the relative undervaluation of the former. He has had a decided impact on the critical fortunes of the Brontës.

There is no surer test as there can be no higher evidence than this of that imperative and primary genius which holds its power in fee of no other mind, which derives of no foreign stream through the conduit of no alien channel. Perhaps we may reasonably divide all imaginative work into three classes; the lowest, which leaves us in a complacent mood of acquiescence with the graceful or natural inventions and fancies of an honest and ingenious workman, and in no mind to question or dispute the accuracy of his transcript from life or the fidelity of his design to the modesty and the likelihood of nature; the second, of high enough quality to engage our judgment in its service, and make direct demand on our grave attention for deliberate assent or dissent; the third, which in the exercise of its highest faculties at their best neither solicits nor seduces nor provokes us to acquiescence or demur, but compels us without question to positive acceptance and belief. Of the first class it would be superfluous to cite instances from among writers of our own day, not undeserving of serious respect and of genuine gratitude for much honest work done and honest pleasure conferred on us. Of the second order our literature has no more apt and brilliant examples than George Eliot and George Meredith. Of the third, if in such a matter as this I may trust my own instinct—that last resource and ultimate reason of all critics in every case and on every question—there is no clearer and more positive instance in the whole world of letters than that supplied by the genius of Charlotte Brontë.

I do not mean that such an instance is to be found in the treatment of each figure in each of her great three books. If this could accurately be said, it could not reasonably be denied that she might justly claim and must naturally assume that seat by the side of Shakespeare which certain critics of the hour are prompt alike to assign alternately to the author of *Adam Bede* and to the author of *Queen Mary*. Only in the eyes of such critics as these, or in the glassy substitutes which serve their singular kind as proxies for a human squint, will it seem to imply a want of serious interest and respect in the former direction, of loyal and grateful admiration in the latter, if I confess that to my unaided organs and limited capacities of sight the one comparison appears as portentously farcical as the other in its superhuman or subsimious absurdity; that I should find it as hard an article of religion to digest and assimilate into the body of a living faith, which bade me believe in the assumption of the goddess as that which bade me believe in the ascension of the god to complete the co-eternal and co-equal personality of English genius at its highest apogee, in its triune and bisexual apotheosis. But, without putting in a claim for the author of *Jane Eyre* as qualified to ascend the height on which a minority of not overwise admirers would fain enthrone a demigoddess of more dubious divinity than hers, I must take leave to reiterate my conviction that no living English or female writer can rationally be held her equal in what I cannot but regard as the highest and the rarest quality which supplies the hardest and the surest proof of a great and absolute genius for the painting and the handling of human characters in mutual relation and reaction. Even the glorious mistress of all forms and powers of imaginative prose, who has lately left France afresh in mourning—even George Sand herself had not this gift in like measure with those great twin sisters in genius who were born to the stern and strong-hearted old Rector of Haworth.

The gift of which I would speak is that of a power to make us feel in every nerve, at every step forward which our imagination is compelled to take under the guidance of another's, that thus and not otherwise, but in all things altogether even as we are told and shown, it was and it must have been with the human figures set before us in their action and their suffering; that thus and not otherwise they absolutely must and would have felt and thought and spoken under the proposed conditions. It is something for a writer to have achieved if he has made it worth our fancy's while to consider by the light of imaginative reason whether the creatures of his own fancy would in actual fact and life have done as he has made them do or not; it is something, and by comparison it is much. But no definite terms of comparison will suffice to express how much more than this it is to have done what the youngest of capable readers must feel on first opening *Jane Eyre* that the writer of its very first pages has shown herself competent to do. In almost all other great works of its kind, in almost all the sovereign masterpieces even of Fielding, of Thackeray, of the royal and imperial master, Sir Walter Scott himself—to whose glorious memory I need offer no apology for the attribution of epithets which I cannot but regret to remember that even in their vulgar sense he would not have regarded as other than terms of honour—even in the best and greatest works of these our best and greatest we do not find this one great good quality so innate, so immanent as in hers. At most we find the combination of event with character, the coincidence of action with disposition, the coherence of consequences with emotions, to be rationally credible and acceptable to the natural sense of a reasonable faith. We rarely or never feel that, given the characters, the incidents become inevitable; that such passion must needs bring forth none other than such action, such emotions cannot choose but find their only issue in such events. And certainly we do not feel, what it seems to me the highest triumph of inspired intelligence and creative instinct to succeed in making us feel, that the mainspring of all, the central relation of the whole, 'the very pulse of the machine',[1] has in it this occult inexplicable force of nature. But when Catherine Earnshaw says to Nellie Dean, 'I *am* Heathcliff!'[2] and when Jane Eyre answers Edward Rochester's question, whether she feels in him the absolute sense of fitness and correspondence to herself which he feels to himself in her, with the words which close and crown the history of their twin-born spirits—'To the finest fibre of my nature, sir'[3]—we feel to the finest fibre of our own that these are no mere words. On this ground at least it might for once be not unpardonable to borrow their standing reference or illustration from that comparative school of critics whose habit of comparison we have treated with something less than respect, and say, as was said on another score of Emily Brontë in particular by Sydney Dobell, in an admirable paper[4] which we miss with regret and with surprise from among the costly relics of his genius, so lovingly set in order and so ably lighted up by the faithful friendship and the loyal intelligence of Professor Nichol—that either sister in this single point 'has done no less' than Shakespeare. As easily might we imagine a change of the mutual relations between the characters of Shakespeare as a corresponding revolution or reversal of conditions among theirs.

If I turn again for contrast or comparison with their works to the work of George Eliot, it will be attributed by no one above the spiritual rank and type of Pope's representative dunces to irreverence or ingratitude for the large and liberal beneficence of her genius at its best. But she alone among our living writers is generally admitted or assumed as the rightful occupant, or at least as the legitimate claimant, of that foremost place in the front rank of artists in this kind which none can hold or claim without challenging such comparison or such contrast. And in some points it is undeniable that she may claim precedence, not of these alone, but of all other illustrious women. Such wealth and depth of thoughtful and fruitful humour, of vital and various intelligence, no woman has ever shown—no woman perhaps has ever shown a tithe of it. In knowledge, in culture, perhaps in capacity for knowledge and for culture, Charlotte Brontë was no more comparable to George Eliot than George Eliot is comparable to Charlotte Brontë in purity of passion, in depth and ardour of feeling, in spiritual force and fervour of forthright inspiration. It would be rather a rough and sweeping than a loose or inaccurate division which should define the one as a type of genius distinguished from intellect, the other of intellect as opposed to genius. But it would, as I venture to think, be little or nothing more or less than accurate to recognise in George Eliot a type of intelligence vivified and coloured by a vein of genius, in Charlotte Brontë a type of genius directed and moulded by the touch of intelligence. No better test of this distinction could be desired than a comparison of their respective shortcomings or failures. These will serve, by their difference in kind and import, in quality and in weight, to show the depth and width of the great gulf between pure genius and pure intellect, even better than a comparison of their highest merits and achievements. . . .

Most children, I suppose, who are at once given to dreaming and capable of devotion, must know the mood of loyal fancy and tender ardour so perfectly expressed in the wish of Mrs. Gaskell's little Maggie[5] that she could have waited as a servant on Don Quixote; and the feeling is akin to this with which at a later age any one of kindred nature, on their first intimate acquaintance, and in a great degree ever after, is certain to regard M. Paul. Supreme as is the spiritual triumph of Cervantes in the person of his perfect knight over all insult and mockery of brutal chance and ruffianly realities, all cudgels and all cheats and all contumely, it is hardly a more marvellous or a completer example of imaginative and moral mastery than the triumph of Charlotte Brontë in the quaint person of her grim little Professor over his own eccentric infirmities of habit and temper, more hazardous to our sense of respect than any outward risk or infliction of alien violence or mockery from duchesses or muleteers; a triumph so naturally drawn out and delicately displayed in the swift steady gradations of change and development, now ludicrous and now attractive, and wellnigh adorable at last, through which the figure of M. Paul seems to pass as under summer lights and shadows, till it gradually opens upon us in human fullness of self-unconscious charm and almost sacred beauty—yet always with the sense of some latent infusion, some tender native admixture of a quality at once loveable and laughable; with something indeed of that quaint sweet kind of earnest affection and half-smiling veneration which all men fit to read him feel to their 'heart's root'[6] for the person even more than for the writings of Charles Lamb. That our smile should in no wise impair for one instant our reverence, that our reverence should in no wise make us abashed or ashamed for one moment at the recollection of our smile—this is the final test and triumph of a genius to which we find no likeness outside the very highest rank of creators in the sphere of spiritual invention or of moral imagination.

All who have ever read it will remember the exquisite saying of Chateaubriand so exquisitely rendered by Mr. Arnold:—'The true tears are those which are called forth by the beauty of poetry; there must be as much admiration in them as sorrow.'[7] The true tears are also those of a yet rarer kind, which are called up at least, if not called forth, by the beauty of goodness; and in such unshed tears as these are the thoughts as it were baptised, which attend upon our memory of some few among the imperishable shadows of men created by man's genius; phantoms more actual and vital than the creators they outlive, as mankind outlives the gods of its own creation. There is or should be for all men such consecration in a great man's tears as cannot but glorify the source and embalm the subject of their flow. We may even, and not unreasonably, suspect and fear that it must be through some defect or default in ourselves if we cannot feel as they do the force or charm of that which touches others, and these our betters as often as our equals, so nearly; if we cannot, for example,—as I may regretfully confess that I never could—feel adequately or in full the bitter sweetness that so many thousands—and most notably among them all a better man by far and a far worthier judge than I—have tasted in those pages of Dickens which hold the story of Little Nell;[8] a story in which all the elaborate accumulation of pathetic incident and interest, so tenderly and studiously built up, has never, to speak truth, given me one passing thrill—in the exquisitely fit and faithful phrase of a great living poet, one 'sweet possessive pang'[9]—of the tender delight and pity requickened wellnigh to tears at every fresh reperusal or chance recollection of that one simpler page in *Bleak House* which describes the baby household tended by the little sister who leaves her lesser charges locked up while she goes out charring; a page which I can imagine that many a man unused to the melting mood would not undertake to read out aloud without a break. But this inability to feel with those who have been most deeply moved by the earlier design of the same great master—sovereign over all competitors of his country and his day in the conterminous provinces of laughter and of tears—this incompetence or obduracy of temper is anything but a source of self-complacent satisfaction when I remember that foremost among these was the illustrious man of lion-hearted genius who but thirteen years since was still our greatest countryman surviving from an age of godlike giants and gods as yet but half divine; the Roman who best knew Greece, the Englishman who best loved England; the friend of Pericles and of Chatham, the associate of Sophocles and of Shakespeare; the heroic poet who retained at the age of Nestor whatever qualities were noblest in the nature of Achilles—all the lightnings of his mortal wrath, and all the tenderness of his immortal tears.

It is certainly no subject for a boast—perhaps it properly should rather be matter for a blush—that Landor's little favourite among all the deathless children begotten by the genius of Dickens should never have had power to work such transformation on my eyes as many a line of his own in verse or prose has wrought so many a time upon them: for if ever that sovereign power of perfection was made manifest in human words, such words assuredly were his, whether English or Latin, who wrote that epitaph on the martyred patriots of Spain,[10] as far exceeding in its majesty of beauty the famous inscription for the Spartan three hundred as the law of the love of liberty exceeds all human laws of mere obedience; who gave back Iphigenia to Agamemnon for ever, and Vipsania for an hour to Tiberius.[11] Before the breath of such a spirit as speaks in his transcendent words, the spirit of a loyal-minded man is bowed down as it were at a touch and melted into burning tears, to be again raised up by it and filled and kindled and expanded into something—or he dreams so—of a likeness for the moment to itself.

Some portion of a faculty such as this, some touch of the same godlike and wonder-working might of imperious moral quality, some flush of the same divine and plenary inspiration, there was likewise in the noble genius and heroic instinct of Charlotte Brontë. Some part of the power denied to many a writer of more keen and rare intelligence than even hers we feel 'to the finest fibre of our nature' at the slight strong touch of her magnetic hand. The phrase of 'passionate perfection',[12] devised by Mr. Tennyson to describe the rarest type of highest human character, is admirably applicable to her special style at its best. The figure of the young missionary St. John Rivers is by no means to be rated as one of her great unsurpassable successes in spiritual portraiture; the central mainspring of his hard fanatic heroism is never quite adequately touched; her own apparent lack of sympathy with this white marble clergyman (counterpart, as it were, of the 'black marble'[13] Brocklehurst, who chills and darkens the dreary dawn of the story) seems here and there as though it scarcely could be held down by force of artistic conscience from passing into actual and avowed aversion; but the imperishable passion and perfection of the words describing the moorland scene of which his eyes at parting take their long last look must have drawn the tears to many another man's that his own were not soft enough to shed.

This instinct (if I may so call it) for the tragic use of landscape was wellnigh even more potent and conspicuous in Emily than in Charlotte. Little need was there for the survivor to tell us in such earnest and tender words of memorial record how 'my sister Emily loved the moors':[14] that love exhales, as a fresh wild odour from a bleak shrewd soil, from every storm-swept page of *Wuthering Heights*. All the heart of the league-long billows of rolling and breathing and brightening heather is blown with the breath of it on our faces as we read; all the wind and all the sound and all the fragrance and freedom and gloom and glory of the high north moorland—'in winter nothing more dreary, in summer nothing more divine'.[15] Even in Charlotte Brontë's highest work I find no touches of such exquisite strength and triumphant simplicity as here. There is nothing known to me in any book of quite equal or similar effect to that conveyed by one or two of these. Take for instance that marvellous note of landscape struck as it seems unconsciously by the heaven-born instinct of a supreme artist in composition and colour, in tones and shades and minor notes of tragic and magic sweetness, which serves as overture to the last fierce rapturous passage of raging love and mad recrimination between Heathcliff and the dying Catherine; the mention of the church-bell that in winter could just be heard ringing right across the naked little glen, but in summer the sound was lost, muffled by the murmur of blowing foliage and branches full of birds. The one thing I know or can remember as in some sort comparable in its effect to this passage is of course that notice of the temple-haunting martlet and its loved mansionry which serves as prelude to the entrance of Lady Macbeth from under the buttresses where its pendant bed and procreant cradle bore witness to the delicate air in which incarnate murder also was now to breed and haunt. Even more wonderful perhaps in serene perfection of subdued and sovereign power is the last brief paragraph of that stormy and fiery tale. There was a dark unconscious instinct as of primitive nature-worship in the passionate great genius of Emily Brontë, which found no corresponding quality in her sister's. It is into the lips of her representative Shirley Keeldar that Charlotte puts the fervent 'pagan' hymn of visionary praise to her mother nature—Hertha, Demeter, '*la déesse des dieux*',[16] which follows on her fearless indignant repudiation of Milton and his Eve. Nor had Charlotte's less old-world and Titanic soul any touch of the self-dependent solitary contempt for all outward objects of faith and hope, for all aspiration after a changed heart or a contrite spirit or a converted mind, which speaks in the plain-song note of Emily's clear stern verse with such grandeur of antichristian fortitude and self-controlling self-reliance, that the 'halting slave'[17] of Epaphroditus might have owned for his spiritual sister the English girl whose only prayer for herself, 'in life and death'—a self-sufficing prayer, self-answered, and fulfilled even in the utterance—was for 'a chainless soul, with courage to endure'. Not often probably has such a petition gone up from within the walls of a country parsonage as this:—

And if I pray, the only prayer
That moves my lips for me,
Is—Leave the heart that now I bear,
And give me liberty![18]

That word which is above every word might surely have been found written on that heart. Her love of earth for earth's sake, her tender loyalty and passionate reverence for the All-mother, bring to mind the words of her sister's friend, and the first eloquent champion of her own genius:—

I praise thee, mother earth! oh earth, my mother!
Oh earth, sweet mother! gentle mother earth!
Whence thou receivest what thou givest I
Ask not as a child asketh not his mother,
Oh earth, my mother![19]

No other poet's imagination could have conceived that agony of the girl who dreams she is in heaven, and weeps so bitterly for the loss of earth that the angels cast her out in anger, and she finds herself fallen on the moss and heather of the mid moor-head, and wakes herself with sobbing for joy.[20] It is possible that to take full delight in Emily Brontë's book one must have something by natural inheritance of her instinct and something by earliest association of her love for the same special points of earth—the same lights and sounds and colours and odours and sights and shapes of the same fierce free landscape of tenantless and fruitless and fenceless moor; but however that may be, it was assuredly with no less justice of insight and accuracy of judgment than humility of self-knowledge and fidelity of love that Charlotte in her day of solitary fame assigned to her dead sister the crown of poetic honour which she as rightfully disclaimed for herself. Full of poetic quality as her own work is throughout, that quality is never condensed or crystallised into the proper and final form of verse. But the pure note of absolutely right expression for things inexpressible in full by prose at its highest point of adequacy—the formal inspiration of sound which at once reveals itself, and which can fully reveal itself by metrical embodiment alone, in the symphonies and antiphonies of regular word-music and definite instinctive modulation of corresponsive tones—this is what Emily had for her birthright as certainly as Charlotte had it not. Here are a few lines to give evidence for themselves on that score.

He comes with western winds, with evening's wandering airs,
With that clear dusk of heaven that brings the thickest stars.
Winds take a pensive tone, and stars a tender fire,
And visions rise, and change, that kill me with desire.

Desire for nothing known in my maturer years,
When Joy grew mad with awe, at counting future tears.

. . . .

Oh, dreadful is the check—intense the agony—
When the ear begins to hear, and the eye begins to see;
When the pulse begins to throb, the brain to think again,
The soul to feel the flesh, and the flesh to feel the chain.[21]

If here is not the pure distinctive note of song as opposed to speech—the 'lyrical cry', as Mr. Arnold calls it—I know not where to seek it in English verse since Shelley. Another such unmistakable note is struck in the verses headed 'Remembrance', where the deep sense of division wellnigh melts and dies into a dream of reunion and revival by the might of memories 'that are most dearly sweet and bitter'. Here too is the same profound perception of an abiding power, but little less if surely less than omnipotence, in the old dumb divinities of Earth and Time—gods only not yet found strong enough to divide long love from death;

Severed at last by Time's all-severing wave.

All these samples are from the little triune publication of 1846;[22] which gave also some witness of the latent and labouring powers, as yet unsure of aim and outlet, but feeling their unquiet way to right and left in the deep underworld of Charlotte Brontë's growing genius. But the final expression in verse of Emily's passionate and inspired intelligence was to be uttered from lips already whitened though not yet chilled by the present shadow of unterrifying death. No last words of poet or hero or sage or saint were ever worthy of longer and more reverent remembrance than that appeal which is so far above and beyond a prayer to the indestructible God within herself; a psalm of trust so strangely (as it seems) compounded of personal and pantheistic faith, at once fiery and solemn, full alike of resignation and of rapture, far alike from the conventions of vulgar piety and the complacencies of scientific limitation; as utterly disdainful of doctrine as of doubt, as contemptuous of hearsay as reverent of itself, as wholly stripped and cleared and lightened from all burdens and all bandages and all incrustations of creed as it is utterly pervaded and possessed by the sublime and irrefutable passion of belief.

The praise of Emily Brontë can be no alien or discursive episode in the briefest and most cursory notice, the least adequate or exhaustive panegyric of her sister; and far less would it have seemed less than indispensable to that most faithful and devoted spirit of indomitable love which kept such constant watch over her memory, and fought so good a fight for her fame. There is no more significant or memorable touch of nature in the records of her noble soul and unalterable heart than we find in her instant and her lifelong thankfulness for the fervent tribute of Mr. Dobell to the profound and subtle genius, then already fallen still and silent, which had moved as a wind upon the tragic and perilous waters of passion overtopped by the shadow of *Wuthering Heights*. Those who would understand Charlotte, even more than those who would understand Emily, should study the difference of tenderness between the touch that drew Shirley Keeldar and the touch that drew Lucy Snowe. This latter figure, as Mr. Wemyss Reid has observed with indisputable accuracy of insight,[23] was doubtless, if never meant to win liking or made to find favour in the general reader's eyes, yet none the less evidently on that account the faithful likeness of Charlotte Brontë, studied from the life, and painted by her own hand with the sharp austere precision of a photograph rather than a portrait. But it is herself with the consolation and support of her genius withdrawn, with the strength of her spiritual arm immeasurably shortened, the cunning of her right hand comparatively cancelled; and this it is that makes the main undertone and ultimate result of the book somewhat mournfuller even than the literal record of her mournful and glorious life. In the house where I now write this there is a picture which I have known through all the years I can remember—a landscape by Crome;[24] showing just a wild sad track of shoreward brushwood and chill fen, blasted and wasted by the bitter breath of the east wind blowing off the eastward sea, shrivelled and subdued and resigned as it were with a sort of grim submission to the dumb dark tyranny of a full-charged thundercloud which masks the mid heaven of midnoon with the heavy muffler of midnight, and leaves but here and there a dull fierce gleam of discomfortable and deadened sunlight along the haggard sky-line or below it. As with all this it is yet always a pleasure to look upon so beautiful and noble a study of so sad and harsh-featured an outlying byway through the weariest waste places of the world, so is it in its kind a perpetual pleasure to revisit the wellnigh sunless landscape of Lucy Snowe's sad, passionate, and valiant life. But to us, knowing what we all now know of the designer, there seems a touch of pathos beyond all articulate expression in the contrast, when we turn from this to the ideal decoration of Shirley Keeldar's, and remember that here is the vision of the life she would fain have realized for her dead and best beloved and most dearly honoured sister; who had had in the days of her actual life as harsh and strange a time of it as her own. From the character of Shirley, as from the character of Lucy Snowe, the artist has naturally as of necessity withdrawn the component element that in its effect and result at least was or is for us now the dominant and distinctive quality of Emily Brontë as of Charlotte—the special gift and application of her creative genius; and on the other hand we can barely imagine that austere and fiery poetess, a creature so admirably and terribly compounded of tragic genius and Stoic heroism, a jester of pleasantry so bitter and so grim in those brief bleak flashes of northern humour that lighten across the byways of her book from the rigid old lips of the Calvinist farm-servant—we can barely, I say, conceive of her as exchanging such rapid passes of light bright fence in a laughing war of words with the reverend and gallant old Cossack Helstone as sharpen and quicken the dialogue and action of the most gracious and joyous interlude in *Shirley*. Yet surely Charlotte should have known as well as she loved her sister; and therefore we may more reasonably and more confidently infer that but for the brilliant study of Shirley Keeldar we should never have seen with the eye of our imagination any other than a misconceived and mutilated portrait, a disfigured and discoloured likeness of Emily Brontë; one curtailed of the fair proportions, if not diminished from the natural stature of her spirit; discrowned and disinherited of its livelier and gentler charm of living feature, though not degraded or dethroned from the august succession to their strength for endurance or rebellion most beseeming a lineal daughter of the earth-born giants, more ancient in their godlike lineage than all modern reigning gods.

The habit of direct study from life which has given us, among its finest and most precious results, these two contrasted figures of Shirley Keeldar and Lucy Snowe, affords yet another point of contrast or distinction between the manner and motive of work respectively perceptible in the design of either sister. Emily Brontë, like William Blake, would probably have said, or at least would presumably have felt, that such study after the model was to her impossible—

an attempt but too certain to diminish her imaginative insight and disable her creative hand; while Charlotte evidently never worked so well as when painting more or less directly from nature. Almost the only apparent exception, as far as we—the run of her readers—know, is the wonderful and incomparable figure of Rochester. For M. Paul she must have had some kind of model, however transfigured and dilated by the splendid influence of her own genius; for such studies as Madame Beck and Miss Fanshawe she doubtless had the sitters in her mind's eye as clearly and as close as under the lens of a photographic machine; but how she came first to conceive and finally to fashion that perfect study of noble and faultful and suffering manhood remains one of the most insoluble riddles ever set by genius as a snare or planned as a maze for the judgment of any lesser intelligence than its own. There in any case is the result—alive at all events, and deathless; defiant alike of explanation or reproduction by any critic or copyist.

NOTES

1 Wordsworth, 'She was a Phantom of delight', l. 22.
2 In *Wuthering Heights*, chapter 9.
3 In the next to the last chapter of *Jane Eyre*.
4 Dobell's article in the *Palladium* for September 1850 was reprinted in *The Life and Letters of Sydney Dobell* (London, 1878), i, 163–86. Dobell assumed that the two novels now known to be by Charlotte and Emily respectively were both the work of 'Currer Bell' (Charlotte's pseudonym).
5 In 'The Moorland Cottage'.
6 Cf. Chaucer's *Wife of Bath's Prologue*, l. 471: 'It tikleth me aboute myn herte roote.'
7 In Arnold's essay on Joubert, *Essays in Criticism*.
8 *The Old Curiosity Shop*.
9 From D. G. Rossetti's sonnet 'For an Allegorical Dance of Women. By Andrea Mantegna', l. 3.
10 'For a Gravestone in Spain', *Poems*, ed. Stephen Wheeler, iv (*Complete Works*, xvi), 41; first published in *Heroic Idyls* (1863).
11 In 'The Shades of Agamemnon and of Iphigeneia' (*Dramas and Dramatic Scenes*; originally in *Pericles and Aspasia*, 1836) and in 'Tiberius and Vipsania', *Imaginary Conversations*.
12 From 'Lancelot and Elaine', l. 122.
13 In *Jane Eyre*, chapter 4, Jane 'looked up at—a black pillar!'—a grown man with a 'stony face', who later proved to be, in chapter 7, where the

phrase 'black marble' describes him, the sanctimonious and harsh treasurer and manager of Lowood.

14 From Charlotte Brontë's introduction to Emily's poems.

15 From *Wuthering Heights*, chapter 32.

16 'The goddess of the gods'; from Victor Hugo's '*Hymne*', l. 106, in *La Légende des Siècles*, I.

17 Said of Epictetus in Arnold's sonnet 'To a Friend'.

18 From Emily Brontë's 'The Old Stoic'.

19 From scene xxiv of Sydney Dobell's *Balder* (London, 1854), 131.

20 In chapter 9 of *Wuthering Heights*.

21 From 'The Prisoner: A Fragment'.

22 *Poems by Currer, Ellis, and Acton Bell.*

23 T. Wemyss Reid, *Charlotte Brontë: A Monograph* (London, 1877), 62.

24 Probably John Crome (1768–1821).

16 Emily Brontë
1883, 1886

The essay on Emily Brontë, who had been considered along with Charlotte in *A Note on Charlotte Brontë*, was published in the *Athenaeum* for 16 June 1883, as a review of Miss Robinson's biography, and in *Miscellanies* (1886). Swinburne's letter to T. Wemyss Reid of 26 September 1877 (Lang, iv, 21–2) contains an interesting defence of the realism of the 'law-defying passion and tyranny' in *Wuthering Heights.*

To the England of our own time, it has often enough been remarked, the novel is what the drama was to the England of Shakespeare's. The same general interest produces the same incessant demand for the same inexhaustible supply of imaginative produce, in a shape more suited to the genius of a later day and the conditions of a changed society. Assuming this simple explanation to be sufficient for the obvious fact that in the modern world of English letters the novel is everywhere and the drama is nowhere, we may remark one radical point of difference between the taste of playgoers in the age of Shakespeare and the taste of novel-readers in our own. Tragedy was then at least as popular as either romantic or realistic comedy; whereas nothing would seem to be more unpopular with the run of modern readers than the threatening shadow of tragedy projected across the whole length of a story, inevitable and unmistakable from the lurid harshness of its dawn to the fiery softness of its sunset. The objection to a novel in which the tragic element has an air of incongruity and caprice—in which a tragic surprise is, as it were, sprung upon the reader, with a jarring shock such as might be given by the actual news of some unforeseen and grievous accident—this objection seems to me thoroughly reasonable, grounded on a true critical sense of fitness and unfitness; but the distaste for high and pure tragedy, where the close is in perfect and simple harmony with the opening, seems not less thoroughly pitiable and irrational.

A later work of indisputable power, in which the freshness of humour is as real and vital as the fervour of passion, was at once on its appearance compared with Emily Brontë's now famous story. And certainly not without good cause; for in point of local colour *Mehalah*[1] is, as far as I know, the one other book which can bear and may challenge the comparison. Its pages, for one thing, reflect the sterile glitter and desolate fascination of the salt marshes, their minute splendours and barren beauties and multitudinous monotony of measureless expanse, with the same instinctive and unlaborious accuracy which brings all the moorland before us in a breath when we open any chapter of *Wuthering Heights*. But the accumulated horrors of the close, however possible in fact, are wanting in the one quality which justifies and ennobles all admissible horror in fiction: they hardly seem inevitable; they lack the impression of logical and moral certitude. All the realism in the world will not suffice to convey this impression: and a work of art which wants it wants the one final and irreplaceable requisite of inner harmony. Now in *Wuthering Heights* this one thing needful is as perfectly and triumphantly attained as in *King Lear* or *The Duchess of Malfy*, in *The Bride of Lammermoor* or *Notre-Dame de Paris*. From the first we breathe the fresh dark air of tragic passion and presage; and to the last the changing wind and flying sunlight are in keeping with the stormy promise of the dawn. There is no monotony, there is no repetition, but there is no discord. This is the first and last necessity, the foundation of all labour and the crown of all success, for a poem worthy of the name; and this it is that distinguishes the hand of Emily from the hand of Charlotte Brontë. All the works of the elder sister are rich in poetic spirit, poetic feeling, and poetic detail; but the younger sister's work is essentially and definitely a poem in the fullest and most positive sense of the term. It was therefore all the more proper that the honour of raising a biographical and critical monument to the author of *Wuthering Heights* should have been reserved for a poetess of the next generation to her own. And those who had already in their mind's eye the clearest and most definite conception of Emily Brontë will be the readiest to acknowledge their obligation and express their gratitude to Miss Robinson for the additional light which she has been enabled to throw upon a great and singular character. It is true that when all has been said the main features of that character stand out before us unchanged. The sweet and noble genius of Mrs. Gaskell did not en-able her to see far into so strange and sublime a problem; but, after all, the main difference between the biographer of Emily and the biographer of Charlotte is that Miss Robinson has been interested and attracted where Mrs. Gaskell was scared and perplexed. On one point, however, the new light afforded us is of the very utmost value and interest. We all knew how great was Emily Brontë's tenderness for the lower animals; we find, with surprise as well as admiration, that the range of this charity was so vast as to include even her own miserable brother. Of that lamentable and contemptible caitiff—contemptible not so much for his commonplace debauchery as for his abject selfishness, his lying pretention, and his nerveless cowardice—there is far too much in this memoir: it is inconceivable how any one can have put into a lady's hand such a letter as one which defaces two pages of the volume, and it may be permissible to regret that a lady should have made it public; but this error is almost atoned for by the revelation that of all the three sisters in that silent home 'it was the silent Emily who had ever a cheering word for Branwell; it was Emily who still remembered that he was her brother, without that remembrance freezing her heart to numbness.'[2] That she saved his life from fire, and hid from their father the knowledge of her heroism, no one who knows anything of Emily Brontë will learn with any mixture of surprise in his sense of admiration; but it gives a new tone and colour to our sympathetic and reverent regard for her noble memory when we find in the depth of that self-reliant and stoic nature a fountain so inexhaustible of such Christlike longsuffering and compassion.

I cannot however but think that Miss Robinson makes a little too much of the influence exercised on Emily Brontë's work by the bitter, narrow, and ignoble misery of the life which she had watched burn down into such pitiful ruin that its memory is hardly redeemed by the last strange and inconsistent flash of expiring manhood which forbids us to regard with unmixed contempt the sufferer who had resolution enough to die standing if he had lived prostrate, and so make at the very last a manful end of an abject history. The impression of this miserable experience is visible only in Anne Brontë's second work, *The Tenant of Wildfell Hall*; which deserves perhaps a little more notice and recognition than it has ever received. It is ludicrously weak, palpably unreal, and apparently imitative, whenever it reminds the reader that it was written by a sister of Charlotte and Emily Brontë; but as a study of utterly flaccid and invertebrate immorality it bears signs of more faithful transcription from life than anything in *Jane Eyre* or *Wuthering Heights*. On the other hand, the intelligent reader of *Wuthering Heights* cannot fail to recognize that what he is reading is a tragedy simply because it is the work of a writer whose genius is essentially tragic. Those who believe that Heathcliff was called into existence by the accident that his creator had witnessed the agonies of a violent weakling in love and in disgrace might believe that Shakespeare wrote *King Lear* because he had witnessed the bad effects of parental indulgence, and that Æschylus wrote the *Eumenides* because he had witnessed the uncomfortable results of matricide. The book is what it is because the author was what she was; this is the main and central fact to be remembered. Circumstances have modified the details; they have not implanted the conception. If there were any need for explanation there would be no room for apology. As it is, the few faults of design or execution leap to sight at a first glance, and vanish in the final effect and unimpaired impression of the whole; while those who object to the violent illegalities of conduct with regard to real or personal property on which the progress of the story does undeniably depend—'a senseless piece of glaring folly', it was once called by some critic learned in the law—might as well complain, in Carlylesque phrase, that the manners are quite other than Belgravian.

It is a fine and accurate instinct that has inevitably led Miss Robinson to cite in chosen illustration of the book's quality at its highest those two incomparable pictures of dreamland and delirium which no poet that ever lived has ever surpassed for passionate and lifelike beauty of imaginative truth. But it is even somewhat less than exact to say that the latter scene 'is given with a masterly pathos that Webster need not have made more strong, nor Fletcher more lovely and appealing'.[3] Fletcher could not have made it as lovely and appealing as it is; he would have made it exquisitely pretty and effectively theatrical; but the depth, the force, the sincerity, recalling here so vividly the 'several forms of distraction' through which Webster's Cornelia passes after the murder of her son by his brother, excel everything else of the kind in imaginative art; not excepting, if truth may be spoken on such a subject, the madness of Ophelia or even of Madge Wildfire.[4] It is hardly ever safe to say dogmatically what can or cannot be done by the rarest and highest genius; yet it must surely be borne in upon us all that these two crowning passages could never have been written by any one to whom the motherhood of earth was less than the brotherhood of man—to whom the anguish, the intolerable and mortal yearning, of insatiate and insuppressible homesickness, was less than the bitterest of all other sufferings endurable or conceivable in youth. But in Emily Brontë this passion was twin-born with the passion for truth and rectitude. The stale and futile epithet of Titaness has in this instance a deeper meaning than appears; her goddess mother was in both senses the same who gave birth to the divine martyr of Æschylean legend: Earth under one aspect and one name, but under the other Righteousness.[5] And therefore was the first and last word uttered out of the depth of her nature a cry for that one thing needful[6] without which all virtue is as worthless as all pleasure is vile, all hope as shameful as all faith is abject—a cry for liberty.

And therefore too, perhaps we may say, it is that any seeming confusion or incoherence in her work is merely external and accidental, not inward and spiritual. Belief in the personal or positive immortality of the individual and indivisible spirit was not apparently, in her case, swallowed up or nullified or made nebulous by any doctrine or dream of simple reabsorption into some indefinite infinity of eternal life. So at least it seems to me that her last ardent confession of dauntless and triumphant faith should properly be read, however capable certain phrases in it may seem of the vaguer and more impersonal interpretation. For surely no scornfuller or stronger comment on the 'unutterable' vanity of creeds[7] could pass more naturally into a chant expressive of more profound and potent faith; a song of spiritual trust more grave and deep and passionate in the solemn ardour of its appeal than the Hymn to God of Cleanthes. Her infrangible self-reliance and lonely sublimity of spirit she had in common with him and his fellows of the Porch;[8] it was much more than 'some shy ostrich prompting'[9] which bade her assign to an old Stoic the most personal and characteristic utterance in all her previous poems; but the double current of imaginative passion and practical compassion which made her a tragic poet and proved her a perfect woman gives as it were a living warmth and sweetness to her memory, such as might well have seemed incompatible with that sterner and colder veneration so long reserved for her spiritual kinsmen of the past. As a woman we never knew her so well as now that we have to welcome this worthy record of her life, with deeper thanks and warmer congratulations to the writer than can often be due even to the best of biographers and critics. As an author she has not perhaps even yet received her full due or taken her final place. Again and again has the same obvious objection been taken to that awkwardness of construction or presentation which no reader of *Wuthering Heights* can undertake to deny. But, to judge by the vigour with which this objection is urged, it might be supposed that the rules of narrative observed by all great novelists were of an almost legal or logical strictness and exactitude with regard to probability of detail. Now most assuredly the indirect method of relation through which the story of Heathcliff is conveyed, however unlikely or clumsy it may seem from the realistic point of view, does not make this narrative more liable to the charge of actual impossibility than others of the kind. Defoe still remains the one writer of narrative in the first person who has always kept the stringent law of possibilities before the eye of his invention. Even the admirable ingenuity and the singular painstaking which distinguish the method of Mr. Wilkie Collins can only give external and transient plausibility to the record of long conversations overheard or shared in by the narrator only a few hours before the supposed date of the report drawn up from memory. The very greatest masters in their kind, Walter Scott and Charles Dickens, are of all narrators the most superbly regardless of this objection. From *Rob Roy* and *Redgauntlet*, from *David Copperfield* and *Bleak House*, we might select at almost any stage of the autobiographic record some instance of detail in which the violation of plausibility, probability, or even possibility, is at least as daring and as glaring as any to be found in the narrative of Nelly Dean. Even when that narrative is removed, so to speak, yet one degree further back—even when we are supposed to be reading a minute detail of incident and dialogue transcribed by the hand of the lay figure Mr. Lockwood from Nelly Dean's report of the account conveyed to her years ago by Heathcliff's fugitive wife or gadding servant, each invested for the nonce with the peculiar force and distinctive style of the author—even then we are not asked to put such an overwhelming strain on our faculty of imaginative belief as is exacted by the great writer who invites us to accept the report drawn up by Mr. Pendennis of everything that takes place—down even to the minutest points of dialogue, accent, and gesture—in the household of the Newcomes or the Firmins[10] during the absence no less than in the presence of their friend the reporter. Yet all this we gladly and gratefully admit, without demur or cavil, to be thoroughly authentic and credible, because the whole matter of the report, however we get at it, is found when we do get at it to be vivid and lifelike as an actual experience of living fact. Here, if ever anywhere, the attainment of the end justifies the employment of the means. If we are to enjoy imaginative work at all, we must 'assume the virtue'[11] of imagination, even if we have it not; we must, as children say, 'pretend' or make believe a little as a very condition of the game.

A graver and perhaps a somewhat more plausible charge is brought against the author of *Wuthering Heights* by those who find here and there in her book the savage note or the sickly symptom of a morbid ferocity. Twice or thrice especially the details of deliberate or passionate brutality in Heathcliff's treatment of his victims make the reader feel for a moment as though he were reading a police report or even a novel by some French 'naturalist' of the latest and brutallest order. But the pervading atmosphere of the book is so high and healthy that the effect even of those 'vivid and fearful scenes'[12] which impaired the rest of Charlotte Brontë is almost at once neutralized—we may hardly say softened, but sweetened, dispersed, and transfigured—by the general impression of noble purity and passionate straightforwardness, which removes it at once and for ever from any such ugly possibility of association or comparison. The whole work is not more incomparable in the effect of its atmosphere or landscape than in the peculiar note of its wild and bitter pathos; but most of all is it unique in the special and distinctive character of its passion. The love which devours life itself, which devastates the present and desolates the future with unquenchable and raging fire, has nothing less pure in it than flame or sunlight. And this passionate and ardent chastity is utterly and unmistakably spontaneous and unconscious. Not till the story is ended, not till the effect of it has been thoroughly absorbed and digested, does the reader even perceive the simple and natural absence of any grosser element, any hint or suggestion of a baser alloy in the ingredients of its human emotion than in the splendour of lightning or the roll of a gathered wave. Then, as on issuing sometimes from the tumult of charging waters, he finds with something of wonder how absolutely pure and sweet was the element of living storm with which his own nature has been for a while made one; not a grain in it of soiling sand, not a waif of clogging weed. As was the author's life, so is her book in all things: troubled and taintless, with little of rest in it, and nothing of reproach. It may be true that not many will ever take it to their hearts; it is certain that those who do like it will like nothing very much better in the whole world of poetry or prose.

NOTES

1 A novel by S. Baring-Gould (1880). Swinburne omitted a sentence about this 'recent' (rather than 'later') work, as he called it in the

Athenaeum essay: 'And the humour is even better: and the passion is not less genuine.' On 21 June 1883 he wrote to John Nichol: 'I did not mean—Heaven forbid!—to set *Mehalah*, on the whole, beside or near *Wuthering Heights*: but it is the only book I know which shows anything of the same power' (Lang, v, 27).

2 A. Mary F. Robinson, *Emily Brontë* (London, 1883), 125.

3 *Ibid.*, 126–7.

4 Cornelia appears in *The White Devil* (from which 'several forms of distraction' is quoted); Madge Wildfire, in Scott's *Heart of Midlothian.*

5 Prometheus was said to be the son of Iapetus and sometimes of Themis, associated as here with Righteousness but also identified with Gaea (Earth).

6 Cf. Luke 10: 42: 'But one thing is needful.'

7 Cf. Emily Brontë's 'No coward soul is mine', ll. 9–10:

> Vain are the thousand creeds
> That move our hearts: unutterably vain.

8 Associated with the Stoics.

9 Robinson, 136: 'a little poem, which, by some shy ostrich prompting, Emily chose to call "The Old Stoic".'

10 In *The Newcomes* and in *The Adventures of Philip*, the Firmins in the latter.

11 Cf. *Hamlet*, III, iv, 160: 'Assume a virtue, if you have it not.'

12 The phrase used by Charlotte Brontë in her preface to Emily's *Wuthering Heights.*

17 Wilkie Collins
1889, 1894

'Wilkie Collins' appeared in the *Fortnightly Review* for November 1889, not long after Collins had died, and in *Studies in Prose and Poetry* (1894). It is still one of the best critical appraisals of the novelist.

The ingratitude of kings and the ingratitude of democracies have often supplied the text of historic or political sermons: the ingratitude of readers and spectators, from Shakespeare's day to our own, is at least as notable and memorable. A man who has amused our leisure, relieved our weariness, delighted our fancy, enthralled our attention, refreshed our sympathies, cannot claim a place of equal honour in our grateful estimation with the dullest or the most perverse of historians who ever falsified or stupefied history, of metaphysicians who ever 'darkened counsel'[1] and wasted time and wearied attention by the profitless lucubrations of pseudosophy. To create is nothing: to comment is much. The commentary may be utterly hollow and rotten, the creation thoroughly solid and alive: the one is nothing less than criticism, the other nothing more than fiction. '*Un âne qui ressemble à monsieur Nisard*'[2] takes precedence, in the judgment of his kind, of the men on whose works, inventive or creative, it is the business of a Nisard to pass judgment and to bray.

Some few students, whose levity or perversity is duly derided and deplored by the Nisards of our time, are of opinion that the age of Shakespeare is well worth studying even in the minor productions of his day and the humblest professors of his art. And, far as the modern novel at its best is beneath the higher level of the stage in the time of Shakespeare, it must be admitted that the appeal to general imagination or to general sympathy, which then was made only by the dramatist, is now made only by the novelist. Middleton, Heywood, and Rowley would now have to undertake the parts so excellently played by Collins, by Trollope, and by Reade. Culture, in their days, was pleased to ignore the drama with a scorn as academic—in Mr. Carlyle's picturesque and fortunate phrase, as 'high-sniffing' a contempt—as it now can pretend to feel for the novel. And yet the name of Shakespeare is now more widely known than the name of Puttenham.[3] And though Dickens was not a Shakespeare, and though Collins was not a Dickens, it is permissible to anticipate that their names and their works will be familiar to generations unacquainted with the existence and unaware of the eclipse of their most shining, most scornful, and most superior critics. To have written *Basil*, though *Basil* is by no manner of means an impeccable work of imperishable art, is something more than to have demonstrated what needs no demonstration—that a writer must do better than this if he wishes to achieve a serious or a memorable success. But, violent and unlovely and unlikely as it is, this early story had in it something more than promise—the evidence of original and noticeable power to constrain and retain attention of a more serious and perhaps a more reasonable kind than can be evoked by many later and more ambitious and pretentious appeals to the same or a similar source of interest. The horrible heroine, beast as she is, is a credible and conceivable beast; and her hapless young husband is a rather pathetic if a rather incredible figure. But the vindictive paramour is somewhat too much of a stage property; and the book would hardly be remembered for better or for worse if the author had not in his future stories excelled its merits and eschewed its faults. Nor would *Hide and Seek*, though a most ingenious and amusing story, have had much chance of a life as long as it deserves if it had been the best that its teller had to tell. But in *The Dead Secret* Wilkie Collins made his mark for the first time as a writer who could do something that no one else could—and something well worth doing. The skill of the plot, the construction, and the narrative, whatever such skill may be worth, was far beyond the reach of any contemporary, however far above him in the loftier and clearer qualities of genius. Dickens never wrote and Thackeray never tried to write a story so excellent in construction and so persistent in its hold on the reader's curiosity—a curiosity amounting, in the case of its younger and more impressible readers, to absolute anxiety. But, good as it is, this book is the first among many examples of the too undeniable and characteristic fact that the remarkable genius of its author for invention and construction and composition of incidents and effects was limited by an incapacity and dependent on a condition which cannot but be regarded as seriously impairing his claims to consideration as an artist or a student. He could not, as a rule, get forward at all without the help of some physical or moral infirmity in some one of the leading agents or patients of the story.[4] Neither *The Dead Secret* nor *The Woman in White* could have run its course for a single volume if Sarah Leeson or Anne Catherick had been sound in mind—not abnormally and constitutionally deficient in nerve and brain. And the suggested or implied suffering of such poor innocent wretches, the martyrdom of perpetual terror and agony inflicted on the shattered nerves or the shaken brain of a woman or a girl, is surely a cruel and a painful mainspring for a story or a plot. Again, if the hero in this story and the heroine in another had not been blind, there could have been no story at all. It is in every case a wonderfully ingenious and interesting story that we enjoy; but the ungrateful reader cannot avoid the reflection that there is something unlovely as well as artificial in the condition of its existence. Madge Wildfire is no more the central and indispensable mainspring —the *cheville ouvrière*[5]—of *The Heart of Midlothian* than Ophelia is of *Hamlet*: their insanity is an important but subordinate point in the working of the story most skilfully and superbly wrought into the texture of its composition; but in neither case is the story made to depend for its very existence on this insanity.

But from first to last, if allowance be duly made for occasional lapses, it will be admitted that Wilkie Collins was in his way a genuine artist. *Basil*, with all its violence and crudity, has something of sustained though not elevated interest; whereas the most successful imitation ever attempted of its author's method has nothing in it whatever beyond one certainly most ingenious idea—that a blind man[6] by accident be the only witness (if witness he can be called) of a murder; the rest of the story being but vehement commonplace, of the spasmodically torpid kind—electrified stupidity, if the phrase may be allowed to pass. All the works of Wilkie Collins which we remember with pleasure are works of art as true as his godfather's pictures,[7] and in their own line as complete. His excellent sense, his perfect self-command, his modest devotion to his art, are qualities not more praiseworthy than they are obvious. And if it were but for their rarity they should command no less attention than respect. His most illustrious friend and contemporary did not always show himself at once so loyal and so rational in observance of intellectual or æsthetic propriety. Collins never ventured to fling down among his readers so shapeless or misshapen a piece of work, though doubtless he could not furnish them with a piece of work so splendid and so excellent in parts and sections, as *Little Dorrit*. Dickens, with his usual straightforward dexterity, laid hold of the objection absurdly raised against the catastrophe of *Little Dorrit* by the carpers who averred that it must have been suggested by an actual accident which occurred just before the close of the periodical publication of his story: he pointed out the intimations conveyed again and again of just such an unforeseen peril in the earlier stages of the story—in numbers which had appeared many months before; and he most satisfactorily and triumphantly stamped out that most fatuous and preposterous suggestion. But he did not prove or even try to prove it possible for his most devoted admirer to believe that when he began the story he meant that so much of it should finally be left hanging in the air; that a figure so admirably and so carefully outlined as that of a malignant 'self-tormentor'[8] should have been intended to justify and expound herself by putting into the hands of a stranger to whom she had conceived a rather virulent antipathy the unsolicited and unexplained revelation of her poisoned nature and her cankered life; or that the ill-mated pair whose miserable tragedy had been so darkly foreshadowed and so elaborately sketched in should have been left in the simply uncomfortable condition to which the great novelist, overburdened with an inartistic multiplicity of episodical and incoherent interests, was finally content to condemn them by default. A writer may let his characters slip for the sake of his story, or he may let his story slip for the sake of his characters: Dickens, in *Little Dorrit*, fell alternately into both errors, and yet achieved such success on both lines that the chaotic magnificence of his work may well be held sufficient to strike even the most rational and rightful criticism into silence. Such triumph and such aberration were alike impossible to Collins; the most plausible objection that could be brought against his best books was that the study of character and the modesty of nature must too surely have been subordinated, if not sacrificed, to the exquisitely mechanical ingenuity of so continuously intricate a plot. And now and then it would certainly seem as if the writer had been struck, and had possibly been irritated, by an apprehension that he might be regarded as a mere mechanic or mechanist of fiction, and had been impelled by this apprehension into some not always fortunate or felicitous attempt to relieve the weft of his story and heighten the tone of his work with somewhat crude and over-coloured effects of character or caricature. But it seems to me grossly and glaringly unjust to deny or to question the merit or the truthfulness of his better studies. By far the best the most thoughtful, serious, and critical article that appeared on the occasion of his death, fair and good as it was in the main, may be cited in example of this injustice. Count Fosco, said the critic, stands revealed as a mechanical non-entity, an ingenious invention never realized or vitalized or informed with humanity by the inventor, who felt at last that he had failed to make a living man of him; the proof of this being simply that at the close of the story two or three different explanations of his conduct and his character are suggested as equally plausible and acceptable. This would be a quite unimpeachable objection if the story had been told in the third person; but such too intelligent criticism overlooks the fact that it is not. The author does not tell us what he thinks of his creature; he gives us the various impressions made on the fellow-creatures of his imagination by the influence or the impact of this particular figure. And the consequence is that we see there are more ways of considering and estimating a man's character than a meaner artist could have suggested or conceived. And the author's especial genius is never more distinctly displayed or more happily employed than in the exposition and the contrast of such varying estimates of character or explanations of event. At the opening of the story which seems to be generally regarded as the masterpiece of his art, we are warned by the worthy old steward who first takes up the narrative to believe nothing that may be said of him by a lady whose recollections and reflections are to follow on the record of his own; and when the Evangelical hag[9] who is one of her creator's most thoroughly and simply successful creations takes up the tale in turn, and sets forth her opinions as to the past and the present and the future of her friends and neighbours, we find that her view of life and character is as dramatically just and appropriate—from the opposite point of view—as his. It is apparently the general opinion—an opinion which seems to me incontestable—that no third book of their author's can be ranked as equal with *The Woman in White* and *The Moonstone*: two works of not more indisputable than incomparable ability. *No Name* is an only less excellent example of as curious and original a talent. It is more elaborately ingenious, but less thoroughly successful, than the finest work of the first Lord Lytton—a story grounded on the same motive, and starting from the same point; the imputation of illegitimacy, the struggle against its consequences, and the final triumph over its disadvantages. But there is nothing—though much is good—so good in the work of the later novelist as the character of Gawtrey;[10] nor anything so effective and impressive as his end.

In this story the complication and alternation of interests and incidents are carried as far as they can reasonably be carried: in *Armadale* they are carried further. That curious and laborious romance must be considered, even by those who cannot consider it successful, as a failure which fell short on the verge of a success. The prologue or prelude is so full of interest and promise that the expectations of its readers may have been unduly stimulated; but the sequel, astonishingly ingenious and inventive as it is, is scarcely perhaps in perfect keeping with the anticipations thus ingeniously aroused. To the average reader, judging by my own impressions, I should imagine that the book must on the whole be a little disappointing; but such a reader should ask himself whether this impression of disappointment is reasonable. The criminal heroine who dies of her own will by her own crime, to save the beloved victim whom it has accidentally brought to the verge of death, is a figure which would have aroused the widest and the deepest sympathy of English readers if only she had not been the creation of an Englishman. Had a Frenchman or an American introduced her, no acclamation would have been too vehement to express their gratitude. The signature of Nathaniel Hawthorne or of Octave Feuillet would have sufficed to evoke a rapture of regret that England could produce no such novelist as this. But neither Feuillet nor Hawthorne could have composed and constructed such a story: the ingenuity spent on it may possibly be perverse, but it is certainly superb. And the studies of character are fair; the fortunate and amiable young hero and heroine may be rather incredibly boyish and girlish, but the two somewhat loathsome figures of the Pedgifts are as good as any studies of ugly dotage in a father and hideous depravity in a son can be made by any dexterity of arrangement to be or to appear. But the weft of the story is perhaps too dense; the web is perhaps too tightly drawn, and the threads of it are perhaps not always harmonious in colour. The superb success of *The Moonstone* may perhaps make even his most cordial admirers unconsciously if not ungratefully unjust to the less unquestionable and the less unqualified successes of its author; just as any one who has thoroughly enjoyed Lord Digby's incomparable *Elvira*[11]—the one dramatic work in the language which may be said to have anticipated the peculiarly lucid method, and the peculiarly careful evolution of a most amusingly complicated story, which we admire in the best works of Wilkie Collins—will find himself disqualified from enjoying Sir Samuel Tuke's *Adventures of Five Hours*; even when he remembers that the recollection of the latter play, recently witnessed on the stage, made Mr. Samuel Pepys reflect after seeing *Othello*—a play which he was wont to think well of—that, 'having so lately seen *The Adventures of Five Hours*, it do seem but a mean thing.'[12] In *Elvira*, as in *The Moonstone*, the skill of construction is so exquisite, so complete, so masterly, that we follow the thread of the story with unflagging enjoyment and a perpetually changeful and delightful perplexity of conjecture as to what the upshot is to be; and when this upshot comes it is all that sympathy could have desired, and more than ingenuity could have conceived. Lord Digby lives—if he can be said to live—by grace of his *Elvira* alone, and for fewer readers, I fear, than he seems to me to deserve; there are many, I believe, who think that Wilkie Collins would have a likelier chance of longer life in the memories of more future readers if he had left nothing behind him but his masterpiece *The Moonstone* and the one or two other stories which may fairly be set beside or but a little beneath it. A man who has written much after writing a book of indisputably great merit in its way, and has never again written anything of merit so indisputable and so great, is apt to be thought all the less of on that account; but if these comparatively inferior works have any real and indisputable merit of their own, they surely ought rather to be set down to his credit than to his discredit. And if no good judge of fiction—in other words, of that creative art which alone can entitle a man to be called, not a discoverer or inventor, a commentator or a thinker, but a maker—will affirm that any later work of this able and loyal workman is so good as not to disappoint us when we compare it with *The Moonstone*, none will deny the real and great merit of this later work at its best. And few will differ, I should think, from the suggestion that the inferiority or imperfection which we cannot ignore or deny in it was due to the lamentable illusion of which most unquestionably there are no traces in his earlier work—work which was always modestly, straightforwardly, and thoroughly loyal to the intellectual dictates of his instinct and the intelligent rules of his art. This illusion was the benevolent and maleficent fancy—the 'devout imagination'—that he might do good service, as Dickens had done and was doing, in the line of didactic fiction and reformatory romance. The shades of Mr. Bumble, Mr. Fang, Mr. Nupkins, Mr. Squeers, Mr. Alderman Cute, Mr. Pecksniff, Mr. Creakle, Mr. Kenge, Mr. Vholes, Mr. Bounderby, Mr. Gradgrind, Mr. Merdle,[13] and I know not how many more immortals, may well have disturbed the literary rest of their great creator's friend and disciple; but that was an evil day for his genius on which he bethought himself to try his hand at the correction of abuses, the castigation of follies, and the advocacy of reforms. It is as noble a work as man can undertake, to improve the conditions of life for other men by writing or by speaking or by example; but in the two former cases, if a man has not the requisite capacity, even the most generous volunteer in the army of progress or reform will be likelier to lose his own way than to lead other men back into theirs.

The first and best of Wilkie Collins's didactic or admonitory novels[14] is so brilliant in exposition of character, so dexterous in construction of incident, so happy in evolution of event, that its place is nearer the better work which preceded than the poorer work which followed it. The subject of marriage law in Scotland is one which it is painfully difficult for any one who has read the most exhaustingly delightful and the most unmercifully side-splitting of all farcical comedies to consider as suggestive of serious or tragic interest. Belinda and her Belvawney, Cheviot and his Minnie, rise up again before the eyes of enraptured if incredulous fancy, in the light —or should we say limelight?—of inextinguishable and irrepressible laughter:[15] and the woes and wrongs of any couple accidentally or otherwise mismarried on the wrong side of the Border are inevitably invested with a lambent halo of ridicule—an ineffaceable aureole of farce. But if Mr. Gilbert had never written *Engaged* (Momus forbid the lamentable fancy!), it might still be possible to follow the fortunes of the singularly frail and singularly stout-hearted heroine of *Man and Wife* with no sense of incongruity or comicality in the mainspring of the action which directs them: and it is still possible to regret the unexplained if not inexplicable incongruity between the physical or moral weakness which could yield up honour and character to the seduction or attraction of a brainless and soulless brute, and the moral and physical courage which could inspire and sustain the devotion of his victim when aware that her self-sacrifice for the sake of others must expose her to the imminent peril of suffering and terror worse than death. The satire on muscle-worship, though neither unprovoked nor unmerited, might have gained in point and force if the method of attack had been a trifle less heavy-handed. The great objection to the muscular Christians and ethical professors of athleticism, as was once remarked by an undergraduate of my acquaintance, is that they are so unhealthily conscious of their unconscious healthiness.[16] But the satirical or controversial note in this book, if not too finely touched, is touched more finely than those which the author attempted to strike in some of his subsequent works. *The New Magdalen* is merely feeble, false, and silly in its sentimental cleverness; but in *The Fallen Leaves* there is something too absurdly repulsive[17] for comment or endurance. The extreme clumsiness and infelicity of Wilkie Collins as a dramatic teacher or preacher may be tested by comparison with the exquisite skill and tact displayed by M. Alexandre Dumas in his studies of the same or of similar subjects. To the revoltingly ridiculous book just mentioned I am loth to refer again: all readers who feel any gratitude or goodwill towards its author must desire to efface its miserable memory from the record of his works. But take even the comparatively successful *New Magdalen* and set it, for instance, beside *Les Idées de Mme Aubray*:[18] it is as the scratching of a savage or a child to the drawing of an all but impeccable artist. Even *Une Visite de Noces*,[19] though not exactly a lovely or a lofty study of noble manners and elevated life, is saved by the author's astonishing gift of dexterity in presentation, 'that can make vile things precious':[20] whereas Mr. Collins, if only by overstating his case, destroys any pathos or plausibility that might otherwise be fancied or be found in it. To the mealy-mouthed modern philopornist the homely and hardy method of the old poet who first discovered or invented the penitent prostitute may seem rough and brutal in its lifelike straightforwardness: but to the wiser eye Bellafront[21] is worth a shoal of her successors in that line of sentimental fiction which provokes from weary humanity the bitter cry of the long-suffering novel-reader: When will the last reformed harlot vanish into space in the arms of the last clerical sceptic—Mercy Merrick and Robert Elsmere destroy each other in a fiery embrace, or in such a duel as that between the princess and the Ifrit, which ended in mutual annihilation?[22]

Less offensive if not less irrational, more amusing if not more convincing, was the childish and harmless onslaught on scientific research attempted if not achieved by the simple-minded and innocent author of *Heart and Science*. The story which bears that most remarkably silly title is the best—after *Man and Wife*, and a good way after—of all its writer's moral or didactic tales. There is a capital child in it, for one thing; her experiences of Scottish life and character, as related on the occasion of her last appearance, are nothing less than delicious.

> Carmina could have Zo all to herself. 'Now, my dear,' she said, in a kiss, 'tell me about Scotland.'
>
> 'Scotland,' Zo answered with dignity, 'belongs to Uncle Northlake. He pays for everything: and I'm Missus.'

'It's true,' said Mr. Gallilee, bursting with pride. 'My lord says it's no use having a will of your own where Zo is. When he introduces her to anybody on the estate, he says, "Here's the Missus." '

Mr. Gallilee's youngest daughter listened critically to the parental testimony. 'You see he knows,' she said to Ovid. 'There's nothing to laugh at.'

Carmina tried another question. 'Did you think of me, dear, when you were far away?

'Think of you?' Zo repeated. 'You're to sleep in my bedroom when we go back to Scotland—and I'm to be out of bed, and one of 'em, when you eat your first Scotch dinner. Shall I tell you what you'll see on the table? You'll see a big brown steaming bag in a dish—and you'll see me slit it with a knife—and the bag's fat inside will tumble out, all smoking hot and stinking. That's a Scotch dinner. Oh!' she cried, losing her dignity in the sudden interest of a new idea, 'oh, Carmina, do you remember the Italian boy, and his song?'

Here was one of those tests of her memory for trifles, applied with a child's happy abruptness, for which Ovid had been waiting. He listened eagerly. To his unutterable relief, Carmina laughed.

'Of course I remember it!' she said. 'Who could forget the boy who sings and grins and says *Gimmee haypenny*?'

'That's it!' cried Zo. 'The boy's song was a good one in its way. I've learnt a better in Scotland. You've heard of Donald, haven't you?'

'No.'

Zo turned indignantly to her father. 'Why didn't you tell her of Donald?'

Mr. Gallilee humbly admitted that he was in fault. Carmina asked who Donald was, and what he was like. Zo unconsciously tested her memory for the second time.

'You know that day,' she said, 'when Joseph had an errand at the grocer's and I went along with him, and Miss Minerva said I was a vulgar child?'

Carmina's memory recalled this new trifle, without an effort. 'I know,' she answered; 'you told me Joseph and the grocer weighed you in the great scales.'

Zo delighted Ovid by trying her again.

'When they put me into the scales, Carmina, what did I weigh?'

'Nearly four stone, dear.'

'Quite four stone. Donald weighs fourteen. What do you think of that?'

Mr. Gallilee once more offered his testimony. 'The biggest Piper on my lord's estate,' he began, 'comes of a Highland family, and was removed to the Lowlands by my lord's father. A great player——'

'And *my* friend,' Zo explained, stopping her father in full career. 'He takes snuff out of a cow's horn. He shovels it up his fat nose with a spoon, like this. He nose wags. He says, "Try my sneeshin." Sneeshin's Scotch for snuff. He boos till he's nearly double when Uncle Northlake speaks to him. Boos is Scotch for bows. He skirls on the pipes—skirls means screeches. When you first hear him, he'll make your stomach ache. You'll get used to that—and you'll find you like him. He wears a purse and a petticoat; he never had a pair of trousers on in his life; there's no pride about him. Say you're my friend, and he'll let you smack his legs——'

Here Ovid was obliged to bring the biography of Donald to a close. Carmina's enjoyment of Zo was becoming too keen for her strength; her bursts of laughter grew louder and louder—the wholesome limit of excitement was being rapidly passed. 'Tell us about your cousins,' he said, by way of effecting a diversion.

'The big ones?' Zo asked.

'No, the little ones, like you.'

'Nice girls—they play at everything I tell 'em. Jolly boys—when they knock a girl down, they pick her up again, and clean her.'

Her father, too, is good; her mother is merely a 'shocking example'. Not quite so much can be said against the leading character of the story: the relentless lover of knowledge who lives for that love alone is at least *un succès manqué*.[23] Now and then he becomes a really living, interesting, and rather memorable figure. The cynomaniacs with whom the death or the suffering of 'that beast man'[24] is of less account than the death or the suffering of a rabbit or a dog must naturally, one would think, have disapproved of a story in which the awkward champion of their preposterous cause has contrived somehow so to concentrate the serious interest of his book on the person of a vivisector, whom he meant to be an object of mere abhorrence, as to leave him an object of something like sympathy and admiration as well as compassion and respect; none the less deserved if he did once feel a desire to vivisect his vicious and thankless idiot of a brother. The cynical sentimentality—cynical in the metaphorical no less than in the literal sense of the word—which winces and whines at the thought of a benefit conferred on mankind at the price of experiments made on the vile or at any rate the viler body of a beast is worth exactly as much as the humanity and sympathy which inspire the advocates of free trade in the most unspeakable kind of pestilence. And it strikes me that Mr. Godfrey Ablewhite (of *The Moonstone*) would have been a fitter champion of free and independent hydrophobia than the creator of that distinguished philanthropist; who would certainly have been a quite ideal chairman at a meeting of the Ladies' Society for the Propagation of the—well, let us say for the Dissemination of Contagious Disease (Unlimited).

> What brought Sir Visto's ill-got wealth to waste?
> Some demon whispered—'Visto! have a taste.'[25]

A slight change in that famous couplet will express and condense the truth about Wilkie Collins the teacher and preacher more happily and aptly than many pages of analysis.

> What brought good Wilkie's genius nigh perdition?
> Some demon whispered—'Wilkie! have a mission.'

Nothing can be more fatuous than to brand all didactic or missionary fiction as an illegitimate or inferior form of art: the highest works in that line fall short only of the highest ever achieved by man. Many of the very truest and noblest triumphs achieved by the matchless genius of Charles Dickens were achieved in this field: but Collins, I must really be allowed to repeat, was no more a Dickens than Dickens was a Shakespeare; and if the example of his illustrious friend misled him into emulation or imitation of such labours, we can only regret that he was thus misguided; remembering nevertheless that 'the light which led astray was light from'[26] Dickens.

In some but by no means in all of his later novels there is much of the peculiar and studious ability which distinguishes his best: but his originally remarkable faculty for writing short stories had undergone a total and unaccountable decay. *After Dark* is one of the most delightful books he has left us: each of the stories in it is a little model, a little masterpiece in its kind: but if we compare the admirable story of *The Yellow Mask* with the hideous fiction of *The Haunted Hotel*, we cannot but acknowledge and deplore in the latter novelette such an absolute eclipse or collapse of all the qualities which we admired in the earlier that it reads rather like a bad parody than like a bad imitation of its author's better work.

It would seem something less than complimentary to say of an industrious and not unambitious writer that the crowning merit, the most distinctive quality, of his very best work was to be sought and would be found in the construction of an interesting and perplexing story, well conceived, well contrived, and well moulded into lifelike and attractive shape; yet this is what we enjoy—it is all, or almost all, that we find to enjoy, to admire, or to approve—in a work of tragic art so admirable to so many generations as was *The Orphan*; it is the supreme quality of a work so far superior to Otway's as *The Maid's Tragedy*.[27] And both these famous poems are faultier in study of character—more false, incoherent, and incredible—than almost any work by Wilkie Collins. It is but right and reasonable that his abilities should find such favour as they find in France; that so fair an example of his conscientious and ingenious workmanship as the story called *I Say No* should have been honoured by the appearance of a masterly translation in the columns of the *Rappel*.[28] His mannerisms and faults of style are much less obvious and obtrusive in a foreign version: his best qualities are commoner, I regret to think, in French than in English fiction. Such lucidity, such order, such care in the adjustment of parts and the arrangement of the whole, would hardly seem so exceptional to a French reader as to claim for the possessor of these merits a place in the Pantheon; nor can it be supposed that a memorial in Westminster Abbey would not be considered by most Englishmen something more than an adequate recognition of his claims. But a friendly and kindly recollection of them is no more than may be hoped for and expected from a later generation than his own.

NOTES

1 Job 38: 2.
2 'A donkey that resembles M. Nisard.' From l. 23 of '*Les Griffonnages de l'écolier*', Hugo's *L'Art d'être grand-père*. Désiré Nisard (1806–88) had passed unfavourable judgment on Hugo.
3 Richard Puttenham (*c.* 1520–*c.* 1601), assumed author of *The Arte of English Poesie*, sometimes ascribed to his brother.
4 Those who are passive, as opposed to 'agents', but Swinburne is playing on the more usual meaning of 'patients'.
5 Mainspring.
6 The *Fortnightly Review* has 'should' after 'man'.
7 Sir David Wilkie (1785–1841), Scottish genre painter, was Collins's godfather.
8 Chapter 21 of Book ii, *Little Dorrit*, 'The History of a Self-Tormentor', is a paper written by Miss Wade.
9 Miss Clack.
10 In Lord Lytton's *Night and Morning*.

11 *Elvira; or, The Worst Not Always True* (1667), a comedy by George Digby, second Earl of Bristol (1612–77).
12 Pepys's entry for 20 August 1666: 'Up, and to Deptford by water, reading "Othello, Moore of Venice", which I ever heretofore esteemed a mighty good play, but having so lately read "The Adventures of Five Hours", it seems a mean thing.'
13 Characters whose social outlook is benighted and whose practices in legal, financial, or educational affairs are evil.
14 *Man and Wife*.
15 A Homeric phrase: *Odyssey*, viii, 326. In Gilbert's play the outcome depends on whether a spot of ground is in England or Scotland.
16 Since Swinburne wrote a letter mentioning 'my old objection' to Kingsley's 'school' of thinkers (Lang, iii, 247), the 'undergraduate' seems to have been Swinburne himself.
17 'Ludicrously loathsome' in Swinburne's original article.
18 'Madame Aubray's Principles', by Alexandre Dumas *fils*.
19 'A Wedding Visit', also by the younger Dumas.
20 King Lear, III, ii, 70–1:

> The art of our necessities is strange,
> And can make vile things precious.

21 In Dekker's *The Honest Whore*.
22 Mercy Merrick, in *The New Magdalen*, is paired with the hero of Mrs Humphry Ward's *Robert Elsmere*. 'The Second Kalandar's Tale' in *The Arabian Nights* contains the episode involving the princess and the Ifrit (a variant of the Jinn and usually malignant).
23 A success that is really failure.
24 Henry St John, Viscount Bolingbroke, letter of 12 September 1742: '. . . that wild beast man'.

'Literal sense of the word', ten lines below, aludes to the derivation of 'cynic' from the Greek word for 'dog'.

25 Pope's *Moral Essays*, iv, 15–16.
26 From Burns's 'The Vision', stanza 40.
27 A play by Beaumont and Fletcher.
28 A journal (1869–1928) established in Paris by Victor Hugo's sons, Auguste Vacquerie, and others.

18 Charles Dickens

1902

'Charles Dickens', in the *Quarterly Review* for July 1902, the text used here, was amalgamated with an essay on *Oliver Twist* in *Charles Dickens* (1913), edited by Theodore Watts-Dunton. The book adds praise of certain characters, notably Mr Bucket, and of 'the genius of George Cruikshank'; a key sentence touches on both Dickens's limitations and his greatness: 'On the literary and sentimental side of his work Dickens was but a type of his generation and his class: on the comic and pathetic, the tragic and the creative side, "he was not of an age, but for all time".' The quotation, of course, tends to put Dickens in the company of Shakespeare.

What Swinburne says on such topics as *Great Expectations*, Little Nell, or *Dombey and Son* and *Little Dorrit* as stories agrees with the opinions of several later critics. Boundless enthusiasm for Dickens from early boyhood may obscure his reservations, nor is his style at its best. As the notes indicate, there were personal reasons for his invective; but he realized that George Henry Lewes's criticism had been influential, and his comments on Lewes in 'Changes of Aspect' may indicate that his other reasons for a long-standing dislike of Lewes were less important to him than Lewes's attitude towards Dickens.

It is only when such names as Shakespeare's or Hugo's rise and remain as the supreme witnesses of what was highest in any particular country at any particular time that there can be no question among any but irrational and impudent men as to the supremacy of their greatest. England, under the reign of Dickens, had other great names to boast of which may well be allowed to challenge the sovereignty of his genius. But as there certainly was no Shakespeare and no Hugo to rival and eclipse his glory, he will probably and naturally always be accepted and acclaimed as the greatest Englishman of his generation. His first works or attempts at work gave little more promise of such a future than if he had been a Coleridge or a Shelley. No one could have foreseen what all may now foresee in the *Sketches by Boz*—not only a quick and keen-eyed observer, 'a chiel amang us takin' notes'[1] more notable than Captain Grose's, but a great creative genius. Nor could any one have foreseen it in the early chapters of *Pickwick*—which, at their best, do better the sort of thing which had been done fairly well before. Sam Weller and Charles Dickens came to life together, immortal and twin-born. In *Oliver Twist* the quality of a great tragic and comic poet or dramatist in prose fiction was for the first time combined with the already famous qualities of a great humorist and a born master in the arts of narrative and dialogue.

Like the early works of all other great writers whose critical contemporaries have failed to elude the kindly chance of beneficent oblivion, the early works of Dickens have been made use of to depreciate his later, with the same enlightened and impartial candour which on the appearance of *Othello* must doubtless have deplored the steady though gradual decline of its author's genius from the unfulfilled promise of excellence held forth by *Two Gentlemen of Verona*. There may possibly be some faint and flickering shadow of excuse for the dullards, if unmalignant, who prefer *Nicholas Nickleby* to the riper and sounder fruits of the same splendid and inexhaustible genius. Admirable as it is, full of life and sap and savour, the strength and the weakness of youth are so singularly mingled in the story and the style that readers who knew nothing of its date might naturally have assumed that it must have been the writer's first attempt at fiction. There is perhaps no question which would more thoroughly test the scholarship of the student than this:—What do you know of Jane Dibabs and Horatio Peltiogrus?[2] At fourscore and ten it might be thought 'too late a week'[3] for a reader to revel with insuppressible delight in a first reading of the chapters which enrol all worthy readers in the company of Mr Vincent Crummles; but I can bear witness to the fact that this effect was produced on a reader of that age who had earned honour and respect in public life, affection and veneration in private.[4] It is not, on the other hand, less curious and significant that Sydney Smith, who had held out against Sam Weller, should have been conquered by Miss Squeers; that her letter, which of all Dickens's really good things is perhaps the most obviously imitative and suggestive of its model, should have converted so great an elder humorist to appreciation of a greater than himself; that the echo of familiar fun, an echo from the grave of Smollett, should have done what finer and more original strokes of comic genius had unaccountably failed to do. But in all criticism of such work the merely personal element of the critic, the natural atmosphere in which his mind or his insight works, and uses its faculties of appreciation, is really the first and last thing to be taken into account.

No mortal man or woman, no human boy or girl, can resist the fascination of Mr and Mrs Quilp, of Mr and Miss Brass, of Mr Swiveller and his Marchioness; but even the charm of Mrs Jarley and her surroundings, the magic which enthrals us in the presence of a Codlin and a Short, cannot mesmerise or hypnotise us into belief that the story of *The Old Curiosity Shop* is in any way a good story. But it is the first book in which the background or setting is often as impressive as the figures which can hardly be detached from it in our remembered impression of the whole design. From Quilp's Wharf to Plashwater Weir Mill Lock, the river belongs to Dickens by right of conquest or creation. The part it plays in more than a few of his books is indivisible from the parts played in them by human actors beside it or upon it. Of such actors in this book, the most famous as an example of her creator's power as a master of pathetic tragedy would thoroughly deserve her fame if she were but a thought more human and more credible. 'The child'[5] has never a touch of childhood about her; she is an impeccable and invariable portent of devotion, without a moment's lapse into the humanity of frailty in temper or in conduct. Dickens might as well have fitted her with a pair of wings at once. A woman might possibly be as patient, as resourceful, as indefatigable in well-doing and as faultless in perception of the right thing to do; it would be difficult to make her deeply interesting, but she might be made more or less of an actual creature. But a child whom nothing can ever irritate, whom nothing can ever baffle, whom nothing can ever misguide, whom nothing can ever delude, and whom nothing can ever dismay, is a monster as inhuman as a baby with two heads.

Outside the class which excludes all but the highest masterpieces of poetry it is difficult to find or to imagine a faultless work of creation—in other words, a faultless work of fiction; but the story of *Barnaby Rudge* can hardly, in common justice, be said to fall short of this crowning praise. And in this book, even if not in any of its precursors, an appreciative reader must recognise a quality of humour which will remind him of Shakespeare, and perhaps of

Aristophanes. The impetuous and irrepressible volubility of Miss Miggs, when once her eloquence breaks loose and finds vent like raging water or fire, is powerful enough to overbear for the moment any slight objection which a severe morality might suggest with respect to the rectitude and propriety of her conduct. It is impossible to be rigid in our judgment of 'a toiling, moiling, constant-working, always-being-found-fault-with, never-giving-satisfactions, nor-having-no-time-to-clean-oneself, potter's wessel,' whose 'only becoming occupations is to help young flaunting pagins to brush and comb and titiwate theirselves into whitening and suppulchres, and leave the young men to think that there an't a bit of padding in it nor no pinching-ins nor fillings-out nor pomatums nor deceits nor earthly wanities.' To have made malignity as delightful for an instant as simplicity, and Miss Miggs as enchanting as Mrs Quickly or Mrs Gamp, is an unsurpassable triumph of dramatic humour.[6]

But the advance in tragic power is even more notable and memorable than this. The pathos, indeed, is too cruel; the tortures of the idiot's mother and the murderer's wife are so fearful that interest and sympathy are wellnigh superseded or overbalanced by a sense of horror rather than of pity; magnificent as is the power of dramatic invention which animates every scene in every stage of her martyrdom. Dennis is the first of those consummate and wonderful ruffians, with two vile faces under one frowsy hood, whose captain or commander-in-chief is Rogue Riderhood; more fearful by far, though not (one would hope) more natural, than Henriet Cousin, who could hardly breathe when fastening the rope round Esmeralda's neck, '*tant la chose l'apitoyait*';[7] a divine touch of surviving humanity which would have been impossible to the more horrible hangman whose mortal agony in immediate prospect of the imminent gallows is as terribly memorable as anything in the tragedy of fiction or the poetry of prose. His fellow hangbird is a figure no less admirable throughout all his stormy and fiery career till the last moment; and then he drops into poetry. Nor is it poetry above the reach of Silas Wegg which 'invokes the curse of all its victims on that black tree, of which he is the ripened fruit'.[8] The writer's impulse was noble; but its expression or its effusion is such as indifference may deride and sympathy must deplore. Twice only did the greatest English writer of his day make use of history as a background or a stage for fiction; the use made of it in *Barnaby Rudge* is even more admirable in the lifelike tragedy and the terrible comedy of its presentation than the use made of it in *A Tale of Two Cities*.

Dickens was doubtless right in his preference of *David Copperfield* to all his other masterpieces; it is only among dunces that it is held improbable or impossible for a great writer to judge aright of his own work at its best, to select and to prefer the finest and the fullest example of his active genius; but, when all deductions have been made from the acknowledgment due to the counter-claim of *Martin Chuzzlewit*, the fact remains that in that unequal and irregular masterpiece his comic and his tragic genius rose now and then to the very highest pitch of all. No son of Adam and no daughter of Eve on this God's earth, as his occasional friend Mr Carlyle might have expressed it, could have imagined it possible—humanly possible—for anything in later comedy to rival the unspeakable perfection of Mrs Quickly's eloquence at its best; at such moments as when her claim to be acknowledged as Lady Falstaff was reinforced, if not by the spiritual authority of Master Dumb, by the correlative evidence of Mrs Keech;[9] but no reader above the level of intelligence which prefers to Shakespeare the Parisian Ibsen and the Norwegian Sardou[10] can dispute the fact that Mrs Gamp has once and again risen even to that unimaginable supremacy of triumph.

At the first interview vouchsafed to us with the adorable Sairey, we feel that no words can express our sense of the divinely altruistic and devoted nature which finds utterance in the sweetly and sublimely simple words—'If I could afford to lay all my feller creeturs out for nothink, I would gladly do it: sich is the love I bear 'em.' We think of little Tommy Harris, and the little red worsted shoe gurgling in his throat; of the previous occasion when his father sought shelter and silence in an empty dog-kennel; of that father's immortally infamous reflection on the advent of his ninth; of religious feelings, of life, and the end of all things; of Mr Gamp, his wooden leg, and their precious boy; of her calculations and her experiences with reference to birth and death; of her views as to the expediency of travel by steam, which anticipated Ruskin's and those of later dissenters from the gospel of hurry and the religion of mechanism; of the contents of Mrs Harris's pocket; of the incredible incredulity of the infidel Mrs Prig; we think of all this, and of more than all this, and acknowledge with infinite thanksgiving of inexhaustible laughter and of rapturous admiration the very greatest comic poet or creator that ever lived to make the life of other men more bright and more glad and more perfect than ever, without his beneficent influence, it possibly or imaginably could have been.

The advance in power of tragic invention, the increased strength in grasp of character and grip of situation, which distinguishes *Chuzzlewit* from *Nickleby*, may be tested by comparison of the leading villains. Ralph Nickleby might almost have walked straight off the boards on which the dramatic genius of his nephew was employed to bring into action two tubs and a pump: Jonas Chuzzlewit has his place of eminence for ever among the most memorable types of living and breathing wickedness that ever were stamped and branded with immortality by the indignant genius of a great and unrelenting master. Neither Vautrin nor Thénardier[11] has more of evil and of deathless life in him.

It is not only by his masterpieces, it is also by his inferior works or even by his comparative failures that the greatness of a great writer may be reasonably judged and tested. We can measure in some degree the genius of Thackeray by the fact that *Pendennis*, with all its marvellous wealth of character and humour and living truth, has never been and never will be rated among his very greatest works. *Dombey and Son* cannot be held nearly so much of a success as *Pendennis*. I have known a man of the very highest genius and the most fervent enthusiasm for that of Dickens who never could get through it. There is nothing of a story, and all that nothing (to borrow a phrase from Martial)[12] is bad. The Roman starveling had nothing to lose, and lost it all: the story of Dombey has no plot, and that a very stupid one. The struttingly offensive father and his gushingly submissive daughter are failures of the first magnitude. Little Paul is a more credible child than little Nell; he sometimes forgets that he is foredoomed by a more than Pauline or Calvinistic law of predestination to die in the odour of sentiment, and says or thinks or does something really and quaintly childlike. But we get, to say the least, a good deal of him; and how much too little do we get of Jack Bunsby! Not so very much more than of old Bill Barley;[13] and yet those two ancient mariners are berthed for ever in the inmost shrine of our affections. Another patch of the very brightest purple sewn into the sometimes rather threadbare stuff or groundwork of the story is the scene in which the dissolution of a ruined household is so tragicomically set before us in the breaking up of the servants' hall. And when we think upon the cherished names of Toots and Nipper, Gills and Cuttle, Rob the Grinder and good Mrs Brown, we are tempted to throw conscience to the winds, and affirm that the book is a good book.

But even if we admit that here was an interlude of comparative failure, we cannot but feel moved to acclaim with all the more ardent gratitude the appearance of the next and perhaps the greatest gift bestowed on us by this magnificent and immortal benefactor. *David Copperfield*, from the first chapter to the last, is unmistakable by any eye above the level and beyond the insight of a beetle's as one of the masterpieces to which time can only add a new charm and an unimaginable value. The narrative is as coherent and harmonious as that of *Tom Jones*; and to say this is to try it by the very highest and apparently the most unattainable standard. But I must venture to reaffirm my conviction that even the glorious masterpiece of Fielding's radiant and beneficent genius, if in some points superior, is by no means superior in all. Tom is a far completer and more living type of gallant boyhood and generous young manhood than David; but even the lustre of Partridge is pallid and lunar beside the noontide glory of Micawber. Blifil is a more poisonously plausible villain than Uriah: Sophia Western remains unequalled except by her sister heroine Amelia as a perfectly credible and adorable type of young English womanhood, naturally 'like one of Shakespeare's women',[14] socially as fine and true a lady as Congreve's Millamant or Angelica. But even so large-minded and liberal a genius as Fielding's could never have conceived any figure like Miss Trotwood's, any group like that of the Peggottys. As easily could it have imagined and realised the magnificent setting of the story, with its homely foreground of street or wayside and its background of tragic sea.

The perfect excellence of this masterpiece has perhaps done some undeserved injury to the less impeccable works of genius which immediately succeeded it. But in *Bleak House* the daring experiment of combination or alternation which divides a story between narrative in the third person and narrative in the first is justified and vindicated by its singular and fascinating success. 'Esther's narrative' is as good as her creator's; and no enthusiasm of praise could overrate the excellence of them both. For wealth and variety of character none of the master's works can be said to surpass and few can be said to equal it. When all necessary allowance has been made for occasional unlikeliness in detail or questionable methods of exposition, the sustained interest and the terrible pathos of Lady Dedlock's tragedy will remain unaffected and unimpaired. Any reader can object that a lady visiting a slum in the disguise of a servant would not have kept jewelled rings on her fingers for the inspection of a crossing-sweeper, or that a less decorous and plausible way of acquainting her with the fact that a scandalous episode in her early life was no longer a secret for the family lawyer could hardly have been imagined than the public narrative of her story in her own drawing-room by way of an evening's entertainment for her husband and their guests. To these objections, which any Helot of culture whose brain may have been affected by habitual indulgence in the academic delirium of self-complacent superiority may advance or may suggest with the most exquisite infinity of impertinence, it may be impossible to retort an equally obvious and inconsiderable objection.

But to a far more serious charge, which even now appears to survive the confutation of all serious evidence, it is incomprehensible and inexplicable that Dickens should have returned no better an answer than he did. Harold Skimpole was said to be Leigh Hunt;[15] a rascal after the order of Wainewright,[16] without the poisoner's comparatively and diabolically admirable audacity of frank and fiendish self-esteem, was assumed to be meant for a portrait or a caricature of an honest man and a man of unquestionable genius. To this most serious and most disgraceful charge Dickens merely replied that he never anticipated the identification of the rascal Skimpole with the fascinating Harold—the attribution of imaginary villainy to the original model who suggested or supplied a likeness for the externally amiable and ineffectually accomplished lounger and shuffler through life. The simple and final reply should have been that indolence was the essential quality of the character and conduct and philosophy of Skimpole—'a perfectly idle man: a mere amateur', as he describes himself to the sympathetic and approving Sir Leicester; that Leigh Hunt was one of the hardest and steadiest workers on record, throughout a long and chequered life, at the toilsome trade of letters; and therefore that to represent him as a heartless and shameless idler would have been about as rational an enterprise, as lifelike a design after the life, as it would have been to represent Shelley as a gluttonous and canting hypocrite or Byron as a loyal and unselfish friend. And no one as yet, I believe, has pretended to recognise in Mr Jarndyce a study from Byron, in Mr Chadband a libel on Shelley.

Of the two shorter novels which would suffice to preserve for ever the fame of Dickens, some readers will as probably always prefer *Hard Times* as others will prefer *A Tale of Two Cities*. The later of these is doubtless the most ingeniously and dramatically invented and constructed of all the master's works; the earlier seems to me the greater in moral and pathetic and humorous effect. The martyr workman, beautiful as is the study of his character and terrible as is the record of his tragedy, is almost too spotless a sufferer and a saint; the lifelong lapidation of this unluckier Stephen[17] is somewhat too consistent and insistent and persistent for any record but that of a martyrology; but the obdurate and histrionic affectation which animates the brutality and stimulates the selfishness of Mr Bounderby is only too lamentably truer and nearer to the unlovely side of life. Mr Ruskin—a name never to be mentioned without reverence—thought otherwise; but in knowledge and insight into character and ethics that nobly minded man of genius was no more comparable to Dickens than in sanity of ardour and rationality of aspiration for progressive and practical reform.

As a social satirist Dickens is usually considered to have shown himself at his weakest; the curious and seemingly incorrigible ignorance which imagined that the proper title of Sir John Smith's wife was Lady John Smith, and that the same noble peer could be known to his friends and parasites alternately as Lord Jones and Lord James Jones, may naturally make us regret the absence from their society of our old Parisian friend Sir Brown, Esquire; but though such singular designations as these were never rectified or removed from the text of *Nicholas Nickleby*, and though a Lady Kew was as far outside the range of his genius as a Madame Marneffe,[18] his satire of social pretension and pretence was by no means always 'a swordstroke in the water' or a flourish in the air. Mrs Sparsit is as typical and immortal as any figure of Molière's; and the fact that Mr Sparsit was a Powler is one which can never be forgotten.

There is no surer way of testing the greatness of a really great writer than by consideration of his work at its weakest, and comparison of that comparative weakness with the strength of lesser men at their strongest and their best. The romantic and fanciful comedy of *Love's Labour's Lost* is hardly a perceptible jewel in the sovereign crown of Shakespeare; but a single passage in a single scene of it—the last of the fourth act—is more than sufficient to outweigh, to outshine, to eclipse and efface for ever the dramatic lucubrations or prescriptions of Dr Ibsen—Fracastoro of the drama[19]—and his volubly grateful patients. Among the mature works of Dickens and of Thackeray, I suppose most readers would agree in the opinion that the least satisfactory, if considered as representative of the author's incomparable powers, are *Little Dorrit* and *The Virginians*; yet no one above the intellectual level of an Ibsenite or a Zolaist will doubt or will deny that there is enough merit in either of these books for the stable foundation of an enduring fame.

The conception of *Little Dorrit* was far happier and more promising than that of *Dombey and Son*; which indeed is not much to say for it. Mr Dombey is a doll; Mr Dorrit is an everlasting figure of comedy in its most tragic aspect and tragedy in its most comic phase. Little Dorrit herself might be less untruly than unkindly described as Little Nell grown big, or, in Milton's phrase, 'writ large'.[20] But on that very account she is a more credible and therefore a more really and rationally pathetic figure. The incomparable incoherence of the parts which pretend in vain to compose the incomposite story may be gauged by the collapse of some of them and the vehement hurry of cramped and halting invention which huddles up the close of it without an attempt at the rational and natural evolution of others. It is like a child's dissected map with some of the counties or kingdoms missing. Much, though certainly not all, of the humour is of the poorest kind possible to Dickens; and the reiterated repetition of comic catchwords and tragic illustrations of character is such as to affect the nerves no less than the intelligence of the reader with irrepressible irritation. But this, if he be wise, will be got over and kept under by his sense of admiration and of gratitude for the unsurpassable excellence of the finest passages and chapters. The day after the death of Mr Merdle is one of the most memorable dates in all the record of creative history—or, to use one word in place of two, in all the record of fiction. The fusion of humour and horror in the marvellous chapter which describes it is comparable only with the kindred work of such creators as the authors of *Les Misérables* and *King Lear*. And nothing in the work of Balzac is newer and truer and more terrible than the relentless yet not unmerciful evolution of the central figure in the story. The Father of the Marshalsea is so pitiably worthy of pity as well as of scorn that it would have seemed impossible to heighten or to deepen the contempt or the compassion of the reader; but when he falls from adversity to prosperity he succeeds in soaring down and sinking up to a more tragicomic ignominy of more aspiring degradation. And his end is magnificent.

It must always be interesting as well as curious to observe the natural attitude of mind, the inborn instinct of intelligent antipathy or sympathy, discernible or conjecturable in the greatest writer of any nation at any particular date, with regard to the characteristic merits or demerits of foreigners. Dickens was once most unjustly taxed with injustice to the French, by an evidently loyal and cordial French critic, on the ground that the one Frenchman of any mark in all his books was a murderer. The polypseudonymous ruffian who uses and wears out as many stolen names as ever did even the most cowardly and virulent of literary poisoners is doubtless an unlovely figure: but not even Mr Peggotty and his infant niece are painted with more tender and fervent sympathy than the good Corporal and little Bebelle. Hugo could not—even omnipotence has its limits—have given a more perfect and living picture of a hero and a child. I wish I could think he would have given it as the picture of an English hero and an English child. But I do think that Italian readers of *Little Dorrit* ought to appreciate and to enjoy the delightful and admirable personality of Cavalletto. Mr Baptist in Bleeding Heart Yard is as attractively memorable a figure as his excellent friend Signor Panco.

And how much more might be said—would the gods annihilate but time and space for a worthier purpose than that of making two lovers happy—of the splendid successes to be noted in the least successful book or books of this great and inexhaustible writer! And if the figure or development of the story in *Little Dorrit*, the shapeliness in parts or the proportions of the whole, may seem to have suffered from tight-lacing in this part and from padding in that, the harmony and unity of the masterpiece which followed it made ample and magnificent amends. In *A Tale of Two Cities* Dickens, for the second and last time, did history the honour to enrol it in the service of fiction. This faultless work of tragic and creative art has nothing of the rich and various exuberance which makes of *Barnaby Rudge* so marvellous an example of youthful genius in all the glowing growth of its bright and fiery April; but it has the classic and poetic symmetry of perfect execution and of perfect design. One or two of the figures in the story which immediately preceded it are unusually liable to the usually fatuous objection which dullness has not yet grown decently ashamed of bringing against the characters of Dickens: to the charge of exaggeration and unreality in the posture or the mechanism of puppets and of daubs, which found its final and supremely offensive expression in the chattering duncery and the impudent malignity of so consummate and pseudosophical a quack as George Henry Lewes.[21] Not even such a past-master in the noble science of defamation could plausibly have dared to cite in support of his insolent and idiotic impeachment either the leading or the supplementary characters in *A Tale of Two Cities*. The pathetic and heroic figure of Sydney Carton seems rather to have cast into the shade of comparative neglect the no less living and admirable figures among and over which it stands and towers in our memory. Miss Pross and Mr Lorry, Madame Defarge and her husband, are equally and indisputably to be recognised by the sign of eternal life.

Among the highest landmarks of success ever reared for immortality by the triumphant genius of Dickens, the story of *Great Expectations* must for ever stand eminent beside that of *David Copperfield*. These are his great twin masterpieces. Great as they are, there is nothing in them greater than the very best things in some of his other books: there is certainly no person preferable and there is possibly no person comparable to Samuel Weller or to Sarah Gamp. Of the two childish and boyish autobiographers, David is the better little fellow though not the more lifelike little friend; but of all first chapters is there any comparable for impression and for fusion of humour and terror and pity and fancy and truth to that which confronts the child with the convict on the marshes in the twilight? And the story is incomparably the finer story of the two; there can be none superior, if there be any equal to it, in the whole range of English fiction. And except in *Vanity Fair* and *The Newcomes*, if even they may claim exception, there can surely be found no equal or nearly equal number of living and everliving figures. The tragedy and the comedy, the realism and the dreamery of life, are fused or mingled together with little less than Shakespearean strength and skill of hand. To have created Abel Magwitch is to be a god indeed among the creators of deathless men. Pumblechook is actually better and droller and truer to imaginative life than Pecksniff: Joe Gargery is worthy to have been praised and loved at once by Fielding and by Sterne: Mr Jaggers and his clients, Mr Wemmick and his parent and his bride, are such figures as Shakespeare, when dropping out of poetry,[22] might have created, if his lot had been cast in a later century. Can as much be said for the creatures of any other man or god? The ghastly tragedy of Miss Havisham could only have been made at once credible and endurable by Dickens; he alone could have reconciled the strange and sordid horror with the noble and pathetic survival of possible emotion and repentance. And he alone could have eluded condemnation for so gross an oversight as the escape from retribution of so important a criminal as the 'double murderer and monster' whose baffled or inadequate attempts are enough to make Bill Sikes seem comparatively the gentlest and Jonas Chuzzlewit the most amiable of men.[23] I remember no such flaw in any other story I ever read. But in this story it may well have been allowed to pass unrebuked and unobserved; which yet I think it should not.

Among all the minor and momentary figures which flash into eternity across the stage of Dickens, there is one to which I have never yet seen the tribute of grateful homage adequately or even decently paid. The sonorous claims of old Bill Barley on the reader's affectionate and respectful interest have not remained without response; but the landlord's Jack has never yet, as far as I am aware, been fully recognised as great among the greatest of the gods of comic fiction. We are introduced to this lifelong friend in a waterside public-house as a 'grizzled male creature, the "Jack"[24] of the little causeway, who was as slimy and smeary as if he had been low watermark too'. It is but for a moment that we meet him: but eternity is in that moment.

> While we were comforting ourselves by the fire after our meal, the Jack—who was sitting in a corner, and who had a bloated pair of shoes on, which he had exhibited, while we were eating our eggs and bacon, as interesting relics that he had taken a few days ago from the feet of a drowned seaman washed ashore—asked me if we had seen a four-oared galley going up with the tide? When I told him No, he said she must have gone down then, and yet she 'took up two', when she left there.
>
> 'They must ha' thought better on't for some reason or another, said the Jack, 'and gone down.'
>
> 'A four-oared galley, did you say?' said I.
>
> 'A four,' said the Jack, 'and two sitters.'
>
> 'Did they come ashore here?'
>
> 'They put in with a stone two-gallon jar for some beer. I'd ha' been glad to pison the beer myself,' said the Jack, 'or put some rattling physic in it.'
>
> 'Why?'
>
> '*I* know why,' said the Jack. He spoke in a slushy voice, as if much mud had washed into his throat.
>
> 'He thinks,' said the landlord, a weakly meditative man with a pale eye, who seemed to rely greatly on his Jack, 'he thinks they was, what they wasn't.'
>
> '*I* knows what I thinks,' observed the Jack.
>
> 'You thinks Custum 'Us, Jack?' said the landlord.
>
> 'I do,' said the Jack.
>
> 'Then you're wrong, Jack.'
>
> 'AM I!'
>
> In the infinite meaning of his reply and his boundless confidence in his views, the Jack took one of his bloated shoes off, looked into it, knocked a few stones out of it on the kitchen floor, and

> put it on again. He did this with the air of a Jack who was so right that he could afford to do anything.
>
> 'Why, what do you make out that they done with their buttons then, Jack?' said the landlord, vacillating weakly.
>
> 'Done with their buttons?' returned the Jack. 'Chucked 'em overboard. Swallered 'em. Sowed 'em, to come up small salad. Done with their buttons!'
>
> 'Don't be cheeky, Jack,' remonstrated the landlord, in a melancholy and pathetic way.
>
> 'A Custum 'Us officer knows what to do with his Buttons,' said the Jack, repeating the obnoxious word with the greatest contempt, 'when they comes betwixt him and his own light. A Four and two sitters don't go hanging and hovering, up with one tide and down with another, and both with and against another, without there being Custum 'Us at the bottom of it.' Saying which, he went out in disdain.

To join Francis the drawer and Cob the water-bearer in an ever-blessed immortality.[25]

This was the author's last great work: the defects in it are as nearly imperceptible as spots on the sun or shadows on a sunlit sea. His last long story, *Our Mutual Friend*, superior as it is in harmony and animation to *Little Dorrit* or *Dombey and Son*, belongs to the same class of piebald or rather skewbald fiction. As in the first great prose work of the one greater and far greater genius then working in the world the cathedral of Notre Dame is the one prevailing and dominating presence, the supreme and silent witness of life and action and passion and death, so in this last of its writer's completed novels the real protagonist—for the part it plays is rather active than passive—is the river. Of a play attributed on the obviously worthless authority of all who knew or who could have known anything about the matter to William Shakespeare, but now ascribed on the joint authority of Bedlam and Hanwell[26] to the joint authorship of Francis Bacon and John Fletcher, assisted by the fraternal collaboration of their fellow-poets Sir Walter Raleigh and King James I, it was very unjustly said by Dr Johnson that 'the genius of the author comes in and goes out with Queen Katherine'. Of this book it might more justly be said that the genius of the author ebbs and flows with the disappearance and the reappearance of the Thames.

That unfragrant and insanitary waif of its rottenest refuse, the incomparable Rogue Riderhood, must always hold a chosen place among the choicest villains of our selectest acquaintance. When the genius of his immortal creator said 'Let there be Riderhood',[27] and there was Riderhood, a figure of coequal immortality rose reeking and skulking into sight. The deliciously amphibious nature of the venomous human reptile is so wonderfully preserved in his transference from Southwark Bridge to Plashwater Weir Mill Lockhouse that we feel it impossible for imagination to detach the water-snake from the water, the water-rat from the mud. There is a horrible harmony, a hellish consistency, in the hideous part he takes in the martyrdom of Betty Higden—the most nearly intolerable tragedy in all the tragic work of Dickens. Even the unsurpassed and unsurpassable grandeur and beauty of the martyred old heroine's character can hardly make the wonderful record of her heroic agony endurable by those who have been so tenderly and so powerfully compelled to love and to revere her. The divine scene in the children's hospital is something that could only have been conceived and that could only have been realised by two of the greatest among writers and creators: it is a curious and memorable thing that they should have shone upon our sight together.

We can only guess what manner of tribute Victor Hugo might have paid to Dickens on reading how Johnny 'bequeathed all he had to dispose of, and arranged his affairs in this world'. But a more incomparable scene than this is the resurrection of Rogue Riderhood. That is one of the very greatest works of any creator who ever revealed himself as a master of fiction: a word, it should be unnecessary to repeat, synonymous with the word creation. The terrible humour of it holds the reader entranced alike at the first and the hundredth reading. And the blatant boobies who deny truthfulness and realism to the imagination or the genius of Dickens, because it never condescended or aspired to wallow in metaphysics or in filth, may be fearlessly challenged to match this scene for tragicomic and everlasting truth in the work of Sardou or Ibsen, of the bisexual George Eliot or the masculine 'Miss Mævia Mannish'.[28] M. Zola, had he imagined it, as undoubtedly his potent and indisputable genius might have done, must have added a flavour of blood and a savour of ordure which would hardly have gratified or tickled the nostrils and the palate of Dickens: but it is possible that this insular delicacy or prudery of relish and of sense may not be altogether a pitiable infirmity or a derisible defect. Every scene in which Mr Inspector or Miss Abbey Potterson figures is as lifelike as it could be if it were foul instead of fair—if it were as fetid with the reek of malodorous realism as it is fragrant with the breath of kindly and homely nature.

The fragmentary *Mystery of Edwin Drood* has things in it worthy of Dickens at his best: whether the completed work would probably have deserved a place among his best must always be an open question. It is certain that if Shakespeare had completed *The Two Noble Kinsmen*; if Hugo had completed *Les Jumeaux*; or if Thackeray had completed *Denis Duval*, the world would have been richer by a deathless and a classic masterpiece. It is equally certain that the grim and tragic humours of the opium den and the boy-devil are worthy of the author of *Barnaby Rudge*, that the leading villain is an original villain of great promise, and that the interest which assuredly, for the average reader, is not awakened in Mr Drood and Miss Bud is naturally aroused by the sorrows and perils of the brother and sister whose history is inwoven with theirs. It is uncertain beyond all reach of reasonable conjecture whether the upshot of the story would have been as satisfactory as the conclusion, for instance, of *David Copperfield* or *Martin Chuzzlewit*, or as far from satisfactory as the close of *Little Dorrit* or *Dombey and Son*.

If Dickens had never in his life undertaken the writing of a long story, he would still be great among the immortal writers of his age by grace of his matchless excellence as a writer of short stories. His earlier Christmas books might well suffice for the assurance of a lasting fame; and the best of them are far surpassed in excellence by his contributions to the Christmas numbers of his successive magazines. We remember the noble 'Chimes', the delightful 'Carol', the entrancing 'Cricket on the Hearth', the delicious Tetterbys who make 'The Haunted Man and the Ghost's Bargain' immortal and unghostly, and even the good stolid figure of Clemency Newcome, which redeems from the torpid peace of absolute nonentity so nearly complete a failure as 'The Battle of Life'; but the Christmas work done for *Household Words* and *All the Year Round* is at its best on a higher level than the best of these. 'The Wreck of the Golden Mary' is the work of a genius till then unimaginable—a Defoe with a human heart. More lifelike or more accurate in seamanship, more noble and natural in manhood, it could not have been if the soul of Shakespeare or of Hugo had entered into the somewhat inhuman or at least insensitive genius which begot Robinson Crusoe on Moll Flanders.

Among the others every reader will always have his special favourites: I do not say his chosen favourites; he will not choose but find them; it is not a question to be settled by judgment but by instinct. All are as good of their kind as they need be: children and schoolboys, soldiers and sailors, showmen and waiters, landladies and cheap-jacks, signalmen and cellarmen: all of them actual and convincing, yet all of them sealed of the tribe of Dickens; real if ever any figures in any book were real, yet as unmistakable in their paternity as the children of Chaucer, of Shakespeare, or of Fielding. A modest and honest critic will always, when dealing with questions of preference in such matters, be guided by the example of the not always exemplary Mr Jingle—'not presume to dictate, but broiled fowl and mushrooms—capital thing!'[29] He may in that case indicate his own peculiar addiction to the society of Toby Magsman and Mr Chops, Captain Jorgan, Mr Christopher (surely one of the most perfect figures ever drawn and coloured by such a hand as Shakespeare's or Dekker's or Sterne's or Thackeray's), Mrs Lirriper and Major Jackman, Dr Marigold, and Barbox Brothers. The incredible immensity, measurable by no critic ever born, of such a creative power as was needed to call all these into immortal life would surely, had Dickens never done any work on a larger scale of invention and construction, have sufficed for a fame great enough to deserve the applause and the thanksgiving of all men worthy to acclaim it, and the contempt of such a Triton of the minnows as Matthew Arnold. A man whose main achievement in creative literature was to make himself by painful painstaking into a sort of pseudo-Wordsworth[30] could pay no other tribute than that of stolid scorn to a genius of such inexhaustible force and such indisputable originality as that of Charles Dickens. It is not always envy, I hope and believe, which disables and stupefies such brilliant and versatile examples of the minor poet and the minor critic when appreciation of anything new and great is found impossible for their self-complacent and self-centred understanding to attain. It is just that they cannot see high enough; they were born so, and will please themselves; as they do, and always did, and always will. And not even the tribute of equals or superiors is more precious and more significant than such disdain or such distaste as theirs.

These Christmas numbers are not, because of their small bulk, to be classed among the minor works of Dickens: they are gems as costly as any of the larger in his crown of fame. Of his lesser works the best and most precious is beyond all question or comparison *The Uncommercial Traveller*; a book which would require another volume of the same size to praise it adequately or aright. Not that there are not other short studies as good as its very best among the 'reprinted pieces' which preserve for us and for all time the beloved figure of

Our Bore, the less delightful figures of the noble savage and the begging-letter writer, the pathetic plaint of Mr Meek, and the incomparable studies and stories of the detective police. We could perhaps dispense with *Pictures from Italy*, and even with *American Notes*, except for the delicious account or narrative or description of seasickness, which will always give such exquisite intensity of rapture to boys born impervious to that ailment and susceptible only of enjoyment in rough weather at sea as can hardly be rivalled by the delight of man or boy in Mrs Gamp herself. But there is only one book which I cannot but regret that Dickens should have written; and I cannot imagine what evil imp, for what inscrutable reason in the unjustifiable designs of a malevolent Providence, was ever permitted to suggest to him the perpetration of *A Child's History of England*. I would almost as soon train up a child on Catholic or Calvinistic or servile or disloyal principles as on the cheap-jack radicalism which sees nothing to honour or love or revere in history, and ought therefore to confess that it can in reason pretend to see nothing on which to build any hope of patriotic advance or progressive endurance in the future.

A word may be added on the everlasting subject of editors and editions: a subject on which it really seems impossible that the countrymen of Shakespeare and of Dickens should ever be aroused to a sense that the matter is really worth care and consideration. Instead of reprinting the valuable and interesting prefaces written by Dickens for the first cheap edition of his collected works (a poor little double-columned reissue), the publishers of the beautiful and convenient Gadshill series are good enough to favour its purchasers with the prefatory importunities of a writer disentitled to express and disqualified to form an opinion on the work of an English humorist. The intrusive condescension or adulation of such a commentator was perhaps somewhat superfluous in front of the reprinted Waverley Novels; the offence becomes an outrage, the impertinence becomes impudence, when such rubbish is shot down before the doorstep of Charles Dickens.[31]

It is curious to compare the posthumous fortune of two such compeers in fame as Dickens and Thackeray. Rivals they were not and could not be: comparison or preference of their respective work is a subject fit only to be debated by the energetic idleness of boyhood. In life Dickens was the more prosperous: Thackeray has had the better fortune after death. To the exquisite genius, the tender devotion, the faultless taste and the unfailing tact of his daughter, we owe the most perfect memorial ever raised to the fame and to the character of any great writer on record by any editor or commentator or writer of prefaces or preludes to his work. A daughter of Dickens has left us a very charming little volume of reminiscences in which we enjoy the pleasure and honour of admission to his private presence: we yet await an edition of his works which may be worthy to stand beside the biographical edition of Thackeray's. So much we ought to have: we can demand and we can desire no more.

NOTES

1 Adapted from Burns's 'On the Late Captain Grose's Peregrinations thro' Scotland' (l. 5), 'us' being substituted for 'you'.
2 Chapter 55 of *Nicholas Nickleby*.
3 *As You Like It*, II, iii, 74: 'But at fourscore it is too late a week.'
4 Swinburne's grandfather.
5 Little Nell.
6 Mrs Quickly appears in the plays dealing with Henry IV and V and in *The Merry Wives of Windsor*; Mrs Gamp, in *Martin Chuzzlewit*.
7 'The thing filled him with such pity'; near the close of Hugo's *Notre Dame de Paris*.
8 Hugh in *Barnaby Rudge* (chapter 77): 'On that black tree, of which I am the ripened fruit, I do invoke the curse of all its victims, past, and present, and to come.' For Silas Wegg, see note 22 below.
9 *2 Henry IV*, II, i.
10 The exchange of nationality is of course intentional.
11 Jacques Collin, alias Vautrin, is a cynical convict and corrupter in Balzac's *Père Goriot*; Thénardier, a scoundrel in Hugo's *Les Miserables*.
12 See, among 'Epigrams Ascribed to Martial', the Loeb Library edition, xiii, 'On Filus'.
13 Jack Bunsby, a friend of Captain Cuttle, in *Dombey and Son*; Bill Barley, Clara's father, in *Great Expectations*.
14 Unidentified.
15 See the Introduction, section II.
16 Thomas Griffiths Wainewright (1794–1852), an art critic and figure in literary circles who became a poisoner.
17 Acts 7: 59.
18 Lady Kew is a dominating old woman in Thackeray's *Newcomes*; Madame Marneffe, in Balzac's *Cousine Bette*, is beautiful and unprincipled.
19 Italian physician (*c.* 1483–1553) who in a Latin poem described 'the terrible disease inflicted by Apollo on the young shepherd Syphilus'. Because of its use of the same disease, Ibsen's *Ghosts* shocked its early audiences and readers.

20 From 'On the New Forces of Conscience': 'New presbyter is but old priest writ large.'

21 Swinburne remembers a central point in Lewes's influential essay 'Dickens in Relation to Criticism' (*Fortnightly Review*, February 1872), which contains a disparaging analysis of Dickens's methods of characterization and reveals a distaste for the novelist's lack of profundity.

22 In chapter 5 of *Our Mutual Friend* Silas Wegg and Mr Boffin discuss the possibility of Wegg's 'dropping into poetry' during the course of his reading to Boffin.

23 Bill Sikes is a villain in *Oliver Twist*; Jonas Chuzzlewit, in *Martin Chuzzlewit*. The allusion is to Dolge Orlick in *Great Expectations*.

24 A male attendant, one who does odd jobs.

25 Francis appears in *1 Henry IV*, II, iv; Cob, in Jonson's *Every Man in His Humour*.

26 There was a large lunatic asylum near Hanwell (in Middlesex), as well as some private asylums in the parish. On *Henry VII*, see p. 19.

27 The divine fiat (cf. Gen. 1: 3) is applied to the creation of Riderhood in *Our Mutual Friend*.

28 'Maevia' from analogy with 'Maevius', one of the bad poets mentioned in Vergil's *Eclogues* (iii, 90–1). The comment on George Eliot may be aimed partly at Lewes (see note 21).

29 In chapter 2 of *Pickwick Papers*.

30 An obvious retort to Arnold's calling Swinburne 'a sort of pseudo-Shelley' in a letter of 1863, not published till after Arnold's death. 'Triton of the minnows' is prompted by Arnold's praise of such minor authors as Eugénie and Maurice de Guérin. As Swinburne may have heard, Arnold's early impressions of Dickens were hardly favourable, but in his chapter on 'The Incompatibles' in *Irish Essays and Others* (London, 1882) he praised *David Copperfield* highly, using three of its characters (Creakle, Murdstone, and Quinion) to illustrate qualities that made the English repellent to the Irish. (Arnold's editor, Professor R. H. Super, supplies this reference.)

31 Swinburne's attitude towards Lang is partly due to Lang's 'To Lord Byron' in his *Letters to Dead Authors* (1895), which deals harshly with Swinburne's reasons (in 'Wordsworth and Byron') for disagreeing with Arnold's ranking Byron above Shelley. Watts-Dunton suggested that Swinburne doubted that a Scot could appreciate Dickensian humour. (Did Swinburne remember Charles Lamb's 'Imperfect Sympathies' and forget that the Scots are countrymen of Robert Burns and Walter Scott, both notable for a sense of humour?) Lang wrote with some awareness that at the moment the vogue of Russian and French fiction had made Dickens seem old-fashioned, but his introductions to volumes of the Gadshill edition are more favourable to Dickens than Swinburne may seem to imply.

Drama

19 Congreve
1877, 1886

Swinburne's first discussion of Congreve, one of his earliest published writings, appeared in the *Imperial Dictionary of Universal Biography* (1857). The sketch below, after being published in the ninth edition of the *Encyclopædia Britannica* (vi, 1877), was included in *Miscellanies* (1886).

William Congreve, the greatest English master of pure comedy, was born, according to the latest and likeliest accounts, in 1670, according to the inscription on his monument, in 1672; and whether in England or in Ireland, at Bardsey near Leeds or at some place unknown beyond St. George's Channel, has likewise been matter of doubt and dispute; but we may presumably accept the authority of Lord Macaulay, who decides against Dr. Johnson in favour of the later date, and dismisses without notice the tradition of an Irish birthplace. To Ireland, at all events, is due the credit of his education,—as a schoolboy at Kilkenny, as an undergraduate at Dublin. From college he came to London, and was entered as a student of law at the Middle Temple.

The first-fruits of his studies appeared under the boyish pseudonym of 'Cleophil',[1] in the form of a novel whose existence is now remembered only through the unabashed avowal of so austere a moralist as Dr. Johnson, that he 'would rather praise it than read it'.[2] In 1693 Congreve's real career began, and early enough by the latest computation, with the brilliant appearance and instant success of his first comedy, *The Old Bachelor*, under the generous auspices of Dryden, then as ever a living and immortal witness to the falsehood of the vulgar charge which taxes the greater among poets with jealousy or envy, the natural badge and brand of the smallest that would claim a place among their kind. The discrowned laureate had never, he said, seen such a first play; and indeed the graceless grace of the dialogue was as yet only to be matched by the last and best work of Etherege, standing as till then it had done alone among the barefaced brutalities of Wycherley and Shadwell. The types of Congreve's first work were the common conventional properties of stage tradition; but the fine and clear-cut style in which these types were reproduced was his own. The gift of one place and the reversion of another were the solid fruits of his splendid success. Next year a better play from the same hand met with worse fortune on the stage, and with yet higher honour from the first living poet of his nation. The noble verses, as faultless in the expression as reckless in the extravagance of their applause, prefixed by Dryden to *The Double Dealer*, must naturally have supported the younger poet, if indeed such support can have been required, against the momentary annoyance of assailants whose passing clamour left uninjured and secure the fame of his second comedy; for the following year witnessed the crowning triumph of his art and life, in the appearance of *Love for Love*. Two years later his ambition rather than his genius adventured on the foreign ground of tragedy, and *The Mourning Bride* began such a long career of good fortune as in earlier or later times would have been closed against a far better work. Next year he attempted, without his usual success, a reply to the attack of Jeremy Collier, the nonjuror, *On the Immorality and Profaneness of the English Stage*—an attack for once not discreditable to the assailant, whose honesty and courage were evident enough to approve him incapable alike of the ignominious precaution which might have suppressed his own name, and of the dastardly mendacity which would have stolen the mask of a stranger's. Against this merit must be set the mistake of confounding in one indiscriminate indictment the levities of a writer like Congreve with the brutalities of a writer like Wycherley; an error which ever since has more or less perverted the judgment of succeeding critics. The general case of comedy was then, however, as untenable by the argument as indefensible by the sarcasm of its most brilliant and comparatively blameless champion. Art itself, more than anything else, had been outraged and degraded by the recent school of the Restoration; and the comic work of Congreve, though different rather in kind than in degree from the bestial and blatant license of his immediate precursors, was inevitably for a time involved in the sentence passed upon the comic work of men in all ways alike his inferiors. The true and triumphant answer to all possible attacks of honest men or liars, brave men or cowards, was then as ever to be given by the production of work unarraignable alike by fair means or foul, by frank impeachment or by furtive imputation. In 1700 Congreve thus replied to Collier with the crowning work of his genius—the unequalled and unapproached masterpiece of English comedy. The one play in our language which may fairly claim a place beside or but just beneath the mightiest work of Molière is *The Way of the World.* On the stage which had recently acclaimed with uncritical applause the author's more questionable appearance in the field of tragedy, this final and flawless evidence of his incomparable powers met with a rejection then and ever since inexplicable on any ground of conjecture. During the twenty-eight years which remained to him, Congreve produced little beyond a volume of fugitive verses, published ten years after the miscarriage of his masterpiece. His even course of good fortune under Whig and Tory Governments alike was counterweighed by the physical infirmities of gout and failing sight. He died, January 29, 1729, in consequence of an injury received on a journey to Bath by the upsetting of his carriage; was buried in Westminster Abbey, after lying in state in the Jerusalem Chamber; and bequeathed the bulk of his fortune to the chief friend of his last years, Henrietta Duchess of Marlborough, daughter of the great duke, rather than to his family, which, according to Johnson, was then in difficulties, or to Mrs. Bracegirdle the actress, with whom he had lived longer on intimate terms than with any other mistress or friend, but who inherited by his will only 200*l.* The one memorable incident of his later life was the visit of Voltaire, whom he astonished and repelled by his rejection of proffered praise and the expression of his wish to be considered merely as any other gentleman of no literary fame. The great master of wellnigh every province in the empire of letters, except the only one in which his host reigned supreme, replied that in that sad case Congreve would not have received his visit.

The fame of our greatest comic dramatist is founded wholly or mainly on but three of his five plays. His first comedy was little more than a brilliant study after such models as were eclipsed by this earliest effort of their imitator; and tragedy under his hands appears rouged and wrinkled, in the patches and powder of Lady Wishfort.[3] But his three great comedies are more than enough to sustain a reputation as durable as our language. Were it not for these we should have no samples to show of comedy in its purest and highest form. Ben Jonson, who alone attempted to introduce it by way of reform among the mixed work of a time when comedy and tragedy were as inextricably blended on the stage as in actual life, failed to give the requisite ease and the indispensable grace of comic life and movement to the action and passion of his elaborate and magnificent work. Of Congreve's immediate predecessors, whose aim had been to raise on French foundations a new English fabric of simple and unmixed comedy, Wycherley was of too base metal and Etherege was of metal too light to be weighed against him; and besides theirs no other or finer coin was current than the crude British ore of Shadwell's brutal and burly talent. Borrowing a metaphor from Landor, we may say that a limb of Molière would have sufficed to make a Congreve, a limb of Congreve would have sufficed to make a Sheridan. The broad and robust humour of Vanbrugh's admirable comedies gives him a place on the master's right hand; on the left stands Farquhar, whose bright light genius is to Congreve's as female is to male, or 'as moonlight unto sunlight'.[4] No English writer, on the whole, has so nearly touched the skirts of Molière; but his splendid intelligence is wanting in the deepest and subtlest quality which has won for Molière from the greatest poet of his country and our age the tribute of exact and final definition conveyed in that perfect phrase which salutes at once and denotes him—'*ce moqueur pensif comme un apôtre*'.[5] Only perhaps in a single part has Congreve half consciously touched a note of almost tragic depth and suggestion; there is something wellnigh akin to the grotesque and piteous figure of Arnolphe himself in the unvenerable old age of Lady Wishfort, set off and relieved as it is, with grace and art worthy of the supreme French master, against the only figure on any stage which need not shun comparison even with that of Célimène.[6]

NOTES

1 *Incognita* (1691).
2 From 'Congreve' in *The Lives of the English Poets.*
3 In *The Way of the World.*
4 From Tennyson's 'Locksley Hall', l. 152.
5 'That mocker as thoughtful as an apostle.' From Hugo's '*Les Pamphlétaires d'église*', l. 98 (in *L'Année terrible*).
6 The heroine of Molière's *Misanthrope*. Arnolphe is the old man in *L'École des femmes.*

20 Chapman's *Bussy D'Ambois*
1875

George Chapman: A Critical Essay (1875), published as a book of some length, also served as the introduction to the third volume of Chapman's *Complete Works*, edited by Richard Herne Shepherd. Swinburne spent much time and effort in helping Shepherd achieve an intelligible text. In addition he wrote a biographical and critical sketch of Chapman for the ninth edition of the *Encyclopædia Britannica* (v, 1876), and included it in *The Age of Shakespeare* (1908). Though the Bonchurch Edition of Swinburne reprinted the other parts of this volume, it omitted that short essay on Chapman. The passage that follows, concerning Chapman's best-known play, is not from it but from the longer work.

The first of Chapman's historic tragedies was published at the age of forty-eight, and stands now sixth on the list of the plays in which he had the help of no partner. He never wrote better and he seldom wrote worse than in this only play of his writing which kept any firm and durable hold on the stage. The impression made on Dryden by its 'glaring colours' in the representation, and the indignant reaction of his judgment 'in the reading', are probably known to more than have studied the work by the light of their own taste. All his vituperation is well deserved by such excerpts as those which alone Sir Walter Scott was careful to select in his editorial note on this passage by way of illustration; not even the sharpest terms in the terrible and splendid arsenal of Dryden's satire can be too vivid or too vigorous in their condemnation of the damnable jargon in which the elder poet was prone to indulge his infirmity; whole sections of his poems and whole scenes of his plays are indeed but shapeless masses of bombast and bulky vacuity, with nothing better in them than most villainous 'incorrect English, and a hideous mingle of false poetry and true nonsense; or at best a scantling of wit, which lies gasping for life and groaning beneath a heap of rubbish'.[1] The injustice of the criticism lies only in the assertion or implication that there was nothing discoverable on all Chapman's ground but such cinder-heaps and wind-bags; whereas the proportion of good to bad in this very play of *Bussy d'Ambois* is enough to outweigh even such demerits as it doubtless shares with too much of its author's work. There is a bright and fiery energy throughout, a vigour of ambitious aspiration, which is transmitted as it were by echo and reflection from the spirit of the poet into the spirit of his hero. The brilliant swordsman of the court of Henri III, who flashes out on us as the joyous central figure of one of the most joyous and vigorous in all the bright list of those large historic groups to which the strong swift hand of Dumas gave colour and life,[2] has undergone at the heavier hand of the old English poet a singular transfiguration. He is still the irresistible duellist and amorist of tradition; but, instead of the grace and courtliness proper to his age and rank, Chapman has bestowed on him the grave qualities of an epic braggart, whose tongue is at least as long as his sword, and whose gasconades have in them less of the Gascon than of our 'Homer-Lucan'[3] himself; who with all his notable interest in the France of his time and her turbulent history had assuredly nothing of the lighter and more gracious characteristics of French genius. But in the broad full outline of this figure, and in the robust handling of the tragic action which serves for environment or for background to its haughty and dilated proportions, there is more proof of greatness than Chapman had yet given. His comic or gnomic poetry may be better or at least less faulty in its kind, but in that kind there is less room for the growth and display of those greater qualities which not unfrequently struggle through the hot and turbid atmosphere of his tragic writing, and show by a stormy and cloudy illumination the higher reaches of his real genius. Nor is there in these rugged outlying highlands of tragedy, and in the somewhat thick and troubled air of the brooding skies above them, no beauty perceptible but the beauty of cloud and flame, of flood and fell: they have intervals of pure sunshine and soft greensward, interludes of grave and tender harmony, aspects of deep and serene attraction. There is a noticeable abruptness and want of ease in the disposal of the incidents, as though the workman were not yet well broken in to his business; and in effect Chapman never did learn to run with perfect ease and grace in tragic harness. Yet if his tragedies were erased from the roll of his works, and only the most perfect of his comedies and the better portions of his other poems were left for our judgment, the sentence that we should then have to pass would assuredly assign him a much lower place among English poets than he now may rightly claim to hold. A greater and a faultier genius finds expression in these tragic poems than in the more general and equable excellence of even his best comic or romantic plays.

The first in order of these, especially at first sight, is beyond question the most effective in point of dramatic interest. With all its tumid and turbid exuberance of speech, the action of this play never actually halts or flags. There is no depth or delicacy of character discernible in any of the leading parts; in some cases indeed it is hard at first to determine whether the author meant to excite the sympathies or the antipathies of his audience for a good or for a bad character; the virtue of the heroine collapses without a touch, and friends and foes change sides with no more reason shown than that the figure of the dance requires it. But the power of hand is gigantic which shifts and shuffles these puppets about the board; there are passages of a sublime and Titanic beauty, rebellious and excessive in style as in sentiment, but full of majestic and massive harmony. The magnificent speech of the hero, stricken to death and leaning on his sword to die, has been often quoted, and as a sample of fiery imagination clothed in verse of solemn and sonorous music it can never be overpraised; the inevitable afterthought that the privilege of tragic poetry to exceed the range of realism is here strained to the utmost and beyond it will recur on reading many of the most memorable passages in these plays, where the epic declamation of the speaker breaks the last limit of law to attain the last limit of license possible to a style which even in outward form keeps up any pretence of dramatic plausibility. Any child may see and object that no man ever died with such a funeral oration on his lips; but any critic qualified to judge of such a poet in his strength and his weakness will temper the reflection with admiration of 'that full and heightened style'[4] which the third among English tragic poets has applauded in the tragedies of Chapman. The height indeed is somewhat giddy, and the fullness too often tends or threatens to dilate into tumidity; sometimes the foot slips and the style stumbles heavily from its height, while for its fullness we find but the emptiness of a burst bladder; but while the writer's head remains clear and his hand sure, the high air of this poetry is fresh and buoyant, and its full cadences have in them a large echo as of mountain winds and waters. And if Webster, with the generous justice proper to a great fellow-craftsman in the highest guild of art, was able to condone the manifest abuse in Chapman's work of rhetoric and mere poetry, those may well be content to do likewise who bear duly in mind the admirable absence of any such defect from the vivid and intense veracity of his own.

NOTES

1 Like the preceding quotation, from Dryden's dedication to *The Spanish Friar.*
2 In Dumas's novel *La Dame de Monsoreau* (1846), as well as in a play.
3 In Samuel Daniel's *Defence of Rhyme* (*c.* 1603).
4 From John Webster's 'To the Reader', prefixed to *The White Devil.*

21 Shakespeare
1880

On 27 August 1879 Swinburne wrote of putting 'the very last touch to the very last sentence of the very last paragraph' of his *Study of Shakespeare* (1880) (Lang, iv, 84). Its nucleus was 'The Three Stages of Shakespeare', in the *Fortnightly Review* for May 1875 and January 1876; of the selections that follow, however, only the first appeared in the periodical. The *Study* begins with Swinburne's most extended analogy. He considered his analysis of Falstaff and of Hamlet and the other great tragic characters to be among the best passages in his book—a judgment with which most readers would agree.

Shakespeare and the Sea

The greatest poet of our age has drawn a parallel of elaborate eloquence between Shakespeare and the sea;[1] and the likeness holds good in many points of less significance than those which have been set down by the master-hand. For two hundred years at least have students of every kind put forth in every sort of boat on a longer or a shorter voyage of research across the waters of that unsounded sea. From the paltriest fishing-craft to such majestic galleys as were steered by Coleridge and by Goethe, each division of the fleet has done or has essayed its turn of work; some busied in dredging along-shore, some taking surveys of this or that gulf or headland, some putting forth through shine and shadow into the darkness of the great deep. Nor does it seem as if there would sooner be an end to men's labour on this than on the other sea. But here a difference is perceptible. The material ocean has been so far mastered by the wisdom and the heroism of man that we may look for a time to come when the mystery shall be manifest of its furthest north and south, and men resolve the secret of the uttermost parts of the sea:[2] the poles also may find their Columbus. But the limits of that other ocean, the laws of its tides, the motive of its forces, the mystery of its unity and the secret of its change, no seafarer of us all may ever think thoroughly to know. No wind-gauge will help us to the science of its storms, no lead-line sound for us the depth of its divine and terrible serenity.

As, however, each generation for some two centuries now or more has witnessed fresh attempts at pilotage and fresh expeditions of discovery undertaken in the seas of Shakespeare, it may be well to study a little the laws of navigation in such waters as these, and look well to compass and rudder before we accept the guidance of a strange helmsman or make proffer for trial of our own. There are shoals and quicksands on which many a seafarer has run his craft aground in time past, and others of more special peril to adventurers of the present day. The chances of shipwreck vary in a certain degree with each new change of vessel and each fresh muster of hands. At one time a main rock of offence[3] on which the stoutest ships of discovery were wont to split was the narrow and slippery reef of verbal emendation; and upon this our native pilots were too many of them prone to steer. Others fell becalmed offshore in a German fog of philosophic theories, and would not be persuaded that the house of words they had built in honour of Shakespeare was 'dark as hell', seeing 'it had bay windows transparent as barricadoes, and the clear-stories towards the south-north were as lustrous as ebony'.[4] These are not the most besetting dangers of more modern steersmen: what we have to guard against now is neither a repetition of the pedantries of Steevens nor a recrudescence of the moralities of Ulrici. Fresh follies spring up in new paths of criticism, and fresh labourers in a fruitless field are at hand to gather them and to garner. A discovery of some importance has recently been proclaimed as with blare of vociferous trumpets and flutter of triumphal flags; no less a discovery than this—that a singer must be tested by his song. Well, it is something that criticism should at length be awake to that wholly indisputable fact; that learned and laborious men who can hear only with their fingers should open their eyes to admit such a novelty, their minds to accept such a paradox, as that a painter should be studied in his pictures and a poet in his verse. To the common herd of students and lovers of either art this may perhaps appear no great discovery; but that it should at length have dawned even upon the race of commentators is a sign which in itself might be taken as a presage of new light to come in an epoch of miracle yet to be. Unhappily it is as yet but a partial revelation that has been vouchsafed to them. To the recognition of the apocalyptic fact that a workman can only be known by his work, and that without examination of his method and material that work can hardly be studied to much purpose, they have yet to add the knowledge of a further truth no less recondite and abstruse than this,[5] that as the technical work of a painter appeals to the eye, so the technical work of a poet appeals to the ear. It follows that men who have none are as likely to arrive at any profitable end by the application of metrical tests to the work of Shakespeare as a blind man by the application of his theory of colours to the work of Titian.

Falstaff

It should on the other hand be noted that the finest touch in the comic scenes, if not the finest in the whole portrait of Falstaff, is apparently an afterthought, a touch added on revision of the original design. In the first scene of the second act Mrs. Quickly's remark that 'he'll yield the crow a pudding one of these days'[1] is common to both versions of the play; but the six words following are only to be found in the revised edition; and these six words the very pirates could hardly have passed over or struck out. They are not such as can drop from the text of a poet unperceived by the very dullest and horniest of human eyes. 'The king has killed his heart.'[2] Here is the point in Falstaff's nature so strangely overlooked by the man of all men who we should have said must be the first to seize and to appreciate it. It is as grievous as it is inexplicable that the Shakespeare of France—the most infinite in compassion, in 'conscience and tender heart',[3] of all great poets in all ages and all nations of the world—should have missed the deep tenderness of this supreme and subtlest touch in the work of the greatest among his fellows. Again, with anything but 'damnable' iteration,[4] does Shakespeare revert to it before the close of this very scene. Even Pistol and Nym can see that what now ails their old master is no such ailment as in his prosperous days was but too liable to 'play the rogue with his great toe'.[5] 'The king hath run bad humours on the knight':[6] 'his heart is fracted, and corroborate.'[7] And it is not thus merely through the eclipse of that brief mirage, that fair prospect 'of Africa, and golden joys',[8] in view of which he was ready to 'take any man's horses'.[9] This it is that distinguishes Falstaff from Panurge; that lifts him at least to the moral level of Sancho Panza. I cannot but be reluctant to set the verdict of my own judgment against that of Victor Hugo's; I need none to remind me what and who he is whose judgment I for once oppose, and what and who am I that I should oppose it; that he is he, and I am but myself; yet against his classification of Falstaff, against his definition of Shakespeare's unapproached and unapproachable masterpiece in the school of comic art and humoristic nature, I must and do with all my soul and strength protest. The admirable phrase of 'swine-centaur' (*centaure du porc*) is as inapplicable to Falstaff as it is appropriate to Panurge. Not the third person but the first in date of that divine and human trinity of humourists whose names make radiant for ever the century of their new-born glory—not Shakespeare but Rabelais is responsible for the creation or the discovery of such a type as this. '*Suum cuique* is our Roman justice';[10] the gradation from Panurge to Falstaff is not downward but upward; though it be Victor Hugo's very self who asserts the contrary.[11] Singular as may seem the collocation of the epithet 'moral' with the name 'Falstaff', I venture to maintain my thesis; that in point of feeling, and therefore of possible moral elevation, Falstaff is as undeniably the superior of Sancho as Sancho is unquestionably the superior of Panurge. The natural affection of Panurge is bounded by the self-same limits as the natural theology of Polyphemus; the love of the one, like the faith of the other, begins and ends alike at one point;

Myself,
And this great belly, first of deities;[12]

(in which line, by the way, we may hear as it were a first faint prelude of the great proclamation to come—the hymn of praise and thanksgiving for the coronation day of King Gaster; whose laureate, we know, was as lovingly familiar with the Polyphemus of Euripides as Shakespeare with his own Pantagruel.) In Sancho we come upon a creature capable of love—but not of such love as kills or helps to kill, such love as may end or even as may seem to end in anything like heartbreak. 'And now abideth Rabelais, Cervantes, Shakespeare, these three; but the greatest of these is Shakespeare.'[13]

I would fain score yet another point in the fat knight's favour; 'I have much to say in the behalf of that Falstaff.'[14] Rabelais, evangelist and prophet of the Resurrection of the Flesh (so long entombed, ignored, repudiated, misconstrued, vilified, by so many generations and ages of Galilean preachers and Pharisaic schoolmen)—Rabelais was content to paint the flesh merely, in its honest human reality—human at least, if also bestial; in its frank and rude reaction against the half brainless and wholly bloodless teachers whose doctrine he himself on the one hand, and Luther on the other, arose together to smite severally—to smite them hip and thigh, even till the going down of the sun;[15] the mock sun or marshy meteor that served only to deepen the darkness encompassing on every side the doubly dark ages—the ages of monarchy and theocracy, the ages of death and of faith. To Panurge, therefore, it was unnecessary and it might have seemed inconsequent to attribute other gifts or functions than are proper to such intelligence as may accompany the appetites of an animal. That most irreverend father in God, Friar John, belongs to a higher class in the moral order of being; and he much rather than his fellow-voyager and penitent is properly comparable with Falstaff. It is impossible to connect the notion of rebuke with the sins of Panurge. The actual lust and gluttony, the imaginary cowardice of Falstaff, have been gravely and sharply rebuked by critical morality; we have just noted a too recent and too eminent example of this; but what mortal ever dreamed of casting these qualities in the teeth of his supposed counterpart? The difference is as vast between Falstaff on the field of battle and Panurge on the storm-tossed deck as between Falstaff and Hotspur, Panurge and Friar John. No man could show cooler and steadier nerve than is displayed in either case—by the lay as well as the clerical namesake of the fourth evangelist. If ever fruitless but endless care was shown to prevent misunderstanding, it was shown in the pains taken by Shakespeare to obviate the misconstruction which would impute to Falstaff the quality of a Parolles or a Bobadil, a Bessus or a Moron.[16] The delightful encounter between the jester and the bear in the crowning interlude of *La Princesse d'Élide* shows once more, I may remark, that Molière had sat at the feet of Rabelais as delightedly as Shakespeare before him. Such rapturous inebriety or Olympian incontinence of humour only fires the blood of the graver and less exuberant humourist when his lips are still warm and wet from the well-spring of the *Dive Bouteille*.[17]

It is needless to do over again the work which was done, and well done, a hundred years since, by the writer whose able essay in vindication and exposition of the genuine character of Falstaff elicited from Dr. Johnson as good a jest and as bad a criticism as might have been expected.[18] His argument is too thoroughly carried out at all points and fortified on all hands to require or even to admit of corroboration; and the attempt to appropriate any share of the lasting credit which is his due would be nothing less than a disingenuous impertinence. I may here however notice that in the very first scene of this trilogy which introduces us to the ever dear and honoured presence of Sir John, his creator has put into the mouth of a witness no friendlier or more candid than Ned Poins the distinction between two as true-bred cowards as ever turned back and one who will fight no longer than he sees reason. In this nutshell lies the whole kernel of the matter; the sweet, sound, ripe, toothsome, wholesome kernel of Falstaff's character and humour. He will fight as well as his princely patron, and, like the prince, as long as he sees reason; but neither Hal nor Jack has ever felt any touch of desire to pluck that 'mere scutcheon' honour 'from the pale-faced moon'.[19]

Hamlet

I trust it will be taken as no breach of my past pledge to abstain from all intrusion on the sacred ground of Gigadibs[1] and the Germans, if I venture to indicate a touch inserted by Shakespeare for no other perceptible or conceivable purpose than to obviate by anticipation the indomitable and ineradicable fallacy of criticism which would find the keynote of Hamlet's character in the quality of irresolution. I may observe at once that the misconception involved in such a reading of the riddle ought to have been evident even without this episodical stroke of illustration. In any case it should be plain to any reader that the signal characteristic of Hamlet's inmost nature is by no means irresolution or hesitation or any form of weakness, but rather the strong conflux of contending forces. That during four whole acts Hamlet cannot or does not make up his mind to any direct and deliberate action against his uncle is true enough; true, also, we may say, that Hamlet had somewhat more of mind than another man to make up, and might properly want somewhat more time than might another man to do it in; but, not I venture to say in spite of Goethe, through innate inadequacy to his task and unconquerable weakness of the will;[2] not, I venture to think in spite of Hugo, through immedicable scepticism of the spirit and irremediable propensity to nebulous intellectual refinement.[3] One practical point in the action of the play precludes us from accepting so ready a solution of the riddle as is suggested either by the simple theory of half-heartedness or by the simple hypothesis of doubt. There is absolutely no other reason, we might say there was no other excuse, for the introduction or intrusion of an else superfluous episode into a play which was already, and which remains even after all possible excisions, one of the longest plays on record. The compulsory expedition of Hamlet to

England, his discovery by the way of the plot laid against his life, his interception of the King's letter and his forgery of a substitute for it against the lives of the King's agents, the ensuing adventure of the sea-fight, with Hamlet's daring act of hot-headed personal intrepidity, his capture and subsequent release on terms giving no less patent proof of his cool-headed and ready-witted courage and resource than the attack had afforded of his physically impulsive and even impetuous hardihood—all this serves no purpose whatever but that of exhibiting the instant and amost unscrupulous resolution of Hamlet's character in time of practical need. But for all that he or Hamlet has got by it, Shakespeare might too evidently have spared his pains; and for all this voice as of one crying in a wilderness, Hamlet will too surely remain to the majority of students, not less than to all actors and all editors and all critics, the standing type and embodied emblem of irresolution, half-heartedness, and doubt.

That Hamlet should seem at times to accept for himself, and even to enforce by reiteration of argument upon his conscience and his reason, some such conviction or suspicion as to his own character, tells much rather in disfavour than in favour of its truth. A man whose natural temptation was to swerve, whose inborn inclination was to shrink and skulk aside from duty and from action, would hardly be the first and last person to suspect his own weakness, the one only unbiassed judge and witness of sufficiently sharp-sighted candour and accuracy to estimate aright his poverty of nature and the malformation of his mind. But the high-hearted and tender-conscienced Hamlet, with his native bias towards introspection intensified and inflamed and directed and dilated at once by one imperative pressure and oppression of unavoidable and unalterable circumstance, was assuredly and exactly the one only man to be troubled by any momentary fear that such might indeed be the solution of his riddle, and to feel or to fancy for the moment some kind of ease and relief in the sense of that very trouble. A born doubter would have doubted even of Horatio; hardly can all positive and almost palpable evidence of underhand instigation and inspired good intentions induce Hamlet for some time to doubt even of Ophelia.

King Lear and *Othello*

Of all Shakespeare's plays, *King Lear* is unquestionably that in which he has come nearest to the height and to the likeness of the one tragic poet on any side greater than himself whom the world in all its ages has ever seen born of time. It is by far the most Æschylean of his works; the most elemental and primæval, the most oceanic and Titanic in conception. He deals here with no subtleties as in *Hamlet*, with no conventions as in *Othello*: there is no question of 'a divided duty'[1] or a problem half insoluble, a matter of country and connection, of family or of race; we look upward and downward, and in vain, into the deepest things of nature, into the highest things of providence; to the roots of life, and to the stars; from the roots that no God waters to the stars which give no man light; over a world full of death and life without resting-place or guidance.

But in one main point it differs radically from the work and the spirit of Æschylus. Its fatalism is of a darker and harder nature. To Prometheus the fetters of the lord and enemy of mankind were bitter; upon Orestes the hand of heaven was laid too heavily to bear; yet in the not utterly infinite or everlasting distance we see beyond them the promise of the morning on which mystery and justice shall be made one; when righteousness and omnipotence at last shall kiss each other. But on the horizon of Shakespeare's tragic fatalism we see no such twilight of atonement, such pledge of reconciliation as this. Requital, redemption, amends, equity, explanation, pity and mercy, are words without a meaning here.

> As flies to wanton boys are we to the gods;
> They kill us for their sport.[2]

Here is no need of the Eumenides, children of Night everlasting,[3] for here is very Night herself.

The words just cited are not casual or episodical; they strike the keynote of the whole poem, lay the keystone of the whole arch of thought. There is no contest of conflicting forces, no judgment so much as by casting of lots: far less is there any light of heavenly harmony or of heavenly wisdom, of Apollo or Athene from above. We have heard much and often from theologians of the light of revelation: and some such thing indeed we find in Æschylus: but the darkness of revelation is here.

For in this the most terrible work of human genius it is with the very springs and sources of nature that her student has set himself to deal. The veil of the temple of our humanity is rent in twain.[4] Nature herself, we might say, is revealed—and revealed as unnatural. In face of such a world as this a man might be forgiven who should pray that chaos might come again.[5] Nowhere else in Shakespeare's work or in the universe of jarring lives are the lines of character and event so broadly drawn or so sharply cut. Only the supreme self-command of this one poet could so mould and handle such types as to restrain and prevent their passing from the abnormal into the monstrous: yet even as much as this, at least in all cases but one, it surely has accomplished. In Regan alone would it be, I think, impossible to find a touch or trace of anything less vile than it was devilish. Even Goneril has her one splendid hour, her fire-flaught[6] of hellish glory; when she treads under foot the half-hearted goodness, the wordy and windy though sincere abhorrence, which is all that the mild and impotent revolt of Albany can bring to bear against her imperious and dauntless devilhood; when she flaunts before the eyes of her 'milk-livered' and 'moral fool' the coming banners of France about the 'plumed helm' of his slayer.[7]

On the other side, Kent is the exception which answers to Regan on this. Cordelia, the brotherless Antigone of our stage, has one passing touch of intolerance for what her sister was afterwards to brand as indiscretion and dotage in their father, which redeems her from the charge of perfection. Like Imogen, she is not too inhumanly divine for the sense of divine irritation. Godlike though they be, their very godhead is human and feminine; and only therefore credible, and only therefore adorable. Cloten and Regan, Goneril and Iachimo,[8] have power to stir and embitter the sweetness of their blood. But for the contrast and even the contact of antagonists as abominable as these, the gold of their spirit would be too refined, the lily of their holiness too radiant, the violet of their virtue too sweet. As it is, Shakespeare has gone down perforce among the blackest and the basest things of nature to find anything so equally exceptional in evil as properly to counterbalance and make bearable the excellence and extremity of their goodness. No otherwise could either angel have escaped the blame implied in the very attribute and epithet of blameless. But where the possible depth of human hell is so foul and unfathomable as it appears in the spirits which serve as foils to these, we may endure that in them the inner height of heaven should be no less immaculate and immeasurable.

It should be a truism wellnigh as musty as Hamlet's half cited proverb, to enlarge upon the evidence given in *King Lear* of a sympathy with the mass of social misery more wide and deep and direct and bitter and tender than Shakespeare has shown elsewhere. But as even to this day and even in respectable quarters the murmur is not quite duly extinct which would charge on Shakespeare a certain share of divine indifference to suffering, of godlike satisfaction and a less than compassionate content, it is not yet perhaps utterly superfluous to insist on the utter fallacy and falsity of their creed who whether in praise or in blame would rank him to his credit or discredit among such poets as on this side at least may be classed rather with Goethe than with Shelley and with Gautier than with Hugo. A poet of revolution he is not, as none of his country in that generation could have been: but as surely as the author of *Julius Cæsar* has approved himself in the best and highest sense of the word at least potentially a republican, so surely has the author of *King Lear* avowed himself in the only good and rational sense of the words a spiritual if not a political democrat and socialist.

It is only, I think, in this most tragic of tragedies that the sovereign lord and incarnate god of pity and terror can be said to have struck with all his strength a chord of which the resonance could excite such angry agony and heartbreak of wrath as that of the brother kings when they smote their staffs against the ground in fierce imperious anguish of agonised and rebellious compassion, at the oracular cry of Calchas for the innocent blood of Iphigenia.[9] The doom even of Desdemona seems as much less morally intolerable as it is more logically inevitable than the doom of Cordelia. But doubtless the fatalism of *Othello* is as much darker and harder than that of any third among the plays of Shakespeare, as it is less dark and hard than the fatalism of *King Lear*. For upon the head of the very noblest man whom even omnipotence or Shakespeare could ever call to life he has laid a burden in one sense yet heavier than the burden of Lear, insomuch as the sufferer can with somewhat less confidence of universal appeal proclaim himself a man more sinned against than sinning.[10]

And yet, if ever man after Lear might lift up his voice in that protest, it would assuredly be none other than Othello. He is in all the prosperous days of his labour and his triumph so utterly and wholly nobler than the self-centred and wayward king, that the capture of his soul and body in the unimaginable snare of Iago seems a yet blinder and more unrighteous blow

Struck by the envious wrath of man or God[11]

than ever fell on the old white head of that child-changed father. But at least he is destroyed by the stroke of a mightier hand than theirs who struck down Lear. As surely as Othello is the noblest man of man's making, Iago is the most perfect evildoer, the most potent demi-devil. It is of course the merest commonplace to say as much, and would be no less a waste of speech to add the half comfortable reflection that it is in any case no shame to fall by such a hand. But this subtlest and strangest work of Shakespeare's admits and requires some closer than common scrutiny. Coleridge has admirably described the first great soliloquy which opens to us the pit of hell within as 'the motive-hunting of a motiveless malignity'.[12] But subtle and profound and just as is this definitive appreciation, there is more in the matter yet than even this. It is not only that Iago, so to speak, half tries to make himself half believe that Othello has wronged him, and that the thought of it gnaws him inly like a poisonous mineral:[13] though this also be true, it is not half the truth—nor half that half again. Malignant as he is, the very subtlest and strongest component of his complex nature is not even malignity. It is the instinct of what Mr. Carlyle would call an inarticulate poet. In his immortal study on the affair of the diamond necklace, the most profound and potent humourist of his country in his century has unwittingly touched on the mainspring of Iago's character—'the very pulse of the machine'.[14] He describes his Circe de la Mothe-Valois as a practical dramatic poet or playwright at least in lieu of play-writer: while indicating how and wherefore, with all her constructive skill and rhythmic art in action, such genius as hers so differs from the genius of Shakespeare that she undeniably could not have written a *Hamlet*. Neither could Iago have written an *Othello*. (From this theorem, by the way, a reasoner or a casuist benighted enough to prefer articulate poets to inarticulate, Shakespeare to Cromwell, a fair Vittoria Colonna to a 'foul Circe-Megæra',[15] and even such a strategist as Homer to such a strategist as Frederic-William, would not illogically draw such conclusions or infer such corollaries as might result in opinions hardly consonant with the Teutonic-Titanic evangel of the preacher who supplied him with his thesis.) 'But what he can do, that he will':[16] and if it be better to make a tragedy than to write one, to act a poem than to sing it, we must allow to Iago a station in the hierarchy of poets very far in advance of his creator's. None of the great inarticulate may more justly claim place and precedence. With all his poetic gift, he has no poetic weakness. Almost any creator but his would have given him some grain of spite or some spark of lust after Desdemona. To Shakespeare's Iago she is no more than is a rhyme to another and articulate poet.[17] His stanza must at any rate and at all costs be polished: to borrow the metaphor used by Mr. Carlyle in apologetic illustration of a royal hero's peculiar system of levying recruits for his colossal brigade. He has within him a sense or conscience of power incomparable: and this power shall not be left, in Hamlet's phrase, 'to fust in him unused'.[18] A genuine and thorough capacity for human lust or hate would diminish and degrade the supremacy of his evil. He is almost as far above or beyond vice as he is beneath or beyond virtue. And this it is that makes him impregnable and invulnerable. When once he has said it, we know as well as he that thenceforth he never will speak word. We could smile almost as we can see him to have smiled at Gratiano's most ignorant and empty threat, being well assured that torments will in no wise ope his lips: that as surely and as truthfully as ever did the tortured philosopher before him, he might have told his tormentors that they did but bruise the coating, batter the crust, or break the shell of Iago. Could we imagine a far other lost spirit than Farinata degli Uberti's endowed with Farinata's[19] might of will, and transferred from the sepulchres of fire to the dykes of Malebolge, we might conceive something of Iago's attitude in hell—of his unalterable and indomitable posture for all eternity. As though it were possible and necessary that in some one point the extremities of all conceivable good and of all imaginable evil should meet and mix together in a new 'marriage of heaven and hell',[20] the action in passion of the most devilish among all the human damned could hardly be other than that of the most godlike among all divine saviours—the figure of Iago than a reflection by hell-fire of the figure of Prometheus.

Between Iago and Othello the position of Desdemona is precisely that defined with such quaint sublimity of fancy in the old English by-word—'between the devil and the deep sea'. Deep and pure and strong and adorable always and terrible and pitiless on occasion as the sea is the great soul of the glorious hero to whom she has given herself; and what likeness of man's enemy from Satan down to Mephistopheles could be matched for danger and for dread against the good bluff soldierly trustworthy figure of honest Iago? The rough license of his tongue at once takes warrant from his good soldiership and again gives warrant for his honesty: so that in a double sense it does him yeoman's service, and that twice told. It is pitifully ludicrous to see him staged to the show like a member—and a very inefficient member—of the secret police. But it would seem impossible for actors to understand that he is not a would-be detective, an aspirant for the honours of a Vidocq, a candidate for the laurels of a Vautrin:[21] that he is no less than Lepidus, or than Antony's horse, 'a tried and valiant soldier'.[22] It is perhaps natural that the two deepest and subtlest of all Shakespeare's intellectual studies in good and evil should be the two most painfully misused and misunderstood alike by his commentators and his fellows of the stage: it is certainly undeniable that no third figure of his creation has ever been on both sides as persistently misconceived and misrepresented with such desperate pertinacity as Hamlet and Iago.

And it is only when Iago is justly appreciated that we can justly appreciate either Othello or Desdemona. This again should surely be no more than the truism that it sounds; but practically it would seem to be no less than an adventurous and audacious paradox. Remove or deform or diminish or modify the dominant features of the destroyer, and we have but the eternal and vulgar figures of jealousy and innocence, newly vamped and veneered and padded and patched up for the stalest purposes of puppetry. As it is, when Coleridge asks 'which do we pity the most' at the fall of the curtain, we can surely answer, Othello. Noble as are the 'most blessed conditions'[23] of 'the gentle Desdemona', he is yet the nobler of the two; and has suffered more in one single pang than she could suffer in life or in death.

NOTES

Shakespeare and the Sea

1 The *Fortnightly Review* has 'the first of living poets'. Hugo's 'parallel' comes near the end of section 1 and in section 2 of *William Shakespeare*.
2 From Psalm 139: 9.
3 From Isaiah 8: 14.
4 From *Twelfth Night*, IV, ii, 38–42.
5 The comma in the *Fortnightly Review* seems better than the semicolon used in the book; the latter could of course be a misprint for a colon.

Falstaff

1 *Henry V*, II, i, 91–2.
2 *Ibid.*, II, i, 93.
3 From Chaucer's *Prologue*, l. 150.
4 *1 Henry IV*, I, ii, 101.
5 *2 Henry IV*, I, ii, 273–4.
6 *Henry V*, II, i, 127–8.
7 *Ibid.*, II, i, 130.
8 *2 Henry IV*, V, iii, 104.
9 *Ibid.*, V, iii, 143.
10 *Titus Andronicus*, I, i, 280.

11 'La dynastie du bon sens, inaugurée dans Panurge, continuée dans Sancho Pança, tourne à mal et avorte dans Falstaff.' (*William Shakespeare*, deuxième partie, livre premier, ch. ii.) (ACS). ['The dynasty of good sense, established in Panurge, continued in Sancho Panza, takes a bad turn and miscarries in Falstaff.']
12 Euripides, *The Cyclops*, ll. 334–6; Rabelais, end of chapter 58 of Book 4.
13 Cf. the pattern of 1 Cor. 13: 13.
14 *1 Henry IV*, II, iv, 531–2.
15 Judges 15: 8.
16 Parolles, *All's Well That Ends Well*; Bobadil, Jonson's *Every Man in His Humour*; Bessus, Beaumont and Fletcher's *A King and No King*; Moron, Molière's *The Princess of Elis.*
17 A sacred bottle in the middle of a fountain (Rabelais, Book v, chapter 42).
18 Dr Johnson on Maurice Morgann's *Essay on the Dramatic Character of Sir John Falstaff* (1777): 'Why, Sir, we shall have the man come forth again; and as he has proved Falstaff to be no coward, he may prove Iago to be a very good character' (Boswell's *Life*, ed. Hill, iv, 192 note).
19 *1 Henry IV*, I, iii, 202.

Hamlet

1 A mediocre journalist in Browning's 'Bishop Blougram's Apology'.
2 *Wilhelm Meister*, Book v.
3 Hugo's *William Shakespeare*, Part II, Book ii, sections III, IV, V.

King Lear *and* Othello

1 *Othello*, I, iii, 181.
2 *King Lear*, IV, i, 38–9.
3 Cf. Æschylus, *Eumenides*, 1033ff.: 'Pass on your way to your abode, O ye mighty children of Night . . .' (tr. Herbert Weir Smith). Apollo and Athene, mentioned by Swinburne in the following paragraph, appear in the play, in which the Erinyes, who pursue Orestes, are the chorus.
4 Cf. Matt. 27: 51; Mark 15: 38; Luke 23: 45.
5 *Othello*, III, iii, 92.
6 A storm of thunder and lightning; figuratively, a sudden burst.
7 *King Lear*, IV, ii, 56ff.
8 Cloten and Iachimo appear in *Cymbeline.*
9 Iphigenia, Agamemnon's daughter, was to be sacrificed in order that the Greek fleet might sail, as the oracle Calchas had decreed. Menelaus was the other 'brother king'.

10 Cf. *King Lear*, III, ii, 59–60.
11 Shelley, 'Adonais', l. 42.
12 In his 'Notes on *Othello*'.
13 *Othello*, II, i, 306.
14 Wordsworth, 'She was a Phantom of delight', l. 22.
15 Carlyle, near the beginning of the last chapter of *The Diamond Necklace*, in the 'Occasional Discourse, by Count Alessandro Cagliostro'.
16 Unidentified.
17 What would at least be partly lust in another man is all but purely hatred in Iago.

> Now I do love her too:
> Not out of absolute lust, (though, peradventure,
> I stand accountant for as great a sin)
> But partly led to diet my revenge.

For 'partly' read 'wholly', and for 'peradventure' read 'assuredly', and the incarnate father of lies, made manifest in the flesh, here speaks all but all the truth for once, to himself alone. (ACS)
18 *Hamlet*, IV, iv, 39.
19 Dante places Farinata among the heretics (*Inferno*, x). Malebolge ('Evil Pouches') is the eighth circle of Hell (xviii ff.).
20 Alluding to Blake's title.
21 François Eugène Vidocq (1775–1857), French detective and adventurer, published *Memoirs* which are supposed to have inspired various men of letters, including Balzac in the creation of his character Vautrin.
22 *Julius Caesar*, IV, i, 28.
23 Cf. *Othello*, II, i, 255: 'full of most blessed condition', 'condition' referring to Desdemona's character.

22 Charles Lamb

1885, 1886

Swinburne wrote on 9 October 1879: 'I have among my choicest treasures a copy of his [Wither's] earlier poems in a wretched reprint, *but* interleaved with quarto sheets of thin paper containing many most characteristic unpublished (as well as published) notes in the autograph of Charles Lamb—one of my very dearest and earliest friends in all the world of books' (Lang, iv, 104). This treasure was the subject of 'Charles Lamb and George Wither', in the *Nineteenth Century* for January 1885, which was reprinted in *Miscellanies* (1886). For us Lamb is most important as an essayist, of course, his plays now being seldom read; but Lamb's *Specimens* was the book that inspired Swinburne's devotion to Elizabethan drama, and to Lamb's memory he dedicated his *Age of Shakespeare* (1908).

'*Iamque opus exegi*,'[1] which I would not have undertaken for love of any other man than Lamb: so much heavier to some hands than to others is the labour of transcription and collation. To those who feel nothing of the attraction which his lovers find in the lightest word, the slightest record, the smallest relic of Charles Lamb, the time and care spent on these fugitive notes will seem deplorably and strangely wasted. As many talk of Robin Hood who never shot in his bow, so do many talk of Charles Lamb who have never entered in spirit into the homely and happy sanctuary of his more private or inward presence. But for all who love him the charm of that companionship is alike indefinable and incomparable. It pervades his work as with an odour of sweet old-world flowers or spices long laid by among fine linens and rare brocades in some such old oaken or cedarn cabinet as his grandmother might have opened to rejoice the wondering senses of her boyish visitor at 'Blakesmoor'. His own words may best express the special feeling of tenderness and delight, familiar reverence and satisfied affection, which the very sound or thought of his 'gentle name'[2] wakes up always anew within us into warmth and freshness of life. 'The names of some of our poets,' avows Elia in one of his last essays, with a graceful touch of apology for the fanciful confession, 'sound sweeter, and have a finer relish to the ear—to mine, at least—than that of Milton or of Shakespeare. It may be, that the latter are more staled and rung upon in common discourse. The sweetest names, and which carry a perfume in the mention, are, Kit Marlowe, Drayton, Drummond of Hawthornden, and Cowley.'[3] And even so do we now find a homely magic in the name of Lamb, a special fragrance in the fame of it, such as hardly seems to hang about the statelier sound of Coleridge's or Wordsworth's or Shelley's. No good criticism of Lamb, strictly speaking, can ever be written; because nobody can do justice to his work who does not love it too well to feel himself capable of giving judgment on it. And if such a reader as this should undertake to enter the lists against any of Lamb's detractors, or to engage in debate with any of his half-hearted and semi-supercilious partisans, he would doubtless find himself driven or tempted to break all bounds of critical reason in his panegyric of a genius so beloved. Question or denial of Lamb's dramatic powers might goad him on to maintain that *John Woodvil* is the only tragedy in the language which may properly be set beside *Hamlet*, and *The Wife's Trial* the one comedy which may hold its own if compared with *Much Ado about Nothing*. Let me not be suspected of any desire to maintain this thesis if I avow my enjoyment and admiration of Lamb's tragedy, his comedy, and his farce. Of his essays and letters, humorous or pathetic, prosaic or fantastic, erratic or composed, what is there to be said but that it would be a feat far easier to surpass all others than to approach the best of these? But the truth is simple and indisputable that no labour could be at once so delightful and so useless, so attractive and so vain, as the task of writing in praise of Lamb. Any man or any child who can feel anything of his charm utters better praise of him in silence than any array of epithets or periods could give. Any man or any woman who can feel nothing of his charm is outside the pale of any possible influence or impression from any reasoning or any enthusiasm of others. Genius and goodness, self-sacrifice and love, sweet and stingless humour, joyful kindness and patient endurance, could not but make of Charles and Mary Lamb two figures most obnoxious and contemptible to that very sorry pair of phenomena, Thomas Cloacinus and his Goody.[4] 'This was a sham strong man,' said Carlyle[5]—very justly—of Byron: and equal justice echoes back the verdict as retorted on Carlyle. The true strong man whose whole life was an act of love, an offering of faithful and grateful affection which gave all it had and felt that it could not give enough, what other recognition or what fitter acknowledgment could he receive from such as these than their distaste and their contempt? What they had to give they gave him; that so nothing might be wanting of the tribute due from inferiors as from equals, from strangers as from friends, to the very sweetest nature that ever gave warmth and fragrance to the quiet and quenchless light of so rare and pure a genius. But it may well be that the Essays of Elia will be found to have kept their perfume, and the letters of Charles Lamb to retain their old sweet savour, when *Sartor Resartus* has about as many readers as Bulwer's *Artificial Changeling* and nine-tenths even of *Don Juan* lie darkening under the same deep dust that covers the rarely troubled pages of the *Secchia Rapita*.[6] One thing is very certain, which it needs no inspiration to foresee and no presumption to foretell: that whether the number of his loving readers be greater or be less in any time to come, be the quantity of their muster what it may, the quality of their affection must always be the same. The 'cordial old man', whose 'tripping tongue', heard 'once, and once only',[7] woke so deep an echo of regard from the noble heart of Landor, will never be loved a little or honoured with a temperate esteem. Not all, it may be, who share his love and his understanding of Shakespeare or of Hogarth, can be expected to love him likewise: but surely nothing less than this may be looked for from all whom he has led to the sealed and hidden fountains[8] of English dramatic poetry; from all to whom he has opened that passionate and stormy paradise, the turbulent and radiant heaven of our elder tragic writers: for a very heaven it is to those who can breathe its 'eager air',[9] a very paradise to such as can walk unhurt among its flaming fires. That a Lamb should have gone in among these lions, and become as it were the keeper of the lions' den, is a chance which provokes the inevitable application of his own favourite form of jest: but it is to be remembered that the one other writer who ever shared with 'the gentle Elia' the common or habitual surname bestowed by that soft-sounding epithet is none other than Shakespeare himself. Gentleness such as Shakespeare's or as Lamb's implies a strength beside which the braggardism of a stoic whose Porch[10] is of stucco, for all his swashing and martial outside of painted blood and imitated iron, proves worse than womanish weakness. Carlyle says of his friend Sterling that during his brief career as a clergyman he was ever striving with all his might 'not to be a moonshine shadow of the first Paul':[11] it may be said—by the disbelievers in his pseudosophy—that Carlyle's own 'realized ideal' was to be a moonshine shadow of the first Knox. No man ever had less about him of pretention, philosophic or other, than Charles Lamb: but when he took on him to grapple in spirit with Shakespeare, and with Shakespeare's fellows or followers, the author of *John Woodvil*, who might till then have seemed to unsympathetic readers of that little tragedy no more than the 'moonshine shadow' of an Elizabethan playwright, showed himself the strongest as well as the finest critic that ever was found worthy to comment on the most masculine or leonine school of poets in all the range of English literature. With the gentler natures among them—with the sweet spirit of Dekker or of Heywood, of Davenport or of Day—we should naturally have expected him to feel and to approve his affinity; but even more than towards these do we find him attracted towards the strongest and most terrible of all the giant brood: and this by no effeminate attraction towards horrors, no morbid and liquorish appetite for visions of blood or images of agony; but by the heroic or poetic instinct of sympathy with 'high actions and high passions',[12] with the sublimity of suffering and the extravagance of love, which gave him power to read aright such poetry as to Campbell was a stumbling-block and to Hallam foolishness.[13] Marlowe with his Faustus, Marston with his Andrugio, Tourneur with his Vindice, Ford with his Calantha, Webster, above all, with his two sovereign types of feminine daring and womanly endurance, the heroine of suffering and the heroine of sin: these are they whom he has interpreted and made known to us in such words as alone could seem deserving, for truth and for beauty, for subtlety and for strength, to be heard by way of interlude between the softer and the sterner harmonies of their Titanic text. Truly and thankfully may those whose boyish tastes have been strengthened with such mental food and quickened with such spiritual wine—the meat so carved and garnished, the cup so tempered and poured out, by such a master and founder of the feast—bear witness and give thanks to so great and so generous a benefactor; who has fed us on lion's marrow, and with honey out of the lion's mouth.[14] To him and to him alone it is that we owe the revelation and the resurrection of our greatest dramatic poets after Shakespeare. All those who have done hard and good work in the same field, from the date of Mr. Collier's supplementary volume to Dodsley down to the present date of Mr. Bullen's no less thankworthy collection of costly waifs[15] and strays redeemed at last from mouldering manuscript or scarce less inaccessible print —all to whom we owe anything of good service in this line owe to Lamb the first example of such toil, the first indication of such treasure. He alone opened the golden vein alike for students and for sciolists: he set the fashion of real or affected interest in our great forgotten poets. Behind him and beneath we see the whole line of conscientious scholars and of imitative rhetoricians: the Hazlitts prattling at his heel, the Dyces labouring in his wake.[16] If the occasional harvest of these desultory researches were his one and only claim on the regard of Englishmen, this alone should suffice to ensure him their everlasting respect and their unalterable gratitude: and this is as small a part as it is a precious one of his priceless legacy to all time. The sweet spontaneous grace of his best poetry has never been surpassed: for subtle and simple humour, for tender and cordial wit, his essays and letters have never been approached: as a critic, Coleridge alone has ever equalled or excelled him in delicacy and strength of insight, and Coleridge has excelled or equalled him only when writing on Shakespeare: of Shakespeare's contemporaries Lamb was as much the better judge as he was the steadier, the deeper, and the more appreciative student. A wise enthusiasm gave only the sharper insight to his love, the keener edge to his judgment: and the rare composition of all such highest qualities as we find scattered or confused in others raised criticism in his case to the level of creation, and made his lightest word more weighty than all the labouring wisdom of any judge less gracious, any reader less inspired than Charles Lamb.

NOTES

1 Ovid's *Metamorphoses*, xv, 871: 'And now I have completed a work [which neither Jove's wrath nor fire nor iron nor devouring time can destroy].'

2 'Gentle name' is used by Lamb himself in the first and last lines of his sonnet on the family name. Others, of course, have referred to him as 'gentle Elia'.

3 From Lamb's 'Detached Thoughts on Books and Reading'.

4 This masculine form suggests 'Cloacina', who, according to Lemprière (Swinburne owned his book on mythology), was a Roman goddess presiding over *cloacae*, receptacles of filth. See the Introduction, note 3. 'Goody' was, according to the *O.E.D.*, a term once applied, especially in Scotland, 'to a woman, usually a married woman, in humble

life'. In writing to Mrs Carlyle, Carlyle sometimes addressed her as 'Goody'.

5 In 'Goethe's Works' (*Critical and Miscellaneous Essays*, ii, 436).

6 Alessandro Tassoni's mock epic, *The Rape of the Bucket* (1622).

7 From Landor's 'Lines on the Death of Charles Lamb', *Poems*, ed. Wheeler, iii (*Complete Works*, xv), 145–6.

8 Cf. the Song of Solomon 4: 12: 'a spring shut up, a fountain sealed.'

9 *Hamlet*, I, iv, 2.

10 Zeno, the ancient founder of the Stoics, met his disciples in the Porch.

11 From Carlyle's *Life of John Sterling*, Part II, chapter 1.

12 Milton's *Paradise Regained*, iv, 266.

13 As indicated by Thomas Campbell's 'Essay on English Poetry' introducing his *Specimens of the British Poets* and by the chapters on dramatic literature in Henry Hallam's *Introduction to the Literature of Europe*. Cf. I Cor. 1: 23: '. . . unto the Jews a stumblingblock, and unto the Greeks foolishness.'

14 Reminiscent of Samson's encounter with a lion in Judges 14.

15 In his edition of Dodsley's *Old Plays*, John Payne Collier (1789–1883) included six early dramas not previously included; he added others in *Five Old Plays*. A. H. Bullen (1857–1920) published new texts in *Old English Plays*.

16 The reference is to W. C. Hazlitt, grandson of the essayist, and to Alexander Dyce.

23 Ben Jonson
1888, 1889

On 8 March 1888 Swinburne wrote of completing his study of Ben Jonson's dramatic works—'the almost exclusive occupation of some months past' (Lang, v, 226), but on 27 April he was 'up to my throat in Ben Jonson's undramatic works, of which I have undertaken to give an account simply because there is not a decently adequate one in existence' (Lang, v, 236). Aware of the merits of Jonson's *Discoveries* and desiring to promote its reading, he overrated it in comparison with Jonson's other writings. Because the work reflects Jonson's robust personality, he might have found it hard to believe what scholars have unearthed regarding the extent of Jonson's borrowings in that attractive mosaic. Of *A Study of Ben Jonson* (1889), of which parts appeared in the *Nineteenth Century* for April and May 1888 and in the *Fortnightly Review* for July and October 1888, Swinburne remarked, 'I never worked harder at anything, but I was never better satisfied with the result' (Lang, v, 282). The distinction between the giants and the gods with which the book opens had been clearly developed in *George Chapman* and earlier suggested in the essay on Coleridge. Jonson is placed among the giants; as Swinburne wrote in the sonnet addressed to Ben, his Muse's feet had danced on a mountain

> Broad-based, broad-fronted, bounteous, multiform,
> With many a valley impleached with ivy and vine.

If poets may be divided into two exhaustive but not exclusive classes,—the gods of harmony and creation, the giants of energy and invention,—the supremacy of Shakespeare among the gods of English verse is not more unquestionable than the supremacy of Jonson among its giants. Shakespeare himself stands no higher above Milton and Shelley than Jonson above Dryden and Byron. Beside the towering figure of this Enceladus[1] the stature of Dryden seems but that of an ordinary man, the stature of Byron—who indeed can only be classed among giants by a somewhat licentious or audacious use of metaphor—seems little higher than a dwarf's. Not even the ardour of his most fanatical worshippers, from the date of Cartwright and Randolph to the date of Gilchrist and Gifford,[2] could exaggerate the actual greatness of his various and marvellous energies. No giant ever came so near to the ranks of the gods: were it possible for one not born a god to become divine by dint of ambition and devotion, this glory would have crowned the Titanic labours of Ben Jonson. There is something heroic and magnificent in his lifelong dedication of all his gifts and all his powers to the service of the art he had elected as the business of all his life and the aim of all his aspiration. And the result also was magnificent: the flowers of his growing have every quality but one which belongs to the rarest and finest among flowers: they have colour, form, variety, fertility, vigour: the one thing they want is fragrance. Once or twice only in all his indefatigable career of toil and triumph did he achieve what was easily and habitually accomplished by men otherwise unworthy to be named in the same day with him; by men who would have avowed themselves unworthy to unloose the latchets of his shoes.[3] That singing power which answers in verse to the odour of a blossom, to the colouring of a picture, to the flavour of a fruit,—that quality without which they may be good, commendable, admirable, but cannot be delightful,—was not, it should seem, a natural gift of this great writer's: hardly now and then could his industry attain to it by some exceptional touch of inspiration or of luck. It is 'above all strangeness'[4] that a man labouring under this habitual disqualification should have been competent to recognize with accurate and delicate discernment an occasion on which he had for once risen above his usual capacity—a shot by which he had actually hit the white: but the lyrical verses which Ben Jonson quoted to Drummond as his best have exactly the quality which lyrical verse ought to have and which their author's lyrical verse almost invariably misses; the note of apparently spontaneous, inevitable, irrepressible and impeccable music. They might have been written by Coleridge or Shelley. But Ben, as a rule,—a rule which is proved by the exception[5]—was one of the singers who could not sing; though, like Dryden, he could intone most admirably; which is more—and much more—than can truthfully be said for Byron. He, however, as well as Dryden, has one example of lyrical success to show for himself, as exceptional and as unmistakable as

Jonson's. The incantation in *Œdipus*, brief as it is, and the first four stanzas of the incantation in *Manfred*, imitative as they are, reveal a momentary sense of music, a momentary command of the instrument employed, no less singular and no less absolute. But Jonson, at all points the greatest and most genuine poet of the three, has achieved such a success more than once; has nearly achieved it, or has achieved a success only less absolute than this, more than a few times in the course of his works. And it should be remembered always that poetry in any other sense than the sense of invention or divination, creation by dint of recollection and by force of reproduction, was by no means the aim and end of his ambition. The grace, the charm, the magic of poetry was to him always a secondary if not always an inconsiderable quality in comparison with the weight of matter, the solidity of meaning, the significance and purpose of the thing suggested or presented. The famous men whose names may most naturally and most rationally be coupled with the more illustrious name of Ben Jonson came short of the triumph which might have been theirs in consequence of their worst faults or defects—of the weaker and baser elements in their moral nature; because they preferred self-interest in the one case and self-indulgence in the other to the noble toil and the noble pleasure of doing their best for their art's sake and their duty's, to the ultimate satisfaction of their conscience; a guide as sure and a monitor as exacting in æsthetic matters—or, to use a Latin rather than a Greek word, in matters of pure intelligence—as in questions of ethics or morality. But with Ben Jonson conscience was the first and last consideration: the conscience of power which undoubtedly made him arrogant and exacting made him even more severe in self-exaction, more resolute in self-discipline, more inexorable in self-devotion to the elected labour of his life. From others he exacted much; but less than he exacted from himself. And it is to this noble uprightness of mind, to this lofty loyalty in labour, that the gravest vices and the most serious defects of his work may indisputably be traced. Reversing the famous axiom of Goldsmith's professional art-critic,[6] we may say of Jonson's work in almost every instance that the picture would have been better if the artist had taken less pains. For in some cases at least he writes better as soon as he allows himself to write with ease—or at all events without elaborate ostentation of effort and demonstrative prodigality of toil. The unequalled breadth and depth of his reading could not but enrich as well as encumber his writings: those who could wish he had been less learned may be reminded how much we should certainly lose—how much of solid and precious metal—for the mere chance of a possible gain in spontaneity and ease; in qualities of lyrical or dramatic excellence which it is doubtful whether he had received from nature in any degree comparable with those to which his learning gave a fresh impulse and a double force of energetic life. And when his work is at its worst, when his faults are most flagrant, when his tediousness is most unendurable, it is not his learning that is to blame, for his learning is not even apparent. The obtrusion and accumulation of details and references, allusions and citations, which encumber the text and the margin of his first Roman tragedy with such a ponderous mass of illustrative superfluity, may undoubtedly be set down, if not to the discredit, at least to the disadvantage of the poet whose resolute caprice had impelled him to be author and commentator, dramatist and scholiast, at once: but however tedious a languid or a cursory reader may find this part of Jonson's work, he must, if not abnormally perverse in stupidity, admit that it is far less wearisome, less vexatious, less deplorable and insufferable, than the interminable deserts of dreary dialogue in which the affectations, pretentions, or idiocies of the period are subjected to the indefatigable and the lamentable industry of a caricaturist or a photographer.

NOTES

1 The giant son of Gaea and Uranus who warred against the gods and was buried under Etna.
2 William Cartwright (*c.* 1611–43) and Thomas Randolph (1605–35) are chiefly remembered for plays. O. G. Gilchrist (1779–1823) was an antiquary who furnished help to William Gifford (1756–1826) for an edition of Jonson.
3 Cf. Luke 3 : 16.
4 *King Lear*, IV, vi, 66.
5 In the proverb giving rise to this common though absurd sophism 'proves' means 'tests'.
6 In *The Vicar of Wakefield*, chapter 20. One of two rules for the critic is 'always to observe that the picture might have been better if the painter had taken more pains'.

24 Christopher Marlowe
1883, 1908

Swinburne often praised the first English poet who he thought deserved to be called sublime. He wrote for the *Undergraduate Papers* at Oxford (cf. the headnote for No. 3) a paper on Marlowe and Webster. In the concluding passage of *George Chapman* he refers to 'the pedestal of a statue reared in thought to the father of our tragic verse', though, as he observed in a letter, the lack of any portrait of Marlowe would have required a Michelangelo 'to conceive and realise' a statue (Lang, v, 245). Swinburne's verses do not appear on the statue ultimately erected in Canterbury, but he did write an 'Inscription for the Four Sides of a Pedestal' in honour of the poet who 'first gave our song a sound that matched our sea'. 'In the Bay' is also mainly in Marlowe's honour. There are several incidental tributes in prose, some of them, as in *A Study of Shakespeare*, on Marlowe's famous passage on poets and poetry. The sketch that follows is the revision of an article in the ninth edition of the *Britannica* (xv, 1883). In revising his article, Swinburne introduced several changes, the chief of these being a new opening paragraph and the remarks on Marlowe's humour.

The first great English poet was the father of English tragedy and the creator of English blank verse. Chaucer and Spenser were great writers and great men: they shared between them every gift which goes to the making of a poet except the one which alone can make a poet, in the proper sense of the word, great. Neither pathos nor humour nor fancy nor invention will suffice for that: no poet is great as a poet whom no one could ever pretend to recognise as sublime. Sublimity is the test of imagination as distinguished from invention or from fancy: and the first English poet whose powers can be called sublime was Christopher Marlowe.

The majestic and exquisite excellence of various lines and passages in Marlowe's first play must be admitted to relieve, if it cannot be allowed to redeem, the stormy monotony of Titanic truculence which blusters like a simoom through the noisy course of its ten fierce acts. With many and heavy faults, there is something of genuine greatness in *Tamburlaine the Great*; and for two grave reasons it must always be remembered with distinction and mentioned with honour. It is the first poem ever written in English blank verse, as distinguished from mere rhymeless decasyllabics; and it contains one of the noblest passages, perhaps indeed the noblest in the literature of the world, ever written by one of the greatest masters of poetry in loving praise of the glorious delights and sublime submission to the everlasting limits of his art. In its highest and most distinctive qualities, in unfaltering and infallible command of the right note of music and the proper tone of colour for the finest touches of poetic execution, no poet of the most elaborate modern school, working at ease upon every consummate resource of luxurious learning and leisurely refinement, has ever excelled the best and most representative work of a man who had literally no models before him, and probably or evidently was often, if not always, compelled to write against time for his living.

The just and generous judgment passed by Goethe on the *Faustus* of his English predecessor in tragic treatment of the same subject is somewhat more than sufficient to counterbalance the slighting or the sneering references to that magnificent poem which might have been expected from the ignorance of Byron or the incompetence of Hallam.[1] And the particular note of merit observed, the special point of the praise conferred, by the great German poet should be no less sufficient to dispose of the vulgar misconception yet lingering among sciolists and pretenders to criticism, which regards a writer than whom no man was ever born with a finer or a stronger instinct for perfection of excellence in execution as a mere noble savage of letters, a rough self-taught sketcher or scribbler of crude and rude genius, whose unhewn blocks of verse had in them some veins of rare enough metal to be quarried and polished by Shakespeare. What most impressed the author of *Faust* in the work of Marlowe was a quality the want of which in the author of *Manfred* is proof enough to consign his best work to the second or third class at most. 'How greatly it is all planned!'[2] the first requisite of all great work, and one of which the highest genius possible to a greatly gifted barbarian could by no possibility understand the nature or conceive the existence. That

Goethe 'had thought of translating it' is perhaps hardly less precious a tribute to its greatness than the fact that it has been actually and admirably translated by the matchless translator of Shakespeare—the son of Victor Hugo; whose labour of love may thus be said to have made another point in common, and forged as it were another link of union, between Shakespeare and the young master of Shakespeare's youth. Of all great poems in dramatic form it is perhaps the most remarkable for absolute singleness of aim and simplicity of construction, yet is it wholly free from all possible imputation of monotony or aridity. *Tamburlaine* is monotonous in the general roll and flow of its stately and sonorous verse through a noisy wilderness of perpetual bluster and slaughter; but the unity of tone and purpose in *Doctor Faustus* is not unrelieved by change of manner and variety of incident. The comic scenes, written evidently with as little of labour as of relish, are for the most part scarcely more than transcripts, thrown into the form of dialogue, from a popular prose *History of Doctor Faustus*; and therefore should be set down as little to the discredit as to the credit of the poet. Few masterpieces of any age in any language can stand beside this tragic poem—it has hardly the structure of a play—for the qualities of terror and splendour, for intensity of purpose and sublimity of note. In the vision of Helen, for example, the intense perception of loveliness gives actual sublimity to the sweetness and radiance of mere beauty in the passionate and spontaneous selection of words the most choice and perfect; and in like manner the sublimity of simplicity in Marlowe's conception and expression of the agonies endured by Faustus under the immediate imminence of his doom gives the highest note of beauty, the quality of absolute fitness and propriety, to the sheer straightforwardness of speech in which his agonising horror finds vent ever more and more terrible from the first to the last equally beautiful and fearful verse of that tremendous monologue which has no parallel in all the range of tragedy.

It is now a commonplace of criticism to observe and regret the decline of power and interest after the opening acts of *The Jew of Malta*. This decline is undeniable, though even the latter part of the play is not wanting in rough energy and a coarse kind of interest; but the first two acts would be sufficient foundation for the durable fame of a dramatic poet. In the blank verse of Milton alone, who perhaps was hardly less indebted than Shakespeare was before him to Marlowe as the first English master of word-music in its grander forms, has the glory or the melody of passages in the opening soliloquy of

Barabas been possibly surpassed. The figure of the hero before it degenerates into caricature is as finely touched as the poetic execution is excellent; and the rude and rapid sketches of the minor characters show at least some vigour and vivacity of touch.

In *Edward the Second* the interest rises and the execution improves as visibly and as greatly with the course of the advancing story as they decline in *The Jew of Malta*. The scene of the king's deposition at Kenilworth is almost as much finer in tragic effect and poetic quality as it is shorter and less elaborate than the corresponding scene in Shakespeare's *King Richard II*. The terror of the death-scene undoubtedly rises into horror; but this horror is with skilful simplicity of treatment preserved from passing into disgust. In pure poetry, in sublime and splendid imagination, this tragedy is excelled by *Doctor Faustus*; in dramatic power and positive impression of natural effect it is as certainly the masterpiece of Marlowe. It was almost inevitable, in the hands of any poet but Shakespeare, that none of the characters represented should be capable of securing or even exciting any finer sympathy or more serious interest than attends on the mere evolution of successive events or the mere display of emotions (except always in the great scene of the deposition) rather animal than spiritual in their expression of rage or tenderness or suffering. The exact balance of mutual effect, the final note of scenic harmony between ideal conception and realistic execution, is not yet struck with perfect accuracy of touch and security of hand; but on this point also Marlowe has here come nearer by many degrees to Shakespeare than any of his other predecessors have ever come near to Marlowe.

Of *The Massacre at Paris* it is impossible to judge fairly from the garbled fragment of its genuine text which is all that has come down to us. To Mr. Collier, among numberless other obligations, we owe the discovery of a striking passage excised in the piratical edition which gives us the only version extant of this unlucky play; and which, it must be allowed, contains nothing of quite equal value. This is obviously an occasional and polemical work, and being as it is overcharged with the anti-Catholic passion of the time, has a typical quality which gives it some empirical significance and interest. That anti-papal ardour is indeed the only note of unity in a rough and ragged chronicle which shambles and stumbles onward from the death of Queen Jeanne of Navarre to the murder of the last Valois. It is possible to conjecture what it would be fruitless to affirm, that it gave a hint in the next century to Nathaniel Lee for his far superior and really admirable tragedy on the same subject, issued ninety-seven years after the death of Marlowe.

The tragedy of *Dido, Queen of Carthage*, was probably completed for the stage after that irreparable and incalculable loss to English letters by Thomas Nash, the worthiest English precursor of Swift in vivid, pure, and passionate prose, embodying the most terrible and splendid qualities of a personal and social satirist; a man gifted also with some fair faculty of elegiac and even lyric verse, but in no wise qualified to put on the buskin left behind him by the 'famous gracer of tragedians',[3] as Marlowe had already been designated by their common friend Greene from among the worthiest of his fellows. In this somewhat thin-spun and evidently hasty play a servile fidelity to the text of Virgil's narrative has naturally resulted in the failure which might have been expected from an attempt at once to transcribe what is essentially inimitable and to reproduce it under the hopelessly alien conditions of dramatic adaptation. The one really noble passage in a generally feeble and incomposite piece of work is, however, uninspired by the unattainable model to which the dramatists have been only too obsequious in their subservience.

It is as nearly certain as anything can be which depends chiefly upon cumulative and collateral evidence that the better part of what is best in the serious scenes of *King Henry VI* is mainly the work of Marlowe. That he is, at any rate, the principal author of the second and third plays passing under that name among the works of Shakespeare, but first and imperfectly printed as *The Contention between the two Famous Houses of York and Lancaster*, can hardly be now a matter of debate among competent judges.[4] The crucial difficulty of criticism in this matter is to determine, if indeed we should not rather say to conjecture, the authorship of the humorous scenes in prose, showing as they generally do a power of comparatively high and pure comic realism to which nothing in the acknowledged works of any pre-Shakespearean dramatist is even remotely comparable. Yet, especially in the original text of these scenes as they stand unpurified by the ultimate revision of Shakespeare, there are tones and touches which recall rather the clownish horseplay and homely ribaldry of his predecessors than anything in the lighter interludes of his very earliest plays. We find the same sort of thing which we find in their writings, only better done than they usually do it, rather than such work as Shakespeare's a little worse done than usual. And even in the final text of the tragic or metrical scenes the highest note struck is always, with one magnificent and unquestionable exception, rather in the key of Marlowe at his best than of Shakespeare while yet in great measure his disciple.

It is another commonplace of criticism to affirm that Marlowe had not a touch of comic genius, not a gleam of wit in him or a twinkle of humour: but it is an indisputable fact that he had. In *The Massacre at Paris*, the soliloquy of the soldier lying in wait for the minion of Henri III has the same very rough but very real humour as a passage in the *Contention* which was cancelled by the reviser. The same hand is unmistakable in both these broad and boyish outbreaks of unseemly but undeniable fun: and if we might wish it rather less indecorous, we must admit that the tradition which denies all sense of humour and all instinct of wit to the first great poet of England is no less unworthy of serious notice or elaborate refutation than the charges and calumnies of an informer who was duly hanged the year after Marlowe's death.[5] For if the same note of humour is struck in an undoubted play of Marlowe's and in a play of disputed authorship, it is evident that the rest of the scene in the latter play must also be Marlowe's. And in that unquestionable case the superb and savage humour of the terribly comic scenes which represent with such rough magnificence of realism the riot of Jack Cade and his ruffians through the ravaged streets of London must be recognisable as no other man's than his. It is a pity we have not before us for comparison the comic scenes or burlesque interludes of *Tamburlaine* which the printer or publisher, as he had the impudence to avow in his prefatory note, purposely omitted and left out.

The author of *A Study of Shakespeare* was therefore wrong, and utterly wrong, when in a book issued some quarter of a century ago he followed the lead of Mr. Dyce in assuming that because the author of *Doctor Faustus* and *The Jew of Malta* 'was as certainly'—and certainly it is difficult to deny that whether as a mere transcriber or as an original dealer in pleasantry he sometimes was—'one of the least and worst among jesters as he was one of the best and greatest among poets', he could not have had a hand in the admirable comic scenes of *The Taming of a Shrew*. For it is now, I should hope, unnecessary to insist that the able and conscientious editor to whom his fame and his readers owe so great a debt was over-hasty in assuming and asserting that he was a poet 'to whom, we have reason to believe, nature had denied even a moderate talent for the humorous'.[6] The serious or would-be poetical scenes of the play are as unmistakably the work of an imitator as are most of the better passages in *Titus Andronicus* and *King Edward III*. Greene or Peele may be responsible for the bad poetry, but there is no reason to suppose that the great poet whose mannerisms he imitated with so stupid a servility was incapable of the good fun.

Had every copy of Marlowe's boyish version or perversion of Ovid's *Elegies* deservedly perished in the flames to which it was judicially condemned by the sentence of a brace of prelates it is possible that an occasional bookworm, it is certain that no poetical student, would have deplored its destruction, if its demerits—hardly relieved, as his first competent editor has happily remarked, by the occasional incidence of a fine and felicitous couplet—could in that case have been imagined. His translation of the first book of Lucan alternately rises above the original and falls short of it; often inferior to the Latin in point and weight of expressive rhetoric, now and then brightened by a clearer note of poetry and lifted into a higher mood of verse. Its terseness, vigour, and purity of style would in any case have been praiseworthy, but are nothing less than admirable, if not wonderful, when we consider how close the translator has on the whole (in spite of occasional slips into inaccuracy) kept himself to the most rigid limit of literal representation, phrase by phrase and often line by line. The really startling force and felicity of occasional verses are worthier of remark than the inevitable stiffness and heaviness of others, when the technical difficulty of such a task is duly taken into account.

One of the most faultless lyrics and one of the loveliest fragments in the whole range of descriptive and fanciful poetry would have secured a place for Marlowe among the memorable men of his epoch, even if his plays had perished with himself. His 'Passionate Shepherd' remains ever since unrivalled in its way—a way of pure fancy and radiant melody without break or lapse. The untitled fragment, on the other hand, has been very closely rivalled, perhaps very happily imitated, but only by the greatest lyric poet of England—by Shelley alone. Marlowe's poem of *Hero and Leander*, closing with the sunrise which closes the night of the lovers' union, stands alone in its age, and far ahead of the work of any possible competitor between the death of Spenser and the dawn of Milton. In clear mastery of narrative and presentation, in melodious ease and simplicity of strength, it is not less pre-eminent than in the adorable beauty and impeccable perfection of separate lines or passages.

The place and the value of Christopher Marlowe as a leader among English poets it would be almost impossible for historical criticism to over-estimate. To none of them all, perhaps, have so many of the greatest among them been so deeply and so directly indebted. Nor was ever any great writer's influence upon his fellows more utterly and unmixedly an influence for good. He first, and he alone, guided Shakespeare into the right way of work; his music, in which there is no echo of any man's before him, found its own echo in the more prolonged but hardly more exalted harmony of Milton's. He is the greatest discoverer, the most daring and inspired pioneer, in all our poetic literature. Before him there was neither genuine blank verse nor genuine tragedy in our language. After his arrival the way was prepared, the paths were made straight, for Shakespeare.[7]

NOTES

1 Byron asserted that he had not read Marlowe's play before writing *Manfred* (*Letters and Journals* [1922], iv, 174).
2 Goethe's comments are reported in Crabb Robinson's diary, 18 August 1829.
3 In Greene's *Groatsworth of Wit* (1592).
4 The question is more controversial than Swinburne implies.
5 Richard Baines (or Bames). But since there seems to have been more than one man of that name in London, the conclusion is uncertain.
6 *The Works of Christopher Marlowe*, ed. Alexander Dyce (London and New York, 1876), lii.
7 Cf. Mark 1 : 3 : 'Prepare ye the way of the Lord, make his paths straight.'

25 John Webster
1886, 1908

'John Webster', which first appeared in the *Nineteenth Century* for June 1886, was included in *The Age of Shakespeare* (1908), so that Webster, who had been discussed by Swinburne while he was a student at Oxford (cf. the headnote for No. 24), was also represented in a book published in the year before his death. In addition, he wrote for the ninth edition of the *Encyclopædia Britannica* (xxiv, 1888) a short sketch of Webster, reprinted in *Studies in Prose and Poetry* (1894).

There were many poets in the age of Shakespeare who make us think, as we read them, that the characters in their plays could not have spoken more beautifully, more powerfully, more effectively, under the circumstances imagined for the occasion of their utterance: there are only two who make us feel that the words assigned to the creatures of their genius are the very words they must have said, the only words they could have said, the actual words they assuredly did say. Mere literary power, mere poetic beauty, mere charm of passionate or pathetic fancy, we find in varying degrees dispersed among them all alike; but the crowning gift of imagination, the power to make us realise that thus and not otherwise it was, that thus and not otherwise it must have been, was given—except by exceptional fits and starts—to none of the poets of their time but only to Shakespeare and to Webster.

Webster, it may be said, was but as it were a limb of Shakespeare: but that limb, it might be replied, was the right arm. 'The kingly-crownèd head, the vigilant eye',[1] whose empire of thought and whose reach of vision no other man's faculty has ever been found competent to match, are Shakespeare's alone for ever: but the force of hand, the fire of heart, the fervour of pity, the sympathy of passion, not poetic or theatric merely, but actual and immediate, are qualities in which the lesser poet is not less certainly or less unmistakably pre-eminent than the greater. And there is no third to be set beside them: not even if we turn from their contemporaries to Shelley himself. All that Beatrice says in *The Cenci* is beautiful and conceivable and admirable: but unless we except her exquisite last words—and even they are more beautiful than inevitable—we shall hardly find what we find in *King Lear* and *The White Devil*, *Othello* and *The Duchess of Malfy*; the tone of convincing reality; the note, as a critic of our own day might call it, of certitude.

There are poets—in our own age, as in all past ages—from whose best work it might be difficult to choose at a glance some verse sufficient to establish their claim—great as their claim may be—to be remembered for ever; and who yet may be worthy of remembrance among all but the highest. Webster is not one of these: though his fame assuredly does not depend upon the merit of a casual passage here or there, it would be easy to select from any one of his representative plays such examples of the highest, the purest, the most perfect power, as can be found only in the works of the greatest among poets. There is not, as far as my studies have ever extended, a third English poet to whom these words might rationally be attributed by the conjecture of a competent reader.

> We cease to grieve, cease to be fortune's slaves,
> Nay, cease to die, by dying.[2]

There is a depth of severe sense in them, a height of heroic scorn, or a dignity of quiet cynicism, which can scarcely be paralleled in the bitterest or the fiercest effusions of John Marston or Cyril Tourneur or Jonathan Swift. Nay, were they not put into the mouth of a criminal cynic, they would not seem unworthy of Epictetus. There is nothing so grand in the part of Edmund; the one figure in Shakespeare whose aim in life, whose centre of character, is one with the view or the instinct of Webster's two typical villains. Some touches in the part of Flamineo suggest, if not a conscious imitation, an unconscious reminiscence of that prototype: but the essential and radical originality of Webster's genius is shown in the difference of accent with which the same savage and sarcastic philosophy of self-interest finds expression through the snarl and sneer of his ambitious cynic. Monsters as they may seem of unnatural egotism and unallayed ferocity, the one who dies penitent, though his repentance be as sudden if not as suspicious as any ever wrought by miraculous conversion, dies as thoroughly in character as the one who takes leave of life in a passion of scorn and defiant irony which hardly passes off at last into a mood of mocking and triumphant resignation. There is a cross of heroism in almost all Webster's characters which preserves the worst of them from such hatefulness as disgusts us in certain of Fletcher's or of Ford's: they have in them some salt of manhood, some savour of venturesome and humorous resolution, which reminds us of the heroic age in which the genius that begot them was born and reared—the age of Richard Grenville and Francis Drake, Philip Sidney and William Shakespeare.

The earliest play of Webster's now surviving—if a work so piteously mutilated and defaced can properly be said to survive—is a curious example of the combined freedom and realism with which recent or even contemporary history was habitually treated on the stage during the last years of the reign of Queen Elizabeth. The noblest poem known to me of this peculiar kind is the play of *Sir Thomas More*, first printed by Mr. Dyce in 1844 for the Shakespeare Society: the worst must almost certainly be that *Chronicle History of Thomas Lord Cromwell* which the infallible verdict of German intuition has discovered to be 'not only unquestionably Shakespeare's, but worthy to be classed among his best and maturest works'.[3] About midway between these two I should be inclined to rank *The Famous History of Sir Thomas Wyatt*, a mangled and deformed abridgment of a tragedy by Dekker and Webster on the story of Lady Jane Grey. In this tragedy, as in the two comedies due to the collaboration of the same poets, it appears to me more than probable that Dekker took decidedly the greater part. The shambling and slipshod metre, which seems now and then to hit by mere chance on some pure and tender note of simple and exquisite melody—the lazy vivacity and impulsive inconsequence of style—the fitful sort of slovenly inspiration, with interludes of absolute and headlong collapse—are qualities by which a very novice in the study of dramatic form may recognise the reckless and unmistakable presence of Dekker. The curt and grim precision of Webster's tone, his terse and pungent force of compressed rhetoric, will be found equally difficult to trace in any of these three plays. *Northward Ho*, a clever, coarse, and vigorous study of the realistic sort, has not a note of poetry in it, but is more coherent, more sensibly conceived and more ably constructed, than the rambling history of Wyatt or the hybrid amalgam of prosaic and romantic elements in the compound comedy of *Westward Ho*. All that is of any great value in this amorphous and incongruous product of inventive impatience and impetuous idleness can be as distinctly traced to the hand of Dekker as the crowning glories of *The Two Noble Kinsmen* can be traced to the hand of Shakespeare. Any poet, even of his time, might have been proud of these verses, but the accent of them is unmistakable as that of Dekker.

Go, let music
Charm with her excellent voice an awful silence
Through all this building, that her sphery soul
May, on the wings of air, in thousand forms
Invisibly fly, yet be enjoyed.

This delicate fluency and distilled refinement of expression ought properly, one would say, to have belonged to a poet of such careful and self-respectful genius as Tennyson's: whereas in the very next speech of the same speaker we stumble over such a phrase as that which closes the following sentence:—

We feed, wear rich attires, and strive to cleave
The stars with marble towers, fight battles, spend
Our blood to buy us names, *and, in iron hold,*
Will we eat roots, to imprison fugitive gold.

Which he who can parse, let him scan, and he who can scan, let him construe. It is alike incredible and certain that the writer of such exquisite and blameless verse as that in which the finer scenes of *Old Fortunatus* and *The Honest Whore* are so smoothly and simply and naturally written should have been capable of writing whole plays in this headlong and halting fashion, as helpless and graceless as the action of a spavined horse, or a cripple who should attempt to run.

It is difficult to say what part of these plays should be assigned to Webster. Their rough realistic humour, with its tone of somewhat coarse-grained good-nature, strikes the habitual note of Dekker's comic style: there is nothing of the fierce and scornful intensity, the ardour of passionate and compressed contempt, which distinguishes the savagely humorous satire of Webster and of Marston, and makes it hopeless to determine by intrinsic evidence how little or how much was added by Webster in the second edition to the original text of Marston's *Malcontent*: unless—which appears to me not unreasonable—we assume that the printer of that edition lied or blundered after the manner of his contemporary kind in attributing on the title-page—as apparently he meant to attribute—any share in the additional scenes or speeches to the original author of the play. In any case, the passages thus added to that grimmest and most sombre of tragicomedies are in such exact keeping with the previous text that the keenest scent of the veriest bloodhound among critics could not detect a shade of difference in the savour.

The text of either comedy is generally very fair—as free from corruption as could reasonably be expected. The text of *Sir Thomas Wyatt* is corrupt as well as mutilated. Even in Mr. Dyce's second edition I have noted, not without astonishment, the following flagrant errors left still to glare on us from the distorted and disfigured page. In the sixth scene a single speech of Arundel's contains two of the most palpably preposterous:—

> The obligation wherein we all stood bound
>
> . . . . . .
>
> Cannot be concealed without great reproach
> To us and to our issue.

We should of course read 'cancelled' for 'concealed': the sense of the context and the exigence of the verse cry alike aloud for the correction. In the sixteenth line from this we come upon an equally obvious error:—

> Advice in this I hold it better far,
> To keep the course we run, than, seeking change,
> Hazard our lives, our honours, and the realm.

It seems hardly credible to those who are aware how much they owe to the excellent scholarship and editorial faculty of Mr. Dyce, that he should have allowed such a misprint as 'heirs' for 'honours' to stand in this last unlucky line. Again, in the next scene, when the popular leader Captain Brett attempts to reassure the country folk who are startled at the sight of his insurgent array, he is made to utter (in reply to the exclamation, 'What's here? soldiers!') the perfectly fatuous phrase, 'Fear not good speech.' Of course—once more—we should read, 'Fear not, good people'; a correction which rectifies the metre as well as the sense.

The play attributed to Webster and Rowley by a publisher of the next generation has been carefully and delicately analysed by a critic of our own time, who naturally finds it easy to distinguish the finer from the homelier part of the compound weft, and to assign what is rough and crude to the inferior, what is interesting and graceful to the superior poet. The authority of the rogue Kirkman may be likened to the outline or profile of Mr. Mantalini's early loves: it is either no authority at all, or at best it is a 'demd' authority.[4] The same swindler who assigned to Webster and Rowley the authorship of *A Cure for a Cuckold* assigned to Shakespeare and Rowley the authorship of an infinitely inferior play—a play of which German sagacity has discovered that 'none of Rowley's other works are equal to this'.[5] Assuredly[6] they are not—in utter stolidity of platitude and absolute impotence of drivel. Rowley was a vigorous artist in comedy and an original master of tragedy: he may have written the lighter or broader parts of the play which rather unluckily took its name from these, and Webster may have written the more serious or sentimental parts: but there is not the slightest shadow of a reason to suppose it. An obviously apocryphal abortion of the same date, attributed to the same poets by the same knave, has long since been struck off the roll of Webster's works.

The few occasional poems of this great poet are worth study by those who are capable of feeling interest in the comparison of slighter with sublimer things, and the detection in minor works of the same style, here revealed by fitful hints in casual phrases, as that which animates and distinguishes even a work so insufficient and incompetent as Webster's 'tragecomœdy' of *The Devil's Law-case*. The noble and impressive extracts from this most incoherent and chaotic of all plays which must be familiar to all students of Charles Lamb are but patches of imperial purple sewn on with the roughest of needles to a garment of the raggedest and coarsest kind of literary serge. Hardly any praise can be too high for their dignity and beauty, their lofty loyalty and simplicity of chivalrous manhood or their deep sincerity of cynic meditation and self-contemptuous mournfulness: and the reader who turns from these magnificent samples to the complete play must expect to find yet another and a yet unknown masterpiece of English tragedy. He will find a crowning example of the famous theorem, that 'the plot is of no use except to bring in the fine things'.[7] The plot is in this instance absurd to a degree so far beyond the most preposterous conception of confused and distracting extravagance that the reader's attention may at times be withdrawn from the all but unqualified ugliness of its ethical tone or tendency. Two of Webster's favourite types, the meditative murderer or philosophic ruffian, and the impulsive impostor who is liable to collapse into the likeness of a passionate penitent, will remind the reader how much better they appear in tragedies which are carried through to their natural tragic end. But here, where the story is admirably opened and the characters as skilfully introduced, the strong interest thus excited at starting is scattered or broken or trifled away before the action is halfway through: and at its close the awkward violence or irregularity of moral and scenical effect comes to a crowning crisis in the general and mutual condonation of unnatural perjury and attempted murder with which the victims and the criminals agree to hush up all grudges, shake hands all round, and live happy ever after. There is at least one point of somewhat repulsive resemblance between the story of this play and that of Fletcher's *Fair Maid of the Inn*: but Fletcher's play, with none of the tragic touches or interludes of superb and sombre poetry which relieve the incoherence of Webster's, is better laid out and constructed, more amusing if not more interesting and more intelligent if not more imaginative.

A far more creditable and workmanlike piece of work, though glorified by no flashes of such sudden and singular beauty, is the tragedy of *Appius and Virginia*. The almost infinite superiority of Webster to Fletcher as a poet of pure tragedy and a painter of masculine character is in this play as obvious as the inferiority in construction and conduct of romantic story displayed in his attempt at a tragicomedy. From the evidence of style I should judge this play to have been written at an earlier date than *The Devil's Law-case*: it is, I repeat, far better composed; better, perhaps, than any other play of the author's: but it has none of his more distinctive qualities; intensity of idea, concentration of utterance, pungency of expression and ardour of pathos. It is written with noble and equable power of hand, with force and purity and fluency of apt and simple eloquence: there is nothing in it unworthy of the writer: but it is the only one of his unassisted works in which we do not find that especial note of tragic style, concise and pointed and tipped as it were with fire, which usually makes it impossible for the dullest reader to mistake the peculiar presence, the original tone or accent, of John Webster. If the epithet unique had not such a tang of German affectation in it, it would be perhaps the aptest of all adjectives to denote the genius or define the manner of this great poet. But in this tragedy, though whatever is said is well said and whatever is done well done, we miss that sense of positive and inevitable conviction, that instant and profound perception or impression as of immediate and indisputable truth, which is burnt in upon us as we read the more Websterian scenes of Webster's writing. We feel, in short, that thus it may have been: not, as I observed at the opening of these notes, that thus it must have been. The poem does him no discredit; nay, it does him additional honour, as an evidence of powers more various and many-sided than we should otherwise have known or supposed in him.

Indeed, the figure of Virginius is one of the finest types of soldierly and fatherly heroism ever presented on the stage: there is equal force of dramatic effect, equal fervour of eloquent passion, in the scene of his pleading before the senate on behalf of the claims of his suffering and struggling fellow-soldiers, and in the scene of his return to the camp after the immolation of his daughter. The mere theatric effect of this latter scene is at once so triumphant and so dignified, so noble in its presentation and so passionate in its restraint, that we feel the high justice and sound reason of the instinct which inspired the poet to prolong the action of his play so far beyond the sacrifice of his heroine. A comparison of Webster's Virginius with any of Fletcher's wordy warriors will suffice to show how much nearer to Shakespeare than to Fletcher stands Webster as a tragic or a serious dramatist. Coleridge, not always just to Fletcher, was not unjust in his remark 'what strange self-trumpeters and tongue-bullies all the brave soldiers of Beaumont and Fletcher are'; and again almost immediately —'all B. and F.'s generals are pugilists, or cudgel-fighters, that boast of their bottom and of the "claret" they have shed'.[8] There is nothing of this in Virginius; Shakespeare himself has not represented with a more lofty fidelity, in the person of Coriolanus or of Brutus, 'the high Roman fashion'[9] of austere and heroic self-respect. In the other leading or dominant figure of this tragedy there is certainly discernible a genuine and thoughtful originality or freshness of conception; but perhaps there is also recognisable a certain inconsistency of touch. It was well thought of to mingle some alloy of goodness with the wickedness of Appius Claudius, to represent the treacherous and lecherous decemvir as neither kindless nor remorseless,[10] but capable of penitence and courage in his last hour. But Shakespeare, I cannot but think, would have prepared us with more care and more dexterity for the revelation of some such redeeming quality in a character which in the act immediately preceding Webster has represented as utterly heartless and shameless, brutal in its hypocrisy and impudent in its brutality.

If the works already discussed were their author's only claims to remembrance and honour, they might not suffice to place him on a higher level among our tragic poets than that occupied by Marston and Dekker and Middleton on the one hand, by Fletcher and Massinger and Shirley on the other. *Antonio and Mellida*, *Old Fortunatus*, or *The Changeling*—*The Maid's Tragedy*, *The Duke of Milan*, or *The Traitor*—would suffice to counterweigh (if not, in some cases, to outbalance) the merit of the best among these: the fitful and futile inspiration of *The Devil's Law-case*, and the stately but subdued inspiration of *Appius and Virginia*. That his place was with no subordinate poet—that his station is at Shakespeare's right hand—the evidence supplied by his two great tragedies is disputable by no one who has an inkling of the qualities which confer a right to be named in the same day with the greatest writer of all time.

Æschylus is above all things the poet of righteousness. 'But in any wise, I say unto thee, revere thou the altar of righteousness':[11] this is the crowning admonition of his doctrine, as its crowning prospect is the reconciliation or atonement of the principle of retribution with the principle of redemption, of the powers of the mystery of darkness with the coeternal forces of the spirit of wisdom, of the lord of inspiration and of light. The doctrine of Shakespeare, where it is not vaguer, is darker in its implication of injustice, in its acceptance of accident, than the impression of the doctrine of Æschylus. Fate, irreversible and inscrutable, is the only force of which we feel the impact, of which we trace the sign, in the upshot of *Othello* or *King Lear*. The last step into the darkness remained to be taken by 'the most tragic' of all English poets. With Shakespeare—and assuredly not with Æschylus—righteousness itself seems subject and subordinate to the masterdom of fate: but fate itself, in the tragic world of Webster, seems merely the servant or the synonym of chance. The two chief agents in his two great tragedies pass away—the phrase was, perhaps, unconsciously repeated—'in a mist':[12] perplexed, indomitable, defiant of hope and fear; bitter and sceptical and bloody in penitence or impenitence alike. And the mist which encompasses the departing spirits of these moody and mocking men of blood seems equally to involve the lives of their chastisers and their victims. Blind accident and blundering mishap—'such a mistake,' says one of the criminals, 'as I have often seen in a play'[13]—are the steersmen of their fortunes and the doomsmen of their deeds. The effect of this method or the result of this view, whether adopted for dramatic objects or ingrained in the writer's temperament, is equally fit for pure tragedy and unfit for any form of drama not purely tragic in evolution and event. In *The Devil's Law-case* it is offensive, because the upshot is incongruous and insufficient: in *The White Devil* and *The Duchess of Malfy* it is admirable, because the results are adequate and coherent. But in all these three plays alike, and in these three plays only, the peculiar tone of Webster's genius, the peculiar force of his imagination, is distinct and absolute in its fullness of effect. The author of *Appius and Virginia* would have earned an honourable and enduring place in the history of English letters as a worthy member—one among many—of a great school in poetry, a deserving representative of a great epoch in literature: but the author of these three plays has a solitary station, an indisputable distinction of his own. The greatest poets of all time are not more mutually independent than this one—a lesser poet only than those greatest—is essentially independent of them all.

The first quality which all readers recognise, and which may strike a superficial reader as the exclusive or excessive note of his genius and his work, is of course his command of terror. Except in Æschylus, in Dante, and in Shakespeare, I at least know not where to seek for passages which in sheer force of tragic and noble horror—to the vulgar shock of ignoble or brutal horror he never condescends to submit his reader or subdue his inspiration—may be set against the subtlest, the deepest, the sublimest passages of Webster. Other gifts he had as great in themselves, as precious and as necessary to the poet: but on this side he is incomparable and unique. Neither Marlowe nor Shakespeare had so fine, so accurate, so infallible a sense of the delicate line of demarcation which divides the impressive and the terrible from the horrible and the loathsome—Victor Hugo and Honoré de Balzac from Eugène Sue and Émile Zola. On his theatre we find no presentation of old men with their beards torn off and their eyes gouged out, of young men imprisoned in reeking cesspools and impaled with red-hot spits. Again and again his passionate and daring genius attains the utmost limit and rounds the final goal of tragedy; never once does it break the bounds of pure poetic instinct. If ever for a moment it may seem to graze that goal too closely, to brush too sharply by those bounds, the very next moment finds it clear of any such risk and remote from any such temptation as sometimes entrapped or seduced the foremost of its forerunners in the field. And yet this is the field in which its paces are most superbly shown. No name among all the names of great poets will recur so soon as Webster's to the reader who knows what it signifies, as he reads or repeats the verses in which a greater than this great poet—a greater than all since Shakespeare—has expressed the latent mystery of terror which lurks in all the highest poetry or beauty, and distinguishes it inexplicably and inevitably from all that is but a little lower than the highest.

> Les aigles sur les bords du Gange et du Caÿstre
> Sont effrayants;

Rien de grand qui ne soit confusément sinistre;
Les noirs pæans,

Les psaumes, la chanson monstrueuse du mage
Ezéchiel,
Font devant notre œil fixe errer la vague image
D'un affreux ciel.

L'empyrée est l'abîme, on y plonge, on y reste
Avec terreur.
Car planer, c'est trembler; si l'azur est céleste,
C'est par l'horreur.

L'épouvante est au fond des choses les plus belles;
Les bleus vallons
Font parfois reculer d'effroi les fauves ailes
Des aquilons.[14]

And even in comedy as in tragedy, in prosaic even as in prophetic inspiration, in imitative as in imaginative works of genius, the sovereign of modern poets has detected the same touch of terror wherever the deepest note possible has been struck, the fullest sense possible of genuine and peculiar power conveyed to the student of lyric or dramatic, epic or elegiac masters.

De là tant de beautés difformes dans leurs œuvres;
Le vers charmant
Est par la torsion subite des couleuvres
Pris brusquement;

A de certains moments toutes les jeunes flores
Dans la forêt
Ont peur, et sur le front des blanches métaphores
L'ombre apparaît;

C'est qu'Horace ou Virgile ont vu soudain le spectre
Noir se dresser;
C'est que là-bas, derrière Amaryllis, Électre
Vient de passer.[15]

Nor was it the Electra of Sophocles, the calm and impassive accomplice of an untroubled and unhesitating matricide, who showed herself ever in passing to the intent and serious vision of Webster. By those candid and sensible judges to whom the praise of Marlowe seems to imply a reflection on the fame of Shakespeare, I may be accused—and by such critics I am content to be accused—of a fatuous design to set Webster beside Sophocles, or Sophocles—for aught I know—beneath Webster, if I venture to indicate the superiority in truth of natural passion—and, I must add, of moral instinct—which distinguishes the modern from the ancient. It is not, it never will be, and it never can have been natural for noble and civilised creatures to accept with spontaneous complacency, to discharge with unforced equanimity, such offices or such duties as weigh so lightly on the spirit of the Sophoclean Orestes that the slaughter of a mother seems to be a less serious undertaking for his unreluctant hand than the subsequent execution of her paramour. The immeasurable superiority of Æschylus to his successors in this quality of instinctive righteousness—if a word long vulgarised by theology may yet be used in its just and natural sense—is shared no less by Webster than by Shakespeare. The grave and deep truth of natural impulse is never ignored by these poets when dealing either with innocent or with criminal passion: but it surely is now and then ignored by the artistic quietism of Sophocles—as surely as it is outraged and degraded by the vulgar theatricalities of Euripides. Thomas Campbell was amused and scandalised by the fact that Webster (as he is pleased to express it) modestly compares himself to the playwright last mentioned; being apparently of opinion that *Hippolytus* and *Medea* may be reckoned equal or superior, as works of tragic art or examples of ethical elevation, to *The White Devil* and *The Duchess of Malfy*; and being no less apparently ignorant, and incapable of understanding, that as there is no poet morally nobler than Webster so is there no poet ignobler in the moral sense than Euripides: while as a dramatic artist—an artist in character, action, and emotion—the degenerate tragedian of Athens, compared to the second tragic dramatist of England, is as a mutilated monkey to a well-made man. No better test of critical faculty could be required by the most exacting scrutiny of probation than is afforded by the critic's professed or professional estimate of those great poets whose names are not consecrated—or desecrated—by the conventional applause, the factitious adoration, of a tribunal whose judgments are dictated by obsequious superstition and unanimous incompetence. When certain critics inform a listening world that they do not admire Marlowe and Webster—they admire Shakespeare and Milton, we know at once that it is not the genius of Shakespeare—it is the reputation of Shakespeare that they admire. It is not the man that they bow down to: it is the bust that they crouch down before. They would worship Shirley as soon as Shakespeare—Glover[16] as soon as Milton—Byron as soon as Shelley—Ponsard[17] as soon as Hugo—Longfellow as soon as Tennyson—if the tablet were as showily emblazoned, the inscription as pretentiously engraved.

The nobility of spirit and motive which is so distinguishing a mark of Webster's instinctive genius or natural disposition of mind is proved by his treatment of facts placed on record by contemporary annalists in the tragic story of Vittoria Accorambuoni, Duchess of Bracciano. That story would have been suggestive, if not tempting, to any dramatic poet: and almost any poet but Shakespeare or Webster would have been content to accept the characters and circumstances as they stood nakedly on record, and adapt them to the contemporary stage of England with such dexterity and intelligence as he might be able to command. But, as Shakespeare took the savage legend of Hamlet, the brutal story of Othello, and raised them from the respective levels of the *Heimskringla* and *The Newgate Calendar* to the very highest 'heaven of invention',[18] so has Webster transmuted the impressive but repulsive record of villainies and atrocities, in which he discovered the motive for a magnificent poem, into the majestic and pathetic masterpiece which is one of the most triumphant and the most memorable achievements of English poetry. If, in his play, as in the legal or historic account of the affair, the whole family of the heroine had appeared unanimous and eager in complicity with her sins and competition for a share in the profits of her dishonour, the tragedy might still have been as effective as it is now from the theatrical or sensational point of view; it might have thrilled the reader's nerves as keenly, have excited and stimulated his curiosity, have whetted and satiated his appetite for transient emotion, as thoroughly and triumphantly as now. But it would have been merely a criminal melodrama, compiled by the labour and vivified by the talent of an able theatrical journeyman. The one great follower of Shakespeare—'*haud passibus æquis*' at all points; '*longo sed proximus intervallo*'[19]—has recognised, with Shakespearean accuracy and delicacy and elevation of instinct, the necessity of ennobling and transfiguring his characters if their story was to be made acceptable to the sympathies of any but an idle or an ignoble audience. And he has done so after the very manner and in the very spirit of Shakespeare. The noble creatures of his invention give to the story that dignity and variety of interest without which the most powerful romance or drama can be but an example of vigorous vulgarity. The upright and high-minded mother and brother of the shameless Flamineo and the shame-stricken Vittoria refresh and purify the tragic atmosphere of the poem by the passing presence of their virtues. The shallow and fiery nature of the fair White Devil herself is a notable example of the difference so accurately distinguished by Charlotte Brontë between an impressionable and an impressible character. Ambition, self-interest, passion, remorse and hardihood alternate and contend in her impetuous and wayward spirit. The one distinct and trustworthy quality which may always be reckoned on is the indomitable courage underlying her easily irritable emotions. Her bearing at the trial for her husband's murder is as dexterous and dauntless as the demeanour of Mary Stuart before her judges. To Charles Lamb it seemed 'an innocence-resembling boldness'; to Mr. Dyce and Canon Kingsley the innocence displayed in Lamb's estimate seemed almost ludicrous in its misconception of Webster's text. I should hesitate to agree with them that he has never once made his accused heroine speak in the natural key of innocence unjustly impeached: Mary's pleading for her life is not at all points incompatible in tone with the innocence which it certainly fails to establish—except in minds already made up to accept any plea as valid which may plausibly or possibly be advanced on her behalf; and the arguments advanced by Vittoria are not more evasive and equivocal, in face of the patent and flagrant prepossession of her judges, than those put forward by the Queen of Scots. It is impossible not to wonder whether the poet had not in his mind the actual tragedy which had taken place just twenty-five years before the publication of this play: if not, the coincidence is something more than singular. The fierce profligacy and savage egotism of Brachiano have a certain energy and activity in the display and the development of their motives and effects which suggest rather such a character as Bothwell's than such a character as that of the bloated and stolid sensualist who stands or grovels before us in the historic record of his life. As presented by Webster, he is doubtless an execrable ruffian: as presented by history, he would be intolerable by any but such readers or spectators as those on whom the figments or the photographs of self-styled naturalism produce other than emetic emotions. Here again the noble instinct of the English poet has rectified the æsthetic unseemliness of an ignoble reality. This 'Brachiano' is a far more living figure than the porcine paramour of the historic Accorambuoni. I am not prepared to maintain that in one scene too much has not been sacrificed to immediate vehemence of effect. The devotion of the discarded wife, who to shelter her Antony from the vengeance of Octavius assumes the mask of raging jealousy, thus taking upon herself the blame and responsibility of their final separation, is expressed with such consummate and artistic simplicity of power that on a first reading the genius of the dramatist may well blind us to the violent unlikelihood of the action. But this very extravagance of self-sacrifice may be thought by some to add a crowning touch of pathos to the unsurpassable beauty of the scene in which her child, after the murder of his mother, relates her past sufferings to his uncle. Those to whom the great name of Webster represents merely an artist in horrors, a ruffian of genius, may be recommended to study every line and syllable of this brief dialogue.

Francisco. How now, my noble cousin? what, in black?
Giovanni. Yes, uncle, I was taught to imitate you
In virtue, and you [? now] must imitate me
In colours of your garments. My sweet mother
Is—
Francisco. How! where?
Giovanni. Is there; no, yonder: indeed, sir, I'll not tell you,
For I shall make you weep.
Francisco. Is dead?
Giovanni. Do not blame me now,
I did not tell you so.
Lodovico. She's dead, my lord.
Francisco. Dead!
Monticelso. Blest lady, thou art now above thy woes!

. . . . . .

Giovanni. What do the dead do, uncle? do they eat,
Hear music, go a hunting, and be merry,
As we that live?
Francisco. No, coz; they sleep.
Giovanni. Lord, Lord, that I were dead!
I have not slept these six nights.—When do they wake?
Francisco. When God shall please.
Giovanni. Good God, let her sleep ever!
For I have known her wake an hundred nights
When all the pillow where she laid her head
Was brine-wet with her tears. I am to complain to you, sir;

I'll tell you how they have used her now she's dead:
They wrapped her in a cruel fold of lead,
And would not let me kiss her.
Francisco. Thou didst love her.
Giovanni. I have often heard her say she gave me suck,
And it should seem by that she dearly loved me,
Since princes seldom do it.
Francisco. O, all of my poor sister that remains!—
Take him away, for God's sake![20]

I must admit that I do not see how Shakespeare could have improved upon that. It seems to me that in any one of even his greatest tragedies this scene would have been remarkable among its most beautiful and perfect passages; nor, upon the whole, do I remember a third English poet who could be imagined capable of having written it. And it affords, I think, very clear and sufficient evidence that Webster could not have handled so pathetic and suggestive a subject as the execution of Lady Jane Grey and her young husband in a style so thin and feeble, so shallow in expression of pathos and so empty of suggestion or of passion, as that in which it is presented at the close of *Sir Thomas Wyatt*.

There is a perfect harmony of contrast between this and the death-scene of the boy's father: the agony of the murdered murderer is as superb in effect of terror as the sorrow of his son is exquisite in effect of pathos. Again we are reminded of Shakespeare, by no touch of imitation but simply by a note of kinship in genius and in style, at the cry of Brachiano under the first sharp workings of the poison:

O thou strong heart!
There's such a covenant 'tween the world and it,
They're loth to break.[21]

Another stroke well worthy of Shakespeare is the redeeming touch of grace in this brutal and cold-blooded ruffian which gives him in his agony a thought of tender care for the accomplice of his atrocities:

Do not kiss me, for I shall poison thee.

Few instances of Webster's genius are so well known as the brief but magnificent passage which follows; yet it may not be impertinent to cite it once again.

Brachiano. O thou soft natural death, that art joint twin
To sweetest slumber! no rough-bearded comet

Stares on thy mild departure; the dull owl
Beats not against thy casement; the hoarse wolf
Scents not thy carrion; pity winds thy corpse,
Whilst horror waits on princes.
Vittoria. I am lost for ever.
Brachiano. How miserable a thing it is to die
'Mongst women howling!—What are those?
Flamineo. Franciscans:
They have brought the extreme unction.
Brachiano. On pain of death, let no man name death to me;
It is a word [? most] infinitely terrible.

The very tremor of moral and physical abjection from nervous defiance into prostrate fear which seems to pant and bluster and quail and subside in the natural cadence of these lines would suffice to prove the greatness of the artist who could express it with such terrible perfection: but when we compare it, by collation of the two scenes, with the deep simplicity of tenderness, the childlike accuracy of innocent emotion, in the passage previously cited, it seems to me that we must admit, as an unquestionable truth, that in the deepest and highest and purest qualities of tragic poetry Webster stands nearer to Shakespeare than any other English poet stands to Webster; and so much nearer as to be a good second; while it is at least questionable whether even Shelley can reasonably be accepted as a good third. Not one among the predecessors, contemporaries, or successors of Shakespeare and Webster has given proof of this double faculty—this coequal mastery of terror and pity, undiscoloured and undistorted, but vivified and glorified, by the splendour of immediate and infallible imagination. The most grovelling realism could scarcely be so impudent in stupidity as to pretend an aim at more perfect presentation of truth: the most fervent fancy, the most sensitive taste, could hardly dream of a desire for more exquisite expression of natural passion in a form of utterance more naturally exalted and refined.

In all the vast and voluminous records of critical error there can be discovered no falsehood more foolish or more flagrant than the vulgar tradition which represents this high-souled and gentle-hearted poet as one morbidly fascinated by a fantastic attraction towards the 'violent delights'[22] of horror and the nervous or sensational excitements of criminal detail; nor can there be conceived a more perverse or futile misapprehension than that which represents

John Webster as one whose instinct led him by some obscure and oblique propensity to darken the darkness of southern crime or vice by an infusion of northern seriousness, of introspective cynicism and reflective intensity in wrongdoing, into the easy levity and infantile simplicity of spontaneous wickedness which distinguished the moral and social corruption of renascent Italy. Proof enough of this has already been adduced to make any protestation or appeal against such an estimate as preposterous in its superfluity as the misconception just mentioned is preposterous in its perversity. The great if not incomparable power displayed in Webster's delineation of such criminals as Flamineo and Bosola—Bonapartes in the bud, Napoleons in a nutshell, Cæsars who have missed their Rubicon and collapse into the likeness of a Catiline—is a sign rather of his noble English loathing for the traditions associated with such names as Cæsar and Medici and Borgia, Catiline and Iscariot and Napoleon, than of any sympathetic interest in such incarnations of historic crime. Flamineo especially, the ardent pimp, the enthusiastic pandar, who prostitutes his sister and assassinates his brother with such earnest and single-hearted devotion to his own straightforward self-interest, has in him a sublime fervour of rascality which recalls rather the man of Brumaire and of Waterloo than the man of December and of Sedan.[23] He has something too of Napoleon's ruffianly good-humour—the frankness of a thieves' kitchen or an imperial court, when the last thin figleaf of pretence has been plucked off and crumpled up and flung away. We can imagine him pinching his favourites by the ear and dictating memorials of mendacity with the self-possession of a self-made monarch. As it is, we see him only in the stage of parasite and pimp—more like the hired husband of a cast-off Creole than the resplendent rogue who fascinated even history for a time by the clamour and glitter of his triumphs. But the fellow is unmistakably an emperor in the egg—so dauntless and frontless in the very abjection of his villainy that we feel him to have been defrauded by mischance of the only two destinations appropriate for the close of his career—a gibbet or a throne.

This imperial quality of ultimate perfection in egotism and crowning complacency in crime is wanting to his brother in atrocity, the most notable villain who figures on the stage of Webster's latest masterpiece. Bosola is not quite a possible Bonaparte; he is not even on a level with the bloody hirelings who execute the orders of tyranny and treason with the perfunctory atrocity of Anicetus or Saint-Arnaud.[24] There is not, or I am much mistaken, a touch of imaginative poetry in the part of Flamineo: his passion, excitable on occasion and vehement enough, is as prosaic in its homely and cynical eloquence as the most fervent emotions of a Napoleon or an Iago when warmed or goaded into elocution. The one is a human snake, the other is a human wolf. Webster could not with equal propriety have put into the mouth of Flamineo such magnificent lyric poetry as seems to fall naturally, however suddenly and strangely, from the bitter and bloodthirsty tongue of Bosola. To him, as to the baffled and incoherent ruffian Romelio in the contemporary play of *The Devil's Law-case*, his creator has assigned the utterance of such verse as can only be compared to that uttered by Cornelia over the body of her murdered son in the tragedy to which I have just given so feeble and inadequate a word of tribute. In his command and in his use of the metre first made fashionable by the graceful improvisations of Greene, Webster seems to me as original and as peculiar as in his grasp and manipulation of character and event. All other poets, Shakespeare no less than Barnfield and Milton no less than Wither, have used this lyric instrument for none but gentle or gracious ends: Webster has breathed into it the power to express a sublimer and a profounder tone of emotion; he has given it the cadence and the colour of tragedy; he has touched and transfigured its note of meditative music into a chord of passionate austerity and prophetic awe. This was the key in which all previous poets had played upon the metre which Webster was to put to so deeply different an use.

Walking in a valley greene,
Spred with Flora summer queene:
Where shee heaping all hir graces,
Niggard seem'd in other places:
Spring it was, and here did spring
All that nature forth can bring.

(*Tullies Loue*, p. 53, ed. 1589.)

Nights were short, and daies were long;
Blossoms on the Hauthorns hung:
Philomele (Night-Musiques King)
Tolde the comming of the spring.

(*Grosart's Barnfield* [1876], p. 97.)

On a day (alack the day!)
Love, whose month is ever May,
Spied a blossom passing fair

Playing in the wanton air.

(*Love's Labour's Lost*, Act iv. Sc. iii.)

And now let us hear Webster.

Hearke, now every thing is still,
The Scritch-Owle, and the whistler shrill,
Call upon our Dame, aloud,
And bid her quickly don her shrowd:
Much you had of Land and rent,
Your length in clay's now competent.
A long war disturb'd your minde,
Here your perfect peace is sign'd.
Of what is't, fooles make such vaine keeping?
Sin their conception, their birth, weeping:
Their life, a generall mist of error,
Their death, a hideous storme of terror.
Strew your haire with powders sweete:
Don cleane linnen, bath[e] your feete,
And (the foule feend more to checke)
A crucifixe let blesse your necke:
'Tis now full tide 'tweene night and day,
End your groane, and come away.

(*The Tragedy of the Dutchesse of Malfy*: 1623: sig. K, K 2.)

The toll of the funereal rhythm, the heavy chime of the solemn and simple verse, the mournful menace and the brooding presage of its note, are but the covering, as it were, or the outer expression, of the tragic significance which deepens and quickens and kindles to its close. Æschylus and Dante have never excelled, nor perhaps have Sophocles and Shakespeare ever equalled in impression of terrible effect, the fancy of bidding a live woman array herself in the raiment of the grave, and do for her own living body the offices done for a corpse by the ministers attendant on the dead.

The murderous humourist whose cynical inspiration gives life to these deadly lines is at first sight a less plausible, but on second thoughts may perhaps seem no less possible a character than Flamineo. Pure and simple ambition of the Napoleonic order is the motive which impels into infamy the aspiring parasite of Brachiano: a savage melancholy inflames the baffled greed of Bosola to a pitch of wickedness not unqualified by relenting touches of profitless remorse, which come always either too early or too late to bear any serviceable fruit of compassion or redemption. There is no deeper or more Shakespearean stroke of tragic humour in all Webster's writings than that conveyed in the scornful and acute reply—almost too acute perhaps for the character—of Bosola's remorseless patron to the remonstrance or appeal of his instrument against the insatiable excess and persistence of his cruelty: 'Thy pity is nothing akin to thee.'[25] He has more in common with Romelio in *The Devil's Law-case*, an assassin who misses his aim and flounders into penitence much as that discomfortable drama misses its point and stumbles into vacuity: and whose unsatisfactory figure looks either like a crude and unsuccessful study for that of Bosola, or a disproportioned and emasculated copy from it. But to him too Webster has given the fitful force of fancy or inspiration which finds expression in such sudden snatches of funereal verse as this:

> How then can any monument say
> 'Here rest these bones till the last day,'
> When Time, swift both of foot and feather,
> May bear them the sexton kens not whither?
> What care I, then, though my last sleep
> Be in the desert or the deep,
> No lamp nor taper, day and night,
> To give my charnel chargeable light?
> I have there like quantity of ground,
> And at the last day I shall be found.[26]

The villainous laxity of versification which deforms the grim and sardonic beauty of these occasionally rough and halting lines is perceptible here and there in *The Duchess of Malfy*, but comes to its head in *The Devil's Law-case*. It cannot, I fear, be denied that Webster was the first to relax those natural bonds of noble metre 'whose service is perfect freedom'[27]—as Shakespeare found it, and combined with perfect loyalty to its law the most perfect liberty of living and sublime and spontaneous and accurate expression. I can only conjecture that this greatest of the Shakespeareans was misguided out of his natural line of writing as exemplified and perfected in the tragedy of Vittoria, and lured into this cross and crooked byway of immetrical experiment, by the temptation of some theory or crotchet on the score of what is now called naturalism or realism; which, if there were any real or natural weight in the reasoning that seeks to support it, would of course do away, and of course ought to do away, with dramatic poetry altogether: for if it is certain that real persons do not actually converse in good metre, it is happily no less certain that they do not actually converse in bad metre. In the hands of so great a tragic poet as Webster a peculiar and impressive effect may now and then be produced by this anomalous and illegitimate way of writing; it certainly suits well with the thoughtful and fantastic truculence of Bosola's reflections on death and dissolution and decay—his 'talk fit for a charnel',[28] which halts and hovers between things hideous and things sublime. But it is a step on the downward way that leads to the negation or the confusion of all distinctions between poetry and prose; a result to which it would be grievous to think that the example of Shakespeare's greatest contemporary should in any way appear to conduce.

The doctrine or the motive of chance (whichever we may prefer to call it) is seen in its fullest workings and felt in its furthest bearings by the student of Webster's masterpiece. The fifth act of *The Duchess of Malfy* has been assailed on the very ground which it should have been evident to a thoughtful and capable reader that the writer must have intended to take up—on the ground that the whole upshot of the story is dominated by sheer chance, arranged by mere error, and guided by pure accident. No formal scheme or religious principle of retribution would have been so strangely or so thoroughly in keeping with the whole scheme and principle of the tragedy. After the overwhelming terrors and the overpowering beauties of that unique and marvellous fourth act, in which the genius of this poet spreads its fullest and its darkest wing for the longest and the strongest of its flights, it could not but be that the subsequent action and passion of the drama should appear by comparison unimpressive or ineffectual; but all the effect or impression possible of attainment under the inevitable burden of this difficulty is achieved by natural and simple and straightforward means. If Webster has not made the part of Antonio dramatically striking and attractive—as he probably found it impossible to do—he has at least bestowed on the fugitive and unconscious widower of his murdered heroine a pensive and manly grace of deliberate resignation which is not without pathetic as well as poetical effect. In the beautiful and well-known scene where the echo from his wife's unknown and new-made grave seems to respond to his meditative mockery and forewarn him of his impending death, Webster has given such reality and seriousness to an old commonplace of contemporary fancy or previous fashion in poetry that we are fain to forget the fantastic side of the conception and see only the tragic aspect of its meaning. A weightier objection than any which can be brought against the conduct of the play might be suggested to the minds of some readers—and these, perhaps, not too exacting or too captious readers—by the sudden vehemence of transformation which in the great preceding act seems to fall like fire from heaven upon the two chief criminals who figure on the stage of murder. It seems rather a miraculous retribution, a judicial violation of the laws of nature, than a reasonably credible consequence or evolution of those laws, which strikes Ferdinand with madness and Bosola with repentance. But the whole atmosphere of the action is so charged with thunder that this double and simultaneous shock of moral electricity rather thrills us with admiration and faith than chills us with repulsion or distrust. The passionate intensity and moral ardour of imagination which we feel to vibrate and penetrate through every turn and every phrase of the dialogue would suffice to enforce upon our belief a more nearly incredible revolution of nature or revulsion of the soul.

It is so difficult for even the very greatest poets to give any vivid force of living interest to a figure of passive endurance that perhaps the only instance of perfect triumph over this difficulty is to be found in the character of Desdemona. Shakespeare alone could have made her as interesting as Imogen or Cordelia; though these have so much to do and dare, and she after her first appearance has simply to suffer: even Webster could not give such individual vigour of characteristic life to the figure of his martyr as to the figure of his criminal heroine. Her courage and sweetness, her delicacy and sincerity, her patience and her passion, are painted with equal power and tenderness of touch: yet she hardly stands before us as distinct from others of her half angelic sisterhood as does the White Devil from the fellowship of her comrades in perdition.[29] But if, as we may assuredly assume, it was on the twenty-third 'nouell' of William Painter's *Palace of Pleasure* that Webster's crowning masterpiece was founded, the poet's moral and spiritual power of transfiguration is here even more admirable than in the previous case of his other and wellnigh co-equally consummate poem. The narrative degrades and brutalises the widowed heroine's affection for her second husband to the actual level of the vile conception which the poet attributes and confines to the foul imagination of her envious and murderous brothers. Here again, and finally and supremely here, the purifying and exalting power of Webster's noble and magnanimous imagination is gloriously unmistakable by all and any who have eyes to read and hearts to recognise.

For it is only with Shakespeare that Webster can ever be compared in any way to his disadvantage as a tragic poet: above all others of his country he stands indisputably supreme. The place of Marlowe indeed is higher among our poets by right of his primacy as a founder and a pioneer: but of course his work has not—as of course it could not have—that plenitude and perfection of dramatic power in construction and dramatic subtlety in detail which the tragedies of Webster share in so large a measure with the tragedies of Shakespeare. Marston, the poet with whom he has most in common, might almost be said to stand in the same relation to Webster as Webster to Shakespeare. In single lines and phrases, in a few detached passages and a very few distinguishable scenes, he is worthy to be compared with the greater poet; he suddenly rises and dilates to the stature and the strength of a model whom usually he can but follow afar off. Marston, as a tragic poet, is not quite what Webster would be if his fame depended simply on such scenes as those in which the noble mother of Vittoria breaks off her daughter's first interview with Brachiano—spares, and commends to God's forgiveness, the son who has murdered his brother before her eyes—and lastly appears 'in several forms of distraction',[30] 'grown a very old woman in two hours',[31] and singing that most pathetic and imaginative of all funereal invocations which the finest critic of all time so justly and so delicately compared to the watery dirge of Ariel.[32] There is less refinement, less exaltation and perfection of feeling, less tenderness of emotion and less nobility of passion, but hardly less force and fervour, less weighty and sonorous ardour of expression, in the very best and loftiest passages of Marston: but his genius is more uncertain, more fitful and intermittent, less harmonious, coherent, and trustworthy than Webster's. And Webster, notwithstanding an occasional outbreak into Aristophanic license of momentary sarcasm through the sardonic lips of such a cynical ruffian as Ferdinand or Flamineo, is without exception the cleanliest, as Marston is beyond comparison the coarsest writer of his time. In this as in other matters of possible comparison that 'vessel of deathless wrath', the implacable and inconsolable poet of sympathy half maddened into rage and aspiration goaded backwards to despair—it should be needless to add the name of Cyril Tourneur—stands midway between these two more conspicuous figures of their age. But neither the father and master of poetic pessimists, the splendid and sombre creator of Vindice and his victims, nor any other third whom our admiration may discern among all the greatest of their fellows, can be compared with Webster on terms more nearly equal than those on which Webster stands in relation to the sovereign of them all.

NOTES

1 *Coriolanus*, I, i, 119.
2 *The White Devil*, V, vi, 252–3.
3 August Wilhelm Schlegel, *A Course of Lectures on Dramatic Art and Literature*, tr. John Black (London, 1846), 445.
4 'There is the graceful outline of her form—there is nothing like it. The two countesses had no outline at all, and the dowager's was a demnd outline' (from *Nicholas Nickleby*, chapter 34). 'The rogue Kirkman' was Francis Kirkman (*fl.* 1674).
5 Swinburne may somehow have learned that Ludwig Tieck, one of the few who have accepted Kirkman's attribution, argued for Shakespeare's collaboration in the play by calling it (*Shakespeare's Vorschule*, Leipzig, 1829, II, xviii) 'by far the best by him [Rowley] that I have seen' (translated from the German).
6 The *Nineteenth Century* adds, 'As far as I know them'.
7 Cf. George Villiers, second Duke of Buckingham, and others, *The Rehearsal*, III, i: 'Why, what a Devil is the Plot good for, but to bring in fine things?'
8 From Coleridge's comment on *The Maid's Tragedy*, in 'Marginalia on Beaumont and Fletcher'.
9 *Antony and Cleopatra*, IV, xv, 87.
10 Cf. *Hamlet*, II, ii, 609: 'Remorseless, treacherous, lecherous, kindless villain!'
11 Swinburne's translation from Æschylus's *Eumenides*, ll. 538–9.
12 *The White Devil*, V, vi, 260; *The Duchess of Malfi*, V, v, 118.
13 *The Duchess of Malfi*, V, v, 119–20.
14 From Victor Hugo's '*Horreur Sacrée*, in *Les Quatre Vents de l'esprit*: 'The eagles on the banks of the Ganges and of the Caÿster [an ancient river of Lydia, the modern Bayindir] are frightful; there is nothing lofty that may not be vaguely sinister. The dark paeans, the psalms, the monstrous songs of the prophet Ezekiel bring before our eye the indistinct image of a ghastly heaven. The Empyrean is an abyss; one plunges into it; one remains there with terror, for to soar is to tremble; if the azure is celestial, it is because of horror. Terror is at the base of the most beautiful things; the blue vales make the fawn-coloured eagles draw back from fear.'
15 'Thence comes so much misshapen beauty in their [certain poets'] works; charming verse is captured brusquely by the sudden twisting of adders. At certain moments all the young flowers in the forest take fright, and shadow falls on the forehead of white metaphors. It is because Horace or Vergil has suddenly seen the black spectre rise; it is because down there, behind Amaryllis, Electra has just passed by.'
16 Richard Glover (1712–85), a poet and author of two plays.

17 François Ponsard (1814–67), a forgotten dramatist who was averse to Hugo's Romantic drama.

18 *Henry V*, Prologue, l. 2.

19 'By no means with equal steps' (*haud* is substituted for the *non* in Vergil's *Aeneid*, ii, 724), 'but next by a long distance' (*Aeneid*, v, 320).

20 From *The White Devil*, III, ii.

21 This and the two following quotations are from *The White Devil*, V, iii.

22 *Romeo and Juliet*, II, vi, 9.

23 Napoleon I rather than Napoleon III.

24 Anicetus (*fl.* 60), one of Nero's tutors, is said to have collaborated in plots to get rid of the Emperor's mother Agrippina and his wife Octavia. Jacques A. C. L. de Saint-Arnaud (1796–1854), French general, assisted Louis Napoleon in the *coup d'état* of December 1851.

25 *The Duchess of Malfi*, IV, i, 166.

26 *The Devil's Law-Case*, II, iii, 137–46.

27 *The Book of Common Prayer*, 'A Collect for Peace'.

28 *The Duchess of Malfi*, IV, ii, 162.

29 The remaining sentences of this paragraph were added to the original article.

30 From a stage direction for the 'funeral invocation' in *The White Devil*, V, iv.

31 *The White Devil*, V, iv, 48.

32 Charles Lamb in his *Specimens*.

Bibliography

ARVIN, NEWTON, 'Swinburne as a Critic', *Sewanee Review*, xxxii (1924), 405–12. (An early article stressing Swinburne's aesthetic sensibility and interpretive skill.)

CHEW, SAMUEL C., *Swinburne* (Boston, 1929). (Contains an informative and judicious chapter on Swinburne's prose.)

CHILD, RUTH C., 'Swinburne's Mature Standards of Criticism', *PMLA* [*Publications of the Modern Language Association*], lii (1937), 870–79. (Dwells on Swinburne's ultimate concern for nobility and loftiness of thought.)

CONNOLLY, THOMAS E., *Swinburne's Theory of Poetry* (State University of New York, 1964). (The first attempt to deal systematically with the 'solid core of principles' forming the basis of Swinburne's criticism.)

ELIOT, T. S., *The Sacred Wood* (New York and London, 1930). (Contains an estimate, on pages 17 ff., of Swinburne's critical powers.)

HYDER, CLYDE K., *Swinburne's Literary Career and Fame* (Durham, N. C., 1933). (Lists early reviews of Swinburne's volumes.)

HYDER, CLYDE K. ed., *Swinburne Replies* (Syracuse, New York, 1966). (A critical edition of *Notes on Poems and Reviews*, *Under the Microscope*, and the *Dedicatory Epistle* of 1904.)

HYDER, CLYDE K. ed., *Swinburne: The Critical Heritage* (London, 1970). (Contains quotations from Swinburne's critics during his lifetime and some of his own comments and defences.)

LAFOURCADE, GEORGES, *La Jeunesse de Swinburne* (Paris, 1928). (Two volumes dealing with Swinburne's early life and work; contains the text of 'Modern Hellenism' and extracts from other writings.)

LANG, CECIL Y. ed., *The Swinburne Letters* (New Haven and London, 1959–62). (The six volumes supply the indispensable commentary on Swinburne's career and opinions.)

LANG, CECIL Y. ed., *New Writings by Swinburne* (Syracuse, New York, 1964). (Contains texts of five critical pieces not readily accessible elsewhere, as well as valuable notes and comments.)

PETERS, ROBERT L., *The Crowns of Apollo: Swinburne's Principles of Literature and Art* (Detroit, 1965). (An extended and skilful discussion of Swinburne's criticism in relation to contemporary aesthetic principles.)

REUL, PAUL DE, *L'Œuvre de Swinburne* (Brussels, 1922). (Deals at some length with Swinburne's criticism.)

WELLEK, RENÉ, *A History of Modern Criticism : 1750–1950* (New Haven and London, 1955–). (Volume iv, appearing in 1965 and dealing with 'the later nineteenth century', is useful for consideration of Swinburne's relationship to other critics.)

Index